Critical Psychiatry and Mental Health

Critical Psychiatry and Mental Health critically explores the current theory and practice of ethno-psychiatry and multicultural mental health practices and policies. Through an in-depth discussion of the work of Suman Fernando, one of the world's leading scholars and researchers in race, culture and mental health, an international selection of contributors discuss and debate issues affecting mental health and minority ethnic individuals and groups.

The book offers a new approach to global mental health, arguing that the use of outdated and outmoded ways in which psychiatry is researched and practised is a thing of the past, that social justice can only be achieved through a more democratic approach to mental health care and emphasizing that the inclusion of cultural and traditional healing methods and practices are vital to meeting diverse needs. Split into five parts, the book covers:

- critique of Western psychiatry and mental health;
- challenges and opportunities in mental health care;
- training and development in mental health practice;
- transnational contexts: engaging the work of Suman Fernando;
- personal reflections on Suman Fernando's life and work.

Critical Psychiatry and Mental Health is ideal for researchers and practitioners in health and mental health, psychiatry, counselling and psychotherapy and anyone interested in the intersection of race, culture and mental health.

Roy Moodley, PhD, is Associate Professor of Counselling Psychology at the Ontario Institute for Studies in Education, University of Toronto, Canada, and Director of the University of Toronto's Centre for Diversity in Counselling and Psychotherapy.

Martha Ocampo is a long-standing community activist, promoting anti-racist action in the mental health field in Toronto, and a founding member of Across Boundaries: An Ethnoracial Mental Health Centre, a community agency for racialized communities. She now works as a freelance consultant and trainer.

Critical Psychiatry and Mental Health

Exploring the work of Suman Fernando in clinical practice

Edited by Roy Moodley and Martha Ocampo

LONDON AND NEW YORK

First published 2014
by Routledge
27 Church Road, Hove, East Sussex BN3 2FA

and by Routledge
711 Third Avenue, New York, NY 10017

Routledge is an imprint of the Taylor & Francis Group, an informa business

© 2014 Roy Moodley and Martha Ocampo

The right of the editors to be identified as the authors of the editorial material, and of the authors for their individual chapters, has been asserted in accordance with sections 77 and 78 of the Copyright, Designs and Patents Act 1988.

All rights reserved. No part of this book may be reprinted or reproduced or utilized in any form or by any electronic, mechanical, or other means, now known or hereafter invented, including photocopying and recording, or in any information storage or retrieval system, without permission in writing from the publishers.

Trademark notice: Product or corporate names may be trademarks or registered trademarks, and are used only for identification and explanation without intent to infringe.

British Library Cataloguing in Publication Data
A catalogue record for this book is available from the British Library

Library of Congress Cataloging in Publication Data
Critical psychiatry and mental health : exploring the work of
Suman Fernando in clinical practice / edited by Roy Moodley and
Martha Ocampo.
   pages cm
   1. Psychiatry, Transcultural. 2. Ethnopsychology. I. Moodley, Roy.
II. Ocampo, Martha, 1947–
   RC455.4.E8C75 2014
   616.89–dc23   2013050551

ISBN: 978-0-415-53247-1 (hbk)
ISBN: 978-1-138-01658-3 (pbk)
ISBN: 978-1-315-78003-0 (ebk)

Typeset in Times New Roman
by Wearset Ltd, Boldon, Tyne and Wear

Printed and bound in Great Britain by
TJ International Ltd, Padstow, Cornwall

Contents

Notes on contributors   ix
Foreword   xiii
Acknowledgements   xv

Introduction   1

PART I
Critique of Western psychiatry and mental health   11

1 **Transcultural psychiatry and mental health**   13
SUMAN FERNANDO

2 **Racism in psychiatry**   22
SUMAN FERNANDO

3 **Ethno-racial representations and the burden of 'Otherness' in mental health**   33
ROY MOODLEY

4 **Is there an emancipatory psychiatry?**   43
JOHN EVERSLEY

PART II
Challenges and opportunities in mental health care   55

5 **The challenge of diversity to mental health services**   57
DAVID INGLEBY

6 **Race, culture and mental health care for refugees** 69
CHARLES WATTERS

7 **Developing mental health policies that address race and culture** 79
HÁRI SEWELL

8 **Religion, race and mental health: the scientific evidence** 90
ALISON GRAY AND JOHN COX

9 **In the therapist's chair is Suman Fernando** 102
CHARMAINE WILLIAMS

PART III
Training and development in mental health practice 109

10 **Institutional racism as a seminal concept of cultural competency training** 111
JASWANT GUZDER

11 **Race equality and cultural capability training in mental health** 123
PETER FERNS

12 **Race and cultural diversity: the training of psychologists and psychiatrists** 134
RACHEL TRIBE

13 **An anti-racism and anti-oppression framework in mental health practice** 145
MARTHA OCAMPO AND FRITZ LUTHER PINO

PART IV
Transnational contexts: engaging the work of Suman Fernando 157

14 **Developing mental health services: the myth of 'global' mental health** 159
SUMAN FERNANDO

15 Critical psychiatry in Canada 170
LAURENCE J. KIRMAYER

16 Culture, race and ethnicity in US psychiatry 182
CARL C. BELL AND DOMINICA F. McBRIDE

17 Race, culture and psychiatry in South Africa 193
NKOKONE TEMA AND THOLENE SODI

18 Mental health services in Sri Lanka 204
CHAMINDRA WEERACKODY AND SUMAN FERNANDO

19 Transcultural psychiatry, psychology and social entrepreneurship in Denmark 215
RASHMI SINGLA

20 Culture and mental health in Aotearoa, New Zealand 227
JUDI CLEMENTS AND WAYNE BLISSETT

PART V
Personal reflections on Suman Fernando's life and work 237

The life and times of Suman Fernando 239
TED LO

Suman Fernando's roots in Sri Lanka 244
CHAMINDRA WEERACKODY

Suman Fernando's contribution to British psychiatry 248
JOHN COX

Satisfy my soul: Suman Fernando's work in mental health 253
KAMALDEEP BHUI

Suman Fernando and university mental health systems 257
SHARON MIER

Suman Fernando foraging a place for disenfranchised populations in mental health 260
OLIVER TREACY

A 'race' against time: Suman Fernando's contribution to clinical psychology
ZENOBIA NADIRSHAW
262

Concluding remarks: future directions of psychiatry and mental health
SUMAN FERNANDO
265

Index 268

Contributors

Editors

Roy Moodley, PhD, is Associate Professor of Counselling Psychology in the Department of Applied Psychology and Human Development at the Ontario Institute for Studies in Education, University of Toronto and Director of the Centre for Diversity in Counselling and Psychotherapy (CDCP). Research interests include: critical multicultural counselling; race, culture and psychotherapy; traditional healing; and gender and identity. Roy has authored and edited several papers and books, including *Outside the Sentence: Readings in Critical Multicultural Counselling and Psychotherapy* (2011).

Martha Ocampo is a Race, Culture and Mental Health consultant with Martha Ocampo and Associates, providing educational and training workshops at mental health agencies, colleges, universities and the general public. Martha was a founding member of Across Boundaries (AB): An Ethnoracial Mental Health Centre in Toronto. She was also the Co-director of Programs and Services, and the Education and Resource Manager at AB. She played a key role in developing the centre's Holistic Model of Care within an anti-racism/anti-oppression framework. She developed leadership and advocacy training for marginalized groups and co-authored *Let's Talk*, a guidebook on education about violence against women in the Filipino community. She is the Advisory Chair of the Board of the Carlos Bulosan Theatre in Toronto.

Contributors

Carl C. Bell, MD, is Clinical Professor of Psychiatry and Public Health and Director of the Institute for Juvenile Research (IJR) at the University of Illinois at Chicago. IJR provides child and family research, training and service, employing numerous academic faculty and support staff, and is the birthplace of child psychiatry.

Kamaldeep Bhui, PhD, is a Professor at the Centre for Psychiatry at the Wolfson Institute of Preventive Medicine, Barts and London School of

Medicine & Dentistry, Queen Mary, University of London. He is Director of Cultural Consultation Service; Director of MSc Transcultural Mental Healthcare and MSc Psychological Therapies.

Wayne Blissett, BSW (Hons), has worked in the area of Maori mental health in New Zealand for 20 years. Wayne specializes in bicultural systems development and working with organizations to be more responsive to cultural needs of Maori communities across all aspects of the mental health system.

Judi Clements, LLB, MA, was Chief Executive at the Mental Health Foundation of New Zealand. From 1991 to 2000, Chief Executive of Mind, the National Association for Mental Health in the UK. In 1999, she was awarded an Honorary Doctorate for services to mental health and local government. Judi relocated to New Zealand in 2005 to lead the Mental Health Foundation.

John Cox, PhD, is past President of the Royal College of Psychiatrists and the immediate past Secretary General of the World Psychiatric Association. Currently, he is Co-chair at the Centre for the Study of Faith, Science and Values in Healthcare at the University of Gloucestershire (where he is Visiting Professor) and Visiting Professor at the Institute of Psychiatry, London.

John Eversley, PhD, is currently a part-time Senior Lecturer at London Metropolitan University, where he leads a Masters in Community Development. He also teaches Public Health and Healthcare Policy at other universities. John undertakes contract research on contemporary and historical public policy through a not-for-profit company.

Peter Ferns, MSc, CQSW, is a social worker, trainer and consultant, and currently works in a front-line Adult Safeguarding and Disabilities service in London. Peter has worked as an independent training consultant for many years with a wide experience of social and health services. Research interests include mental health, learning disabilities, advocacy, equality issues, social work education, service quality and organizational development.

Alison Gray, MRCPsych, MMedSci, is a Consultant in Liaison Psychiatry in Hereford and an ordained priest in the Church of England. As the secretary to the Royal College of Psychiatrists' Spirituality Special Interest Group Dr Gray organizes teaching and training in spirituality. She lectures at Birmingham University and is also the secretary to the Whole Person Health Network. Dr Gray can often be found walking the Malvern Hills.

Jaswant Guzder, PhD, is Associate Professor, McGill University, Department of Psychiatry; Head of Child Psychiatry and Director of Childhood Disorders, Jewish General Hospital, Center for Child Development and Mental Health in Montreal. She is on the Board of *Transcultural Psychiatry* journal and the Board of theatre company, Tseesri Duniya.

David Ingleby, PhD, is Emeritus Professor of Intercultural Psychology at Utrecht University, the Netherlands, where he works at the European

Research Centre on Migration and Ethnic Relations. He acted as Consultant to the Council of Europe's Expert Committee on Mobility, Migration and Access to Health Care, as well as Temporary Advisor on migration- and ethnicity-linked health inequities to the WHO Regional Office (Europe).

Laurence J. Kirmayer, MD, FRCPC, is James McGill Professor and Director, Division of Social and Transcultural Psychiatry, McGill University, Editor-in-Chief of *Transcultural Psychiatry* and directs the Culture and Mental Health Research Unit at the Jewish General Hospital in Montreal. He co-directs the National Network for Aboriginal Mental Health Research.

Ted Lo, MBBS, MRCPsych, FRCPC, is a community psychiatrist in Toronto, active in ethnocultural mental health. He was an Assistant Professor at the University of Toronto, and a member of the Mental Health Commission of Canada. He founded the Hong Fook Mental Health Association. He provides cultural competence education for health professionals.

Dominica F. McBride, PhD, is Founder/CEO of Become, Inc. She has conducted domestic and international programme development and evaluation projects with marginalized communities. She has led multiple multicultural initiatives, with a focus on community participation and empowerment; and published on various topics including cultural competence, prevention and human rights.

Sharon Mier, PsyD, is in private practice in Ithaca, New York after 10 years working at Cornell University. While at Cornell, Sharon developed an innovative advocacy programme for students who were unable to access mental health services. Prior to Cornell, Sharon lived in Leeds, England working in Community Mental Health.

Zenobia Nadirshaw, PhD, is Professor and Head of Psychology at Kensington and Chelsea Primary Care Trust, London. She is a Consultant Clinical Psychologist with 35 years of clinical and management NHS experience of Health and Social Care Services in Learning Disabilities and mental health care.

Fritz Luther Pino, MA, is currently a PhD candidate in the Department of Humanities, Social Sciences and Social Justice Education, at the Ontario Institute for Studies in Education, University of Toronto. He completed his undergraduate and Masters degrees in psychology in the Philippines.

Hári Sewell, CQSW, DMS, is honorary Senior Visiting Research Fellow at the University of Central Lancashire and Buckinghamshire New University and Editor of the journal *Ethnicity and Inequalities in Health and Social Care*. He is the Director of HS Consultancy.

Rashmi Singla, PhD, is an Associate Professor at the Department of Psychology and Educational Research, as well as at interdisciplinary studies in Health Promotion at Roskilde University, Denmark. She is a member of the Society for Intercultural Psychology board and Global Health network. She has published a number of books and articles in these areas.

Tholene Sodi, PhD, is a registered clinical psychologist with more than 25 years of clinical, university teaching and management experience. He is a Full Professor and Head of the Department of Psychology at the University of Limpopo (Turfloop Campus), South Africa. He has published extensively in the areas of culture and mental health.

Nkokone Tema, MD, is Specialist Psychiatrist and Head of Psychiatry at Rahima Moosa Mother and Child Hospital, Gauteng, South Africa, and Lecturer for medical students and allied professionals, University of Witwatersrand, South Africa.

Oliver Treacy, RMN/RGN, MA, is a registered mental and general nurse. He is currently Service Director at Barnet, Enfield and Haringey Mental Health Trust. He has recently worked in Sri Lanka with the National Institute of Mental Health (NIMH) and the People's Rural Development Association (PRDA).

Rachel Tribe, PhD, is a Professor and Programme Director for the Professional Doctorate in Counselling Psychology at the University of East London, UK. She is an HPC-registered Counselling and Organizational Psychologist, and has published widely in the areas of mental health and diversity.

Charles Watters, PhD, is a Professor in the Department of Childhood Studies, Rutgers State University of New Jersey. He is Visiting Professor at the University of Brasilia and acts as a scientific advisor to the Portuguese Presidency of the European Union and international advisor to the Nordic Research Group on Refugee Children. He is the Founding Editor of the *International Journal of Migration, Health and Social Care*.

Chamindra Weerackody, BA (Hons), is a consultant sociologist in Sri Lanka and Project Lead in Sri Lanka of the Trauma and Global Health (TGH) Program coordinated by McGill University and Douglas Mental Health University Institute, Canada, in partnership with the PRDA.

Charmaine Williams, PhD, is the Associate Dean Academic and the Factor-Inwentash Chair in Health and Mental Health at the Factor-Inwentash Faculty of Social Work, University of Toronto. Her research bridges health and equity of access to primary health care for racial minority women, HIV prevention in black communities, discrimination against LGBTQ individuals in the international context and individual and family experience of living with serious and persistent mental illnesses.

Foreword

The most powerful critiques of bio-medical psychiatry originated in those groups most directly affected and constrained by its power – survivors and service user groups, feminists and women, black people, and others across the globe, who were once subjected to Western colonialism and placed under the lens and authority of psychiatry. These groups have been responsible for unleashing powerful criticism, protest and direct action, academic writing and a coming together in solidarity, resistance and defiance to the right of psychiatric discourse to determine how we should think, act, behave and interpret our experiences. The life and work of Suman Fernando is at the heart of this resistance.

This collection of essays, papers and reflections by luminaries of critical thought in the field of culture and mental health is a fitting tribute to and warm appreciation of Suman's outstanding work and life. It also happens to come at a turning point in the history of psychiatry. The furore that greeted the launch of *DSM-V* in May 2013 is still reverberating in our minds. Allied to this is the repeated failure of neuroscience and genetics to reveal the biological basis of madness and distress. Furthermore, recent work from within the evidence-based medicine paradigm has revealed the dubious effectiveness of most drug treatment in psychiatry, and in addition the evidence now indicates that the long-term use of neuroleptic drugs is fraught with risk and danger. The rise of the global mental health movement, although seemingly innocent enough, threatens a new wave of neo-colonialism. All this is an indication that psychiatry is in crisis, and that it is time to rethink its ethics, epistemology and practice.

Suman Fernando's work has been leading the way in our attempts to rethink psychiatric knowledge and clinical work for over a quarter of a century. My first encounter with it came in the early 1990s, when I was struggling to make sense of the shameful over-representation of young African-Caribbean men on the acute admission ward I worked on in my first consultant post in Manchester. I read *Mental Health, Race and Culture*, and was introduced to drapetomania and the baleful work of the American pro-slavery alienist Samuel Cartwright. Suman's book helped to change the way I saw the world. He opened my eyes, and reinforced my commitment to a path that I had already taken my first hesitant steps down – that of reaching out to and supporting Black and Minority Ethnic (BME) communities. This of course was a process to which Suman was already committed.

In time I came to recognize the cogency of his conceptual analyses of psychiatry and Western therapy. He is, to my knowledge, the first psychiatrist to draw attention to the influence of Enlightenment thought on the Western concept of the self. It wasn't until I read Charles Taylor's *Sources of the Self* (1989) in the late 1990s that I began fully to appreciate the depths to be found in Suman's work, and its implications for my work as a psychiatrist in a multicultural society. Shortly after reading *Mental Health, Race and Culture* I heard Suman speak at a conference, and as we got to know each other my admiration for his humanity, personal integrity, intellectual rigour and humour grew. And these characteristics are bound together by the single most important personal attribute necessary to work ethically as a psychiatrist today – humility.

His work also stands in the tradition of another great psychiatrist and post-colonial critic, that of Frantz Fanon. Suman's work may not have inspired liberatory struggles against colonialism in the way that Fanon's did; nevertheless it has drawn attention to the value and importance of indigenous systems of meaning and support for people who experience mental health problems (Fernando, 2005). These are grounded in local values and understanding, and draw on non-Western traditions of healing, such as Ayurveda. His work with the People's Rural Development Association in Colombo has demonstrated the importance of these systems for Sri Lanka's displaced communities following recent conflicts and natural disasters in the country (Weerackody and Fernando, 2008; Fernando & Weerackody, 2011). This principle of respect of local understandings of distress lies at the heart of the work that I and others have undertaken in Bradford's diverse cultures.

I can count on the fingers of one hand the psychiatrists whose work has left an ineradicable impression on my own, and Suman Fernando is one of them. For me he is like a much wiser, older brother, a close family friend whose opinion and support I have greatly valued throughout my career. He is in my view the first psychiatrist before all others worthy of the adjective "critical". His contributions to the struggles of service users and survivors across the globe will far outlast the tarnished, fading spectre of bio-medical psychiatry.

Philip Thomas
Honorary Visiting Professor
Social Science and Humanities
University of Bradford

References

Fernando, S. (2005). Mental health services in low-income countries: Challenges and innovations. *International Journal of Migration, Health and Social Care, 1*, 13–18.

Fernando, S. & Weerackody, C. (Eds.). (2011). *Aspects of mental health in Sri Lanka.* Colombo: People's Rural Development Association.

Taylor, C. (1989). *Sources of the self: The making of modern identity.* Cambridge: Cambridge University Press.

Weerackody, C. and Fernando, S. (2008). Perceptions of social stratification and well-being in refugee communities in North-Western Sri Lanka. *International Journal of Migration, Health and Social Care, 4*, 47–56.

Acknowledgements

First, our deepest gratitude and appreciation to Suman Fernando for being open and welcoming to the possibility of having his work, exposed, critiqued, reflected upon and written about. Usually a very private person, he was generous with his time and expertise to us as editors, as well as to individual contributors.

To all the authors of the chapters and personal reflective sections of this book, we greatly appreciate your expert contributions, reflecting on Suman Fernando's research and writings in a critical, creative and engaging way. All chapters have analysed Suman's work and set it in particular contexts: in training, in community settings, in research, in practice and transnationally.

Our sincere thanks to several colleagues, friends and family members who were supportive of this project in many different ways through its process. They are: Anissa Talahite, Ramon Ocampo, Charmaine Williams, Daniel Harry, Frances Fernando, Maya Florence, Philip Thomas, Roisin Anna, Sharon Mier, Sharon Moonsamy, Tara Isabelle, Ted Lo, Zina Claude.

A special thanks to Ruth Tellis and Vicki Lee, Catherine Gray and Palgrave Macmillan for granting permission to republish a shortened version of "Racism in Psychiatry", a chapter from Suman Fernando's book, *Mental Health, Race and Culture* (3rd ed., 2010).

Also particular thanks to Routledge for permission to republish Charmaine Williams' interview with Suman Fernando, which was first published in *Counselling Psychology Quarterly*, 25 (2), 167–174; June 2012.

Finally, our sincere thanks and appreciation to Joanne Forshaw, Susannah Frearson, Kirsten Buchanan at Routledge, Georgina Boyle, and Allie Hargreaves and all at Wearset for the help and support we received during the making of this book.

Introduction

The increase and growth of Black and Minority Ethnic (BME) communities in the West, sometimes referred to as Diaspora communities, will have a significant impact on the kinds of health and mental health services that are required for a diverse group of people. In some countries, such as the United States and Canada, the changes in their national demography over the next two decades will markedly shift the ways in which psychiatry and mental health care are theorized, researched and practised so that the needs of the various ethnic, racial and transnational communities are met. For example, in 35 of the United States' 50 largest cities, for instance, non-Hispanic whites are or soon will be the minority (according to United States Census 2006). These new racial/ethnic/cultural configurations inevitably bring about different worldviews, belief systems, values, customs and lifestyles that necessitate myriad responses from health and mental health care providers; among these are to integrate patients' ethno-racial and ethnic attitudes and beliefs into diagnosis and treatment, and to respect and incorporate patients' religious experiences into treatment.

At the same time, globalization and the indulgence of Western health and mental health care practices are making in-roads into low and middle income countries in ways that tend to disseminate and dominate a particular ideology of health and mental health care, sometimes driven by a neo-colonial project directed not by governments, as was colonialism, but by multinational pharmaceutical companies. Very little or no opportunity has been given to research and use indigenous and cultural knowledge of health and mental health care practices.

Suman Fernando's work, which critically examines the current theory, research and practices of mental health policies of racialized and disadvantaged communities, is an important starting point to interrogate the understanding of these practices, which affect not only BME communities in the Diaspora but also those countries these groups come from. In other words, critically examining Western psychological, psychiatric and mental health theories that are deemed to be the standard approach to healing in health and mental health care is paramount to constructing a wellness and healing approach that is global, transnational and holistic. *Critical Psychiatry and Mental Health* therefore offers scholars from various countries – the United Kingdom, United States, Canada, Netherlands, Denmark, India, Sri Lanka and South Africa – to use Suman

Fernando's ideas and theories as the basis to examine their own countries' practices and construct new ways forward in this field.

As a leading scholar in the area of critical mental health, Suman Fernando has been highly influential not only in the United Kingdom, but globally, as the chapters in this book will attest. Moreover, it is not just the academic world that has acknowledged Suman Fernando for his expertise and scholarship; much appreciation for his lifetime efforts has come from the users of mental health care. Some of us, if we are lucky enough, get to receive one or more honours, tributes, accolades or material rewards for our achievements and accomplishments in our lifetime. Many of us are content with simple praises and compliments for our hard work and creativity, and live with the hope that our dreams of glory do not turn into nightmares. When the British Crown offers to appoint someone an OBE (the Most Excellent Order of the British Empire; an honour that ranks just below knighthood in the order of chivalry), most ordinary people happily and respectfully accept the honour. But it is not every day that someone says "No" to the British monarchy and the Order of Empire. One such person is Suman Fernando, who turned down the OBE "for services to black and minority ethnic mental healthcare". Suman Fernando wrote to Tony Blair, the British prime minister at the time, rejecting the award (this letter can be found on Suman Fernando's website: www.sumanfernando.com). The answer he received from Tony Blair's office was to regret his refusal, saying that "the govt was aware of problems in the mental health services and was doing its best to make changes".

In his refusal, Suman Fernando joins the ranks of people like Albert Finney (actor), Caryl Churchill (playwright), David Bowie (musician), John Cleese (actor), Doris Lessing (author), Jennifer Saunders (actress), Dawn French (actress), and the poet Benjamin Zephaniah, who said: "I get angry when I hear the word 'empire'; it reminds me of slavery, it reminds me of thousands of years of brutality, it reminds me of how my foremothers were raped and my forefathers brutalised". Suman Fernando's reasons are complex and multidimensional. On the surface he argues that his refusal of the OBE was a rejection of British policies in mental health care in the United Kingdom. He is a strong advocate for changes in the legislation to end discrimination in the mental health system; however, he felt that practices were going from bad to worse. A *Guardian* article entitled "Psychiatrist snubs OBE in mental health protest" (James, 2007) summarized the situation thus:

> An eminent psychiatrist has turned down an OBE in protest at the government's "deeply flawed" plans to extend compulsory powers of detention over the mentally ill. Dr. Suman Fernando was told last week by Downing Street that he had been nominated for the honour for his "services to black and minority ethnic mental healthcare". But he has publicly rejected the award, accusing NHS mental health services of being institutionally racist. He fears that changes proposed in the mental health bill going through parliament will fail to address the disproportionate rate at which black people are admitted to and detained in psychiatric hospitals. Suman says: "What

seems most strange is that the government say they want to recognise my services to black and minority healthcare at a time when they are trying to push through legislation that would make things worse for black people caught up in the mental health system ... I cannot possibly accept it [the OBE] while the government is pursuing its present policy regarding mental health legislation ... the government bill currently before parliament is deeply flawed".

Suman Fernando's response is thus political, and it arises from his childhood. In a personal conversation with Martha Ocampo, one of the editors, he recalls his parents being very critical of people who accepted such honours during and after the British colonial rule in Sri Lanka. However, when the University of Toronto, in December 2010, sent Suman Fernando a letter confirming that he was offered the OISE/University of Toronto's Lifetime Achievement Award for his work on "Culture, Race and Mental Health", Suman Fernando did not hesitate to travel to Canada to accept this honour, and acknowledge the respect that the Canadian and North American academy and its scholars bestowed upon him. So on 7 June 2011, at the 6th Critical Multicultural and Diversity Counselling Psychology and Psychotherapy Conference, Suman Fernando received the Lifetime Achievement Award for his work on "Culture, Race and Mental Health", presented by Dr Julia O'Sullivan, Dean of the Ontario Institute for Studies in Education (OISE), at the University of Toronto. Here is an excerpt of the citation:

> For his outstanding contribution to the field of cross-cultural, multicultural and diversity psychology, psychiatry, counseling and psychotherapy, particularly to culture, race and mental health concerns ... an outstanding, remarkable and leading expert in his field; as a researcher, mentor and teacher he has inspired a whole generation of scholars who are following in his footsteps examining and critiquing the outdated ways in which mental health care is provided, researched and theorized. Indeed, his creative and inspiring insights into the human spirit have been provocative and challenging to the orthodoxy of traditional psychiatry, psychology, counseling, and psychotherapy. Through his innovative research and lucid writings on the many varied and diverse topics in psychology.... It exemplifies a multilevel, multidisciplinary and also a poetic response to the ways in which we can embrace the big questions of life; yet his focus begins not with the abstract questions of existential theory but with the suffering and pain of particular communities and individuals.

Suman Fernando has a long history with Canada. He has been undertaking training and consultancy work there every year since 1994. Without a break in this annual record of visits, he has been in the city of Toronto for a week or sometimes two, and sometimes accompanied by his life partner, Frances, to engage with the questions that confront race, culture and mental health services in the city. His primary involvement in Toronto has been at Across Boundaries: An

Ethnoracial Mental Health Centre, which he helped launch with the Coalition. During his Toronto visits, he offered seminars on race, culture and mental health at the University of Toronto, on several occasions holding discussions on research, theory, practice and community engagement concerning race, culture and psychiatry. The other Canadian city that Suman Fernando frequently visited was Montreal, engaging in research and international work with colleagues in the Transcultural Psychiatry Department at McGill University.

In 1994, Suman Fernando gave a presentation on Mental Health, Race and Culture at the Clarke Institute of Psychiatry, now the Centre for Addiction and Mental Health (CAMH) in Toronto. This was the start of a collaboration between Suman Fernando and mental health practitioners, who were so impressed and inspired by his critique of race, culture and psychiatry that he was inducted into their hall of fame, the Ethnoracial Mental Health Coalition in Toronto. This began the discussion of developing and setting up a mental health centre to provide appropriate services for people from racialized communities who are experiencing mental health distress.

In March 1995, Across Boundaries: An Ethnoracial Mental Health Centre was launched with Suman Fernando as the guest speaker. His presentation included a critical analysis of Western psychiatry, innovative care and practices and future directions in mental health. Since the launch of Across Boundaries, Suman Fernando has continued to visit the centre every year. He has been a guest speaker in well-attended conferences organized by the centre; made himself available to the clients and staff at Across Boundaries and similar groups for consultations; provided formal and informal consultations; and shared his rich knowledge of race, culture and mental health care to mental health service providers in Toronto. His passion and dedication to make meaningful systemic changes and to improve the care for people from racialized groups have been influential in the development of appropriate services for both racialized and non-racialized communities.

This has been the work of Suman Fernando every year since 1994. Most recently, in July 2012, Suman Fernando was the keynote presenter at a conference organized by a coalition of consumers and family groups and mental health agencies to talk about his latest involvement in the "Inquiry into the Schizophrenia Label". Having reached the grand age of wisdom and enlightenment, being 80, his energy and commitment has not faltered; in fact his last visit in 2013 to Toronto and Montreal has been to continue his life's work of bringing awareness of race, culture and mental health to scholars, researchers and practitioners alike. Critiquing Eurocentric theory, practice and research in the mental health field has become Suman Fernando's lifelong passion. He could be regarded a post-colonial critic of psychiatry, psychology and mental health.

Critique of Western psychiatry and mental health

Although well articulated and documented for several decades now by critics such as Paul Gilroy, Stuart Hall, Homi Bhabha and many others, post-colonial theory has not had the impact in psychology and psychiatry to the extent that we have seen in sociology, literature and contemporary cultural studies. There appear to have been very few, if any, inroads made in mental health research, the theory and practice of psychology, psychiatry and psychotherapy. Psychiatric and mental health provision in the West is still as racist as it was when it first emerged as a discipline. Among the small handful of dedicated and committed researchers and scholars engaging in race, culture, ethnicity and mental health is Suman Fernando, whose work has been the foundation and springboard for transcultural research, theory and practice in psychiatry, counselling and psychotherapy. Thus, some progress has been made to dent the armour of institutional racism and colonial thinking in the mental health profession, but it appears not enough to prevent the stigmatization of blackness as madness, the overrepresentation and misdiagnosis of BME people as mad, bad, sad and so on. As Suman Fernando (2010, p. 68) says:

> The influence of racism in the social construction of commonly diagnosed categories of mental disorder is not always easy to discern. Political, social and ideological pressures current in society always impinge on the diagnostic process by influencing questions of intelligibility, common sense, clinical opinion, pragmatism and tradition. And racism acts through these pressures.

Suman Fernando's critique of psychiatric and mental health care practice is reiterated by other scholars and researchers, such as Aggrey Burke, Arthur Kleinman, Jafar Kareem, John Cox, Kamaldeep Bhui, Laurence Kirmayer, Sashi Sashidahran, Roland Littlewood, and many others. This volume in part brings together some of this research and scholarship. In celebrating the achievements of one single individual we hope that it will make larger statements about current policies and practices and lead to changes that Suman Fernando has advocated. We begin this discussion in Part I, "Critique of Western Psychiatry and Mental Health", which offers a social, cultural and political critique of race, culture and ethnicity, starting with two chapters by Suman Fernando himself, followed by chapters by two of his colleagues. In Chapter 1, "Transcultural Psychiatry and Mental Health", Suman Fernando suggests that there are many limitations in psychiatry when dealing with people from diverse socio-cultural backgrounds. He argues that these limitations are more pronounced when attempting to deal with human suffering and social disharmony by postulating disorders of the mind. These categories ultimately fail as they do not take into account individual differences but rather depend on group stereotyping and racist articulations of BME groups. In Chapter 2, "Racism in Psychiatry", he offers a detailed overview of race and racism by applying social and cultural theories to the practice of psychiatry. Suman Fernando has spent his career noticing the observable but overlooked facts that link race, racialization and mental health status and care experiences. The consequences for such a policy are the themes in Chapter 3, "Ethno-racial Representations and the Burden of 'Otherness' in Mental Health", in which Roy Moodley, drawing on anthropological pronouncements, colonial literature and travel writing, explores the projection and prejudice that has

6 *Introduction*

shaped not only the historical and literary landscape but remains a bastion of our current thinking in health and mental health care. In Chapter 4, "Is There an Emancipatory Psychiatry?", John Eversley raises the question of psychiatry as a social movement. Through his critique of psychiatry and mental health practices, he argues that psychiatry can go back to the basic scientific understanding of human health – the relationships between mind, body and society and what is "normal"; thus making it possible for patients to play a key role in diagnosis, treatment and outcomes.

Challenges and opportunities in mental health care

The second part of this book attempts to explore the challenges and opportunities in mental health care, beginning with David Ingleby in Chapter 5, "The Challenge of Diversity to Mental Health Services", in which he takes on the issues of how diversity is accommodated, but not before drawing attention to the marginalization and social exclusion of many ethnic minority people in mental health services. David argues that there is a need to tackle the social roots rather than simply diagnosing individuals and reaching for therapies. The chapter also offers insights and parallels between the situation of black and ethnic minorities in Western countries and that of populations in low- and middle-income countries. Using Suman Fernando's work as the basis of a critique on psychiatry and mental health, the next chapter, "Race, Culture and Mental Health Care for Refugees", by Charles Watters, focuses on mental health issues in refugee populations, which are widely regarded as having significantly high rates of mental disorders and are in particular associated with significant levels of post-traumatic stress disorder, depression and anxiety disorders. In Chapter 7, "Developing Mental Health Policies That Address Race and Culture", Hári Sewell continues the discussion of how race, culture and mental health can be accommodated with clear policies and guidelines that will ensure equity and social justice. He highlights the challenges and opportunities that practitioners will encounter when making such attempts. One of the competencies that seems critical to transcultural work in mental health is explored in depth in Chapter 8, "Religion, Culture and Mental Health", by Alison Gray and John Cox. They argue that taking into account a patient's religious and spiritual beliefs is of paramount importance if psychiatry is to sustain an empathic and compassionate person-centred healing practice. The final word in this part goes to Suman Fernando, who discusses the challenges and opportunities he has had to make changes to the health and mental health care system. He does this in an interview with Charmaine Williams, in Chapter 9, "In the Therapist's Chair Is Suman Fernando". In this interview Suman Fernando talks about his early life in the United Kingdom, his research and his involvement in transcultural psychiatry. He also discusses his research and writings in critical psychiatry. Charmaine concludes her conversation with this comment on Suman Fernando:

> one can see how his gentle yet persistent assertions of the rights of patients, the link between justice and psychiatry, and the capacity of the system to

deliver anti-racist mental health care has made him so influential. Dr. Fernando is reflective and critical of his field, but also optimistic that awareness, new knowledge and the right kind of alliances can transform it.

Training and development in mental health practice

In Part III, Jaswant Guzder, Peter Ferns, Rachel Tribe, Martha Ocampo and Fritz Luther Pino explore the possibilities for training and development in mental health practice. Drawing on Suman Fernando's work, Jaswant Guzder, in Chapter 10, "Institutional Racism as a Seminal Concept of Cultural Competency Training", places cultural competency at the heart of therapeutic work. Institutional racism, she argues, shapes both the external landscapes (the training and policy) and the internal positioning (the therapist's transference and counter-transference issues) of contemporary psychiatric practice. These remain crucial matters in training and role modelling. Peter Ferns in Chapter 11, "Race Equality and Cultural Capability Training in Mental Health", using Suman Fernando's historical analysis of racism in psychiatry and mental health, explores key practice issues such as the limitations of diagnosis in transcultural situations; working positively with cultural differences; engaging in holistic assessment; greater service user participation in training; and promoting a whole-systems approach to race and culture training. This theme is further explored in Chapter 12, "Race and Cultural Diversity: The Training of Psychologists and Psychiatrists", in which Rachel Tribe reflects on the ways in which training is organized and implemented. She emphasizes the need for issues of diversity, race and culture to be foregrounded in training institutions and in clinical practice to ensure that mental health services are accessible and appropriate to all patient groups in the population. Finally in this part, Martha Ocampo and Fritz Luther Pino, in Chapter 13, "An Anti-racism/Anti-oppression Framework in Mental Health Practice", using a case study from the Across Boundaries centre (in Toronto) explore an anti-racism/anti-oppression framework for mental health care. They suggest that by recognizing the failure of the dominant Western medical model to effectively meet the mental health needs of racialized communities, we can begin to develop programmes and services that promote new and alternative ways of healing.

Transnational contexts: engaging the work of Suman Fernando

Suman Fernando's work has been foundational to the case against colonial psychiatry in many English-speaking countries, many of them former colonies of the British Empire. In Part IV of this volume we invited several colleagues from Canada, the United States, South Africa, Sri Lanka and New Zealand to reflect on the work of Suman Fernando in their country contexts. In this part, entitled "Transnational Contexts: Engaging the Work of Suman Fernando", these colleagues discuss how race, culture and psychiatry in their respective countries intersect to provide mental health services. We begin this part with Suman Fernando offering his thoughts on the "Myth of Global Mental Health" in

Chapter 14. Suman is emphatic about the fact that mental health promotion and alleviation of subjective distress and problems (seen by psychiatrists as "mental illness") are difficult to unravel in relation to low- and middle-income countries with mainly non-Western cultural backgrounds because the language of mental health and illness derives largely from Western cultural sources. Using recent studies (e.g. South India) Suman argues that sometimes traditional healing can be more beneficial for patients than psychiatric treatments. There appears to be growing awareness that traditional and cultural healing practices are now becoming not just an alternative choice for many patients, but a mainstream avenue to seek healing and curing. This fact is borne out by the discussion in Chapter 15, "Critical Psychiatry in Canada", by Laurence J. Kirmayer, who critically examines race, culture and multiculturalism in Canada in relation to health disparities and culturally responsive mental health services. His explores how Aboriginal and First Nation communities are marginalized in mainstream mental health care and resort to traditional ways of healing. In Chapter 16, "Culture, Race and Ethnicity in US Psychiatry", Carl C. Bell and Dominica F. McBride discuss how cultural imperialism and a stark mono-ethnocentrism that mirrored historical colonialism characterized psychiatry in the United States. After the Civil Rights Movement, multiculturalism increased and the appreciation of diversity in psychiatry grew. This chapter intersects the work of Suman Fernando in US psychiatry and describes the pre- and post-Civil Rights Movement and future directions. Many of the themes reflected in the previous chapter are explored by Nkokone Tema and Tholene Sodi in Chapter 17, "Race, Culture and Psychiatry in South Africa". Of significance for psychiatry in South Africa are the issues of colonialism, apartheid, HIV/AIDS and democracy. The negative health and mental health effects of the apartheid era and struggles in the post-apartheid period are critical to the evolution of an equitable and culturally competent practice. In Chapter 18, "Mental Health Services in Sri Lanka", Chamindra Weerackody and Suman Fernando introduce us to the personal and professional roots of Suman Fernando in Sri Lanka. It elaborates on Suman's contribution to introducing transcultural psychiatry in Sri Lanka and his work in promoting participatory approaches for community consultations and research, facilitating a range of global mental health professionals to work alongside local professionals to provide capacity building training to psychiatrists, nurses and social workers and many more. In Chapter 19, "Transcultural Psychiatry, Psychology and Social Entrepreneurship in Denmark", Rashmi Singla emphasizes the impact of Suman Fernando's conceptualizations as well as inspiring dialogues in Scandinavia, especially in the Danish context, during the past two decades. Rashmi shows how Suman's concepts of structural and institutional racism have been useful ideas in transcultural mental health work in Denmark. Finally, in Chapter 20, "Culture and Mental Health in Aotearoa, New Zealand", Judi Clements and Wayne Blissett consider the complex relationships of power and struggles for identity, dominance and place in the diverse communities in Aotearoa, New Zealand, with a particular focus on the history, colonization and racial oppression of the Maori community and its impacts on health and mental health.

Personal reflections on Suman Fernando's life and work

It seems that medicine and politics have been the mainstay in Suman Fernando's life; both his father and grandfather trained as medical practitioners and were also deeply involved in Sri Lankan politics. His grandfather, who had been one of the early Asian doctors to have qualified in the United Kingdom, at Edinburgh University in the 1870s or so, was involved in Sri Lankan politics but sadly died at an early age, suffering a heart attack at a political rally. His father trained as a medical doctor at Cambridge University in the early 1900s and was a founder member of the Ceylon Labour Party, one of the first left-wing parties in the country during British rule. Both his parents were nominal Christians; the family spoke both English and Sinhalese (Sinhala), although his mother could not write in Sinhala since she had gone to a missionary school where the use of Sinhala was forbidden.

Suman Fernando followed in his family's footsteps, gaining his medical degree at Cambridge University. His father educated Suman Fernando about the Indian Freedom Movement and named him after Mahatma Gandhi (Mohandas as his second name). It is not a coincidence that Suman Fernando's practice as a psychiatrist and his writings all point towards changing an unjust system that has political implications that inspire local and worldwide movements, just like the work of the man he was named after. Chamindra Weerackody, in Part V of this volume, writes about the early life and times of Suman Fernando in Sri Lanka. As this volume is also a celebration of his work, Part V, "Personal Reflections on Suman Fernando's Life and Work", attempts to do just that. Several colleagues, friends, research partners and collaborators reflect on their relationship with Suman Fernando. They are: Ted Lo, Chamindra Weerackody, John Cox, Kamaldeep Bhui, Sharon Mier, Oliver Treacy and Zenobia Nadirshaw. Their reflections range from Suman Fernando's life in Sri Lanka to the impact of his work in the United Kingdom and globally. Finally, this book ends with Suman Fernando meditating on the future of mental health in the West and globally. He suggests that

> a psychiatry of the future will maintain "illness" as the basis for understanding many human problems of a personal nature but illness will be seen (theoretically) as the result of a variety of influences in dynamic balance/imbalance – an illness model very different from that in psychiatry today.

References

Fernando, S. (2010). *Mental health, race and culture* (3rd ed.). Basingstoke: Palgrave Macmillan.

James, A. (2007, 17 May). Psychiatrist snubs OBE in mental health protest. *Guardian*. Retrieved from www.theguardian.com/society/2007/may/17/mentalhealth.socialcare.

United States Census. (2006). *Population estimates*. Retrieved from www.census.gov/popest/data/historical/2000s/vintage_2006.

Part I
Critique of Western psychiatry and mental health

1 Transcultural psychiatry and mental health

Suman Fernando

Introduction

There are fundamental differences between, on the one hand, Western psychology and psychiatry and, on the other, non-Western approaches to 'mind' that were derived in non-Western cultural traditions, particularly those of Asia, Africa and Pre-Columbian America. Although there are various systems of medicine, it is only in Western medicine that a system has developed to identify a group of 'disorders' or 'illnesses' located in the 'mind' alone, as psychiatry does. But mind itself is both socially constructed in diverse ways depending on (social) context (Coulter, 1979) and imbued with culturally determined meaning forming the basis of a variety of 'folk psychologies' (Bruner, 1990).

Historically, both Western psychology and psychiatry emerged from Western thinking after the (European) Enlightenment of the 18th century reflecting a paradigm (see Kuhn, 1962, for the meaning of 'paradigm') characterized by: (1) positivism, the belief that reality is rooted only in what can be observed and knowledge is limited to events and to verifiable connections to events; (2) causality yielding a mechanical cause-and-effect model, implying that nothing is truly random and nothing beyond understanding (that is, supernatural); (3) objectivism, where feelings become things 'out there' to be studied as objects, and moral judgements are not valid; and (4) rationality, where the final arbiter of truth is reason and all assertions are verifiable by logical reasoning. The methods of study promoted by scientific thinking were (1) the mechanistic approach of Newtonian physics; (2) reducing complex systems into its parts; and (3) logical reasoning as opposed to any other type of understanding, such as intuition (for discussion, see Fernando, 2010). In the 19th century, Western psychology became biological under the influence of Darwinism (Murphy, 1938); and Morel's theory of degeneration (Morel, 1852) built upon by Kraepelin (1899) drove psychiatry in Europe into a genetic mode, giving rise to the German–British school of bio-medical psychiatry. But it was not until this bio-medical approach was adopted in the United States in the 1970s and 1980s that it became the standard system promoted as the 'scientific' approach (for detailed discussion, see Fernando, 2010). However, it is noteworthy that, although Western medicine and psychiatry started in a Western setting, the development of these disciplines is no longer confined to geographical locations in the West; medical and psychiatric research and theorizing, as well as development of allied techniques and treatments, are now sometimes located in Asian countries like Japan and increasingly in China and India, as a part of the globalization of science and technology. Because of this, it is preferable to speak of bio-medicine (rather than 'Western medicine') and 'bio-medical psychiatry' – or just psychiatry – rather than '*Western* psychiatry'. Yet, it is important to note that because of fundamental conflict between, on the one hand, Western psychology and bio-medical psychiatry and, on the other hand, the psychologies that come from non-Western cultural traditions – the cultures of the majority world – very different (culturally determined) understandings prevail of what problems of the mind entail, and how they may relate to concepts of illness and health. This means that a unitary, global system of 'mental health and illness' is not sustainable.

In this chapter, I shall start with a critical analysis of Western psychology and bio-medical psychiatry. Then I shall present a précis of how the transcultural psychiatry movement developed in the West. And finally, I shall consider briefly the practical application of current Western psychology, appertaining to what is generally understood as 'mental health' and the way psychiatry as a practical discipline allied to (Western) medicine functions today.

Western psychology and (bio-medical) psychiatry: a critical analysis

Western psychology covers 'the scientific study of the human mind and its functions, especially those affecting behaviour in a given context', while psychiatry is 'the branch of medicine concerned with the study and treatment of mental illness, emotional disturbance, and abnormal behaviour' (Soanes and Stevenson, 2008, pp. 1158–1159). Among the important questions that go begging is one concerning the nature of 'mind' and another about the socio-political purposes fulfilled by psychiatry (as a part of a medical system). The question of whether a particular approach is 'scientific' or not is a moot point; and the study of the human mind, closely linked to the concept of 'self', is recognizable in many seemingly 'non-scientific' (non-Western) cultural traditions (see Marsella, Devos and Hsu, 1985; Jahoda, 1992; Kirmayer, 2007). In other words, there are many psychologies in the world today, although admittedly the non-Western systems are mostly located in religion or philosophy. Examples are Indian (Hindu) psychology (Rama, 1985; Safaya, 1976) and its development in Buddhism (Rhys Davids, 1978) as a specific Buddhist psychology (Kalupahana, 1992) or the psychology of Zen (Fromm, Suzuki and de Martinal, 1960) and Tibetan Buddhism (Rinbochay and Napper, 1980); traditions in Chinese medicine that amount to a psychology (Hammer, 1990); African ways of interpreting the spirit/mind (Mbiti, 1969) and its relationship with Egyptian traditions (see Nobles, 1986); and the psychology discernible in the folklore and spiritualities of the first nations of the American continent (e.g. see Ross, 1992; Simmons, 1986).

In considering 'psychiatry' transculturally, the terrain is different. There are many different well-established systems of medicine as well as many others that are not yet standardized into clearly defined written forms, such as those practised in many parts of Africa and America (dating from pre-Columbian times), Ayurveda and Unani medicine (mainly practised in the Indian subcontinent and the Middle East) and Chinese medicine (predominantly used in China and neighbouring countries); but there is only one version of a *medical* speciality concerned with disorder of mind as distinct from body, and that is psychiatry – the system developed in the Western tradition emanating from 19th-century science. It is only in this (Western) system that feelings, beliefs and behaviours are interpreted as 'pathological' (abnormal), indicating the presence of 'illnesses' of the mind (see Fernando, 2010). Analogies between descriptions of treatment in some non-Western medical systems and those in psychiatry, such as that drawn by Clifford (1984) writing about (what she called) 'Tibetan Psychiatry', are in reality far-fetched when one considers their practical applications. What reigns supreme as 'psychiatry' is the Western variety – bio-medical psychiatry.

The major difference between Western and other traditions in relation to psychology and religion is the emphasis in the latter on a holistic perspective of health and the exclusion in the former of spirituality. As psychology developed in the West within philosophy, the stage was set by one of its early founders, Descartes, declaring that mind (seen by Descartes as an indestructible 'soul') and the impermanent body matter were fundamentally separate (the so-called Cartesian philosophy). Capra (1982) describes how as 'scientific' psychology developed, it excluded anything that smacked of 'religion' and produced, under the influence of Newtonian physics, a mechanistic understanding of all aspects of human nature and even of human societies. Although Descartes advocated that the mind should be studied by introspection and body by methods of natural science, both methods were used subsequently. The culmination of (Western) psychology in clinical work was that 'structuralists studied the mind through introspection and tried to analyse consciousness into its basic elements, while behaviourists concentrated exclusively on the study of behaviour and so were led to ignore or deny the existence of mind altogether' (Capra, 1982, p. 166). The result today is some confusion in Western thought about the role and nature of mind, as distinct from that of brain (for detailed discussion of the development of psychology from Descartes onwards, see Capra, 1982; for the relevance of all of this to mental health, see Fernando, 1991, 2002).

Psychiatry developed on the back of a power base resulting from the great confinement – the name given by Foucault (1967) to the institutionalization in asylums from around the middle of the 17th century of large numbers of people in Europe and North America considered deviant or mad. As medical jurisdiction was established over the asylums, the inmates of the asylums were deemed to suffer from various illnesses (see Porter, 1987, 1990; Scull, 1993; Castel, 1988, for interplay between custody and diagnosis of illness) and these became standardized over the years. Ultimately, 'mental illness' became the most popular model in the West to use in categorizing people regarded (in the West) as 'mad' and this model of 'illness' located in the mind became the model for seemingly understanding various problems that human beings had with regard to their feelings, behaviour and beliefs. A variety of therapies have emerged over the years, latterly dominated by psychotropic drugs given designations such as 'anti-psychotics', 'anti-depressants' and so on, on the premise that they antagonize specific types of illnesses.

Both Western psychology and psychiatry have had far-reaching consequences beyond the clinical mental health field. According to Capra (1982, p. 45), psychology arising from the Cartesian division between mind and body has

> taught us to be aware of ourselves as isolated egos existing 'inside' our bodies; it has led us to set a higher value on mental than manual work; it has enabled huge industries to sell products – especially to women – that would make us owners of the 'ideal body'; it has kept doctors from seriously considering the psychological dimensions of illness and psychotherapists from dealing with their patients' bodies.

The influence of psychiatry (see Fernando, 2010) has resulted in a way of thinking – a 'culture' – that tends to reduce complex human problems attributable to a mixture of social, political and biological issues to diagnoses that assume biological causes, thereby reducing our ability to grapple with them realistically. Although its approach to human problems of living has occurred predominantly in the Western tradition, the economic, political and military power of Western nations has resulted in the spread of this 'culture' over many parts of the world, putting at risk the health and welfare of people in many parts of the world (for further discussion of the themes mentioned, see Fernando, 2010).

Brief history of the transcultural psychiatry movement

Although a medical approach to madness and hospitals for people deemed to suffer from illness of the mind go back to the Islamic period of European civilization between the 10th and 12th centuries (Dols, 1992; Ellenberger, 1974), the medical movement that developed into (Western) 'psychiatry' did not emerge until the 18th century (Shorter, 1997). As a discipline developed by (racially) white people in a Western Judeo-Christian cultural framework post-Enlightenment, problems in applying its practices became obvious as the discipline encountered people from 'other' cultures often identified as not being 'white'. The encounter in Asia and Africa gave rise to 'cultural' studies and theorizing that was racist (see Chapter 2, this volume), while some colonial powers introduced the asylum system into their colonies.

In the 1950s an academic interest stimulated by anthropological studies (mainly outside Europe and North America) fed into developing what became known as 'transcultural psychiatry', centred at McGill University led by Eric Wittkower (Murphy, 1983). As the McGill group developed, the 'Transcultural Psychiatry Section' of the World Psychiatric Association (WPA) was formed

(Murphy, 1986). My first book (Fernando, 1988) describes how 'transcultural psychiatry' arrived in the United Kingdom when the Transcultural Psychiatry Society (UK), which soon became known as TCPS, was inaugurated soon after an International Congress on Transcultural Psychiatry was held in 1976. In that book I go on to state that

> The term transcultural psychiatry is used loosely to cover two interrelated topics namely, (a) cultural aspects of psychiatry – or 'cultural psychiatry' – and (b) psychiatry in non-Western cultures. Although the former can ignore race – and frequently does so – the latter cannot possibly do so.
>
> (Fernando, 1988, p. xiii)

In fact, the transcultural psychiatry movement in the United Kingdom stood out from other similar movements (usually called 'cultural psychiatry') to give prominence to issues of discrimination affecting people seen as 'non-white' (see Kirmayer and Minas, 2000); and meetings and conferences in the United Kingdom convened by the TCPS in the 1980s and 1990s served to highlight the nature and effect of racism and power exercised through the practice of biomedical psychiatry. However, with many other groups with similar aims coming on stream in the United Kingdom from the late 1990s onwards, the TCPS itself closed down in 2008 (Vige, 2008).

The influence of the transcultural psychiatry movement in the United Kingdom is difficult to pinpoint. In the 1980s, it formed as it were the bedrock that supported many individuals in challenging the British system of psychiatry and calling for changes in mental health services. The main strength of the movement was its persistence in identifying institutional racism as the basis for many of the problems faced by (what came to be called) 'Black and Minority Ethnic' (BME) people. Also, the TCPS supported individuals and groups to establish training courses for professionals and to take action at various levels of professional practice and management in the National Health Service. Some of the ideologies of transcultural psychiatry, especially the viewpoint that both 'race' *and* 'culture' are issues to be confronted, have been taken on to some extent by institutional processes in the United Kingdom, although there is clearly a long way to go in bringing about mental health services that are both culturally sensitive and racially neutral.

Understanding health and illness: lessons for practice in psychology and psychiatry

The search for understanding the human condition, the yearning for knowing the 'truth' about ourselves, characterizes human societies the world over. But the ways in which societies and individuals have gone about this search are diverse, representing the diversity of 'cultures' themselves. So, although all societies the world over recognize health and a departure from health ('illness') (McQueen, 1978), the concepts underpinning them differ in a variety of ways (Currer and Stacey, 1986) mostly derived from cultural traditions.

In simple shorthand, most non-Western traditions see health as a harmonious balance between various forces in the person and the social context, while the post-Enlightenment Western tradition sees health as an individualized sense of well-being, sometimes called 'subjective wellbeing' (Diener, 1984, 2000). For example, the Chinese way of thinking sees all illness as an imbalance of *yin* and *yang* (two complementary poles of life energy) to be corrected by attempts to re-establish 'balance' (Aakster, 1986); the Indian tradition emphasizes the harmony between the person and their group as indicative of health (Kakar, 1984); and the concept of health in African culture is more social than biological (Lambo, 1969) (for discussion, see Fernando, 2002, 2010). The non-Western ideal of health could be seen then as a sense of subjective well-being (see above) that is widened to include 'the satisfaction of personal, relational and collective needs' as described by Nelson and Prilleltensky (2005, p. 56). However, it is not just that concepts of health and illness are different across cultural traditions; what is important for many societies is that the ways in which illness is perceived – what Kleinman (1977) called the 'explanatory model' for understanding the experience of being 'ill' – are different. And these differences come through in modern multicultural societies resulting in variations between different members of society or different families in the way illness is handled.

In the case of mental health problems, the dominant theme in the Western traditions (reflected in psychiatry and Western psychology) is that problems identified (by the person concerned or by a 'specialist') as being concerned with thinking, emotional reactions, feelings, fears, anxieties, depressions etc. are conceptualized in terms of illness dealt with – 'treated' – by a variety of interventions aimed at 'cure' or alleviation of 'symptoms' (of illness). Even family problems and social behaviour (as in 'psychopathy') and hatred and jealousy (as in 'pathological jealousy') are sometimes fitted into the illness model. Clearly, this Western approach is alien to traditional Asian and African cultural worldviews; in these non-Western traditions, a much narrower range of problems nearly always identified by bodily changes are seen as illness, even then conceptualized as disharmonies within a total (holistic) self.

All this has an important bearing on how mental health professionals, especially psychologists and psychiatrists, should go about their work. When presented with a client who may be regarded by wider society as having problems located in the 'mind' – madness or mental health problems – and hence requiring 'mental health services', it is necessary to bear in mind that attention to 'mental health' may be at variance with – and in conflict with – what some people expect and respect. Therefore it is important for mental health professionals to understand 'illness' from the point of view of the person and their family – or indeed 'cultural group' (if this can be reliably identified) rather than the norms of society at large, which in most Western societies derive from the Western tradition. In other words, it is important in clinical practice, as much as in research, that personal meaning of illness is elicited by an 'emic' (culture-specific) approach to individual distress (for discussion of personal and social meanings of illness, see Kleinman, 1988). Further, transcultural studies suggest that professionals need to go even further than that – to take on board the 'socio-political context and moral predicament of patients [and clients] ... and "what's at stake" for individuals and communities' (Kirmayer, 2006, p. 127).

Conclusions

The transcultural psychiatry movement, which began in Canada and then spread to other parts of the Western world, has fed into a critical approach to Western psychology and psychiatry, which is now largely a bio-medical discipline with only marginal input from socio-psychological knowledge. The spread of these two (Western) disciplines on the back of (Western) allopathic medicine (regarded as scientific and 'modern'), and more general Western power including that of the pharmaceutical industry, has resulted in serious conflicts and injustices – often seen as 'cultural' or 'racial' – in both theoretical discourse (presented in contentious debates) and practical actions (in the provision of mental health services) in non-Western settings and in multicultural societies in the Western world. This chapter outlines the challenge that this situation presents – to practitioners and academics in the mental health field, managers of mental health services, politicians in positions of power and influence and the informed public. The question to be answered now centres on how change can be brought about in the present situation in psychology and psychiatry because clearly fairly fundamental change is indeed necessary.

References

Aakster, C. W. (1986). Concepts in alternative medicine. *Social Science and Medicine*, 22, 265–273.
Bruner, J. (1990). *Acts of meaning*. Cambridge, MA: Harvard University Press.
Capra, F. (1982). *The turning point: Science, society, and the rising culture*. London: Wildwood House.
Castel, R. (1988). *The regulation of madness: The origins of incarceration in France* [*L'Ordre Psychiatrique*] (W. D. Halls, Trans.). Berkeley: University of California Press.
Clifford, T. (1984). *Tibetan Buddhist medicine and psychiatry: The diamond healing*. York Beach, ME: Samuel Weiser.
Coulter, J. (1979). *The social construction of mind: Studies in ethnomethodology and linguistic philosophy*. Basingstoke: Macmillan.
Currer, C. and Stacey, M. (Eds.). (1986). *Concepts of health, illness and disease: A comparative perspective*. Leamington Spa, Hamburg and New York: Berg.
Diener, E. (1984). Subjective well-being. *Psychological Bulletin*, 96, 542–575.
Diener, E. (2000). Subjective well-being: The science of happiness and a proposal for a national index. *American Psychologist*, 55, 34–43.
Dols, M. W. (1992). *Majnūn: The madman in medieval Islamic society* (D. E. Immisch, Ed.). Oxford: Clarendon Press.
Ellenberger, H. F. (1974). Psychiatry from ancient to modern times. In S. Arieti (Ed.), *American handbook of psychiatry* (2nd ed., Vol. 1, pp. 3–27). New York: Basic Books.
Fernando, S. (1988). *Race and culture in psychiatry*. London: Croom Helm.
Fernando, S. (1991). *Mental health, race and culture*. Basingstoke: Macmillan.

Fernando, S. (2002). *Mental health, race and culture* (2nd ed.). Basingstoke: Palgrave.
Fernando, S. (2010). *Mental health, race and culture* (3rd ed.). Basingstoke: Palgrave Macmillan.
Foucault, M. (1967). *Madness and civilization: A history of insanity in the Age of Reason.* London: Tavistock [originally published in French as *Histoire de la Folie*. Paris: Libraire Plon, 1961].
Fromm, E., Suzuki, D. T. and de Martinal, R. (1960). *Zen Buddhism and psychoanalysis.* London: George Allen.
Hammer, L. (1990). *Dragon rises red bird flies: Psychology and Chinese medicine.* New York: Station Hill Press.
Jahoda, G. (1992). *Crossroads between culture and mind: Continuities and change in the theories of human nature.* New York: Harvester Wheatsheaf.
Kakar, S. (1984). *Shamans, mystics and doctors: A psychological inquiry into India and its healing tradition.* London: Unwin Paperbacks.
Kalupahana, D. J. (1992). *The principles of Buddhist psychology.* Delhi: Sri Satguru Publications.
Kirmayer, L. J. (2006). Beyond the 'new cross-cultural psychiatry': Cultural biology, discursive psychology and the ironies of globalisation. *Transcultural Psychiatry, 42*(1), 126–144.
Kirmayer, L. J. (2007). Psychotherapy and the cultural concept of the person. *Transcultural Psychiatry, 44*(2), 232–257.
Kirmayer, L. J. and Minas, H. (2000). The future of cultural psychiatry: An international perspective. *Canadian Journal of Psychiatry, 45,* 438–446.
Kleinman, A. (1977). Depression, somatization and the 'new cross cultural psychiatry'. *Social Science and Medicine, 11,* 3–10.
Kleinman, A. (1988). *The illness narratives: Suffering, healing and the human condition.* New York: Basic Books.
Kraepelin, E. (1899). *Psychiatrie: ein Lehrbuch fur Studirende and Artze,* 6te Auf. Leipzig: Verlag von Johann Ambrosius Barth.
Kuhn, T. S. (1962 [1996]). *The structure of scientific revolutions* (3rd ed.). Chicago and London: University of Chicago Press.
Lambo, A. (1969). Traditional African cultures and Western medicine. In F. N. L. Poynter (Ed.), *Medicine and culture.* London: Wellcome Institute.
Marsella, A. J., Devos, G. and Hsu, F. L. K. (1985). *Culture and self: Asian and Western perspectives.* New York and London: Tavistock.
Mbiti, J. S. (1969). *African religions and philosophy.* New York: Doubleday [reprinted 1988 by Heinemann, London].
McQueen, D. V. (1978). The history of science and medicine as theoretical sources for the comparative study of contemporary medical systems. *Social Science and Medicine, 12,* 69–74.
Morel, B. A. (1852). *Traite des Mentales.* Paris: Masson.
Murphy, G. (1938). *An historical introduction to modern psychology* (4th ed.). London: Routledge & Kegan Paul.
Murphy, H. B. M. (1983). In Memoriam Eric D. Wittkower 1899–1983. *Transcultural Psychiatric Research Review, 20*(1), 81–86.
Murphy, H. B. M. (1986). The mental health impact of British cultural traditions. In J. Cox (Ed.), *Transcultural psychiatry.* London: Croom Helm.
Nelson, G. and Prilleltensky, I. (2005). *Community psychology: In pursuit of liberation and well-being.* Basingstoke: Palgrave Macmillan.

Nobles, W. W. (1986). Ancient Egyptian thought and the renaissance of African (Black) psychology. In M. Karenga and J. H. Carruthers (Eds.), *Kemet and the African worldview: Research, rescue and restoration* (part 3). Los Angeles: University of Sankore Press.

Porter, R. (1987). *A social history of madness: Stories of the insane*. London: Weidenfeld & Nicolson.

Porter, R. (1990). *Mind-Forg'd manacles: A history of madness in England from the Restoration to the Regency*. Harmondsworth: Penguin.

Rama, Swami. (1985). *Perennial psychology of the Bhagavad Gita*. Honesdale, PA: Himalayan International Institute.

Rhys Davids, C. A. F. (1978). *The birth of Indian psychology and its development in Buddhism*. New Delhi: Oriental Books.

Rinbochay, L. and Napper, E. (1980). *Mind in Tibetan Buddhism*. New York: Snow Lion Publications.

Ross, R. (1992). *Dancing with a ghost: Exploring Indian reality*. Markham, Ont.: Reed Books.

Safaya, R. (1976). *Indian psychology*. New Delhi: Munshiram Manoharlal.

Scull, A. (1993). *The most solitary of afflictions: Madness and society in Britain 1700–1900*. New Haven, CT: Yale University Press.

Shorter, E. (1997). *A history of psychiatry from the era of the asylum to the age of Prozac*. New York: John Wiley.

Simmons, W. S. (1986). *Spirit of the New England tribes: Indian history and folklore*. Hanover, NH and London: University Press of New England.

Soanes, C. and Stevenson, A. (2008). *The concise Oxford English dictionary* (11th ed., rev.). Oxford: Oxford University Press.

Vige, M. (Ed.). (2008). *Goodbye TCPS*. Special edition of *Diverse Minds*, 33 Winter.

2 Racism in psychiatry[1]

Suman Fernando

When the basis of psychiatry was being laid down in the mid nineteenth century, psychiatrists and psychologists, like others around them, had very definite ideas on which races were civilized and which were not. A paper published at the time in the *Journal of Mental Science*, which later became the *British Journal of Psychiatry*, by a former physician superintendent of Norfolk County Asylum (England) who was working in Turkey referred to that land as 'a country which forms the link between civilization and barbarism' (Foote, 1858, p. 444); in the same journal, another eminent British psychiatrist, Daniel H. Tuke (1858), denoted Eskimos, Chinese, Egyptians and American blacks as 'uncivilized' people, but with a grudging reference to China as 'in some respects decidedly civilized' (1858, p. 108). The description of Africans as 'child-like savages' by Arrah B. Evarts (1913, p. 393), a physician at the Government Hospital for the Insane in Washington, DC (USA), was typical of opinion among psychiatrists in the USA during the early twentieth century.

Nineteenth-century sociologists 'assumed that when they were studying human society they were studying innate racial characteristics at the same time; white skin and "Anglo-Saxon" civilization were seen as the culmination of the evolutionary process' (Fryer, 1984, p. 179). Francis Galton (1869), a cousin of Charles Darwin and the founder of eugenics, claimed that the 'Negro race' included a large number 'of those whom we should call half-witted' (p. 339). The main thrust of the pseudo-science of eugenics was to identify 'inferior' races; and eminent people, such as Karl Pearson (1901), saw the extermination of such races as an inevitable part of the evolutionary process. The view that black people had inferior brains and/or defective personalities were commonplace in the nineteenth century and early part of the twentieth (see later); these ideas were taken on board very easily and naturally by psychiatry and western psychology. Although overt racism has been less obvious since the Second World War, racism persists currently in the common sense of traditional European thinking. Thus in British society today, pairs of words such as 'culture' and 'race', 'primitive' and 'underdeveloped', 'advanced' and 'western', 'alien' and 'inferior', 'immigrant' and 'black', etc. are often confounded or used purposefully to obscure racist contentions. Further, racial images are raised in references to 'muggers', 'inner-city decay', 'alien cultures', and most recently in the UK, 'terrorists'.

Mind and mental illness

Three distinct views about the mind of non-western peoples, usually identified in racial terms, were discernible during the development of psychiatry. In the mid eighteenth century, Rousseau's concept of the 'noble savage' proposed the view that 'savages' who lacked the civilizing influence of western culture were free of mental disorder; later, in the late eighteenth and nineteenth centuries, Daniel Tuke (1858) and Maudsley (1867, 1879) in England, Esquirol (cited by Jarvis, 1852) in France and Rush (cited by Rosen, 1968) in the United States voiced similar views, expressed most firmly by J. C. Prichard (1835) in his *Treatise on Insanity*: "In savage countries, I mean among such tribes as the negroes of Africa and the native Americans, insanity is stated by all ... to be extremely rare" (p. 349). Lewis (1965) pointed out that a second, somewhat different stance was also evident in Europe about that time, namely, the view that non-Europeans were mentally degenerate because they lacked western culture. A third viewpoint was voiced in the United States by psychiatrists arguing for the retention of slavery: Epidemiological studies based on the Sixth USA Census of 1840 (Anon., 1851) were used to justify a claim that the black person was relatively free of madness in a state of slavery, 'but becomes prey to mental disturbance when he is set free' (Thomas and Sillen, 1972, p. 16). The underlying supposition was that inherent mental inferiority of the African justified slavery. However, Benjamin Rush, the father of American psychiatry, refuted such arguments and maintained that the mental capacity of black people could not be evaluated while they were slaves because of the effect on the mind of the condition of slavery (Plummer, 1970).

From the mid nineteenth century onwards, racist ideas were evident in many scientific theories. For example, the seminal paper by John Langdon Down (1866) claimed to have found physical characteristics of Malays, Ethiopians, Natives of America and Mongols among so-called idiots and imbeciles in hospitals in South London, concluding that a 'very large number of congenital idiots are typical Mongols' (p. 16). German psychiatrist, Kraepelin (1913), claimed that people of Java seldom became depressed and that when they were depressed they rarely felt sinful. Kraepelin (1920) perceived the differences in terms of genetic and physical influences rather than cultural ones – a reflection not only of the biological orientation in German psychiatry at the time, but also of the acceptance of racial explanations for cultural difference. In fact, Kraepelin (1921) saw the Javanese as 'a *psychically underdeveloped* population ... [akin to] ... *immature* European youth', and looked to racial–cultural comparison as a method of scientific study (p. 171; italics in original).

Psychological and intellectual differences

The nineteenth-century anthropological and medical view that the brains of black people were inferior to those of white people was supported by dubious research. For example, even as late as early in the twentieth century, Robert

Bean (1906) claimed that in studying 103 brains from American Negroes and 49 white Americans he found that: '[The] Negro is more objective and the Caucasian more subjective. The Negro has lower mental faculties (smell, sight, handcraftsmanship, body-sense, melody) well developed, the Caucasian the higher (self-control, will-power, ethical and aesthetic senses and reason)' (p. 412). Significantly, reports that did not support the ethos of white superiority, such as the report that brains of Eskimos were larger than those of the average white person (Connolly, 1950), were ignored.

A racist ideology was evident very early in the development of modern psychology, from the nineteenth century onwards. Francis Galton (1865) claimed that European 'civilized races' alone possessed the 'instinct of continuous steady labour' while non-European 'savages' showed an innate 'wild untameable restlessness' (p. 157). A classic text on adolescence written by Stanley Hall, the founder of the *American Journal of Psychology*, and published in 1904, had a chapter on 'Adolescent Races' in which the supposed psychological characteristics of Indians, Africans and North American 'Aborigines' were likened to those of immature children who 'live a life of feeling, emotion and impulse' (Hall, 1904, p. 80). The author of a standard textbook on social psychology, McDougall (1921), formulated the concept that different races produced different 'group minds'; Nordics showed a propensity for scientific work, Mediterraneans for architecture and oratory and Negroes an 'instinct for submission' (p. 119).

In *Totem and Taboo*, Freud (1913/1950) saw similarities between 'the mental lives of savages and [European] neurotics' (title page); and he wrote of the 'great world-dominating nations of white race on whom the leadership of the human species has fallen' (Freud, 1915, p. 276). Freud merely reflected prevalent ideas of his time, and it was Carl Jung who fancied himself as a specialist on black people since he had actually visited Asia and Africa. In 1939, Jung (1964) wrote that India was a 'dream-like world' where 'people carry on an apparently meaningless life ... a gigantic monotony of endlessly repeated life' (pp. 516–517). On visiting the USA, Jung (1930) felt dissatisfied at being unable to 'size them up' – referring to the white population; he could not, at first, understand 'how the Americans descending from European stock have arrived at their striking peculiarities'. He focused on 'the Negro' as the cause. In postulating a psychological danger to white people of living in close proximity to blacks, Jung (1930) deduced the theory of 'racial infection': 'The inferior man exercises a tremendous pull upon civilized beings who are forced to live with him, because he fascinates the inferior layers of our psyche, which has lived through untold ages of similar conditions' (pp. 195–196).

The study of intelligence is another field with a long history of racism. Army data on cognitive test results gathered during the 1914–1918 war led to a discussion of the reasons for racial differences in scores on intelligence tests (IQs) done in the USA; a 'racist IQ movement' that envisaged genetic inferiority of blacks in comparison to whites (Thomas and Sillen, 1972) developed, but died down after the horrors perpetrated by the Nazis in the name of race. But Arthur Jensen (1969), professor of educational psychology at the University of California, revived the argument with a paper in the *Harvard Educational Review* proposing that differences between blacks and whites on scores on IQ tests were genetically determined. Further, he postulated two categories of mental ability – abstract reasoning ability characteristic of white people and rote learning among blacks. Eysenck (1971, 1973) supported Jensen's views while he was professor of psychology at the Institute of Psychiatry (London), but other British psychologists (Kamin, 1974; Stott, 1983) opposed them as scientifically invalid. The racist tradition in studies of intelligence carried on into the 1990s in books such as *The Bell Curve* (Herrnstein and Murray, 1994) and numerous publications by Rushton in the 1990s quoted by Howitt (1991) and Richards (1997). And to cap it all, in October 2007 James Watson, renowned scientist and Nobel Laureate, claimed in an interview to the *Sunday Times* newspaper published in London that black people were less intelligent than white people (Nugent, 2007).

Post-war psychiatry and psychology

A British colonial psychiatrist who achieved the distinction of producing a monograph for WHO, *The African Mind in Health and Disease*, was J. C. Carothers (1953). His first paper (Carothers, 1947) was an analysis of Africans admitted to a mental hospital in Kenya between 1939 and 1943. He proposed several explanations for the 'peculiarities' he observed: He deduced that

> the rarity of insanity in primitive life is due to the absence of problems in the social, sexual and economic spheres ... [and that] ... the African may be less heavily loaded with deleterious genes than the European ... [because] ... natural selection might be expected to eliminate the genes concerned more rapidly in a primitive community.
>
> (pp. 586–587)

After commenting upon the lack of pressure on Africans because they (allegedly) had no long-term 'aims' in life, he deduced the reason for the apparent lack of depression among Africans: 'Perhaps the most striking difference between the European and African cultures is that the former demands self-reliance, personal responsibility, and initiative, whereas there is no place in the latter for such an attitude' (Carothers, 1947, p. 592).

Apart from the publications by Carothers, overt expression of racism has been rare in post-war psychiatric and psychological literature. But a theory that has been propagated over several years and now even in psychiatric textbooks is concerned with the 'differentiation of emotions'. The original study (Leff, 1973) from the Institute of Psychiatry in London used data collected for the International Pilot Study of Schizophrenia (IPSS) (WHO, 1973, 1975) on measures of anxiety and depression made by psychiatrists, supplemented by data on black Americans and white Americans from the US–UK study (Cooper *et al.*, 1972). The conclusion arrived at by Leff (1973) was that '[people from] developed countries show a greater differentiation of emotional states than [do people from] developing countries' (p. 305), except for African Americans who resemble the latter. The racial undertones in Leff's initial presentations become more overt when he later presented his theory as representing an evolutionary process (Leff, 1981).

Bebbington (1978), who, like Leff, was at the British Institute of Psychiatry at the time, concludes a review of the 'epidemiology of depressive disorder' by arguing for 'a provisional syndromal definition of depression as used by a consensus of Western psychiatrists against which cross-cultural anomalies can be tested', claiming that the World Health Organization supports this. In other words, the 'depression' of non-western peoples is hailed as an 'anomaly', and their emotional states as 'anomalies' (p. 303). It is not necessarily the racial prejudices of individual research workers but the pervasive influence of a racist ideology within which they carry out their work that is expressed in these theories and ideas. But what goes for depression goes also for other diagnoses.

Racism in diagnosis

The social construction of mental illness was shown up dramatically in the political abuses of psychiatry in the Soviet Union (Bloch and Reddaway, 1984) and the decision of the American Psychiatric Association in 1973 that homosexuality should cease to be an 'illness' (Bayer, 1981). In both instances, political forces determined the nature of what constituted illness. Similarly, racist considerations are evident in the construction of two diagnostic categories reported in the USA at the time of slavery and described by Cartwright (1851) as peculiar to black people.

Dysaesthesia Aethiopis was described as a disease affecting both mind and body, with 'insensibility' of the skin and 'hebetude' of mind. Cartwright reckoned it to be commoner 'among free slaves living in clusters by themselves than among slaves in our plantations, and attacks only such slaves as live like free negroes in regard to diet, drinks, exercise, etc.', but stating his disinterest in treating the 'disease' among 'free negroes'. The symptoms were clear-cut:

> they break, waste, and destroy everything they handle – abuse horses and cattle, – tear, burn, or rend their clothing, and paying no attention to the rights of property, they steal from others to replace what they have destroyed.... They raise disturbances with their overseers and fellow servants without cause or motive, and seem to be insensible to pain when subject to punishment.
>
> (1851, p. 321)

The second disease described by Cartwright was more straightforward: *Drapetomania*, or the disease 'that induces the negro to run away from service'. After attributing the condition to 'treating them as equal' or frightening them by cruelty, Cartwright advocated a mixture of 'care, kindness, attention and humanity', with punishment 'if any one or more of them, at any time, are inclined to raise their heads to a level with their master or overseer ... until they fall into that submissive state which was intended for them to occupy' (1851, pp. 319–320).

The influence of ideological and political forces in determining diagnosis, and sometimes treatment, is not usually as obvious as it is in the four examples given above, namely, the illness contained in dissenting politically in the Soviet Union, the de-medicalization of homosexuality in the USA, the illness induced by freedom given to black slaves and the disease of running away that affected black slaves. The influence of racism in the social construction of commonly diagnosed categories of mental disorder is not always easy to discern. Political, social and ideological pressures current in society always impinge on the diagnostic process by influencing questions of intelligibility, common sense, clinical opinion, pragmatism and tradition. And racism acts through these pressures.

Psychiatric diagnoses carry their own special images which may connect up with other images derived from, say, common sense. Thus, alienness is linked to schizophrenia (as a diagnosis) and to racial inferiority (as a human type). The result may be an overdiagnosis of schizophrenia among black people who are seen as both 'alien' and 'inferior'. Similarly, if psychiatry is called upon to 'diagnose' dangerousness, common-sense images of dangerous people are taken on – and black people are seen as excessively dangerous. In some situations, pragmatic considerations may promote the denial of illness if political influences encourage some types of behaviour to be ignored or punished. Racist images of the 'lazy black' may lead to the ignoring of self-neglect as indicative of illness among black people; the idea that blacks should not smoke cannabis, but do so, enters into the construction of the disease of 'cannabis psychosis' – a British diagnosis that is given almost exclusively to blacks (McGovern and Cope, 1987). In a context in Britain where public images, fostered by the media and police, associate race with drug abuse and attribute the anger of black youth to their use of cannabis, value judgements attached to drug abuse and the need to 'pathologize' the anger of black people seem to come together in this diagnosis. Diagnoses specific to groups of people identified racially may carry racism within them, when they are derived in a racist context.

In addition to the (racist) pressures arising from the context in which diagnoses are made, the diagnostic process is affected by racism at various points: during the recognition and evaluation of symptoms or psychopathology; in their assessment for the purpose of illness recognition; and in making the decision on the propriety of designating illness. For example, the failure to acknowledge racism as a real threat to black people may result in the designation of anger and fear as 'paranoia'; and the dismissal of culturally determined ways of emotional expression by a black person as an 'inferior' mode of expression may negate the value of 'symptoms' that are identified. Also, the context of the diagnostic interview itself may be significant: For example, in transactions between a black patient and a white professional, the former may be unwilling to divulge information because of the racist misperceptions (held by the latter) of his/her family life and culture, while the white professional may have very little knowledge of, or 'feeling' for, black lifestyles and attitudes. Indeed, the rapport between the participants of an interracial psychiatric interview may be totally disjointed in a racist context.

Post-war social and cultural studies

Although sociology had shown little interest in issues around racism in the early part of the twentieth century, social science studies after the Second World War appeared to recognize the importance of doing so. A renowned study that focused on the effects of discrimination and social conditions on the personalities of black people was the book *The Mark of Oppression* by Kardiner and Ovesey (1951). The book was based on a psychodynamic assessment of twenty-five case records of black people considered against a background of the history of African Americans in American society. The authors argued that the original (African) culture of black people in America had been 'smashed, be it by design or accident' (p. 39); African Americans were seen as people living in a sort of cultural vacuum, their family life as disorganized and the dominance of African American women as disturbing family cohesion. The authors concluded that racial discrimination had resulted in a low self-esteem and self-hatred within the black personality, partly dealt with by being 'projected' as aggression and anxiety. 'There is not one personality trait of the Negro the source of which cannot be traced to his difficult living conditions. There are no exceptions to this rule ... the final result is a wretched internal life' (p. 81).

American ideas about black families have been transferred across the Atlantic to be represented in British research as negative images about African Caribbean and Asian families. According to Lawrence (1982), the former are seen as having a family life that was weak and unstable, with a lack of a sense of paternal responsibility towards children; and the latter as strong 'but the very strength of Asian culture ... [was seen as] ... a source of both actual and potential weaknesses' (p. 118). The American 'Moynihan Report' (Moynihan, 1965) called the black American family 'a tangle of pathology'; in the UK, a Select Committee on Race Relations (1977) reported a connection between the problems of African Caribbean British families and family life in the Caribbean, which was seen as unsuited to British society.

Fortunately, the decade beginning in the 1980s saw a shift away from the racist notions of the earlier years. This change resulted not from academic studies using scientific methods but from black people themselves striving for equality by political action – for example, in challenging police brutality and psychiatric racism – supplemented by writings of black and Asian authors on both sides of the Atlantic, such as (to mention a few) Stuart Hall (in Hall *et al.*, 1978), Paul Gilroy (1993), Homi Bhabha (1994), Edward Said (1994), bell hooks (1994) and Cornel West (1994). A review of their work and other relevant literature is beyond the scope of this chapter. The main lessons for the mental health field that come through are about the positive results of the struggles of black people during the many years of slavery; the richness and variety of black and Asian cultures that have developed in the UK and USA; the interaction and melding together of cultures; the changing nature of racism; the forging of new identities and ethnicities; and the struggles against racism. Unfortunately, mainstream psychiatry and psychology have so far failed on the whole to take on board the insights available in the progressive thinking that has flooded the British and American scene at the end of the twentieth century.

Conclusion

What happens at the coal face of every-day psychiatric practice is characterized by: (a) the failure by most professionals in the mental health field, whatever their ethnicity, to allow for racial bias in practice and institutional racism in the delivery of services; (b) institutional practices, such as mental health assessments and risk-assessments that are inherently institutionally racist, being put through in a colour-blind fashion that does not allow for bias; (c) social pressures that apply differentially to people from BME communities not being picked up so that, for example, justified anger arising from racism in society is not taken into the equation when mental health assessments are made; (d) the sense of alienation felt by many people from BME communities being interpreted as a sign of illness – often seen as *their problem*, rather than a problem for society as a whole. The net result of the problems outlined above is that a disease model (reflected in symptoms of illness) or criminal model (requiring control) – or both – is seen as the most appropriate response to many BME people presenting to the services, or brought into the service compulsorily. Institutional racism lies at the heart of a pattern in British society whereby there are three inter-connected happenings: (a) disproportionate numbers of black men being compulsorily detained and diagnosed as 'schizophrenic' by the mental health system; (b) disproportionate numbers of black youngsters being subject to stop and search, arrest and then being charged, leading to magistrates and judges disproportionately sending them to prison; (c) disproportionate numbers of black children being excluded from school. All this adds up to failures in three social systems, mental health, criminal justice and education, reflecting institutional racism in society as a whole.

Note

1 This chapter is a shortened version of chapter 4 in *Mental Health, Race and Culture*, third edition, by Suman Fernando (2010). Reproduced with permission of Palgrave Macmillan.

References

Anon. (1851). Startling facts from the census. *American Journal of Insanity*, 8(2), 153–155.
Bayer, R. (1981). *Homosexuality and American psychiatry: The politics of diagnosis*. New York: Basic Books.
Bebbington, P. E. (1978). The epidemiology of depressive disorder. *Culture, Medicine and Psychiatry*, 2, 297–341.

Bean, R. B. (1906). Some racial peculiarities of the Negro brain. *American Journal of Anatomy, 5*, 353–415.
Bhabha, H. (1994). *The location of culture.* London: Routledge.
Bloch, S. and Reddaway, P. (1984). *The shadows over world psychiatry.* London: Gollancz.
Carothers, J. C. (1947). A study of mental derangement in Africans and an attempt to explain its peculiarities, more especially in relation to the African attitude to life. *Journal of Mental Science, 101*, 548–597.
Carothers, J. C. (1953). *The African mind in health and disease: A study in ethnopsychiatry* (WHO Monograph Series No. 17). Geneva: WHO.
Cartwright, S. A. (1981/1851). Report on the diseases and physical peculiarities of the Negro race. In A. C. Caplan, H. T. Engelhardt and J. J. McCartney (Eds.), *Concepts of health and disease* (pp. 305–325). Reading, MA: Addison-Wesley [reprinted from *New Orleans Medical and Surgical Journal*, May 1851, 691–715].
Connolly, C. J. (1950). *External morphology of the primate brain.* Springfield, IL: C. C. Thomas.
Cooper, J. E., Kendall, R. E., Garland, B. J., Sharpe, I., Copeland, J. R. M. and Simon, R. (1972). *Psychiatric diagnosis in New York and London*, Maudsley Monograph No. 20. Oxford: Oxford University Press.
Down, J. L. M. (1987/1866). Observations on an ethnic classification of idiots. In C. Thompson (Ed.), *The origins of modern psychiatry* (pp. 15–18). Chichester: Wiley [originally printed in *Lectures and Reports from the London Hospital for 1866*].
Evarts, A. B. (1913). Dementia precox in the colored race. *Psychoanalytic Review, 14*, 388–403.
Eysenck, H. J. (1971). *Race, intelligence and education.* London: Temple Smith.
Eysenck, H. J. (1973). *The inequality of man.* London: Temple Smith.
Foote, R. F. (1858). The condition of the insane and the treatment of nervous diseases in Turkey. *Journal of Mental Science, 4*, 444–450.
Freud, S. (1913/1950). *Totem and taboo.* London: Routledge & Kegan Paul [originally published Vienna: Hugo Heller, 1913].
Freud, S. (1915). Thoughts for the times on war and death. In *The Standard Edition of the Complete Psychological Works of Sigmund Freud* (Vol. 14, pp. 273–300) (J. Strachey, Trans.). London: Hogarth Press.
Fryer, P. (1984). *Staying power: The history of black people in Britain.* London: Pluto Press.
Galton, F. (1865). Hereditary talent and character. *MacMillan Magazine*, 157–166.
Galton, F. (1869). *Hereditary genius: An inquiry into its laws and consequences.* London: Macmillan.
Gilroy, P. (1993). *Small acts: Thoughts on the politics of black cultures.* London: Serpent Tail.
Hall, G. S. (1904). *Adolescence: Its psychology and its relations to physiology, anthropology, sociology, sex, crime, religion and education* (Vol. 2). New York: D. Appleton.
Hall, S., Critcher, C., Jefferson, T., Clarke, J. and Roberts, B. (1978). *Policing the crisis: Mugging, the state, and law and order.* London: Macmillan.
Herrnstein, R. J. and Murray, C. (1994). *The bell curve: Intelligence and class structure in American life.* New York: Free Press.
hooks, bell. (1994). *Outlaw culture: Resisting representations.* New York: Routledge.
Howitt, D. (1991). *Concerning psychology: Psychology applied to social issues.* Milton Keynes and Philadelphia: Open University Press.

Jarvis, E. (1852). On the supposed increase of insanity. *American Journal of Insanity, 8*, 333–364.
Jensen, A. R. (1969). How much can we boost IQ and scholastic achievement? *Harvard Educational Review, 39*, 1–123.
Jung, C. G. (1930). Your Negroid and Indian behaviour. *Forum, 83*(4), 193–199.
Jung, C. G. (1964). The dreamlike world of India. Reprinted in H. Read, M. Fordham and G. Adler (Eds.), *Civilization in transition: Collected works of C. G. Jung* (vol. 10). London: Routledge & Kegan Paul.
Kamin, L. J. (1974). *The science and politics of IQ*. London: Wiley.
Kardiner, A. and Ovesey, L. (1951). *The mark of oppression: A psychosocial study of the American Negro*. New York: Norton.
Kraepelin, E. (1913). *Manic depressive insanity and paranoia* (R. M. Barclay, Trans.). Edinburgh: Livingstone [translation of *Lehrbuch der Psychiatrie*, 8th ed., Vols. 3 and 4].
Kraepelin, E. (1920). Die Erscheinungsformen des Irreseins. *Zeitschrift für die gesamte Neurologie and Psychiatrie, 62*, 1–29 [reprinted 1974 as Patterns of Mental Disorder (H. Marshall, Trans.). In S. Hirsch and M. Shepherd (Eds.) *Themes and Variations in European Psychiatry* (pp. 7–30). Bristol: John Wright].
Kraepelin, E. (1921). *Manic-depressive insanity and paranoia* (R. M. Barclay and G. M. Robertson, Ed. and Trans.). Edinburgh: Livingstone.
Lawrence, E. (1982). In the abundance of water the fool is thirsty: Sociology and Black 'pathology'. In Centre for Contemporary Cultural Studies (Ed.), *The empire strikes back: Race and racism in 70s Britain*. London: Hutchinson.
Leff, J. (1973). Culture and the differentiation of emotional states. *British Journal of Psychiatry, 123*, 299–306.
Leff, J. (1981). *Psychiatry around the globe: A transcultural view*. New York: Marcel Dekker.
Lewis, A. (1965). Chairman's opening remarks. In A. V. S. De Rueck and R. Porter (Eds.), *Transcultural psychiatry*. London: Churchill.
Maudsley, H. (1867). *The physiology and pathology of mind*. New York: D. Appleton.
Maudsley, H. (1879). *The pathology of mind*. London: Macmillan.
McDougall, W. (1921). *Is America safe for democracy?* New York: Scribner.
McGovern, D. and Cope, R. (1987). The compulsory detention of males of different ethnic groups, with special reference to offender patients. *British Journal of Psychiatry, 150*, 505–512.
Moynihan, D. (1965). *The Negro family in the United States: The case for national action*. Washington: US Governmental Printing Office.
Nugent, H. (2007, October 17). Black people 'less intelligent' scientist claims. *The Times*. Retrieved 31 July 2008 from www.timesonline.co.uk/tol/news/uk/article2677098.ece.
Pearson, K. (1901). *National life from the standpoint of science*. London: A. & C. Black.
Plummer, B. L. (1970). Benjamin Rush and the Negro American. *American Journal of Psychiatry, 127*, 793–798.
Prichard, J. C. (1835). *A treatise on insanity and other disorders affecting the mind*. London: Sherwood, Gilbert & Piper.
Richards, G. (1997). *Race, racism and psychology: Towards a reflexive history*. London: Routledge.
Rosen, G. (1968). *Madness in society*. New York: Harper & Row.
Said, E. W. (1994). *Culture and imperialism*. London: Vintage.
Select Committee on Race Relations and Immigration. (1977). *The West Indian community*. London: Her Majesty's Stationery Office.

Stott, D. H. (1983). *Issues in the intelligence debate.* Windsor: NFER-Nelson Publishing.
Thomas, A. and Sillen, S. (1972). *Racism and psychiatry.* New York: Brunner/Mazel.
Tuke, D. H. (1858). Does civilization favour the generation of mental disease? *Journal of Mental Science, 4,* 94–110.
West, C. (1994). *Race matters.* New York: Random House.
WHO. (1973). *Report of the International Pilot Study of Schizophrenia* (vol. 1). Geneva: WHO.
WHO. (1975). *Schizophrenia: A Multinational Study – A summary of the initial evaluation phase of the International Pilot Study of Schizophrenia.* Geneva: WHO.

3 Ethno-racial representations and the burden of 'Otherness' in mental health

Roy Moodley

Introduction

Some of the chief criticisms made against psychiatric and mental health practice are the tensions and contradictions that the profession experiences in relation to Black and Minority Ethnic (BME) communities. The critique takes various forms depending on socio-economic and geo-political arguments that are made in relation to the health and mental health discourses of race which appear to be prevalent in psychiatry. The underlying basis for this interpretation is the way in which psychological discomforts, mental distress and physical illnesses are represented and presented in the context of race, culture, ethnicity and the intersectionality of one or many of the "Group of Seven socio-cultural identities" (Moodley, 2011), such as gender, sexual orientation, religion, class and disability. What arises, it seems, is a process of multiple projections of otherness, within which misdiagnosis, over-medication and over-representation are acted out on a grand scale. For example, in both North America and the United Kingdom racialised clients are still often over-diagnosed for psychological difficulties and mental health issues, particularly for schizophrenia (see Fernando, 1988, for discussion). Fernando argues that the over-diagnosis is not just about how institutionally racist the psychiatric profession is, but is reflective of "the social function of this diagnosis within society" (1988, p. 96); in other words, psychiatry provides a discourse within which isolation, alienation and chronic institutionalisation is normalised in current society (Fernando, 2010).

Indeed, psychiatry's function appears to engage beyond the remit of medicine and the healing arts; as a result of its executive engagement with the mind it enters the realm of culture and society, which gives it control over institutional life that is deemed outside conventional medicine. For example, socio-political and economic relational normativity is constructed through psychiatry's negotiations with the environment. Economic production depends on an ever-present and available workforce that is 'normalised' (capitalised) through the pharmaceutical industry. Yet, its pervasiveness goes even further than just the power and control of people's minds and bodies; it infuses, infiltrates and adjudicates in a deterministic way larger existential and ontological questions of what it is to be human. In some ways psychiatry tends to subsume an epistemological character that governs our sense of reality and the symbolic order and consciousness, as well as the imaginary and the unconsciousness through its preoccupation with madness and the Other. This, perhaps unconscious, preoccupation seems also to be the habitat of anthropology, psychology, literary studies, cultural studies and many others.

In this chapter, I will explore how ethnographic pronouncements, literary theory, travel writings and other scholarly meanderings have created racial and ethnic stereotypes that have stigmatised, marginalised and racialised ethnic minority groups. Indeed, while many in psychiatry have scientifically and intellectually laid to rest the outdated and racist pseudo-scientific theories, thus making way for a liberal humanist approach to mental health care (Fernando, 1988, 1995, 2010; Thomas and Sillen, 1972), it seems that psychiatry as a transformative mental health discourse continues to promote the authority and sovereignty of Europe's past legacy of racist ideology. The liberal humanist philosophy within which critical and transcultural psychiatry monitors and modifies psychiatry's engagement of the mind, illness and the Other is itself a product of the very same source that gave rise to the construction of the Other in the first place.

The process of othering ethnic minority groups can be seen as a developmental and evolutionary process, the templates of which were formed long before colonialism when class and gender constructions and projections were the dominant configurations of the self and the Other. With these templates acting as foundations for the negative projections of race and ethnicity stereotyping, it is not difficult to see how institutional racism became the next stage in the racialisation of the Other. For the institution of psychiatry, a tension exists between holding onto a historical structure that shapes the society within which it functions and addressing the complexity of an ethically competent practice which is also anti-oppressive in relation to black and minority patients; a tension compounded many times when human rights questions are added to this dilemma. The chapter will consider Suman Fernando's writings and articulations about race, culture and mental health in the context of BME health care. But, first, we begin by exploring how BME peoples are constructed as Other.

Ethno-racial construction of the Other

The concept of the Other is now widely used in the social sciences (see Theunissen, 1977),[1] as a location where marginalised groups are situated. As mentioned earlier, long before race became an issue for the West, gender served as a receptacle for the negative projections that ensued as a result of a hegemonic masculine and patriarchal society. Within Western European consciousness the unconscious fantasies found, through the centuries, different crucibles and containers into which the negative internalised objects were projected. More notably, since the Christian era these negative internalised objects were externalised onto selected sub-groups of the Other, namely women, BME people, the blind, the deaf, the gay, the lesbian, and so on. For example, women who challenged the patriarchal consciousness and who attempted to communicate an inner creative and subjectivity reality were trapped in the 'gaze' of a society that incarcerated or burnt them at the stake, as a defence against deep negative anxieties that surfaced through collective ego identification (Moodley, 2011). These 'witches or folk devils' became the represented image of an aspect of the internal negative object. This objectification of women, in later centuries like the Victorian period, manifested itself in the representation of working-class women as sexual objects. Similarly, race and ethnicity, and in more recent times homosexuality, became the receptacles of the collective projections of the Western mind.

With the onset of colonialism, race and ethnicity became a dominating preoccupation in the consciousness of the West, with race as a concept, category or lived reality providing yet another crucible for the negative projections of a dominant white, heterosexual, masculine and capitalist culture. These Western European collective projections were justified and articulated in pseudo-scientific racist discourses in which arguments from science and religion were used to justify slavery, oppression and racism. For example: (1) scriptural authority – Noah and his son Ham; (2) primal difference – skull measurements and superiority by leading scientists and physicians; (3) phylogenetic concept of race; (4) the superficial readings of Darwin; (5) genetic fallacy; (6) the mark of oppression (Thomas and Sillen, 1972).[2] Moreover, Fanon (1952, 1965) maintains that Europe's phallic desire to atomise power and generate its civilisation was concretised in the "corporeality" of black people, while Said (1978) suggests that "European culture gained in strength and identity by setting itself off against the orient as a surrogate and underground self" (p. 3) to establish "a relationship of power, of domination, of varying degrees of a complex hegemony" (p. 5) as a "collective notion identifying 'us' Europeans as against all those non-Europeans" (p. 7). This polarised cognitive template then forms the basis of what becomes natural ways of thinking and being in the world. When highly subjective and irrational thoughts are experienced it is justified through a socio-political and economic analysis of otherness: racial prejudice, ethnic stereotyping and dehumanising of the other. In his book *Mental Health, Race and Culture* (2010), Suman Fernando elaborates in much detail the complexities of race and culture, arguing that as a concept it arrives in European history and social thought at the same time as Christianity was becoming significant as a spiritual and social discourse. He argues that racial superiority emerges as a complex set of post-Enlightenment ideologies that establishes the West as civilised compared with non-Westerners; the consequences of this have given rise to the institutionalisation of racism in society.

To interrogate the macro- and micro-level subtleties of racist practices currently in health and mental health care institutions is a difficult task, to say the least, especially when we consider that it is a challenge to an ideology with historical roots; science and psychology being the originators of the pseudo-scientific racist ideologies that were deployed to construct the notions of the noble savage, the uncivilised native, the dangerous Arab and so on. Indeed, when reduced to a conventional Cartesian dialectic, the notion of seeing the

Other exclusively in black-and-white terms, in fixed and stable categories of race, gender and class, "leads to a reductionist's aggregation ... confuses practice through oversimplification, generating stereotypes and fostering ethnocentrism" (Williams, 1999, p. 213). Indeed, our ethnicity (like gender, sexual orientation, class, disability) location is never fixed; it is always shifting and changing according to our evolutionary, socio-cultural and geo-political needs. Individuals are often torn between the need to experience themselves existentially in the "here and now" and the desire to be historically, psychically and environmentally connected (Whitehead, Talahite and Moodley, 2013). Fernando (2010) argues that, "athough the Eurocentric view of identity embodied in western psychology refers to a unique quality, a less individualistic worldview would see identity as part of group solidarity – implying that there is a political dimension" (p. 16). This political dimension, he asserts, is institutionally embedded, taking its cue from Europe's Enlightenment through ethnology, history, anthropology and early psychiatric pronouncements of what it is to be human.

Ethnographic notebooks in khaki pockets: representations of the Other

The European Enlightenment also manifested a darker side in its evolution to engage science as the sovereign authority that explained the world and life experiences. The colonial period offered the principal investigators of human sciences the opportunity to be part of this philosophical, anthropological and literary adventure. Anthropology's and ethnology's enterprise to shape the language and ideas about the Other has been influential in providing support to the race-based ideas that are foundational to the ways in which psychiatry, psychology and mental health care has evolved in the West. The ethnographer's books in "khaki pockets" mapped out the kinds of interpretations that support the ideas and ideologies of European post-Enlightenment thinking. That is, the self as a rational and objective being is at the centre of what is defined as being human, and, as an extension of this idea, that European rational consciousness is at the centre of what makes the human 'civilised'. This position clearly marks non-Europeans as the Other; positioned at the margins and away from the centre, outside civilization and therefore inferior (Moodley, 2011). The image of the anthropologist/ethnographer in khaki shorts and knee-high socks of the early period of colonialism represents a profound metaphor of an erect European biro inseminating and disseminating into pocket books theoretical possibilities of how to humanise the natives, referred to as 'savages', and will always be indelibly fixed in the postmodern imagination. Their so-called objective gaze and scientific observations merged with their own subjective realities of physical, emotional and, in some cases, spiritual essences to produce a plethora of analysis on the life and times of the natives. Indeed, some of it challenged the discourse of objective rationality of the European Enlightenment arguing for a cross-cultural analysis of the non-European; most of it, however, ensured that the cultural deciphering and interpretations remained ethnocentric and Eurocentric. In reflecting on this process, Trinh T. Minh-ha (1989) argues that it

> is not his inheritance of a power he so often disclaims, disengaging himself from a system he carries with him, but his ear, eye, and pen, which record in his language while pretending to speak through mine, on my behalf ... trying to find the other by defining otherness or by explaining the other through laws and generalisations is, as Zen says, like beating the moon with a pole or scratching an itching foot from outside of a shoe.
>
> (pp. 48, 76)

And it is precisely this that Europeans claimed to have accomplished, thus manufacturing a particular truth and universalising it.

Field accounts like those of Frazer's (1922) *Golden Bough*, Mead's (1928) *Coming of Age in Samoa* and *Growing up in New Guinea* (1930), Malinowski's (1922) *The Sexual Life of Savages*, Benedict's (1935) *Patterns of Culture* and many others have become classic (pocket) textbooks.[3] The ways in which these texts portrayed racialised people became etched in the social sciences, the sciences, medicine and the psycho-therapies. Peeps into these diaries and pocket books begin to reveal an endless spiral in pursuit of a single truth: not how different the "natives" are from us, nor why the rituals and myths are situated in a particular context, although this was done as a matter of course, but a truth that engaged with the negative projections of the European mind. Indeed, it became a racist chant that moved from anthropology to literary studies to psychology and psychiatry. This journey from discipline to discipline was to confirm an inventory, an image, a feeling and a fantasy to normalise and eventually demonise and control the Other. Its validation and verification was achieved through a pseudo-scientific discourse, Eurocentric observation and analysis of native behaviours and comparing and contrasting different worlds as though they were the same.

In addition to the culture of anthropology there has been in the last 50 years a growing body of critical writing that has uncovered the negative projections and constructions of otherness presented in canonical works of literature, such as Conrad's *Heart of Darkness* (1899), Van Der Post's *Venture to the Interior* (1952), Defoe's *Robinson Crusoe* (1719), Shakespeare's *The Tempest* (1611) and Rider Haggard's *King Solomon's Mines* (1885) and *She* (1887). These texts have been known to allegorise the unconscious as the other place – as Africa and its people as the 'absolute other'.[4] Similar projections of the repressed unconscious can be found in the volumes of travel and exploration writings.[5] In these writings, constructions of blackness and cultural difference are mediated through the white characters, always male, 'civilised' heroes and protagonists, while the racialised people were perceived as cannibals, evil and satanic. Writers at the time offered a justification for slavery and the economic exploitation of the colonies. The equation of the unconscious of Europeans with the consciousness of black people is clearly evident throughout these literary texts, such as *Robinson Crusoe*, where the island has been interpreted as a larger metaphor of otherness and constructed as a metaphor for the other place inhabited by Friday, the dark, child-like, erotic innocent Other, who represents the repressed features of Crusoe. It is the shipwreck, a metaphor for the breakdown or failure of white consciousness, that allows for the surfacing of these repressed qualities. In his critique on European writing on Africa, Dominique Mannoni (1956) asserted that Europeans "projected upon ... colonial peoples the obscurities of their own unconscious – obscurities they would rather not penetrate" (p. 19).[6] Even Freud seems to have failed to "self-analyse" this process in himself; or his "self", perhaps, was also a product of his time (Moodley, 2011). Freud's contention that the unconscious was a place below, different, timeless, primordial, libidinal, separated from consciousness, unmapped, dark and without light was said to be "discovered" at the same time that Africa was being explored. This insistence on understanding the unconscious as a dark negative region and equated to the "darker races" prompts white projections onto the Other; in so doing it results in the creation of a vacuum that fills itself with fantasies of white supremacy, cultural purity and an imperialistic ethno-universality. Throughout history, these fantasies and negative projections externalised themselves through such projects as the slave trade, the mass genocide of the Australian Aboriginal, the indiscriminate lynching of American blacks, the extermination of the Incas and the North American Indians and other crimes against humanity such as colonialism, the holocaust and in more recent years apartheid.

The burden of Otherness

The West's imposition of a particular history, its tradition of thought and its philosophical and moralistic conjunctions have certainly contributed a great deal to the ways in which the Other – racialised people – is constructed. In a hegemonic way the West has pursued an ideology of difference where European whiteness has been hierarchical order with a sovereignty of human superiority above all others; to acknowledge its own difference and construct a true (but imagined) self it subverts and relegates non-European voices. Historically, it seems that for Western consciousness difference has been constructed as a binary that imagines a negative image of the Other; at times demonising the Other to validate its perception that the Other is less than human. As discussed earlier, this construction and projection of otherness pervades European historical, social and cultural life over time; its consequences on health and mental health care practices and policies are currently experienced as a significant impact on racialised patients, in the diaspora and globally. As Fernando (2010) says, "as Euro–American influence and political domination spread into Asia and African countries, psychiatry has followed ... [engaging in an] active suppression of ... indigenous systems of medicine and healing as part of the colonial/imperial approach" (p. 112). As critics of the neo-colonial bio-political models of mental health argue, it is not just the suppression of traditional healing systems that constitute this colonial crime, but also, in its place, "the promotion of drugs manufactured in the West" (p. 113).

Throughout his works Fernando has made a clear case for deinstitutionalising the racism that is prevalent in psychiatry. Applying a historical lens he lays bare the underbelly of a racist mental health care that appears resistant to change; although in more recent times the discourse of psychology and psychiatry has given the impression that it is part of the liberal humanist discourse of empathy and compassion in mental health care, there are nevertheless mental health practices that still marginalise, misdiagnose, and disproportionately label racialised people as "mad", "bad" and "sad". For example, he suggests that there are three interconnected issues at play when it comes to stigmatising, marginalising and racially institutionalising BME people. These are:

> (a) disproportionate numbers of black men being compulsorily detained and diagnosed as "schizophrenic" by the mental health system; (b) disproportionate numbers of black youngsters being subject to stop and search, arrest and then being charged, leading to magistrates and judges disproportionately sending them to prison; (c) disproportionate numbers of black children being excluded from school. All this add up to failures in three social systems, mental health, criminal justice and education, reflecting institutional racism in society as a whole.
> (Fernando, 2010, p. 73)

Conclusion

Suman Fernando argues vociferously and in painstaking detail against the ways in which institutional racism has informed theory, practice and research on mental health, and eventually mental health policy itself. His work has exposed racial prejudice and discrimination, and the cyclical nature of institutional racism in mental health care practices. He argues that a vicious cycle has developed within which Western culture has for decades become normalised to the degree that very little resistance is offered by the majority of the professionals, except for a few voices, mainly those professionals, but not exclusively, from the communities most affected by the racialised experience. Fernando, while not the only voice among the concerned few, is still nevertheless a strong voice that addresses the issue of institutional racism with government bodies and policy makers.

Indeed, Fernando's contribution to the field has been to historicise the psychiatric and mental health process by showing the interconnectedness of past (colonial) and present (multiculturalism) constructions of otherness. He debunks the myth that we have a society that is racially different from that of the past. And he debunks the myth that we have a liberal humanistic and compassionate profession in which all are treated equally irrespective of race, gender and class. Fernando's analysis adds a socio-historical and ethical dimension to what is otherwise a medical, Eurocentric and highly North American influenced model that posits itself as absolute truth. As he says:

first, psychiatry is ethnocentric and carries in it the ideologies of western culture, including racism; second, the practice of psychiatry, including its ways of diagnosing, is influenced by the social ethos and the political system in which it exists and works.

(p. 35)

It reminds us of the necessity to constantly examine and critique our mental health practices so that we are cognisant of the negative ideas from the past – from anthropology, literature, travel writings, etc. – when working with racialised individuals whose histories are enmeshed in the troubled relation with the West that has led to the concept of 'otherness'. Indeed, Fernando's critical writings play a significant role in helping researchers and practitioners lend their voices to the anti-psychiatry, the transcultural and cross-cultural psychiatric movements; thus making sure that the large pharmaceutical multinationals are not completely overwhelming and limiting patient's health care strategies and opportunities and that the intellectual and academic discourses of psychiatry are free from the psychopathology of capitalism and the neurosis of Wall Street, and eventually the psychosis of a global mental health enterprise.

Notes

1 Using the philosophy of Husserl, Heidegger, Sartre and Buber, Theunissen (1977) offers a complex theoretical and philosophical understanding of the problem of the Other through magnifying the extremely minute abstract concept of intersubjectivity – the relationship of the "I" and the "other" and its role individually and in groups. Indeed, these ideas, which have been at the foundation of post-Enlightenment thinking on social thought and practice, have provided the historical and theoretical framework from which psychoanalysis, psychotherapy and psychiatry have understood the problem of the Other (see Moodley, 2011).
2 See also Peter Fryer's *Staying Power: The History of Black People in Britain* (1984, pp. 133–190), and *Our Story: A Handbook of African History and Contemporary Issues*, edited by Akyaaba Addai-Sebo and Ansel Wong (1988).
3 Frazer's *The Golden Bough*, for example, an allegory of primitive life and ritual, was a methodological advance over Tylor's *Primitive Culture* (1871), a one-dimensional reportage that reduced the text of non-literate religions to belief in the pervasive agency of spirit matters, the primitive doctrine of animism (Boon, p. 11). The multidimensional representation in *The Golden Bough*, for instance, attracted writers and poets, notably Eliot, Joyce, Lawrence and others (Moodley, 2011).
4 *Heart of Darkness*, for instance, was regarded by Green (1980) as being rich in political and psychological insights into the sins and follies of imperialism, and Defoe, on the other hand, was responsible for the energising myths of English imperialism. The fact that these were "collectively, the story England told itself as it went to sleep at night; and, in the form of its dreams, charged England's energy to go out into the world and explore, conquer, and rule" (Green, 1980, p. 4) strongly suggests that a connection is made between the Western unconscious and the Other. It also points clearly to the fact that in literary analysis the projection of otherness still seeps through the cracks of a supposedly post-colonial, modernist objective and critical view of the colonial era (Moodley, 2011).
5 Notable examples are: Livingstone and Livingstone (1865) and Burton (1910), which textualised the 'negative projection' experiences of Europeans in the 17th and 18th

centuries in Africa and the Asian sub-continent. Pratt (1986), in her lucid study of otherness in John Barrow's *Account of Travels into the Interior of Southern Africa in the Years 1797 and 1798*, reminds us that the manners and customs in a normal discourse is nowhere in greater jeopardy than on the imperial frontier where the Europeans confront not only unfamiliar Others but unfamiliar selves, in not just the reproduction of the capitalist mode of production but also its expansion through displacement of previously established modes (Moodley, 2011).

6 Mannoni (1956) points to Shakespeare's *The Tempest* as a paternalistic colonial representation; he defines the process as a "Prospero complex" (p. 109), a condition reflecting the repressed unconscious "which draws from the inside, as it were, a picture of the paternalist colonial ... his desire to dominate, at the same time portrays the racialist whose daughter has suffered an attempted rape at the hands of an inferior being" (p. 110). In Fanon's (1952/1967) critique of Mannoni's analysis of *The Tempest* a paradox is uncovered. Fanon makes the point that Mannoni "takes it upon himself to explain colonialism's reason for existence" (p. 107), and infers that the analysis fails to see the missing dimension of capitalist exploitation, which Fanon feels is a prime reason for arousing in the people "the feeling of inferiority" (p. 108). These literary texts not only presented an individual's unconscious neurotic tendencies but also reflected the collective unconscious of that period and seems not far from the foundations of racism experienced by society decades later. Davis (1981) demonstrates how these notions proliferated racist ideologies in the United States, especially the Deep South, and justified the mass lynching of black men for the "myth of the black rapist" (p. 172). Another myth transposed Freud's theory of the Oedipus Complex, which implies that the black man wants to kill his father, the white man, and sleep with his mother, the white woman (Davis, 1981, p. 181; Moodley, 2011).

References

Addai-Sebo, A. and Wong, A. (1988). *Our story: A handbook of African history and contemporary issues*. London: Strategic Policy Unit.
Appiah, K. A. (1989). The conversation of "race". *Black American Literature Forum, 23*, 37–60.
Benedict, R. (1935/1961). *Patterns of culture* (7th ed.). London: Routledge & Kegan Paul.
Boon, J. A. (1982). *Other tribes, other scribes: Symbolic anthropology in the comparative study of cultures, histories, religions and texts*. Cambridge: Cambridge University Press.
Burton, R. (1910/1966). *First footsteps in East Africa* (Gordon Waterfield, Ed.). London: Routledge & Kegan Paul.
Conrad, J. (1899/1983). *Heart of darkness*. London: Penguin.
Davis, A. (1981). *Women, race and class*. London: Women's Press.
Defoe, D. (1719/1903). *Robinson Crusoe*. London: J. M. Dent.
Fanon, F. (1952/1967). *Black skins, white masks* (C. L. Markmann, Trans.). New York: Grove Press.
Fanon, F. (1965/1973). *The wretched of the Earth* (C. Farrington, Trans.). London: MacGibbon & Kee.
Fernando, S. (1988). *Race and culture in psychiatry*. London: Croom Helm.
Fernando, S. (Ed.). (1995). *Mental health in a multi-ethnic society: A multidisciplinary handbook*. London: Routledge.
Fernando, S. (2010). *Mental health, race and culture* (3rd ed.). Basingstoke: Palgrave Macmillan.

Frazer, J. G. (1922). *The golden bough: A study in magic and religion*. London: Macmillan.

Fryer, P. (1984). *Staying power: The history of black people in Britain*. London: Pluto.

Green, M. (1980). *Dreams of adventure, deeds of empire*. London: Routledge & Kegan Paul.

Haggard, H. R. (1885/1989). *King Solomon's mines*. Oxford: Oxford University Press.

Haggard, H. R. (1887/1992). *She*. Oxford: Oxford University Press.

Livingstone, D. and Livingstone, C. (1865). *Narrative of an expedition to the Zambezi and its tributaries and the discovery of the Lakes Shirwa and Nyassa, 1858–1864*. London: John Murray.

Malinowski, B. (1922). *The sexual life of savages in North-Western Melanesia: An ethnographic account of courtship, marriage, and family life among the natives of the Trobriand Islands, British New Guinea*. London: Routledge.

Mannoni, O. (1956). *Prospero and Caliban: The psychology of colonization* (P. Powesland, Trans.). London: Metheun.

Mead, M. (1928). *Coming of age in Samoa*. Harmondsworth: Penguin.

Mead, M. (1930). *Growing up in New Guinea*. Harmondsworth: Penguin.

Minh-ha, T. T. (1989). *Woman, native, other (writing, postcoloniality and feminism)*. Bloomington: Indiana University Press.

Moodley, R. (2011). *Outside the sentence: Readings in critical multicultural counselling and psychotherapy*. Toronto: CDCP.

Pratt, M. L. (1986). Scratches on the faces of the country; or, What Mr Barrow saw in the island of the Bushman. In Henry L. Gates Jr. (Ed.), *"Race", writing and difference*. Chicago: University of Chicago Press.

Said, E. W. (1978). *Orientalism*. London: Routledge & Kegan.

Shakespeare, W. (1611/1971). *The Tempest*. London: Macmillan.

Theunissen, M. (1977/1984). *The Other* (C. Macann, Trans.). Cambridge, MA: Massachusetts Institute of Technology.

Thomas, A. and Sillen, S. (1972). *Racism and psychiatry*. Secaucus, NJ: Citadel.

Van Der Post, L. (1952). *Venture into the interior*. London: Hogarth Press.

Whitehead, S., Talahite, A. & Moodley, R. (2013). *Gender and identity: Key themes and new directions*. Toronto: Oxford University Press.

Williams, C. (1999). Connecting anti-racist and anti-oppressive theory and practice: Retrenchment or reappraisal. *British Journal of Social Work, 29*, 211–230.

4 Is there an emancipatory psychiatry?

John Eversley

Introduction

In reviewing the development of anti-psychiatry and critical psychiatry, Cohen (2009, p. 4), quoting Szasz (1961), posits that '[t]he institution of psychiatry, like the institution of slavery, consists of a socially sanctioned relationship between a class of superiors coercively controlling a class of inferiors'. The argument that Black and Minority Ethnic people and women have been oppressed by psychiatry has been made by many people within and outside the profession (e.g. Fernando, 2010a; Tomes, 1994). In this chapter I explore whether there is a commonality in what these and other critiques stand for that amounts to an 'emancipatory psychiatry' movement, specifically in the United Kingdom, and consider Suman Fernando's part in developing this analysis.

In 2008, the present author organised a seminar on 'Psychiatry and Emancipation: The Last 50 Years'. The seminar took place at Kingsley Hall, London, where R. D. Laing and the Philadelphia Association had operated (SUMEHR, 2008). The speakers were Suman Fernando and David Ingleby. Ingleby (1998) had previously argued that the post-war development of psychiatry in the Netherlands had taken a very different turn from that of the United Kingdom because it occurred in the context of emancipatory values that were part of the cultural climate in the Netherlands.

Critiques of psychiatry

There are a number of critiques of psychiatry that come from within the profession. In 1967, David Cooper talked about 'a germinal anti-psychiatry': i.e. something not yet developed. On the other hand, his experiment in Villa 21 at Shenley hospital had already ended (Cooper, 1967). Although R. D. Laing is associated in many people's minds with anti-psychiatry, he, apparently, did not regard himself as an anti-psychiatrist (Nasser, 1995). Many accounts of Cooper and Laing highlight that they moved away from a concern with clinical practice to a more general critique of how society in general operates and the need for social change (Appignanesi, 2008; Ticktin, 1986).

Ingleby used the term 'critical psychiatry' as the title of his 1981 edited volume; a critique of traditional psychiatry, it challenges psychiatry's claims to be scientific by drawing on a variety of disciplines outside psychiatry and its positivist stance. Critical psychiatry clearly has a focus on clinical practice. It is concerned with how psychiatry can move from 'fundamental conservative goals' to how 'psychiatry can incorporate social structure not as constant but as a variable' (Ingleby, 1981a, p. 70).

The Transcultural Psychiatry Society (TCPS) was established in the United Kingdom in the 1970s, though the term was used earlier (Fernando, 2008; Kirmeyer, 2007). Suman Fernando was an early member. He and others expanded the notions around transcultural psychiatry in the United Kingdom to address racism to derive a critique of psychiatry and psychology from a race and culture perspective. A number of books emerged from the TCPS; see, for example, Cox (1986), Fernando (1988), Lipsedge and Littlewood (1997). Other chapters in this volume explore transcultural psychiatry in depth.

Critiques of psychiatry and alternative practices challenging oppression based on gender and sexuality emerged in the 1970s, although earlier roots are clear (Chesler, 1972; Roberts, 2011; Tatchell, 1972; Tomes, 1994). For example, one of the earliest 'functional' groups of the Gay Liberation Front (formed in 1970) was the Counter-Psychiatry Group. It saw itself as part of the anti-psychiatry movement and took as its mentors people like R. D. Laing and David Cooper (Weeks, 1977, p. 198).

Active engagement of mental health service users in their treatment through therapeutic groups (led by psychiatrists) goes back to the 1940s (Andrews, 1998; Foulkes, 1983). 'Survivors' movements' emerged in the 1970s in the United Kingdom (Hughes, 2006), but the idea of a Mental Patients Union and some initiatives began much earlier (Survivors History Group, n.d.).

The influence of the United Kingdom on international movements, and vice versa, are of course important. Although the American Thomas Szasz did not identify himself with anti-psychiatry, he clearly influenced both it and critical psychiatry (Ingleby, 1981b). In Italy, Franco Basaglia's 'democratic psychiatry' *was* influenced by a variety of ideas (such as those of Goffman and Foucault) and practices including anti-psychiatry (Tantam, 1999).

Policy and practice

Movements and policy making are often messy. They often have no clear beginnings and ends, defined memberships or clear manifestos. Thus, on the one hand, Cooper traced back 'therapeutic communities' to pre-Christian times in Egypt (Cooper, 1967). On the other hand, Laing exaggerated how bad things were at the hospital where he worked in the 1950s and did not acknowledge other work going on (Andrews, 1998).

Policy is a process of sense-making, negotiation and settlements made between different parties with a stake in an issue. The visible positions of the stakeholders, their underlying interests and needs interact to be forces and drivers of policy

(John, 1998; Moran, Rein and Goodin, 2006). Practitioners often play an important and unrecognised role (Lipsky, 1980; Peck and 6, 2006). Sometimes debates in psychiatry are between practitioners seeking to find ways of reforming practice and people seeking wider social change. Theorists and ideologists do not always practise what they preach (Cooper, 1968; Ingleby, 1998; Peters, 1996).

Policy making operates on a number of levels (Parsons, 1995; Thompson, 2003). Meta-level drivers are big ideas, often found in books. A number of authors have provided ideologies for emancipatory psychiatry (de Beauvoir, 1971; Fanon, 1967; Foucault, 1965; Goffman, 1961; Szasz, 1961). The counter-culture was an inspiration to Cooper and Laing (Freeman, 2005; Ingleby, 1981b; Shorter, 1998). On the other hand, for practitioners ideological or academic treatises could be of marginal interest. Suman Fernando described transcultural psychiatry in the 1960s as 'a sort of passive subject, respected academically but somewhat dead, of little relevance to practical matters such as the treatment of patients or the organisation of mental health services' (2008, p. 2).

On the macro level the movement away from institutional care was driven by costs, overcrowding, difficulties in staff recruitment and retention and changing inter-professional relations (Freeman, 2005).

On the micro level policy making often comes from changes in practice, prefigurative of a wider change – embodying the relationships and political forms of the desired society. It can be through intentional projects or experiments such as Cooper's Villa 21 at Shenley, or Laing at Kingsley Hall. It can also be less self-conscious as, it has been argued, was the case with 'social psychiatry' (Freeman, 2005).

On the nano level there may be many autobiographical forces and drivers that make people conform or break with tradition. Thus Laing's belief that the family is responsible for much emotional distress is said to come from his own upbringing (Society for Laingian Studies, n.d.). On the other hand, criticising existing practice could threaten career advancement. Fernando has said, 'I could not afford to admit to being anti-psychiatry as well as being seen as some sort of alien' (2008, p. 2), and Ingleby was victimised for his ideas (Ingleby, 2006; Sedgewick, 1981).

Is there an emancipatory psychiatry?

Having identified the different threads in psychiatry that might be seen as working towards emancipation, we now turn to whether they can be woven together to form a coherent set of principles or values that can be translated into action.

Anti-oppressive science

A fundamental criticism shared by many of the critics is that psychiatry is based on 'bad' science or pseudo-science. Science has been used as a tool of discrimination and prejudice (Kirmeyer, 2007) and its scientific claims to objectivity have been deconstructed (Tomes, 1994). Underpinning many of the claims for psychiatry is a positivist view that there are unique objective truths to be uncovered (Cooper, 1967; Foucault, 1965; Ingleby, 1981a; Laing, 1960; Social Perspectives Network, 2003). Much of the positivist canon of knowledge is drawn from (Western) bio-mechanical medicine. The alternative paradigm is an interpretivist scientific one (Ingleby, 1981b). It recognises that there can be multiple perspectives. These include individual and social but also academic and professional viewpoints. The critics of psychiatric orthodoxy often draw on a broad knowledge base including the social sciences and non-Eurocentric knowledge.

Mental illness as a social construction

A major motivation for a move towards an interpretivist science has been the view that diagnostic categories, for example, schizophrenia, hysteria or homosexuality, are social constructions that reflect the social order, not diseases. Much of the feminist and anti-racist critique of psychiatry has challenged the idea that there is any biological or psycho-dynamic mechanistic causality about mental ill health. Very often that has been expressed as a challenge to 'binary oppositions': mind/body, masculine/feminine, black/white, straight/gay. Western medicine has been built around the separation of body and mind. Western philosophy and theology has also counter-posed 'mind' and 'spirit' and 'individual' and 'collective'. These socially constructed distinctions obscure what makes people feel ill or healthy (Fernando, 2010a; Tomes, 1994).

Within the various critiques there have been differences about whether there is any 'mind' disease at all. Thomas Szasz made a distinction between diseases of brain (such as syphilis) and diseases of the mind (Appignanesi, 2008). Others have distinguished between disease and illness, with disease being the biological 'reality' and illness being the interpretations of it. Some have taken the view that mental illness in general or specific illnesses are simply metaphors (Cohen, 2009). The work on schizophrenia that Fernando is currently involved in suggests that the majority of respondents to their inquiry do not think that it is scientifically based (valid) or useful (Schizophrenia Inquiry, n.d.). Between the biological medical model and a pure constructivist model are 'critical realists' who see material reality constraining but not determining actions or interpretations (Ingleby, 1981b; Pilgrim and Rogers, 1999).

For people who think mental ill health has some basis in disease, there remains a question about why it should be unevenly distributed among population groups. It is suggested that there is stratification in diagnosis and treatment: labelling and victimising of the least powerful in societies and exemption or toleration of people with similar conditions of behaviour from more powerful groups. Thus it is argued that shell-shocked soldiers in the First World War displaced the traditional female connotations of hysteria when 'respectable' men went mad, leading to a new kind of psychiatry (Shephard, 1999). Tomes (1994) identifies the sick role and specifically the 'mad' role as a consequence and expression of restricted lives, a refuge from abuse and also as a means of following unconventional lives.

Explanations of what it is that makes individuals and social groups behave, think or feel differently has been addressed on a number of different levels. The transcultural psychiatry movement has put a lot of emphasis on the differences that exist between cultures. Fernando has highlighted that much of the writing on cultural psychiatry focuses on minority cultures within Western/Northern societies; it is generally not applied to the dominant cultures within those societies (Fernando, 2010a).

Much of the emphasis is on the intra-cultural relations rather than inter-group relations. Fernando illustrates this omission from his own experience:

> when I was sorting out what was related to life experience and what was about culture, I soon realized that Jews of the East End had in fact experienced a very different 'environment' to that experienced by other East Enders. 'Culture' and 'environment' were inextricably linked and the link was through anti-Semitism. Jewish life experiences were different to that of others not because of their culture or their family-life or their personal inclinations but because of what other people did to them.
>
> (Fernando, 2008, p. 1)

When inter-group relations are considered, the focus is often on cultural competences and cultural capability rather than discrimination and disadvantage. The feminist analysis of morbidity highlights relations between the sexes and also ways in which notions of femininity such as body image may be transmitted by mothers to daughters (Appignanesi, 2008). This reflects an understanding that power is a series of relationships in which both doctor and patient may be constrained but they also have potential to exert control. This is also evident in debates about whether families are a major source of mental illness and/or have a central role in healing or recovery (Fernando, 2010a; Tomes, 1994).

Support based on human rights

The application of the concept of universal human rights to public policy is relatively recent. The 1948 UN Declaration of Human Rights set out areas in which individuals have rights but also recognised that groups faced discrimination (United Nations, 1948).

Since then, thinking about human rights has evolved. Of particular significance is the 'capability' approach of Amartya Sen. He has wrestled with how human rights can be universal in widely different economic and social contexts and within different belief systems. Having started with the idea that freedom is at the heart of universal rights, he identified capability – the right 'to be and to do' – as being the underlying principle. He has observed that different social groups endure different 'penalties' because of their characteristics (Sen, 2009; Vizard, 2005). These penalties include the results of health status. Fernando draws on Sen's idea of development as freedom when talking about 'recovery as freedom' (Fernando, 2010b).

It has been noted that although nobody is one-dimensional, society is often organised as if they were. For instance, black people and women have been treated as exclusive and homogeneous categories. 'Intersectionality' has come to be used to reflect the multidimensional nature of all social groups (Anthias and Yuval-Davies, 1993; hooks, 1982). Morris explored the issues in relation to people with physical impairments and mental health support needs. Of particular significance is the experience of 'Humerah', a disabled Muslim woman who endured discrimination as a Muslim and as a woman with both physical impairments and mental health issues – but also encountered services that were able to meet her needs (Morris, 2004).

Psychiatry founded on the principles of human rights and equality has the potential to be emancipatory for all social groups. However, this does not resolve the issues of what psychiatry is for and how it should work, to which we now turn.

Recovery as freedom

David Cooper was scathing about psychiatry's pretensions to 'cure'. While Cooper and others rejected the aim of curing, they argued for interventions to support healing or recovery (Cooper, 1967). Fernando suggests that 'If recovery ... is a journey for freedom, then the role of services – the "recovery approach" is to liberate' – a concept he relates to the work of Fanon (Fernando, 2010b, p. 8). For Fernando, recovery is 'healing' as defined by the user: 'the pursuit of personally (not professionally) defined goals, making sense of experiences, understanding oneself, taking power into one's own hands, and above all hoping for a better future' (Fernando, 2010b, p. 1). If it is part of the argument that mental illness is socially constructed, then the challenge is to embrace a user-led goal of recovery incorporating social dimensions. The methods of intervention need to reflect the goals.

Anti-oppressive practice

In relation to social work, Dominelli suggests that there are three established approaches. First, the 'therapeutic' approaches: helping the client better to understand themselves and their relationships with others, particularly close relatives and friends; second, 'maintenance' approaches: ensuring that people can cope or deal adequately with their lives; and third, 'emancipatory' approaches: working towards social justice encouraging users to see their situation in the context of power relationships and either through individual or collective action to take greater control of their lives (Dominelli, 1998).

Therapeutic and maintenance approaches might be seen as part of a paradigm of emancipatory psychiatry. The emphasis on the service user making sense of their situation rather than (simply) being diagnosed and treated and working towards 'recovery' is still relatively a new concept in psychiatry. Many psychiatrists do not see their role as challenging existing social structures and processes.

The literature on professional practice in psychiatry often focuses on questions of differences relating to either identity or socio-economic status but not both. Dominelli argues that the way to look at structural divisions and inequality is through 'a methodology [which focuses] on both process and outcome ... a way of structuring relationships between individuals that aims to empower users by reducing the negative effects of hierarchy in their immediate interaction and the work they do together' (1998, p. 3). Practitioners and service users have to overcome the hierarchical barriers between them.

Cooper and Szasz noted that psychiatry has often been a study of social invalidation: 'patients' are marginalised and pacified (Cooper, 1967; Szasz, 1961). Some critics of mainstream psychiatry have it as part of a wider pattern of oppression, coercion and control, especially sexual control. Established forms of psychiatric practice undermine autonomy in a variety of ways, including by incarceration in all-embracing institutions and labelling (Cooper, 1967; Fanon, 1967; Foucault, 1965; Goffman, 1961; Szasz, 1961).

Holistic interventions and concordance

Emancipatory Psychiatry requires turning a medical model based on diagnosing what is 'wrong' with people to a social model that focuses on realisation of what people can be and do. This requires going back to the most basic scientific understanding of human health: the relationships between mind, body and society and what is 'normal'.

Psychiatry was one of the first health services to recognise that outcomes could be improved by the active involvement of users in decisions about treatment. However, it is not always attempted or successfully practised. As Fernando says, engaging users means a view based on lived experience rather than something that is located in the 'mind', which means '[b]acking user choice and that means a variety of different types of treatment and support being available from which to choose, and a partnership to work out what is best' (Fernando, 2010b, p. 6).

The idea that users should not simply consent or comply with a diagnosis or treatment but should actively choose them – concordance – is neither new nor limited to mental health (Digby, 1985; Street, O'Malley, Cooper and Haidet, 2008). Cooper and Powe define concordance as a state of agreement or harmony between patients and providers. Their research suggested that congruence in language, ethnicity and culture between physicians and patients could all improve outcomes (Cooper and Powe, 2004). Street and colleagues suggest that patients' belief that they are similar to their physicians in personal beliefs, values and communication is important (Street *et al.*, 2008). Within mental health care this view is contested: Bhui and Bhugra (2007) suggest that sharing ethnicity and cultural background may help, but Loewenthal (2007) says there is almost no research to support this.

For many people, this is one of the most challenging aspects of an emancipatory approach. Do users have an unlimited right to choose to say whether they are well or not – can they be wrong? Must all interventions be entirely voluntary? One human rights perspective is that no individual right and no one person's or group's right 'trumps' any other, so it is a matter of balancing rights; there are degrees of voluntariness and voluntary acceptance of restrictions on freedom can be encouraged. Some of the main strategies for doing so are now considered.

The power of people who have similar experiences is now widely recognised in health and social care systems. Examples include the 'Expert Patient' programme, user-led advocacy, therapeutic communities (Campling, 2001), the Survivors movement (Survivors History Group, n.d.) and co-production (New Economics Foundation, 2008). 'Nothing about us, without us' (popularised by the disability movement) is even said to be UK government policy (Lansley, 2010). However, as Karran (2009) says, the more radical ideas of the anti-psychiatry movement have been watered down to a consumer or customer role in relation to health care.

Shared experience and concordance may reflect a community development strategy. Fernando has argued that community development is part of a recovery approach, arguing that

> For many people what matters is a holistic wellbeing of the total person as part of community ... Community Development is a sort of model for what mental health services should do in a recovery approach to support people on the journey of recovery.
>
> (Fernando, 2010b, p. 4)

A recent issue of the *Community Development Journal* has argued for and examined this while noting the mutual suspicions of both community development and mental health practitioners (Carpenter and Raj, 2012). Community development practitioners are expected to work towards a set of core values and display a range of competences to achieve them (England Standards Board, 2009). Reflective practice is part of this (Schön, 1983).

Conclusion

This chapter has explored the nature of a number of initiatives that have tried to change psychiatry. These include anti-psychiatry, critical and transcultural psychiatry from within the profession. Critiques and organisations have come from feminist, Black and Minority Ethnic, gay and disabled people's and service users' perspectives. There are some conscious connections between them but also many opportunities for integration that have not been exploited fully. However, there are enough compatible ideas underlying them sufficient to make a case for an emancipatory psychiatry. Suman Fernando has played a significant role in developing both the underlying rationale and therapeutic interventions. However, there is still much to be done to develop a consistent set of principles underpinning both an alternative clinical practice and an engagement with achieving the wider social change that is necessary to promote good mental health.

To address the role of clinicians in promoting social change, the first principle should be the promotion of healthy public policy (WHO, n.d.). It is one thing to note that the determinants of mental ill health are social and another to be directly involved in tackling them. The idea that doctors have a political role is neither new nor revolutionary. In 1848, Rudolf Virchow, a public health doctor and political Liberal, declared that 'medicine is a social science, and politics is nothing more than medicine on a grand scale' (McNeely, 2002, p. 25). The second principle is not to accept that the status quo is inevitable. Fernando quotes Martin Luther King Jr writing from jail during the Civil Rights Movement:

> Today psychologists have a favourite word, and that word is maladjustment. I tell you today that there are some things in our social system to which I am proud to be maladjusted.... The salvation of the world lies in the maladjusted.
>
> (Fernando, 2010b, p. 5)

We must rise to the challenge.

References

Andrews, J. (1998). R. D. Laing in Scotland: Facts and fictions of the 'rumpus room' and interpersonal psychiatry. In M. Gijswijt-Hofstra and R. Porter (Eds.), *Cultures of Psychiatry* (pp. 121–150). Amsterdam: Rodopi.

Anthias, F. and Yuval-Davies, N. (1993). *Racialized boundaries: Race, nation, colour and class and the anti-racist struggle*. London: Routledge.

Appignanesi, L. (2008). *Mad, bad and sad*. London: Virago.

Bhui, K. and Bhugra, D. (2007). Ethnic inequalities and cultural capability framework in mental healthcare. In D. Bhugra and K. Bhui (Eds.), *Textbook of cultural psychiatry* (pp. 81–92). Cambridge: Cambridge University Press.

Campling, P. (2001). Therapeutic communities. *Advances in Psychiatric Treatment, 7*, 365–372.

Carpenter, M. and Raj, T. (Eds.). (2012). Special issue: Mental health and community development. *Community Development Journal, 47*(4), 451–651.

Chesler, P. (1972). *Women and madness*. Garden City, NY: Doubleday.

Cohen, D. (2009, 22 June). *Whither critical psychiatry?* Paper presented at the Critical Psychiatry Network Conference, Norwich.

Cooper, D. (1967). *Psychiatry and anti-psychiatry*. London: Paladin.

Cooper, D. (Ed.). (1968). *The dialectics of liberation conference*. Harmondsworth: Penguin.

Cooper, L. and Powe, N. (2004). *Disparities in patient experiences, health care processes, and outcomes: The role of patient–provider in racial, ethnic and language concordance*. New York: Commonwealth Fund.

Cox, J. (1986). *Transcultural psychiatry*. London: Croom Helm.

De Beauvoir, S. (1971). *The second sex*. New York: Alfred A. Kopf.

Digby, A. (1985). Moral treatment at the Retreat, 1796–1846. In W. Bynum, R. Porter and M. Shepherd (Eds.), *The anatomy of madness, Vol 2: Institutions and Society* (pp. 52–72). London: Tavistock.

Dominelli, L. (1998). Anti-oppressive practice in context. In R. Adams, L. Dominelli and M. Payne (Eds.), *Social work: Themes, issues and critical debates* (pp. 3–22). Basingstoke: Palgrave Macmillan.

England Standards Board. (2009). *Community development national occupational standards*. Sheffield: ESB. Retrieved 2 January 2013 from www.fcdl.org.uk/nos/45-cd-nos-2009-summary-4-pages-1/download.

Fanon, F. (1967). *Black skin, white masks*. New York: Grove Press.

Femia, L. (1981). *Gramsci's political thought: Hegemony, consciousness and the revolutionary process*. Oxford: Clarendon.

Fernando, S. (1988). *Race and culture in psychiatry*. London: Croom Helm.

Fernando, S. (2008). *50 years in the struggle against racism in psychiatry: From asylums to transcultural psychiatry*. Unpublished manuscript.

Fernando, S. (2010a). *Mental health, race and culture* (3rd ed.). Basingstoke: Palgrave Macmillan.

Fernando, S. (2010b). *Recovery as a quest for freedom*. Paper presented at the Recovery Approaches to Trauma, Mental Illness/Addiction in Racialized Communities: A Community Perspective Conference, organised by Across Boundaries, Toronto.

Foucault, M. (1965). *Madness and civilization: A history of insanity in the Age of Reason*. New York: Random House.

Foulkes, S. (1948/1983). *Introduction to group analytic therapy*. London: Maresfield.

Freeman, H. (Ed.). (1999). *A century of psychiatry*. London: Mosby-Wolfe.

Freeman, H. (2005). Psychiatry and the state in Britain. In M. Gijswijt-Hofstra, H. Oosterhuis, J. Vijselaar and H. Freeman (Eds.), *Psychiatric cultures compared* (pp. 116–140). Amsterdam: Amsterdam University Press.

Goffman, E. (1961). *Asylums*. Harmondsworth: Penguin.

hooks, bell. (1982). *Ain't I a woman: Black women and feminism*. London: Pluto Press.

Hughes, J. (2006). Movements in the 70s. In *Survivors History Group*. Retrieved 2 January 2013 from http://studymore.org.uk/mpu.htm#Hughes1970s.

Ingleby, D. (Ed.). (1981a). *Critical psychiatry: The politics of mental health*. Harmondsworth: Penguin.

Ingleby, D. (1981b). Understanding mental illness. In D. Ingleby (Ed.), *Critical psychiatry: The politics of mental health*. Harmondsworth: Penguin.

Ingleby, D. (1998). The view from the North Sea. In M. Gijswijt-Hofstra and R. Porter (Eds.), *Cultures of psychiatry and mental health care in post-war Britain and Netherlands* (pp. 295–314). Amsterdam: Clio Medica.

Ingleby, D. (2006). Transcultural mental health care: The challenge to positivist psychiatry. In D. Double (Ed.), *Critical psychiatry: The limits of madness*. Basingstoke: Palgrave Macmillan.

John, P. (1998). *Analysing public policy*. London: Continuum.

Karran, J. (2009). *What impact has anti-psychiatric thought had on the structures it attempted to reform and where anti-psychiatry has succeeded or failed in its goals, why has this been the case?* London: UCL/Wellcome.

Kirmeyer, L. (2007). Cultural psychiatry in historical perspective. In D. Bhugra and K. Bhui (Eds.), *Textbook of cultural psychiatry* (pp. 3–19). Cambridge: Cambridge University Press.

Laing, R. (1960). *The divided self*. Harmondsworth: Penguin.

Lansley, A. (2010). *My ambition for patient centred care* [Speech]. Retrieved 1 January 2013 from http://webarchive.nationalarchives.gov.uk/+/www.dh.gov.uk/en/MediaCentre/Speeches/DH_116643.
Lipsedge, M. and Littlewood, R. (1997). *Aliens and alienists: Ethnic minorities and psychiatry*. London: Routledge.
Lipsky, M. (1980). *Street level bureaucracy*. New York: Russell Sage Foundation.
Loewenthal, K. (2007). Spirituality and psychiatry. In D. Bhugra and K. Bhui (Eds.), *Textbook of cultural psychiatry* (pp. 59–71). Cambridge: Cambridge University Press.
McNeely, I. (2002). *'Medicine on a grand scale': Rudolf Virchow, liberalism and the public health*. London: Wellcome UCL.
Mitchell, J. (1974). *Psychoanalysis and feminism*. Harmondsworth: Penguin.
Moran, M., Rein, M. and Goodin, R. (Eds.). (2006). *The Oxford handbook of public policy*. Oxford: Oxford University Press.
Morris, J. (2004). *One town for my body, another for my mind*. York: Joseph Rowntree Foundation.
Nasser, M. (1995). The rise and fall of anti-psychiatry. *Psychiatric Bulletin, 19*, 743–746.
New Economics Foundation. (2008). *Co-production: A manifesto for growing the core economy*. London: New Economics Foundation.
Parsons, W. (1995). *Public policy: An introduction to the theory and practice of policy analysis*. Cheltenham: Edward Elgar.
Peck, E. and 6, P. (2006). *Beyond delivery: Policy implementation as sense-making and settlement*. Basingstoke: Palgrave.
Peters, U. (1996). The emigration of German psychiatrists to Britain. In H. Freeman and G. Berrios (Eds.), *150 years of British Psychiatry, Vol. II: The aftermath*. London: Athlone.
Pilgrim, D. and Rogers, A. (1999). *A sociology of mental health and illness* (3rd ed.). Buckingham: Open University Press.
Roberts, A. (2011). Shifting attitudes to homosexuality. *History Today, 61*(10), 4–6.
Royal College of Psychiatrists. (n.d.) *Gay and Lesbian Group: About us*. Retrieved 2 January 2013 from www.rcpsych.ac.uk/rollofhonour/specialinterestgroups/gaylesbian/aboutus.aspx#past.
Schizophrenia Inquiry. (n.d.). *Inquiry into the schizophrenia label*. Retrieved 1 January 2013 from www.schizophreniainquiry.org.
Schön, D. (1983). *The reflective practitioner: How professionals think in action*. London: Temple Smith.
Sedgewick, P. (1981). The grapes of Roth. *New Society*, 30 April.
Sen, A. (2009). *The idea of justice*. London: Allen Lane.
Shephard, B. (1999). Shell shock. In H. Freeman (Ed.), *A century of psychiatry* (pp. 33–40). London: Mosby-Wolfe.
Shorter, E. (1998). *A history of psychiatry: From the era of the asylum to the age of Prozac*. Chichester: John Wiley.
Social Perspectives Network. (2003). *Where you stand affects your point of view: Emancipatory approaches to mental health research*. SPN paper 4. Retrieved 2 January 2013 from www.spn.org.uk/fileadmin/SPN_uploads/Documents/Papers/SPN_Papers/SPN_Paper_4.pdf.
Society for Laingian Studies. (n.d.) *Biography*. Retrieved 2 January 2013 from http://laingsociety.org/biograph.htm.
Street, R., O'Malley, K., Cooper, L. and Haidet, P. (2008). Understanding concordance in patient–physician relationships: Personal and ethnic dimensions of shared identity. *Annals of Family Medicine, 6*, 198–205.

SUMEHR. (2008). *Psychiatry and emancipation: The last 50 years*. London: Support Unit for Ethnic Minority Health Research.

Survivors History Group. (n.d.). *Mental health and survivors' movements and context*. Retrieved 2 January 2013 from http://studymore.org.uk/mpu.htm#History.

Szasz, T. (1961). *The myth of mental illness*. New York: Hoeber-Harper.

Tantam, D. (1996).The anti-psychiatry movement. In G. Berrios and H. Freeman (Eds.), *150 years of British psychiatry 1841–1991*. London: Athlone Press.

Tantam, D. (1999). R. D. Laing and anti-psychiatry. In H. Freeman (Ed.), *A century of psychiatry* (pp. 202–207). London: Mosby-Wolfe.

Tatchell, P. (1972). Aversion therapy is 'like a visit to the dentist'. *Gay News*, No. 11. Retrieved 2 January 2013 from www.petertatchell.net/lgbt_rights/psychiatry/dentist.htm.

Terrence Higgins Trust. (2010). *Rewriting history: Key moments and issues of the last 50 years of LGBT history*. Retrieved 2 January 2013 from www.tht.org.uk/~/media/Files/Publications/Resources/rewriting-history-resource.ashx.

Thompson, N. (2003). *Promoting equality: Challenging discrimination and oppression*. Basingstoke: Palgrave Macmillan.

Ticktin, S. (1986). Brother beast: A personal memoir of David Cooper. *Asylum Magazine for Democratic Psychiatry, 1*(3). Retrieved 2 January 2013 from http://laingsociety.org/colloquia/inperson/davidcooper/brotherbeast2.htm.

Tomes, N. (1994). Feminist histories of psychiatry. In M. Micale and R. Porter (Eds.), *Discovering the history of psychiatry* (pp. 348–383). New York: Oxford University Press.

United Nations. (1948). *The universal declaration of human rights*. Retrieved 1 January 2013 from www.un.org/en/documents/udhr.

Vizard, P. (2005). *The contributions of Professor Amartya Sen in the field of human rights*. London: LSE STICERD. Retrieved 1 January 2013 from http://sticerd.lse.ac.uk/dps/case/cp/CASEpaper91.pdf.

Weeks, J. (1977). *Coming out: Homosexual politics in Britain, from the nineteenth century to the present*. London: Quartet.

Williamson, I. (2000). Internalized homophobia and health issues affecting lesbians and gay men. *Health Education Research, 15*(1), 97–107.

WHO (World Health Organization). (n.d.). *The Ottawa Charter*. Retrieved 1 January 2013 from www.who.int/healthpromotion/conferences/previous/ottawa/en/index.html.

Part II
Challenges and opportunities in mental health care

5 The challenge of diversity to mental health services

David Ingleby

Introduction

During the last half-century many Western countries have begun to respond to the challenge presented to health services by ethnic and cultural diversity. This challenge has been perceived very differently in different times and places. Nevertheless, international links have developed between those working on this issue in different countries, to the extent that we can speak of the emergence of a movement to adapt health services to diversity and combat inequalities in health care.

For several decades Suman Fernando has been an important contributor to this movement, both within the United Kingdom and internationally. Recently, he has also turned his attention to the topic of global inequalities in mental health and health care. This chapter will try to sketch something of the historical background to his work, so that it can be appreciated in its wider context.

Different approaches to diversity and (mental) health

Developments in the United States originated with the Civil Rights Movement in the decade (roughly speaking) between 1955 and 1965. The 1964 Civil Rights Act, perhaps the crowning achievement of this movement, continues to provide the legal basis of many interventions to improve health care for minorities. The segregated, third-rate health care available to most African Americans was one of the major grievances of the Civil Rights Movement. However, half a century went by before the main source of racial injustice in health care – the fact that a disproportionate number of non-whites could not afford health insurance – was tackled by the America's first black president in the Patient Protection and Affordable Care Act of 2010.

The Civil Rights Movement started a tradition of vigorous criticism of racial bias in American (mental) health care. Racist ideas and practices abounded in traditional psychiatry, exemplified by such oddities as the syndrome of 'drapetomania' – the pathological tendency of slaves to run away from their owners. Psychology also came under fire and in 1968 the Association of Black Psychologists was founded. A landmark article entitled 'Towards a Black Psychology'

(White, 1970) claimed that mainstream psychology was incapable of doing justice to the world of African Americans, whom it systematically misrepresented as 'deviant' or 'inferior'. Significantly, the article called for recognition of the special characteristics of African American culture. The book *Even the Rat Was White* (Guthrie, 1976) exposed the systematic exclusion of African American subjects from psychological research. Similar biases were exposed in the medical sciences, resulting in regulations imposed by the National Institutes of Health (NIH, 1994) that obliged researchers to include both women and ethnic minorities in their samples.

Like the Civil Rights Movement itself, the movement against racism in American mental health focused mainly on the exclusion and oppression of African Americans. However, both movements took on board other racial or ethnic groups, in particular Hispanics and Native Americans. Much less attention was paid to the needs of recent migrants, including refugees and asylum seekers.

Apart from politics, demography has also contributed to the increasing attention for ethnic minorities in American health care. More than one-third of the current population classify themselves as belonging to a minority group; what is more, these groups were responsible for 92% of the population growth in 2000–2010 (Passel, D'Vera and Hugo Lopez, 2011). Many demographers expect that within two or three decades the traditional 'white majority group' will actually be in the minority. No health service provider, whether public or commercial, can therefore afford to ignore the needs of ethnic minorities.

Although the attention paid to diversity has been particularly strong in mental health, the existence of discrimination and inequalities in the entire health care sector became an increasingly important preoccupation of government agencies towards the end of the 20th century. In 1984 the US Department of Health and Human Services (DHHS) established the 'Task Force on Black and Minority Health', which reported serious health disadvantages among several minority groups, especially blacks (Nickens, 1986). Later, a major report by the Institute of Medicine concluded that racial and ethnic minorities receive a systematically lower quality of health care than non-minorities, even when differences in income and health insurance are controlled for (Smedley, Stith and Nelson, 2003). Since 2003 the DHHS's Agency for Healthcare Research and Quality (AHRQ) has produced regular editions of the *National Healthcare Quality Report* (*NHQR*) and the *National Healthcare Disparities Report* (*NHDR*). Ethnic disparities in health and health care have thus been firmly placed on the American public health agenda.

The development of 'cultural competence'

As White's (1970) article illustrates, the concept of 'culture' played a central role in the anti-racist movement within mental health. Promoting the acceptance of minority cultures as different, but equally valid, was seen as essential for eradicating racism. Indeed, for the last 40 years 'cultural sensitivity' (or 'competence') has been viewed as the royal road to inclusiveness in health care. To

Europeans this preoccupation has often seemed a little strange, when a disproportionate number of minority citizens in the United States were not even entitled to *use* health care. Even under the 2010 legislation the 11 million undocumented migrants in the United States, despite their crucial importance to the economy, still have no health care coverage. Giving 'culturally competent care' to those who manage to get into the system seems to ignore the elephant in the room – the plight of those condemned to stay outside it.

However, 'cultural competence' continues to be the key concept in American efforts to promote health equity. The concept was officially embraced by the federal government in 2000, when the Office of Minority Health published the *National Standards on Culturally and Linguistically Appropriate Services (CLAS) in Health Care* (OMH, 2000). Within a decade, the CLAS standards had been adopted in a wide range of health service organizations. Some of the standards were already mandated by the Civil Rights Act, while others are increasingly being incorporated in state legislation, accreditation schemes and professional codes of conduct (Goode and Like, 2012).

By 2000, however, the realization had dawned that racial or ethnic groups are anything but culturally homogeneous, and that 'five sizes fit all' (for example) was not much improvement on 'one size fits all'. Many argued that far from combating stereotyping, this approach to cultural competence actively encouraged it (see Like and Goode, 2012). Immigration from all parts of the world has vastly increased the number of different ethnic groups in the United States, which also show considerable internal variations – resulting in the phenomenon of 'super-diversity' noted by Vertovec (2008).

At the same time, under the influence of Clifford Geertz and 'interpretative anthropology' (Geertz, 1973) the traditional static concept of 'culture' was gradually being abandoned in favor of a fluid, dynamic and multi-layered one. Instead of trying to learn about cultures from books or courses, professionals were now encouraged to adopt an attitude of 'cultural humility', starting from a critical awareness of their *own* culture. They were encouraged to cultivate openness, improve their communication skills and take time to get to know their minority patients better (Tervalon and Murray-Garcia, 1998). At this point, as noted by Beach, Saha and Cooper (2006), the concept of 'cultural competence' started to show a strong resemblance to that of 'patient centered care'.

In the third and most recent development of the concept, there is a growing realization that 'culture' is not the only factor relevant to the health of migrants and ethnic minorities. Their social position, income, occupation, education and migrant status (e.g. as asylum seeker or undocumented migrant) may (among other things) also be crucial. Biological differences sometimes need to be considered as well. At the same time the emphasis on migrants and ethnic minorities is coming to be seen as too narrow: 'diversity' is not something that only these groups exemplify, but exists throughout the population. Gender, religion, age, disability, sexual orientation and place of residence (for example) may also be related to inequalities in health. In Europe, this broadening of perspective is seen as implying a shift *away* from 'culture' (Chiarenza, 2012); in the United States, by contrast, the response has been to greatly expand the concept of 'culture'. According to the 'Enhanced CLAS Standards' (DHHS, 2013), culture is not only associated with racial, ethnic or linguistic groups – the traditional sense of the term – but also with 'religious, spiritual, biological, geographical, or sociological characteristics'. In this way, 'cultural competence' can continue to be the central concept in the health system's response to human diversity – though some would argue that its content has been made so broad as to render the term meaningless.

Mental health care and diversity in other Western countries

Although US approaches have perhaps had the strongest influence on approaches to diversity in other Western countries, other important traditions have developed. Here we have space for only a hasty sketch of the situation in these countries.

In the other traditional 'countries of immigration', *Canada, Australia* and *New Zealand*, much attention has been paid to the theme of migration, ethnicity and health. All these countries host large numbers of migrants, and their inclusion in the health system is seen as an essential aspect of their integration. In addition, each country harbors indigenous or aboriginal minorities that suffered grievously during the colonial era and still have to contend with racial prejudice and social exclusion. Like the descendants of slaves in the United States, these minorities occupy a central, iconic position in the movements to tackle health inequalities.

Although these countries have been strongly influenced by American approaches (in particular by the emphasis on 'culture'), there are important differences. All of them have primarily tax-based health systems aiming at universal coverage, thus removing one of the major discrepancies affecting the health of minorities in the United States. The level of social protection is higher and income inequality is lower, protecting vulnerable groups from extremes of poverty and social exclusion. Nevertheless, migrants often suffer a decline in health as the length of time they have lived in these countries increases (the 'healthy migrant effect' – see Fennelly, 2007).

Turning to Europe, we will examine the *United Kingdom* separately from other countries, because of its strong historical ties with all the countries discussed so far – the most important of these ties being perhaps the use of the English language. Concern with minority health developed rapidly in postwar Britain with the arrival of many post-colonial migrants. 'Guest workers' from Southern Europe complemented these groups during the economic boom of the 1950s and 1960s. As in the United States, the most extreme ethnic tensions were between whites and blacks (though racism in the United Kingdom had more to do with the legacy of colonialism than with that of slavery). It is in this context that Suman Fernando's work on mental health services in multi-ethnic societies is rooted. Characteristically, his first major book (Fernando, 1988) starts not with a discussion of ethnic minority patients, but of 'the culture of psychiatry': this reflexive stance led him to a critical examination of psychiatry's historical involvement in colonialism and racist practices. Although focusing strongly on culture, his work also emphasizes political and economic realities and – in particular – the power relations between groups.

'Black and Minority Ethnic' (BME) groups, as they came to be known in the United Kingdom, have been an important driving force for adapting services to diversity. BME organizations received a paradoxical boost in the 1980s from Margaret Thatcher's drastic cuts in welfare provisions. This attack on vulnerable social groups encouraged collective opposition and the formation of self-help organizations. NGOs such as Black Mental Health UK continue to advocate energetically on behalf of African Caribbean communities. This activism, plus the strong representation of minority ethnic groups in the National Health Service (NHS) workforce (14%), has strengthened the drive to adapt health services to the needs of diverse groups. Nevertheless, as in the United States it is noticeable that new migrants, refugees, asylum seekers and undocumented migrants receive less attention than long-established ethnic groups. The central place accorded to the concepts of race, ethnicity and 'cultural competence' forms another similarity to the United States.

Initiatives to adapt UK health services to diversity, though they thus enjoy 'grass-roots' support, are fairly 'top-down' in nature: they are backed up both by the NHS leadership and by the legal system. The relevant legislation on equalities derives partly from concern about 'institutional racism' at the end of the 1990s and partly from EU anti-discrimination legislation. One integrated legal framework, the Equality Act, now covers all public sector organizations and multiple strands of inequality (age, disability, gender reassignment, race, religion or belief, sex, sexual orientation, marriage and civil partnership, and pregnancy and maternity). In practice, however, there is little cooperation between the different initiatives to combat inequalities in health.

An important feature of the current global scene is the 'social determinants of health' movement (see CSDH, 2008). This has strong roots in the United Kingdom; so far, this movement has shown little concern with the relevance of migration and ethnicity to health inequalities: the drives to combat socio-economic inequalities, on the one hand, and racism, on the other, occupy – somewhat bizarrely – different silos. This split has led to strong criticism from those working on race, ethnicity and health (Salway et al., 2010).

Continental Europe. Nations on the European mainland have strongly resisted the idea that they are 'countries of immigration' – despite the fact that in 2010, the percentage of immigrants in seven European countries was higher than that in the United States (UN DESA, 2011). Multicultural policies were introduced in Sweden (1975) and the Netherlands (1983), but to the extent that pluralist, inclusive policies are to be found at all in Europe, there has been a backlash against them since the late 1990s, accompanied by a revival of nationalist, xenophobic sentiment. The recent financial and economic crisis has intensified this shift. In many countries there are indigenous or national minorities, the largest group being the Roma (mainly concentrated in Central and Eastern Europe). These groups are also suffering from increased levels of intolerance.

The first conference to discuss the health of migrants in Europe was organized by the World Health Organization (WHO) and the Dutch government in 1983 (Colledge, Van Geuns and Svensson, 1986). A few countries subsequently made efforts to tackle this issue, but most managed to ignore them until the end of the century. By contrast, certain countries where immigration did not reach significant levels until the 1980s and 1990s, such as Italy, Spain and Portugal, responded rapidly to the health needs of migrants. Only in the last decade has systematic attention been paid to the acute health problems of many Roma communities.

A variety of approaches to diversity and health can be distinguished on the European mainland. France and Germany developed specialized approaches to mental health problems, whose influence was, however, confined to a few individual clinics and hospitals. In the Netherlands, ideas were imported from the United States and United Kingdom; urban mental health centers showed particular interest in 'interculturalization' (as it was known). However, the recent turn away from multiculturalism has led to the demise of many initiatives (Ingleby, 2012a).

Many Europeans respond with disbelief and dismay to the American and British habit of classifying people according to racial categories, in defiance of the fact that the concept of race has been widely denounced as pernicious and scientifically invalid. There is also much opposition to the notion of 'ethnicity' – particularly in France and Sweden, where the idea of an ethnically segmented society clashes with national ideologies. The use of ethnic data by the Nazis in order to oil the machinery of genocide has left behind a legacy of taboos and prohibitions in Europe that sometimes make research on diversity and health very difficult.

International and intergovernmental authorities have been active in supporting work on migrant and ethnic minority health in Europe (as well as elsewhere). The Council of Europe (COE) has published two sets of recommendations in this area (COE, 2006, 2011), while the WHO has published a policy briefing (WHO, 2010a) and the proceedings of a Global Consultation (WHO, 2010b). The International Organization for Migration (IOM) has been continuously active in this area.

Recently, however, attention for migration and ethnicity has been eclipsed by the increasing influence of the Social Determinants of Health (SDH) program, which focuses almost exclusively on socio-economic drivers of health inequalities. In a recent paper (Ingleby, 2012b) I have argued that the schism between the two approaches is counter-productive. Ethnicity and migration status are increasingly important markers and determinants of socio-economic stratification in Europe, so it is essential for the success of both approaches to forge alliances with each other.

Other countries. The phenomenon of immigration is no longer confined to high-income industrialized countries in what we call 'the West'. Although there is no space to discuss the most recent developments worldwide, attention is beginning to be paid to the health of migrants and ethnic minorities in many other areas, such as Asia, Central and South America, Africa and Russia (see WHO, 2010b). However, it is not yet clear to what extent distinctive new approaches are being developed in these countries

Critical versus technical approaches

Regarding the content of different approaches to diversity and health, I wish to argue here that it is very important to distinguish 'critical' from merely 'technical' approaches. The latter do not really challenge the basic assumptions and principles of mainstream (mental) health care: their basic aim is to deliver this care more efficiently to migrants and ethnic minorities, thus increasing the utilization of health care and the cooperation of patients. No questions are asked about the power imbalance between social groups and between providers and users of health care, or whether the care is in fact beneficial to those who receive it, or whether other forms of care would be better. Indeed, the technical approach to diversity and health is not essentially different from that used to sell any other goods and services to ethnic minorities or Third-World consumers.

Many issues in health care delivery can be tackled in this way. Indeed, if one is sure that a treatment is effective and safe, there may be little to say against encouraging its uptake by improving the way it is presented and delivered. In the current political climate, adopting a technical approach and justifying it in terms of cost-effectiveness may indeed be the best way to get necessary changes made in service provision (such as attention to linguistic and cultural barriers), rather than trying to appeal to political or human-rights considerations.

Critical approaches, by contrast, ask more fundamental questions about what is going on when interventions developed for one population are applied to another. What are the underlying power relations? Whose interests are being served? Is there a covert attempt to impose the values and perspective of the dominant group? Becoming a user of mainstream Western health care involves accepting its underlying philosophy and values: to give this process the euphemistic label of 'acquiring health literacy' obscures the *moral* issues that are at stake (Ingleby, 2012a). Moreover, the benefits of many current treatments are highly controversial. Health care regards itself increasingly as an industry, and, as with any industry, searching questions have to be asked about what it is doing for its customers – and what they are doing for it.

Although such questions can be asked about any area of health care, there is probably no area in which they have been raised more persistently than in mental health. Psychiatry, in particular, has been a heavily contested specialty as long as it has existed. In the first place, its scientific status has always been controversial. Moreover, available pharmacological treatments are unable to achieve success rates much higher than those of placebos: there has also been widespread misrepresentation of research results and suppression of evidence about damaging side effects. Second, because psychiatry deals with 'abnormal' behavior and experience, it is continually open to the charge of covertly imposing norms and values. Although it is too simplistic to regard psychiatry as a 'mental police force' in the sense popularized by Thomas Szasz, there is a vast historical and sociological literature describing its role in regulating and managing the social and personal problems arising in modern societies. 'Critical psychiatry' (Ingleby, 1980; Double, 2006) seeks to uncover the normative and political dimensions of these activities.

It will be clear from the above that a critical approach to diversity and health will have much to do. Despite this, much work on diversity and mental health does not go beyond a technical perspective: it assumes that mainstream psychiatric concepts, theories and treatments are applicable to all patients, and that 'adaptation to diversity' simply involves overcoming linguistic and cultural barriers, packaging and labeling care sensitively, being polite to people from minority groups and disseminating knowledge among the ignorant.

Suman Fernando himself is one of the most energetic exponents of the critical version of transcultural psychiatry. He has highlighted the disempowering, marginalizing potential of psychiatry and shown how easily this comes into play when mental services deal with minority users. Although 'racism' is a key concept in his work, this does not simply refer to individual acts of disrespect or hostility. Rather, it refers to the assumption that modern Western perspectives are superior to all others – the notion that 'our' ideas and way of life are the goal in relation to which other cultures are merely pathways or transitional phases.

Psychosis and compulsory treatment

It has been repeatedly found that members of marginalized ethnic groups have a greatly increased risk of being diagnosed with schizophrenia and subjected to compulsory treatment and incarceration. This has been established for blacks in the United Kingdom, as well as in the United States and several European countries. In the Netherlands, the phenomenon mainly concerns people of Moroccan origin. It does not seem to be explainable by genetic factors and many studies have implicated social exclusion and disadvantage as a cause (see Ingleby, 2008, for a review).

The response to this phenomenon demonstrates the split between the 'technical' and 'critical' approaches. Suman Fernando, who has specialized in forensic psychiatry, is the most active representative of the latter approach in the United Kingdom and sees racism as the most important factor. In his view, psychiatrists without an understanding of the cultural and social situation of blacks will be more likely to deem their behavior to be unintelligible, threatening and thus a symptom of psychosis. The self-fulfilling stereotype 'big, black and dangerous' will lead to more frequent use of coercive measures. By contrast, defenders of psychiatric orthodoxy, such as Singh and Burns (2006), claim that accusations of racism merely increase the gap between psychiatry and minority communities. The suggestion of diagnostic bias is rejected by authors such as Fearon *et al.* (2006), who argue that diagnoses based on clinical notes in which ethnicity is concealed show the same differences.

These counter-arguments, however, serve only to show the inability of the psychiatric mainstream to understand the criticisms (Ingleby, 2008). If 'institutional racism' exists within psychiatry, then acknowledging and combating it – rather than sweeping its existence under the carpet – is the only way to improve relations with minority communities.

Global mental health

The WHO's *World Health Report* on mental health (2001) argued fervently for 'scaling up' the implementation of psychiatric approaches developed in the West in low- and middle-income countries. Since then, a powerful global campaign has been organized, mainly based in American and British institutions, to support this process. The 'global mental health' (GMH) campaign claims to be both evidence-based and rights-based; critics are portrayed as being 'in denial' and callously indifferent to the suffering of their fellow human beings.

At present, critical views on GMH go virtually unheard against the background of a veritable propaganda barrage from powerful and wealthy institutions, supported by industrial backers. However, a selection of counter-arguments can be found in, for example, Summerfield (2008), Fernando (2011) and Timimi (2012). What these arguments boil down to is that to a large extent, psychiatry has been an expensive failure in the West, and its implementation in low- and middle-income countries is not in the interest of the people who live in those countries. Even in the West, its evidence base and its record on human rights is strongly contested; the validity of its diagnostic concepts, theories and treatments in other social and cultural contexts is questionable. The universalistic approach of GMH is reflected in the movement's commitment to a bio-medical approach and pharmaceutical treatments as the mainstay of mental health services. Drug company profits in high-income countries are falling – but exporting 'Western' psychiatric approaches to low- and middle-income countries can open up a market that is potentially five times bigger than that in the high-income countries. Again, Suman Fernando is vigorously involved in efforts to champion truly indigenous, 'grass-roots' mental health practices that could offer an alternative to this 'scaling up' of conventional bio-medical psychiatry.

Conclusion

The above two examples illustrate the contrast between 'technical' and 'critical' approaches to mental health care at (respectively) national and global levels. The majority of existing approaches to mental health and diversity should probably be classified as 'technical' ones: they aim at increasing the consumption of psychiatric services, either by minority ethnic groups or by the population of poorer countries, without stopping to consider whether such care is in the best interests of these groups. Suman Fernando's tireless and sustained critical work on both fronts constitutes a lasting challenge to those who try to sidestep these questions.

References

Beach, M. C., Saha, S. and Cooper, L. A. (2006). *The role and relationship of cultural competence and patient-centeredness in health care quality*. New York: The Commonwealth Fund.

Chiarenza, A. (2012). Developments in the concept of 'cultural competence'. In D. Ingleby, A. Chiarenza, W. Devillé and I. Kotsioni (Eds.), *Inequalities in health care for migrants and ethnic minorities*, COST Series on Health and Diversity (Vol. 2, pp. 9–28). Antwerp/Apeldoorn: Garant.

COE (2006). *Recommendation Rec(2006)18 of the Committee of Ministers to Member States on health services in a multicultural society*. Strasbourg: Council of Europe. Retrieved June 16, 2013, from http://tinyurl.com/39bxw2.

COE (2011). *Recommendation CM/Rec(2011)13 of the Committee of Ministers to member states on mobility, migration and access to health care*. Strasbourg: Council of Europe. Retrieved June 16, 2013, from http://bit.ly/rKs2YD.

Colledge, M., Van Geuns, H. A. and Svensson, P. G. (Eds.). (1986). *Migration and health: Towards an understanding of the health care needs of ethnic minorities*. Proceedings of a consultative group on ethnic minorities (The Hague, Netherlands, November 28–30, 1983). Copenhagen: WHO Regional Office for Europe.

CSDH (2008). *Closing the gap in a generation: Health equity through action on the social determinants of health*. Final report of the Commission on the Social Determinants of Health. Geneva: World Health Organization. Retrieved June 16, 2013, from http://bit.ly/17Z0G3.

DHHS (2013). *National standards for culturally and linguistically appropriate services in health and health care: A blueprint for advancing and sustaining CLAS policy and practice*. Washington, DC: US Department of Health and Human Services, Office of Minority Health. Retrieved from http://1.usa.gov/1hS8SAv.

Double, D. B. (2006). *Critical psychiatry: The limits of madness*. Basingstoke: Palgrave Macmillan.

Fearon, P., Kirkbride, J. B., Morgan, C., Dazzan, P., Morgan, K., Lloyd, T. *et al.* (2006). Incidence of schizophrenia and other psychoses in ethnic minority groups: Results from the MRC AESOP Study. *Psychological Medicine, 36*, 1541–1550.

Fennelly, K. (2007). The 'healthy migrant' effect. *Minnesota Medicine, 90*(3), 51–53.

Fernando, S. (1988). *Race and culture in psychiatry*. London: Croom Helm.

Fernando, S. (2011). A 'global' mental health program or markets for Big Pharma? *Open Mind*, September–October 2011, 22. Retrieved June 16, 2013, from http://bit.ly/17P618k.

Geertz, C. (1973). *The interpretation of cultures*. New York: Basic Books.

Goode, T. C. and Like, R. C. (2012). Advancing and sustaining cultural and linguistic competence in the American health system: Challenges, strategies, and lessons learned. In D. Ingleby, A. Chiarenza, W. Devillé and I. Kotsioni (Eds.), *Inequalities in health care for migrants and ethnic minorities*. COST Series on Health and Diversity (Vol. 2, pp. 49–65). Antwerp/Apeldoorn: Garant.

Guthrie, R. (1976). *Even the rat was white: A historical view of psychology*. New York: Harper & Row.

Ingleby, D. (1980). *Critical psychiatry: The politics of mental health*. New York: Pantheon.

Ingleby, D. (2008). *New perspectives on migration, ethnicity and schizophrenia*. Willy Brandt Series of Working Papers in International Migration and Ethnic Relations 4/07.

Malmö: IMER/MIM, Malmö University, Sweden. Retrieved June 16, 2013, from http://bit.ly/14D6ozQ.
Ingleby, D. (2012a). Acquiring health literacy as a moral task. *International Journal of Migration, Health and Social Care, 8*(1), 22–32.
Ingleby, D. (2012b). Migration, ethnicity and the 'social determinants of health' agenda. *Psychosocial Intervention/Intervención Psicosocial, 21*(3), 331–341. Retrieved June 26, 2013, from http://bit.ly/11bqhNP.
Like, R. C. and Goode, T. (2012). Promoting cultural and linguistic competence in the American health system: Levers of change. In D. Ingleby, A. Chiarenza, W. Devillé and I. Kotsioni (Eds.), *Inequalities in health care for migrants and ethnic minorities*. COST Series on Health and Diversity (Vol. 2, pp. 29–48). Antwerp/Apeldoorn: Garant.
Nickens, H. (1986). Report of the Secretary's Task Force on Black and Minority Health: A summary and a presentation of health data with regard to blacks. *Journal of the National Medical Association, 78*(6), 577–580.
NIH (1994). *NIH guidelines on the inclusion of women and minorities as subjects in clinical research*. Bethesda, MD: National Institutes of Health. Retrieved June 16, 2013, from http://1.usa.gov/13Pcri1.
OMH (2000). *National standards on culturally and linguistically appropriate services (CLAS) in health care*. Washington, DC: United States Department of Health and Human Services. Retrieved June 16, 2013, from http://1.usa.gov/9Tw2v1.
Passel, J., D'Vera, C. and Hugo Lopez, M. (2011). *Hispanics account for more than half of nation's growth in past decade*. Washington, DC: Pew Research Center.
Salway, S., Nazroo, J., Mir, G., Craig, G., Johnson, M. and Gerrish, K. (2010). Fair society, healthy lives: A missed opportunity to address ethnic inequalities in health. Rapid response, 12 April 2010. *British Medical Journal*. Retrieved June 16, 2013, from http://bit.ly/reymMN.
Singh, S. P. and Burns, T. (2006). Race and mental health: There is more to race than racism. *British Medical Journal, 333*, 648–651.
Smedley, B. D., Stith, A. Y. and Nelson, A. R. (2003). *Unequal treatment: Confronting racial and ethnic disparities in health care*. Washington, DC: The National Academies Press, Institute of Medicine.
Summerfield, D. (2008). How scientifically valid is the knowledge base of global mental health? *British Medical Journal, 337*, 992–994.
Tervalon, M. and Murray-Garcia, J. (1998). Cultural humility versus cultural competence: A critical distinction in defining physician training outcomes in multicultural education. *Journal of Health Care for the Poor and Underserved, 9*(2), 117–125.
Timimi, S. (2012). Globalising mental health: A neoliberal project. *Ethnicity and Inequality in Health and Social Care, 4*, 154–160.
UN DESA (2013). *Trends in international migrant stock: The 2013f revision – wallchart data*. New York: United Nations, Department of Economic and Social Affairs, Population Division. Retrieved from http://esa.un.org/unmigration/wallchart2013.htm.
Vertovec, S. (2008). Super-diversity and its implications. *Ethnic and Racial Studies, 30*(6), 1024–1054.
White, J. L. (1970). Towards a black psychology. In R. L. Jones (Ed.), *Black psychology* (pp. 5–17). Oakland, CA: Cobb & Henry.
WHO (2001). *World health report 2001: Mental health –New understanding, new hope*. Geneva: World Health Organization. Retrieved June 16, 2013, from www.who.int/whr/2001/en.

WHO (2010a). *Health of migrants: The way forward.* Report of a global consultation, Madrid, Spain, March 3–5, 2010. Geneva: World Health Organization. Retrieved June 16, 2013, from http://bit.ly/c00uEe.

WHO (2010b). *How health systems can address health inequities linked to migration and ethnicity.* Copenhagen: WHO Regional Office for Europe. Retrieved June 16, 2013, from http://bit.ly/hKAe3T.

6 Race, culture and mental health care for refugees

Charles Watters

Introduction

Suman Fernando's work has been influential on research on the mental health and social care of refugees from the 1980s through to the 2010s. The present author's initial sphere of interest is in culture and mental health and particularly in the way culture shapes the parameters of mental health and illness in specific Black and Minority Ethnic (BME) communities. The work of Fernando, and Littlewood and Lipsedge, has been influential, as has a wide range of anthropological writings on topics such as spirit possession, evil eye and, more broadly, on mental health and healing in disparate societies (Fernando, 1988; Kleinman, 1980; Lipsedge and Littlewood, 1989; Rack, 1982). Within medical anthropology in this period there have been intense discussions of culturally specific concepts and behaviours in the spheres of health and healing. While there has often been a tendency to focus on what, from one cultural perspective, may be seen as rather 'exotic' practices, the author's fieldwork suggests a rich and complex interplay between 'epistemologies of care' (Watters, 2008), whereby groups were ascribed certain characteristic 'problems' according to 'common sense assumptions' (Lawrence, 1982) and what were perceived as indigenous concepts of mental health and illness. BME groups were not, as such, passive recipients of diagnosis but made sense of clinical encounters and mental health services in strategic ways (Watters, 2001).

The critique of multiculturalism that has infused much sociological writing in the United Kingdom from the 1980s challenges an orientation towards viewing cultures as fixed and unshakably inscribed within BME communities. Numerous academics have viewed the emphasis on culture within multiculturalism as one that fails to acknowledge and examine the role of racism in power relations in society (Hall 1992; Lawrence, 1982). Within this context, Fernando's work offers a detailed unpacking of the role of racism within mental health, both historically and within contemporary politics and social policies. Thus, in Foucauldian terms, the clinical gaze has shifted from investigation of the perceived cultures of BME groups towards racism within the institutions that categorize certain BME groups as having particular mental health problems (Foucault, 2003). The impact of institutionalized racism on the lives of BME communities has become a central focus for academic research. While Fernando's work in the mental health sphere was, and remains, vital and influential with respect to what may be termed settled minority ethnic groups, work on the mental health care of refugees has engaged much more rarely with issues of racism and the role of institutional power.

Fernando and refugee mental health

Discourses that link refugees with mental health problems, without reference to power relations and discrimination, have been ubiquitous in academic research and in programmes of service provision to refugees. The emphasis here has often been to view refugees as victims of severely adverse circumstances within their countries of origin that have resulted in trauma and high rates of PTSD. Indeed, a notable feature of academic scholarship in the field is a preoccupation with mental health in contexts in which refugees have wide-ranging needs for an array of services such as housing, legal support, food, education and family reconciliation (Aspinall and Watters 2010; Summerfield 1999). A related area of concern is the limited extent to which investigation into the mental health of refugees takes circumstances in 'host' societies into account. Mental health problems are commonly seen as the product of experiences in refugees countries of origin or in the processes of flight from conflict. Here Fernando's work presents a powerful corrective to this orientation. While studies of the mental health of refugees have tended to emphasize the impact of past events as key factors, scant attention has been paid to the impact of post-migration experiences on mental health, including the impact of racism within host societies. This is surprising in that asylum seekers and refugees often face a combination of severe economic circumstances, intractable problems in accessing basic services and hostile political and public responses to their presence (Watters, 2001). These institutional and societal factors are associated with an exacerbation of mental health problems, as are the lack of social networks and social isolation asylum seekers and refugees often face. A predominant focus on their problems prior to arrival in host societies fails to do justice to the impact of life in the host societies in causing or exacerbating mental health problems.

There are of course some exceptions to this orientation, including Silove's examinations of the impact of post-migration factors on asylum seekers (Silove *et al.*, 1998; Silove, Steel and Watters, 2000). In a survey of 62 Tamil asylum seekers from Sri Lanka, Silove and colleagues (1999) noted the negative impact on mental health of factors such as fears of being sent home, interviews with immigration officials, separation from a spouse, threats to family, poverty and discrimination. They argue that those refugees who had experienced the higher levels of trauma in their country of origin were more susceptible to experiencing mental health problems as a result of post-migration stressors within discriminatory institutional environments. In another study conducted in Australia the impact of post-migration experiences, such as separation from family, under-employment, loneliness and isolation and concerns about the refugee application were identified as having a negative impact on mental health (Sinnerbrink, 1997). Further research indicates not only the psychological impact of specific social policies directed towards refugees, but also the ways in which social policies and their implementation constructs refugees as pathologized individuals and has a deleterious impact on their well-being and treatment (Watters, 2008).

Moreover, an approach that is fundamental to Fernando's work is to link racism at an institutional level with its impact on the level of the day-to-day lives of BME groups. This can be unpacked and formalized into a methodological and analytical approach towards the study of the mental health of refugees that combines an examination of micro- and macro-level analysis through examining mental health interventions with refugees in the context of a three-dimensional model (Watters 2001a; Watters *et al.*, 2003). On a macro level there is a broad legal and policy context in which institutionalized views about the health needs of particular populations influence decisions about the allocation of resources. At a secondary 'service' level, arrangements are put in place within localities for the deployment of health and social care professionals and arrangements governing the interaction between these professionals. The third level is identified as the 'treatment level', which focuses on the direct interaction between health and social care professionals and their clients/patients. The model suggests ways in which a 'macro level', in which 'common sense assumptions' regarding the needs of these groups constructs the very contexts in which services are available, crucially influences the context in which refugees receive mental health treatment.

Consistent with Fernando's observations with resect to BME groups, studies of refugees suggest that the broad social policy context of receiving societies may have a direct bearing on refugees' mental health. Ager has noted that policies which seek to rapidly integrate asylum seekers into their host society have poor mental health outcomes. According to Ager, the best approach may be one in which the particular cultural characteristics of groups are recognized and efforts are made to ensure the maintenance of refugees' cultural identities and networks while, at the same time, encouraging a positive relationship between refugees and the host society (Ager, 1993). The question of the maintenance of cultural identities is, of course, a thorny one and may do little justice to the dynamic nature of the cultures of refugees and migrant groups. In my own fieldwork among refugees and asylum seekers in Europe, I have been struck by how perturbed and bemused asylum seekers have been by the attempts of host societies to place them in tightly defined cultural contexts. In one case, some asylum-seeking teenagers in the UK were placed in accommodation near a mosque and Afghani cultural centre. They expressed the view that this was not why they had come to the United Kingdom and that they wanted to be part of 'English families' and English culture. Fernando (1995) has offered a useful check on tendencies to seek to encapsulate migrant groups within unitary cultural identities, arguing that BME communities should be able to define their own cultures in their own terms.

Moreover, Fernando's emphasis on examining the role of social factors in mental health is consistent with Goldberg and Huxley's broader identification of poor social relationships and social adversity as factors that made individuals vulnerable to mental health problems (Goldberg and Huxley, 1992, p. 101). Drawing on Rutter's work, Goldberg and Huxley identify resilience to mental health problems as being linked to 'a sense of self-esteem and self-confidence; an ability to deal with change and adaptation; and a repertoire of social problem solving approaches' (1992, p. 100). They go on to say that in order to develop resilience, 'an individual needs experience of secure, stable, affectionate responses, and an experience of success and achievement' (p. 100). Goldberg and Huxley's description of the conditions necessary to foster resilience could hardly be more unlike the conditions of asylum seekers in receiving societies in which insecurity, instability and a lack of a sense of achievement and participation is commonplace.

Summerfield's examination of refugees' own perceptions of what would be helpful to them appears consistent with broader findings on factors that enhance resilience. For example, in commenting on war-injured ex-soldiers in Nicaragua, Summerfield observes that 'what interested them was their prospects for work and training'; in other words, opportunities to enhance their material base and participation in society (Summerfield, 1999, p. 1454). Summerfield's engagement with seeking to determine refugees' own perceptions of need accords with Fernando's continuing emphasis on user involvement. The United States, Canada and the Netherlands have been identified as being at the forefront of the development of user involvement in mental health services and user involvement is now widely regarded as a cornerstone of good practice in mental health care. Within the United Kingdom the involvement of users has been advocated in mental health policies and was, for example, identified as a key component of the government's National Service Framework for Mental Health (Department of Health, 1999). As Fernando has noted, despite the emphasis in policy documents, many members of BME communities do not feel involved in user movements. The reasons for this absence of involvement range from the debilitation caused by high levels of medication to stigma surrounding mental illness among some groups. Moreover, the service user movement is normally dominated by white mental health service users who may be unaware or insensitive to the experiences and needs of black service users (Sassoon and Lindow, 1995, p. 100).

These challenges to user involvement are present in relation to asylum seekers and refugees but here take a distinctive form. Asylum seekers are widely seen within Europe as making illegitimate claims upon limited welfare resources (Castles and Miller, 2008). As Sassoon and Lindow (1995) have noted, many of the attitudes widely held in society are also present among service users. Given this, it is likely that the widespread hostility towards asylum seekers in the press throughout Europe have permeated into user groups (Kaye, 2001). A further factor that may militate against asylum seekers' and refugees' involvement in user groups is the fact that problems are rarely perceived by asylum seekers and refugees themselves in terms of mental health and span a wide range of mental health, health and social care agencies. As such, it seems unlikely that an asylum seeker or refugee would locate his/her problem in the context of being a mental health user or survivor. Furthermore, if the user group or user consultation exercise has, or is perceived to have, links to official agencies, there may be a tremendous barrier of trust to overcome before refugees will participate in it. As Daniel and Knudsen (1995, p. 4) have remarked, 'refugees feel they have no control over how caseworkers, government organisations, or strangers use the information they have provided'. Given this range of potential barriers, it is hardly surprising that asylum seekers and refugees are rarely present in the service user movement. While some barriers are common between refugees and BME communities, there are distinctive issues that relate to the political and legal positions of refugees.

Race and culture in refugee mental health services

The evidence from studies of the mental health care of migrant groups and refugees suggest that there may be a range of common problems in terms of access to mental health services and the appropriateness of the services that are received. As Fernando has repeatedly pointed out, within the United Kingdom there is convincing evidence that black people are significantly more likely to enter mental health services through the route of compulsory admission. Furthermore, once in the mental health system they are significantly more likely to receive a diagnosis of schizophrenia (Harrison, Owens, Holton, Neilson and Boot, 1988). This evidence emerges in a context in which black people are less likely than white people to 'receive appropriate or acceptable diagnosis or treatment for possible mental illness at an early stage' (Bingley, 1985, p. 58). There is some evidence to suggest that in the Netherlands high rates of compulsory admissions for minority ethnic groups is coupled with low utilization of community-based resources or RIAGGs (Fernando, 1995, p. 21). The deficiencies in services are viewed by a number of prominent psychiatrists as by-products of a mental health system in which institutional racism is a common and historically conditioned feature (Fernando, 1988; Lipsedge and Littlewood, 1989). Within this context there are a number of particular factors to consider in terms of mental health services for asylum seekers and refugees. The latter are placed within particular legal and epistemological contexts in which a diagnosis of a mental health problem may have a significant bearing on their asylum claim. Here having a mental health problem can be a tool for the development of what I have referred to as strategies of resistance to measures such as the detention and deportation of asylum seekers. Moreover, in the United Kingdom arguments regarding the mental vulnerability of asylum seekers have also played a part in challenging moves towards their dispersal to different parts of the country (Watters, 2001b).

A further challenge alluded to above is that of offering 'culturally sensitive services'. In the context of mental health services, the provision of 'culturally sensitive services' may mean little more than the provision of mental health workers who speak the relevant languages. Culture may be seen as something of a smokescreen that the professional has to move beyond in order to identify the 'real' mental health problem (Ong, 1995). A common response to the existence of a large number of clients from minority ethnic or refugee groups is to employ mental health workers from a similar cultural background. However, such workers may only have the role of 'translators' in the sense of translating symptoms expressed in particular cultural idioms into categories derived from the diagnostic and statistical manual of mental disorders, which are then treated by psychiatrists (Ong, 1995). As such, culturally specific means of describing distress are reduced to 'universal' bio-medical categories in a process that, according to Summerfield (1999, p. 1453), 'emphasises similarity and plays down difference and diversity'. In so doing the mental health professional may 'level down each refugee to a common denominator' in ways that undermine the potential for developing a trusting relationship (Daniel and Knudsen, 1995, p. 5). Fernando's writings offer a corrective to tendencies towards seeing refugees' cultures as a central problem in mental health service delivery, instead advocating a cultural reflexivity in which professionals examine the prejudices that may emanate from their own cultural orientations. In this context, professionals are urged to reflect back on themselves, including examining the epistemological basis of their particular orientation towards refugee groups.

As Fernando has shown, approaches that focus exclusively on learning about the cultures of minority ethnic groups can been criticized on the grounds that they fail to tackle racial discrimination and may indeed add to negative stereotypes. Moreover, he has argued that this bio-medical orientation in mental health services has had profound implications for the training of mental health professionals and the appropriateness of the services received by minority ethnic groups. Instead of the predominantly bio-medical approach of traditional psychiatry, Fernando recommends the development of a 'socio-cultural psychiatry' and the reorganization of mental health and social care services so that they can be closely integrated. He has advocated a radical overhaul of mental health professionals' training to emphasize the centrality of the experience of racism among minority ethnic groups and focus on the way this can be addressed in mental health services (Fernando, 1988, p. 115).

The concerns expressed by Fernando have been raised with respect to the quantity and quality of training with respect to refugees' health and mental health care (Aldous et al., 1999). According to Aldous et al., areas that should be addressed include: the raising of awareness of asylum seekers' and refugees' rights to services and the raising of awareness of the problems faced by asylum seekers and refugees in interaction with health professionals. While evidence indicates that mental health professionals feel they do not know enough about the needs of migrant groups there is little evidence of involvement of migrant groups directly in training initiatives (Watters, 1998). Against this background, the challenges facing mental health services can appear overwhelming. The needs of refugees challenge the very basis of professionals' attitudes to mental health work. However, effective steps can be taken to address the mental health needs of refugees even if these may involve something of a paradigm shift in professional thinking.

Refugees or asylum seekers are rarely talked about except in terms of being a 'problem' or a 'drain on limited resources'. Attention has been given to the fact that refugees have often displayed considerable resilience to make the journeys they have and to cope with new and alien cultures (Muecke, 1992). However, while Muecke and others have supported the emergence of a new paradigm in the health care of refugees that emphasizes their resourcefulness, this has had limited impact beyond the academic literature. Fernando's engagement with a critique of dominant modes of service provision coupled with proposals for the practical development of programmes offers ways forward applicable to both BME groups and refugees. A central shift here is to view refugees as resources in the building of mental health and social care services rather than simply recipients of these services. Following Fernando, models for user participation should avoid the tokenism that may be present in various consultation exercises, and instead introduce durable and influential mechanisms that are routinely evaluated by service users themselves (Watters, 2008).

In this context it may be noted that many refugees arriving in Western countries made significant contributions to their home countries prior to flight and a significant proportion are well educated. Considering refugees as a *resource* rather than a problem opens the possibility of drawing on the experience and expertise of refugees themselves in designing and implementing services. As such it is inextricably linked to an emphasis on *consultation*. Imaginative programmes have already been established in the United Kingdom to train refugees in fields such as medicine and counselling and to establish groups of refugee advisors for service development and research projects. The advantages of this approach are numerous: not only does it empower refugees by making them feel valued in society, it also potentially offers a way of addressing some of the complexities arising from the sheer diversity of refugee groups. Treating refugees as a resource and engaging actively in consultation may have consequences in promoting mental health. As noted above, Goldberg and Huxley argue that 'a sense of self-esteem and self-worth' are important protective factors against mental ill health (1992, p. 100).

This approach also has considerable potential benefits in the training of mental health professionals. There is a widespread view among professionals that there is inadequate training in working with refugees. A European survey indicated that mental health professionals throughout Europe felt that the quality and quantity of training in this area was very poor (Watters, 2002). This has been addressed to some extent in recent years in the United Kingdom through the development of postgraduate and post-qualifying programmes on the mental health and social care of refugees, including, for example, courses at the universities of Kent and Essex. The University of Kent course incorporated a partnership with Utrecht University and Orebro University, allowing students to have direct experience of service provision in Sweden and the Netherlands as well as the United Kingdom. Fernando was a strong supporter of this programme and an intellectual inspiration.

Central to the establishment of appropriate mental health services is a willingness to *integrate* mental health and social care into a holistic approach. Refugees rarely view their problems as relating primarily to mental health. As noted above, when questioned most refugees will describe their problems in terms of basic needs such as housing, employment, education and being able to re-establish links with family members (Summerfield, 1999). If professionals concentrate too much on perceived mental health problems they risk alienating refugee clients who may regard mental illness as highly stigmatizing. It is widely accepted that central to the development of an effective therapeutic relationship is the building of trust. Within the present context this can often only be achieved if mental health professionals initially engage in helping refugees to address pressing practical problems. Such an approach has been adopted successfully within the Breathing Space Project at the Refugee Council in London and underpins the approach of many integrated mental health and social care projects for refugees around the globe.

Conclusion

Suman Fernando's work has been pivotal in proposing a new paradigm in the mental health care of refugees. This challenges professionals to develop a reflexive practice that investigates the epistemological framework used in refugee mental health care and opens to an engagement with refugees as consultants in the development of mental health care. It implies a fundamental shift away from professionals predetermining refugees' problems to one in which refugees are empowered to identify their own problems, to define their own cultural worlds and the actions from service providers that they would find most beneficial. This principle moves beyond that of consultation to one in which refugees are fully participative and valued in determining what mental health and social care services would best meet their needs. It offers a challenge to institutionalized practices that frame refugees' needs within distinctive 'problem spaces' and therapeutic approaches that act within the parameters of predetermined clinically defined problems. The participative and receptive model of refugee care indicated here reflects a positive engagement with Fernando's critique of the epistemological assumptions in psychiatry and his call for a radical reassessment of appropriate mental health care among disadvantaged communities.

References

Ager, A. (1993). *Mental health issues in refugee populations: A review.* Working paper. Cambridge, MA: Harvard University, Harvard Center for the Study of Culture and Medicine.

Aldous, J., Bardsley, M., Daniell, R., Gair, R., Jacobson, B., Lowdell, C. *et al.* (1999). *Refugee health in London: Key issues for public health.* London: Health of Londoners Project.

Aspinall, P. and Watters, C. (2010). *Refugees and asylum seekers: A review from an equality and human rights perspective.* Research Report 52. London: Equality and Human Rights Commission.

Bingley, W. (1985). The Mental Health Act 1983: How is it working? *Journal of the Medical Defence Union, 1,* 9–10.

Castles, S. and Miller, M. (2008). *The age of migration* (4th ed.). London: Macmillan.
Daniel, V. E. and Knudsen, J. C. (Eds.). (1995). *Mistrusting refugees*. Berkeley: University of California Press.
Department of Health. (1999). *The national service framework for mental health: Modern standards and service models*. London: Department of Health.
Fernando, S. (1988). *Race and culture in psychiatry*. London: Croom Helm.
Fernando, S. (Ed.). (1995). *Mental health in a multi-ethnic society: A multi-disciplinary handbook*. London: Routledge.
Foucault, M. (2003). *The birth of the clinic* (3rd ed.). London: Routledge.
Goldberg, D. and Huxley, P. (1992). *Common mental disorders: A bio-social model*. London: Routledge.
Hall, S. (1992). New ethnicities. In J. Donald and A. Rattansi (Eds.), *'Race', culture and difference* (pp. 252–259). London: Sage in association with the Open University.
Harrison, G., Owens, D., Holton, A., Neilson, D. and Boot, D. (1988). A prospective study of severe mental disorder in Afro-Caribbean patients. *Psychological Medicine, 18*(3), 643–657.
Kaye, R. (2001). Blaming the victim: Analysis of press representations of refugees and asylum seekers in the United Kingdom in the 1990s. In R. King and N. Wood (Eds.), *Media and migration: Constructions of mobility and difference*. London: Routledge.
Kleinman, A. (1980). *Patients and healers in the context of culture*. Berkeley: University of California Press.
Lawrence, E. (1982). In the abundance of water the fool is thirsty: Sociology and black 'pathology'. In Centre for Contemporary Cultural Studies (Ed.), *The empire strikes back* (pp. 95–142). London: Hutchinson.
Lipsedge, M. and Littlewood, R. (1989). *Aliens and alienists: Ethnic minorities and psychiatry*. London: Unwin Hyman.
Muecke, M. (1992). New paradigms for refugee health problems. *Social Science and Medicine, 35*(4), 515–523.
Ong, A. (1995). Making the biopolitical subject: Cambodian immigrants, refugee medicine and cultural citizenship in California. *Social Science and Medicine, 40*(9), 1243–1257.
Rack, P. (1982). *Race, culture and mental disorder*. London: Tavistock.
Sassoon, M. and Lindow, V. (1995). Consulting and empowering Black mental health system users. In S. Fernando (Ed.), *Mental health in a multi-ethnic society: A multi-disciplinary handbook* (pp. 89–106). London: Routledge.
Silove, D. and Steel, Z. (1998). *The mental health and well-being of on-shore asylum seekers in Australia*. Liverpool, Australia: Psychiatry Research and Teaching Unit, University of New South Wales.
Silove, D., Steel, Z., McGorry, P. and Dobny, J. (1999). Problems Tamil asylum seekers encounter in accessing health and welfare services in Australia. *Social Science and Medicine, 49*, 951–956.
Silove, D., Steel, Z. and Watters, C. (2000). Policies of deterrence and the mental health of asylum seekers. *Journal of the American Medical Association, 284*(5), 604–611.
Sinnerbrink, I., Silove, D., Field, A., Steel, Z. and Manicavasagar, V. (1997). Compounding of premigration trauma and postmigration stress in asylum seekers. *Journal of Psychology, 131*(5), 463–470.
Summerfield, D. (1999). A critique of seven assumptions behind psychological trauma programmes in war affected areas. *Social Science and Medicine, 48*, 1449–1462.
Watters, C. (1998). The mental health needs of refugees and asylum seekers: Key issues

in research and service development. In F. Nicholson and P. Twomey (Eds.), *Current issues of UK asylum law and policy* (pp. 282–297). London: Avebury.

Watters, C. (2001a). Emerging paradigms in the mental health care of refugees. *Social Science and Medicine, 52*, 1709–1718.

Watters, C. (2001b). Avenues of access and the moral economy of legitimacy. *Anthropology Today, 17*(2), 22–23.

Watters, C. (2002). Migration and mental health care in Europe: Report of a preliminary mapping exercise. *Journal of Ethnic and Migration Studies, 28*(1),153–172.

Watters, C. (2008). *Refugee children: Towards the next horizon.* London: Routledge.

Watters, C., Ingleby, D., Bernal, M., De Freitas, C., De Ruuk, N., Van Leeuwen, M. and Venkatesan, S. (2003). *Good practices in mental health and social care for asylum seekers and refugees.* Final report of project for the European Commission: European Refugee Fund. Canterbury: University of Kent.

7 Developing mental health policies that address race and culture

Hári Sewell

Introduction

Mental health policy in England since the 1980s has been expressly concerned with shifting the emphasis of care from hospitals to community-based treatments and support. Alongside this has been a focus on ensuring that risk is managed effectively through coordinated care, with a high-quality tiered system of forensic services. Attention given to race equality in mental health had, until 2003, been through references to the need to promote equal opportunities and cultural awareness within mainstream mental health documents. The breakthrough in 2003 was the policy document *Inside Outside* (National Institute for Mental Health in England, 2003). *Inside Outside* described racial inequalities in mental health in a direct way, including explicit references to institutional discrimination. It urged those inside and outside mental health services to make changes to reduce the factors that lead to variations both in mental ill health and in utilisation of mental health services. The *Inside Outside* policy was followed by a policy document called *Delivering Race Equality in Mental Health Care*, known as DRE (Department of Health, 2005). DRE was accompanied by millions of pounds of investment and a centralised programme of work, with a regional structure. This was the first time that there was a government-driven discrete programme of work to redress racial inequality in mental health. This raised expectations that, notwithstanding the poor track record of successive governments, there was a real possibility that improvements would be seen. The DRE programme was scheduled to run from 2005 to 2010. It was led by a national director. Partway through the programme this discrete race equality programme became subsumed at the national level within an 'equalities' programme. The equalities programme covered age, disability, gender, race, religion and sexual orientation. This six-stranded new programme was created incrementally and was formally established in April 2009. Leadership of this new programme was by the former national director for the DRE programme, a post that became the national programme lead for equalities, losing the 'director' title.

The extent to which the policy aim of reducing race inequality in mental health in England would be successful depended not solely on the strength of the content of the policy but also on its implementation. Fernando and Keating

(2009, p. 238) offer a summary of their criticism of the content (including the fact that it was described as a plan to address racial equality but did not consider racism within it). DRE included a set of intended outcomes but the only concrete target was the appointment of a specific number of workers to engage with Black and Minority Ethnic (BME) communities. A critical aspect of the implementation of DRE was the leadership by both politicians and officials. Politicians, noted Fernando (2009, p. 55), 'made much of the fact that it was led by people from BME communities'.

This chapter focuses on challenges faced in trying to support the implementation of government policies to tackle race inequality in mental health. The works of Suman Fernando are used to inform the analysis around two themes, namely the choice of the only quantitative target and the emphasis given to BME leadership of DRE.

Race equality and the historical context

A key stage in the development of health policy in England was the publication of *A Hospital Plan for England and Wales* (Ministry of Health, 1962), which was informed by optimistic predictions about the possible reduction in psychiatric beds (Boardman, 2005). Advances in psychopharmacology was suggested as a means to managing (reducing) psychiatric beds, but Bentall (2004) presents evidence that shows that claims about what could be achieved through drugs were over-optimistic or exaggerated. Policies subsequent to *A Hospital Plan for England and Wales* continued to develop and refine approaches to reduce the reliance on treatment and care within large hospital-based institutions for people with mental health problems.

The policy *Health and Welfare: The Development of Community Care* (Ministry of Health, 1963) set out the model for what later became widely known as 'care in the community'. Boardman (2005) states that the first clear policy of government to emphasise the shift from hospital care to community care was *Hospital Services for the Mentally Ill* (Department of Health and Social Security, 1971). This policy contained the provisions to close the large asylums, which had legacies outside of the National Health Service established in 1948, and to locate treatment and caring functions within district general hospitals (Boardman, 2005). Two notable consequences arose. One was the increased visibility of mental health problems as a concern for society and, second, a shift in clinical understandings of risk management. High-profile service or case reviews had an impact on emerging policy. Examples include the government-commissioned Reed Review, *Health and Social Services for Mentally Disordered Offenders and Others Requiring Similar Services* (Department of Health and Home Office, 1992) and the review of the treatment and care of Christopher Clunis, who killed a stranger on a train platform in the London Underground (Ritchie, 1994).

The *Building Bridges* policy (Department of Health, 1995) sought solutions to risk and ineffective coordination of treatment and care by introducing requirements for integrated services across health and social care as well as the Care

Programme Approach (CPA), which remains the bedrock of coordinated practice.

Race equality and the political context

Governmental approaches to address racial inequalities in mental health in England were, until *Inside Outside* (2003), elements within other strategies. For example, the National Service Framework for Mental Health (Department of Health, 1999) included a commitment that service users could expect a non-discriminatory service. Nowhere before *Inside Outside* was there a clear statement by the government in policy or strategy that institutional racism existed in mental health and that specific action was needed to tackle it. For campaigners this was a watershed, but the concerns of sceptics were fuelled by the response of the government to the David Bennett inquiry (NSCSTHA, 2003) which was published soon after. David Bennett was a man of Jamaican heritage who died in a psychiatric hospital while being restrained in the prone position by several nurses following an episode of what was the culmination of a series of events in which race and unchallenged racism were central. The *Guardian*'s Social Affairs Editor reported on 7 February 2004 that 'The government was preparing last night to reject or water down three recommendations from the official inquiry into the death of David "Rocky" Bennett, exposing institutional racism in NHS treatment of mental health patients' (*Guardian*, 2004). The government's response to the David Bennett inquiry was part of the national policy framework discussed above, *Delivering Race Equality in Mental Health Care*, known as DRE (Department of Health, 2005).

At the time of the launch, the then Secretary of State for Health wrote to Members of Parliament in a convoluted avoidance of accepting institutional racism in mental health services while at the same time using words that describe the process itself (see Sewell, 2009, p. 24). The DRE initiative included a framework of three building blocks (better information; community engagement; more appropriate and responsive services) for improving mental health services for BME groups and 12 characteristics of what good mental health services would look like after the effective implementation of DRE (Department of Health, 2005). Accompanying the initiative was a commitment to the appointment of 500 community development workers nationally and also millions of pounds of resources that allowed for a central and regional support structure and exemplar projects known as Focused Implementation Sites. A contradiction therefore ran through the announcements and policy framework; an evident commitment to do something but a sensitivity about naming and confronting racism as part of addressing ethnic inequalities in mental health.

The content of the policy DRE has been discussed by Fernando and Keating (2009) and RAWOrg (2011). There is consensus that DRE focused on information at the expense of action and on research at the expense of reform. For example, Fernando and Keating (2009) point out that the emphasis of DRE was on information and then further state that 'although called a plan to deliver "racial equality" there was no strategy within the document to address racism' (p. 238). The reforming function of DRE was limited to operating within the pre-existing constructs of mental health services and Fernando's works have consistently argued that the legacy of psychiatry as a means of social control and its ethnocentric development weakened its cross-cultural application and potential for truly addressing race inequality in mental health (Fernando, 2003, 2009). Individuals appointed at all levels, from those close to government to those on the front line, worked with DRE as it was, with varying levels of enthusiasm, being grateful that a national programme was in place to address their concerns.

The formal end of DRE came in January 2010, marking the close of the last discrete race equality government initiative for mental health. Alongside the official review of the DRE policy initiative (National Mental Health Development Unit, 2010) were more critical perspectives (see RAWOrg, 2011). The remainder of this chapter looks at concerns with the implementation of the already flawed DRE policy and offers critical analysis informed by the works of Suman Fernando, including suggestions for the way forward.

A critique of the implementation of *Delivering Race Equality in Mental Health Care* initiative

The *Delivering Race Equality* (DRE) programme achieved an unprecedented degree of optimism among black and Asian staff and activists. This was driven largely by the investment of millions of pounds in a national programme, led successively by people from BME backgrounds.

The optimism was short-lived, however, and the critical analyses of Suman Fernando provide useful constructs for understanding the flaws and potential solutions in relation to DRE. Among many others, there were three key concerns that became apparent over time: namely, (1) the implications for BME staff running national programmes; (2) the impact on implementation arising from the wrong choice of quantitative performance measure for DRE; and (3) the short life (five years) of the programme given the scale of issues to be addressed.

A typical question surrounding the appointment of BME staff in supposedly influential positions is whether their appointment is purely tokenistic. Fernando, discussing this issue in relation to the caring professions, wrote 'The issues of tokenism by the establishment was seen as a problem because some of the black professionals did not seem to join the struggle that gradually developed, at least did not do so openly' (2003, p. 83). Fernando highlights a pernicious issue. Critical thinking and the challenging of conventional models gives BME people profile, and this is sometimes a factor in them being appointed to visible positions. However, once in these positions conformity becomes a requirement. Politicians and very senior officials are usually concerned with reputation management and consequently messages that emanate from the establishment are tightly controlled. The freedom of senior BME staff to challenge racial discrimination inside or outside the establishment can become restricted. BME people find that they are appointed without the support necessary to deliver the role effectively, thus allowing the establishment to claim glory for its apparent commitment without bearing the disruption and discomfort of real change.

People of any background who work in official positions are often required to make some internal compromise, often over matters of conscience. Fernando (2003) acknowledges the particular challenge for black and Asian professionals in white institutions: 'In my view, effective change [of white institutions] "from the inside" is a necessary approach and one that black and Asian people must continue to pursue. However, the difficulties of being involved are not something to be taken lightly' (p. 84). This situation of being conflicted was highlighted prior to DRE, when Fernando (2003) suggested that there were sometimes 'uneasy alliances between black people located in "white systems" that were racist in one way or other, and black people outside these systems' (p. 83). This conflicted position leads to self-censorship and this may have (in the eyes of senior civil servants and government ministers) strengthened the managerial standing of those heading up DRE. However, Fernando (2009) writes about those who were appointed to lead DRE that 'they were handpicked by government and did not necessarily carry the confidence of BME communities' (p. 55).

White institutions *actively* restrict the potency of senior BME roles and *unthinkingly* fail to appreciate the internal dissonance that BME people in these roles face. The consequences are problems not just for the individual post-holder but for the organisations that employ them. The leadership of DRE changed during its five-year life and campaigners raised questions about the authenticity and commitment of both the Department of Health and the individuals directly and behind their back. This inability to bring along key partners and stakeholders, argues Fernando, is one reason for the failure of DRE to achieve its stated objectives (2009).

As well as the issues relating to the BME leadership of the programme, the implementation of DRE was hampered also by the wrong choice of quantitative performance measure (the recruitment of community development workers – CDWs) and the inevitable priority that was privileged upon that target by services. The end-of-programme review of DRE was explicit: 'The recruitment of 500 CDWs by primary care trusts (PCTs) was the only hard target in the DRE action plan' (National Mental Health Development Unit, 2010, p. 28). The problem with the positioning of these posts as the key delivery mechanism for DRE is captured well in a contribution to Fernando and Keating's edited volume:

> there was no precedent at the time for community development worker positions. We had been assigned to a junior nursing scale, with few prospects for progression, and yet assigned the complex tasks of developing the service, building links with community organisations, delivering a service to 'hard-to-reach' clients bilingually, and developing culturally competent ways of working. This trap of proposing sweeping changes to be delivered by low-paid and inexperienced staff is common amongst innovating projects.
> (Malik, Fateh and Haque, 2009, p. 179)

The burden of expectation on the CDW roles was great. The experience and impact of the CDW roles was researched and critiqued by RAWOrg, an affiliation of people with lived experience of mental health problems, campaigners, professionals and academics who operate as a virtual think tank to challenge race discrimination in the mental health system. Suman Fernando has been at the forefront of RAWOrg since its inception. Research by RAWOrg referred to an 'over-reliance' on CDWs and stated further: 'although CDWs carried out some remarkable work, the massive emphasis on their efforts as means to achieving DRE's goals may be both a symptom and a cause of where the programme went wrong' (2011, p. 23). RAWOrg's comments point to what was perhaps an unintended consequence of the design of DRE. The setting of the sole quantitative target in relation to the appointment of relatively junior workers rather than in relation to something strategic meant that senior management attention was focused on hitting this target. Subordinate to this was attention given to the transformation of strategic leadership of race equality in organisations and system-level change. This led to some obfuscation by those with executive leadership responsibilities that would have incorporated DRE. The perception held by leaders in mental health about the central role of CDWs is reflected in the findings of the research about progress on race equality in mental health following the end of DRE (Sewell and Waterhouse, 2012).

The RAWOrg report concludes by emphasising that their analysis echoes other critiques of DRE and offers a summary of why the initiative failed to achieve some of its big objectives, i.e. 'the limitations of the CDW role, the lack of focus on institutional reform, the restrictive time and resources committed to the cause' (RAWOrg, 2011, p. 23).

The fixed time frame for the DRE defied logic. First, such a model failed to acknowledge the dynamic nature of racial inequalities in mental health. Even if metrics in mental health services had shown a closure of the equality gap at a certain point in time, the nature of inequalities suggests that if unchecked, a gap would reopen. This is because of the well-established knowledge that key drivers of mental health problems significantly include those in society and in early development (Cooper *et al.*, 2008; McKenzie, Fearon and Hutchinson, 2008). The second reason why the five-year time frame was flawed links precisely to this point. Implementation of DRE was informed by medical research that perpetuated a view that higher rates of diagnosed mental health problems in black groups was individualised pathology for which treatment and cure was required (Fernando and Keating, 2009). Academics who had the ear of government moved to blaming communities rather than looking at societal failures and weaknesses in models of psychiatry (*Guardian*, 2010). This was a confounding factor in the time-limited implementation of DRE. The end-of-programme review acknowledged in the conclusion that earlier intervention and wider public health approaches were required (National Mental Health Development Unit, 2010). This realisation was not an epiphany at the end of DRE but a growing awareness throughout the life of the programme but with no time to adapt.

On the ground, the CDWs whose appointments were heralded as pivotal were towards the end of the five years electing to leave their posts due to uncertainty about their contracts, despite the fact that the funding streams supporting their posts were permanent. Many saw their post changed from race-based roles to incorporate wider equalities issues (National Mental Health Development Unit, 2011); a rationale stated by employers was that DRE was soon to end. In effect, the time-limited nature of DRE gave employers an apparently legitimate reason for amending the posts. However, Fernando (2009) points out that mainstreaming remains a powerful 'euphemism for abolishing' (p. 52). The tenures of these apparently valuable workers were not able to run their course.

The implementation of DRE was partly about creating evidence for effective approaches. This is explored in discussions about focused implementation (pilot) sites and community engagement projects in the end-of-programme five-year review (National Mental Health Development Unit, 2010). Reports with evidence were emerging towards the end of DRE but in a context of crumbling organisational structures and dwindling resources in services, ahead of predicted major change and austerity in the NHS. DRE had an implementation model that was grand in scale, focused on system change and reliant on the creation of a new body of evidence about what works – all to be achieved within five years!

Getting the strategy right and having people in place who are able to lead (without being hamstrung) is key to success of any programme and more so when it is accompanied by millions of pounds of tax-payers' money and relating to a subject imbued with such contention. Creating the correct focus and having a logical implementation timescale is essential.

Policy development and implementation that successfully addresses race equality

Political leadership and policies that create improvements proportionate to the scale of inequality are essential. Racial inequality in mental health has been acknowledged in government statements and in policy documents which become dissipated in the translation prior to practice on the front line (Fernando, 2003).

The works of Suman Fernando provide a steer for overcoming the challenges that beset DRE. When considering solutions for dealing with the challenges and conflicts in roles such as the national director of DRE, wisdom can be found in the following:

> black people who wish to fight racism must become involved in British institutions pushing their way forward if necessary, but once they are involved, they must (in order of priority) (a) be constantly vigilant and not mistake words for actions; (b) push the frontiers of anti-racism as far as possible, making alliances with anyone who wished to co-operate and (c) be prepared to confront racism thoughtfully and realistically.
> (Fernando, 2003, p. 84; cited in Fernando, 1996).

For a leader of a race equality national programme to feel as emboldened as Fernando suggests would require that the politicians to whom they are accountable are fully prepared to accept past mistakes, including the role of racism in society and services. They would need to be able to convince others in their party and the professional bodies in mental health that repair of trust by BME communities (highlighted as a problem by Fountain and Hicks, 2010 and Sainsbury Centre for Mental Health, 2002) is a critical issue, to be addressed through candour. Such an approach would go some way towards addressing the critical success factors for empowered BME leaders of a programme and focus on the right things.

A successful future policy would not misplace emphasis by setting a target on an apparently arbitrary measure such as the appointment of community development workers but would look to measures of bigger-scale changes. In the section entitled 'Lesson from History' in their conclusion, Fernando and Keating (2009) highlight the fact that a review of improvements in mental health care over the past 150 years have been more to do with public pressure for more humane treatment and care and rights for the 'insane', which in shorthand could be referred to as civil rights. These types of issues have more resonance with the kinds of concerns expressed by many clinicians and campaigners who are still at the forefront of tackling race inequality in mental health (e.g. Bhui, 2002; RAWOrg, 2011).

Policies that address such issues are likely to be unpalatable because, as Fernando (2003, p. 210) points out,

> Psychiatry functions in a society that expects psychiatrists, psychologists and other professionals involved in mental health work to deliver certain outcomes. If psychiatrists generally become culturally sensitive, liberal and anti-racist, they are likely to come into conflict with society.

The outcomes being sought of mental health professionals are largely cure, care and containment (Perkins, 2012). A future policy to successfully address race equality in mental health would need to incorporate into its objectives plans to transform society's interpretation of mental distress and its contributory causes. An approach to de-medicalising distress, as described in Rapley, Moncrieff and Dillon (2011) (e.g. genuinely locating people's presentations in the context of emotional and social trauma rather than in a biologically dominated medical paradigm), is not the business of traditional psychiatric services as we know them. A change of society's views would require leadership from professional bodies that would be able to convince politicians and the masses that a new alternative approach was possible and effective. It is important then for governments, policy makers, the mental health system and activists to think more broadly than the boundaries of psychiatric services.

Rather than a large injection of cash into mental health, with implementation over a short timescale, future policy to reduce racial inequality in mental health will need to locate its mission more in the realm of human and civil rights and public health, which is a long-term change that takes decades rather than years.

Conclusion

The critique of policy implementation in this chapter points to a persistence of racial inequalities in mental health in England. The most prominent and well-resourced race equality policy in mental health emerged from a crisis, namely the death of a black patient at the hands of nurses. This may not have been the best start for the policy. There were paradoxes in the content, such as the claim that DRE was a policy to address racial inequality but there was nothing in the policy intended to tackle racism. The intention of DRE to tackle whole-system change was not clearly set out.

The Department of Health sponsored review of DRE (National Mental Health Development Unit, 2010) was largely positive, highlighting successful initiatives and progress on process measures. The lack of demonstrable improved outcomes at the service user level is acknowledged and the rationale for this put forward, which rightly included the over-optimism about what DRE could achieve, particularly in the five-year timescale.

Suman Fernando's central argument throughout his writings is that for all the promises of governments and policies such as DRE, the ultimate measure of success will be improvements in outcomes that are important to black and Asian service users themselves (see Fernando, 2003, 2009, 2010). The content of policy is just part of the picture. The implementation happens in real time and the weaknesses unfold as the timescale ebbs away. The obstacles, both personal and political, that the leaders of the DRE implementation faced hampered the potential for the initiative to deliver the impacts hoped for. This was compounded by the diversion of attention away from major system change onto the arbitrary sole concrete target to appoint 500 community development workers. The five-year timescale allocated to DRE was evidently naive and this flaw in the design of the policy had implications for the implementation that should have been foreseen. For example, the problems with the reliance on newly commissioned research within DRE to create an evidence base for implementation of the same policy, within five years, could have been easily predicted.

It is clear that political leadership, as well leadership from the professional bodies, is needed to engender in society an outrage and intolerance for the perpetuation of race inequality in mental health. This is in direct conflict with the orthodoxy of psychiatry and the progress being made towards the globalisation of psychiatry, which sees medical interventions as the solution.

References

Bentall, R. (2004). *Madness explained: Psychosis and human nature.* London: Penguin.

Bhui, K. (2002). Contemporary dilemmas. In K. Bhui (Ed.), *Racism and mental health: Prejudice and suffering.* London: Jessica Kingsley.

Boardman, J. (2005). New services for old: An overview of mental health policy. In A. Bell and P. Lindley (Eds.), *Beyond the Water Towers: The unfinished revolution in mental health services 1985–2005.* London: Sainsbury Centre for Mental Health.

Cooper, C., Morgan, C., Byrne, M., Dazzan, P., Morgan, K., Hutchinson, G. *et al.* (2008).

Perceptions of disadvantage, ethnicity and psychosis. *British Journal of Psychiatry, 192*, 185–190.

Department of Health. (1995). *Building bridges: A guide to arrangements for inter-agency working for the care and protection of severely mentally ill people*. London: HMSO.

Department of Health. (1999). *National service framework for mental health: Modern standards and service models*. London: Department of Health. Retrieved 31 May 2013 from www.dh.gov.uk/prod_consum_dh/groups/dh_digitalassets/@dh/@en/documents/digitalasset/dh_4077209.pdf.

Department of Health. (2005). *Delivering race equality in mental health care: An action plan for reform inside and outside services and the government's response to the death of David Bennett*. London: Department of Health.

Department of Health and Home Office. (1992). *Review of health and social services for mentally disordered offenders and others requiring similar services*. London: HMSO.

Department of Health and Social Security. (1971). *Hospital services for the mentally ill*. London: HMSO.

Fernando, S. (1996). Black people working in white institutions: Lessons from personal experience. *Human Systems: The Journal of Systemic Consultation and Management, 7*(2–3), 143–154.

Fernando, S. (2003). *Cultural diversity, mental health and psychiatry: The struggle against racism*. Hove: Brunner-Routledge.

Fernando, S. (2009). Inequalities and the politics of race. In S. Fernando and F. Keating (Eds.), *Mental health in a multi-ethnic society*. Hove: Routledge.

Fernando, S. (2010). *Mental health, race and culture* (3rd ed.). London: Palgrave Macmillan.

Fernando, S. and Keating, F. (2009). Conclusion. In S. Fernando and F. Keating (Eds.), *Mental health in a multi-ethnic society*. Hove: Routledge.

Fountain, J. and Hicks, J. (2010). *Delivering race equality in mental health care: Report on the findings and outcomes of the Community Engagement Programme 2005–2008*. Lancashire: ISCRI.

Guardian (2004, 7 February). Officals to resist NHS racism finding. Retrieved 31 May 2013 from www.guardian.co.uk/politics/2004/feb/07/uk.race?INTCMP=ILCNETTXT3487.

Guardian (2010, 3 February). Poor research or an attack on black people. Retrieved 31 May 2013 from www.guardian.co.uk/society/2010/feb/03/mental-health-bme-schizophrenia-letter.

Malik, R., Fateh, R. and Haque, R. (2009). The Marlborough Cultural Therapy Centre. In S. Fernando and F. Keating (Eds.), *Mental health in a multi-ethnic society*. Hove: Routledge.

McKenzie, K., Fearon, P. and Hutchinson, G. (2008). Migration, ethnicity and psychosis. In C. Morgan, K. McKenzie and P. Fearon (Eds.), *Society and psychosis*. Cambridge: Cambridge University Press.

Ministry of Health. (1962). *A hospital plan for England and Wales*. London: HMSO.

Ministry of Health. (1963). *Health and welfare: The development of community care*. London: HMSO.

National Institute for Mental Health in England. (2003). *Inside outside: Improving mental health services for black and minority ethnic communities in England*. London: Department of Health. Retrieved 31 May 2013 from www.dh.gov.uk/prod_consum_dh/groups/dh_digitalassets/@dh/@en/documents/digitalasset/dh_4019452.pdf.

National Mental Health Development Unit. (2010). *Delivering Race Equality Action Plan: A five year review.* London: NMHDU.
National Mental Health Development Unit. (2011). *National evaluation of the Community Development Workers.* London: NMHDU.
NSCSTHA. (2003). *Independent inquiry into the death of David Bennett.* Norfolk, Suffolk and Cambridgeshire Strategic Health Authority.
Perkins, R. (2012). UK mental health policy development: A counter-argument. In P. Phillips, T. Sandford and C. Johnston (Eds.), *Working in mental health: Policy and practice in a changing environment.* Abingdon: Routledge.
Rapley, M., Moncreiff, J. and Dillon, J. (Eds.). (2011). *De-medicalizing misery: Psychiatry, psychology and the human condition.* Basingstoke: Palgrave.
RAWOrg. (2011). *The end of Delivering Race Equality: Perspectives of frontline workers and service users from radicalised groups.* London: RAWOrg.
Ritchie, J., Dick, D. and Lingham, R. (1994). *The report of the inquiry into the care and treatment of Christopher Clunis.* London: HMSO.
Sainsbury Centre for Mental Health. (2002). *Breaking the circles of fear: A review of the relationship between mental health services and African Caribbean communities.* London: SCMH.
Sewell, H. (2009). *Working with ethnicity, race and culture in mental health: A handbook for practitioners.* London: Jessica Kingsley.
Sewell, H. and Waterhouse, S. (2012). *Making progress on race equality in mental health.* London: NHS Confederation.

8 Religion, race and mental health
The scientific evidence

Alison Gray and John Cox

Introduction

Understanding the nature and relevance of religious belief and spiritual practice (R/S) to the experience of health and illness has always been central to the clinical practice of transcultural psychiatry. Different cultures interacting in our cities can lead to a sense of uncertainty, and even anomie, which may be particularly acute for those who are marginalized and discriminated against. Fernando (1986) suggested that the provision of coping and support strategies to safeguard self-esteem and strengthen ethnic identity are important. Church attendance improves resilience in black people and protects against depression (Reese, Thorpe, Bell, Bowie and Laveist, 2012). Although transcultural psychiatry is now more mainstream in the training of psychiatrists in the United Kingdom, the socio-cultural background of patients is still often overlooked. Enquiring into R/S in a mental health setting can be regarded as taboo or even as unethical (Poole and Higgo, 2011). The reasons for avoiding this topic include fear of boundary violations and proselytizing, respecting privacy, inadequate knowledge and avoiding a difficult subject. This hesitancy is bolstered by the current adherence to the dominant scientific/biological explanatory model for illness that tends to view patients as biological machines.

Psychiatry has nevertheless become more open to understanding the relevance of R/S beliefs, even in secular Sweden (De Marinis, 2008). This is partly due to the impact of migrants from more religious countries who publicly express their faith adherence, and also to the greater accessibility of the literature on R/S and health (Koenig, King and Carson, 2012). Furthermore, religious belief is less likely to be explained away by psychoanalytic theorizing; nor can its positive effect on health be ignored. Religions share many fundamental spiritual practices and moral values that can have a positive impact on health, such as meditation and hospitality, moderation and compassion (Stoneham, 2012). Yet misguided religious beliefs can be harmful to mental health, and stressful and novel transformations, for example, conversion, can trigger mental illness in some people (Swaab and Verweij, 2010). Exploring a patient's religious or spiritual belief is facilitated by transcultural psychiatric skills such as recognizing cultural relativity as well as being a 'reflective practitioner' and 'participant observer'.

Critique of Western psychiatry and psychology

Western medicine is a great success story; however, the mechanistic and depersonalized nature of much of modern medicine has often left patients feeling not listened to, and treated as objects, not people. In the United Kingdom junior doctors work shifts with multiple handovers and frequent ward rotations. Patients get moved from ward to ward for administrative reasons. This disrupts the development of trusting relationships between patient, carers and clinicians, inevitably affecting quality of care, rate of recovery and compliance/concordance (Cornwell, Levenson, Sonola and Poteliakhoff, 2012).

Continuity of care is fragmenting in mental health services; the service user is under one consultant when an inpatient, another in the community, another for crisis intervention and a different team for assertive outreach. Each change of team is an opportunity for information to be lost and duplication of effort in getting to know the patient (or not). Some argue that psychiatry needs to focus more on hard medicine and the neurosciences (Craddock et al., 2008); others hold that relationships, meaning and values are most important (Bracken et al., 2012). What we need, throughout healthcare, is both scientific medical expertise and good relationship skills; both technical competence and compassion, which for many is founded in and sustained by their religious practice (Fulford, Campbell and Cox, 2007).

Religious beliefs, illness representations and wellness

Research in the area of spirituality, religion and health is complex, and care must be taken to properly define and operationalize terms. One hundred years ago in the West, 'spiritual' was a subsection of the general category 'religion'; 'spiritual' people were particularly committed and dedicated to their religion. Over the last 30 years 'spirituality' has become unmoored from religion and now refers to a much broader category, often defined to include many of the features of positive mental health. Many now say they are 'spiritual but not religious'. Fernando (1975) was reluctant to cut spirituality loose from its religious moorings, but like many transcultural psychiatrists he has, alas, not pursued further research in this field.

There are many definitions of spirituality, emphasizing different features and encompassing different aspects of life. Spirituality is linked to having a meaning and purpose in life, feeling integrated, connected to others and feeling peaceful and fulfilled. This over-inclusiveness renders spirituality a usefully vague term for clinical use, to encourage consideration of aspects of human life that are not covered by the standard bio-psycho-social model (Engel, 1977; Swinton and Pattison, 2010). However, for research purposes a clear distinction is needed between spirituality and positive mental health. Some definitions of spirituality exclude people living with severe and enduring mental illnesses (SEMI) from the possibility of being 'spiritual'. Many people with SEMI cite spiritual practices as important in their recovery (Cornah, 2006).

Religion refers to a collection of beliefs, practices and rituals related to the transcendent and sacred, arising out of an established tradition and from a community with common beliefs and practices. The definition of religion is not contested, can be easily operationalized and allows for replication in different populations. In northern Europe many are secular humanists and would deny the relevance of religion or spirituality (Salander, 2006). Scandinavian researchers use the term 'existential meaning making' to cover this area (La Cour, 2010). The term 'worldviews' can be helpful as a more neutral and inclusive concept. Everyone has a worldview, while not everyone adheres to a religion or uses spiritual practices. People may hold a religious worldview, or a non-religious, secular worldview, such as scientific materialism (Gray, 2011). Clearly, 'spirituality', 'existential meaning making' and 'worldviews' are difficult terms to operationalize; most researchers work with 'religion' instead (Koenig, McCullough and Larson, 2001), investigating the three dimensions of religious belief, religious practice and individual spiritual experiences.

Research into the impact of R/S on health has developed and matured over the last 20 years. The earliest work tended simply to give a questionnaire survey to, for example, a church congregation, with mixed results (Gray 2001). Fernando's (1975) early work recorded the frequency of church attendance as a measure of Christian practice; whereas in the Jewish tradition family practices are more informative. He concluded that social marginalization of recent second-generation immigrants was associated with depression in Jews, particularly single Jewish men. Fernando (1975, 1978) did not attempt to measure intrinsic religious practice, not having access to the numerous measures that now exist (Hill and Dwiwardani, 2010; Koenig 2011). According to Koenig, King and Carson (2012), religious commitment level can be assessed through religious activities (e.g. attendance at meetings, individual prayer or meditation, reading scriptures). There are many self-report scales looking at different aspects of R/S (Koenig, 2011). The spiritual well-being scale taps into salience of religion (Paloutzian and Ellison, 1982). The spiritual transcendence scale (Piedmont, 2001) measures individual capacity for spiritual experience, and is applicable across cultures (Piedmont and Leach, 2002). 'Religious coping' refers to the degree to which the spiritual practices and beliefs of an individual's religion are helpful in coping with life (Fiala, Bjorck and Gorsuch, 2002). Negative religious coping describes when the person feels victimized or abandoned by God (Koenig et al., 2012). Spiritual, religious and personal beliefs can be usefully tapped into in eight minutes with the WHO Quality of Life questionnaire (Skevington, Gunson and O'Connell, 2012).

The health impacts of belonging to a faith group differ from culture to culture. While much of the research and debate on religion and spirituality has come from the United States, work in the United Kingdom may differ from such identification in the more religion-friendly United States. This raises questions about how applicable the US research on religion and health is to the rest of the world.

So with all these caveats, what do we know about religion and mental health? In the United States, Jews have the highest overall well-being, those with no religious identity the lowest (Gallup, 2012); the more religious you are the higher your sense of well-being (Levin, 2012).

Many people experiencing psychosis will describe religious delusions and hallucinations – from the manic man convinced he is a prophet to the psychotic mother who cut off the arms of her child believing she was giving the child to God (Falkenberg, 2004). If someone is religious, then their psychotic breakdown may well contain religious themes. Some religious groups discourage their members from contact with mental health services. Most vocal are the Scientologists and Christian Scientists, but conservative evangelical Christian groups can also encourage people to pray and fast instead of using medication.

Religious coping is common among those with psychotic illnesses, and non-pathological religious involvement predicts better outcome in patients with SEMI (Benda, 2002; Tepper, Rogers, Coleman and Maloney, 2001). Many service users value the social integration and sense of control over their lives that regular attendance at religious activities give (Fukui, Starnino and Nelson-Becker, 2011).

Up to 2011 there were 443 quantitative studies published on the impact of religion on depression. Of these, 61% show a positive association – less depression and more rapid recovery with more religious practice; 22% report no association; and just 6% link religious involvement with greater depression, despite many turning to religion when struggling (Koenig et al., 2012). Those who attended services at least weekly were most likely to recover from depression and had better health behaviours over 30 years (Strawbridge, Shema, Cohen and Kaplan, 2001), and showed faster recovery from depression associated with physical illness (Koenig, 2007). Intrinsic religiosity significantly predicted lower depression scores at a 24-month follow-up in Australian elders (Payman and Ryburn, 2010). African Americans have one-third lower rates of depression than whites matched on demographic factors and health behaviours (Reese et al., 2012). Religiosity was closely linked to well-being in groups from Egypt and Kuwait, with men having higher well-being than women (Abdel-Khalek, 2011).

Many studies find that those with a religious belief are at lower risk of suicide than those with weak or no such beliefs. Nisbet studied 584 people who committed suicide and matched them with 4,279 people who had died naturally in the United States (Nisbet, Duberstein, Conwell and Seidlitz, 2000). Those who attended religious activities regularly were less likely to have committed suicide, with the most religious being most protected.

Looking at the highest-quality studies (as defined by Koenig et al., 2012), greater religiosity was associated with lower anxiety in 38 studies, and with greater anxiety in 10 studies. Muslim spiritual practices were associated with lower rates of anxiety in a sample from Afghanistan (Cardozo et al., 2004). Observational studies demonstrate an inverse relationship between religiosity and alcohol or drugs usage, with Catholics drinking the most, then Christians, Hindus, Muslims and Jews the least (Koenig et al., 2012). Spirituality is at the base of the 12-step model for recovery from addictions. A Christian spiritual awakening led to the foundation of Alcoholics Anonymous (Alcoholics Anonymous, 2011; Alexander, 1941). The 12-step model is used for many different addictions and forms part of modern treatment programmes (Longabaugh *et al.*, 2005).

Stress and religious coping

At times of stress people commonly turn to spirituality for comfort and inspiration. Buddhist practices were found helpful by 53% of the people surveyed after the Sri Lankan tsunami (Hollifield, 2008). An American survey after the 9/11 attacks reported that 90% had turned to religion for support (Schuster *et al.*, 2001). Some 386 women were enrolled in a psychological study prior to Hurricanes Katrina and Rita hitting; the more religious had better social resources, higher optimism and sense of purpose and better outcomes after the disasters (Chan, Rhodes and Perez, 2012). Religious coping is more prevalent in some countries than others: 95% of 1,600 newly diagnosed cancer patients in Morocco resumed or intensified Muslim practices (Errihani *et al.*, 2008). In Norway, of 253 terminal cancer patients 45% reported that religion provided 'no comfort whatsoever' (Ringdal, 1996). The prevalence of religious coping in a country parallels the numbers who agree that 'religion is important to me' on a World Gallup poll (Crabtree and Pelham, 2009), with high rates in the Middle East and Asia, slightly lower in the United States, down to 27% in the United Kingdom, with the lowest scores in Scandinavia. Religious coping is important for many African American people in facing ongoing racial inequalities (Clark, 2004; Graham and Roemer, 2012).

The transformative nature of religious experience, and the possibility that spiritual practices put people in touch with a powerful reality beyond themselves, is attested to by many religious texts and conversion stories. This possibility cannot be tested by science and must be respectfully laid on one side when considering the mechanisms for the interaction of religion and health. The research evidence is limited and does not yet allow clear elucidation of these mechanisms. We would consider the following factors significant: religious structures provide social and emotional support; communities and congregations provide practical and economic support, decrease loneliness and give people a valued social role; attendance at religious meetings keeps people physically active; and most religious and spiritual traditions protect health by teaching against sexual promiscuity, alcohol excess and drug usage (Cox and Verhagen, 2011).

Multiple studies have shown that religion and spirituality are positively linked to purpose and meaning in life (Ysseldyk, Matheson and Anisman, 2012), to increased social capital (Lewis, Macgregor and Putnam, 2013), relationship stability and positive personality and psychological traits (Koenig *et al.*, 2012). Religions generally provide a narrative of hope and eventual positive outcome. Such positive emotions and cognitions are linked to better immune, endocrine and cardiovascular functioning (Koenig *et al.*, 2012).

Religion may have negative effects on health. This may be because of specific teachings, for example, the Jehovah's Witness prohibition on blood transfusion, and avoidance of medical care by those from the Christian Scientist church (Hughes, 2004). Religious people may have a sense of guilt, shame or failure about their health difficulties, or may feel they cannot go against Karma or God's will by seeking treatment. Some religious fundamentalist mis-identify major mental distress as possession (e.g. demons or djinn), potentially leading to increased suffering. There can be manipulative leaders and false healers in all faith traditions. There is undoubted harm caused by religious leaders who commit sexual abuse, or dominate their congregation, or support apartheid and teach intolerance and racism. Religious fundamentalism sometimes leads to terrorist violence. However, we would contend that such deplorable things occur in a relatively small number of cases, compared to the vast amount of positive actions undertaken by those motivated by their faith.

Race/ethnicity, culture and mental health

Several studies have linked specific ethnicities with higher rates of anxiety and depression. When reviewed by Rosenthal and Wilson (2012), it was found that these data were old, confounding variables were not controlled for and overall ethnicity accounted for less than 1% of observed variance. These authors studied 1,000 youth in a racially mixed area and showed no mean differences in psychological distress between members of different racial/ethnic groups. The limited available evidence suggests that religious discrimination increases the risk of anxiety and depression and lowers life satisfaction (Klocker, Trenerry and Webster, 2011; Pascoe and Richman, 2009). Many people perceived to be Muslim reported harassment following the Twin Towers attacks of 11 September 2001 (Khan and Ecklund, 2012). Women with Arabic-sounding names had poorer birth outcomes in the six months after 11 September 2001 compared to the previous year (Lauderdale, 2006).

Religious discrimination is often tangled up with racism. Racial discrimination in general restricts access to society's goods, such as housing and employment, which has a direct impact on health. Discrimination reduces social cohesion and damages individual flourishing; there is a strong association between perceived discrimination and poorer physical and mental health on multiple measures (Bhui et al., 2005; Williams, Mohammed, Leavell and Collins, 2010). Many people still experience racial discrimination within the NHS (Campbell, 2012).

Discrimination may seem normal to the recipient; such internalized discrimination can lead to lower self-esteem and acceptance of second-class status. Stereotype threat is a source of stress when stereotypes are invoked and the possibility of failing one's group become activated: for example, when race is highlighted before an IQ test (Steele and Aronson, 1995). Stereotype threat leads to anxiety and takes up limited working-memory capacity, resulting in poorer performance. Responding to stereotype threats could deplete self-control resources, leading to self-defeating behaviour later the same day (Inzlicht and Kang, 2010). This gives one possible mechanism for the actions of discrimination on health

(Pascoe and Richman, 2009). A large percentage of those who are politically active, and those who undertake voluntary work regularly, do so from religious motivations (Birdwell and Littler, 2012; Lewis *et al.*, 2013). Historically, in the West, hospitals were built from the Christian imperative to 'love your neighbour', nursing sisters were originally literally sisters of a Christian religious order – nuns (Nelson, 2001). In Brazil, Spiritist hospitals provide health care for the poorest (Schumann, Stroppa and Moreira-Almeida, 2011). People of faith helped motivate the establishment of Amnesty International, the Hospice Movement, Oxfam, Save the Children Fund, the National Health Service, the Red Cross/Red Crescent, the YMCA and the Samaritans, among many others, as revealed on their websites.

Faith has motivated major political movements, such as the abolition of the slave trade. Many charismatic leaders and movements were sustained by their various faiths to achieve freedom for their people and improvement in their health. Examples include Mohandas Ghandi, Martin Luther King, Jr, the 'Velvet Revolution' in Czechoslovakia, the 'Orange Revolution' in Ukraine and Burmese opposition leader Aung San Suu Kyi.

Health professionals working in a multi-faith post-modern society, attentive to the needs of users can no longer dismiss all religious belief and spiritual practice as pathological. Psychiatrists in the West are increasingly being consulted by patients whose faith is a fundamental part of their cultural identity and worldview. Their firmly held religious beliefs may determine their choice of symptoms, their adherence to treatment and their support systems, and be a significant factor in their eventual outcome. All health care workers need awareness of and skills in working with people from different faith communities. This understanding starts with recognizing their own worldview and values (Woodbridge and Fulford, 2004).

Conclusion

We believe it is likely that improving support for people of faith working in health care would enhance quality of life and job satisfaction for many health care workers and noticeably assist many patients. This support is often provided by hospital chaplains, by individuals and by religious communities, through religious services, discussion groups and personal conversations. Hospital chaplain posts are particularly vulnerable during a time of austerity, but many value their input (Sokol, 2009). All the world religions provide a metaphysical framework to sustain care and compassion (Charter for Compassion, 2012). These are values noted to be missing at the present time in the target-driven managed health care system in the United Kingdom (Freeth, 2007), as exemplified by the latest care home scandals. Nevertheless there is hope. In the United Kingdom, we are fortunate to have a comprehensive health service, but it is failing many (Francis, 2010). We need a health service in which continuity of care is improved, basic counseling skills are taught to all practitioners, sufficient time is made available to really listen to patients and relatives, and staff are supported as well as service users. This restoration of compassion will also alter the culture of much present-day health care and can improve outcomes (Campling and Ballat, 2011). Religion and spirituality are important in the majority of people's lives worldwide. There is strong evidence that R/S has a positive impact on many aspects of physical and mental health. All health care workers need to be aware of their own worldviews and values, and of how to elicit and work with the worldviews of others. Reductionist technological medicine has been experienced as damaging and dehumanizing by many. We can be skilled in both the technical and the interpersonal aspects of health care; we can be both competent professionals and whole people. Spiritual practice and support from their religious community are important in sustaining care and compassion for many health workers. Ignoring the R/S dimension in health care provision is a neglect of the key tasks of medicine linked to care, recovery and compassion. The evidence is strong that mainstream religiosity is an enabler of health and a protection against mental illness.

References

Abdel-Khalek, A. (2011). Associations between religiosity, mental health, and subjective well-being among Arabic samples from Egypt and Kuwait. *Mental Health, Religion and Culture, 15*(8), 741–758.

Alcoholics Anonymous. (2011). *About us.* Retrieved from www.alcoholics-anonymous.org.uk?PageID=43.

Alexander, J. (1941). *The Jack Alexander article about AA.* Retrieved from www.aa.org/catalog.cfm?origpage=180&product=35.

Benda, B. B. (2002). Factors associated with re-hospitalization among veterans in a substance abuse treatment program. *Psychiatric services, 53*(9), 1176–1178.

Bhui, K., Stansfield, S., Mckenzie, K., Karlsen, S., Nazroo, J. and Welch, S. (2005). Racial/ethnic discrimination and common mental disorders among workers: Findings from the EMPIRIC study of ethnic minority groups in the United Kingdom. *American Journal of Public Health, 95*(3), 496–501.

Birdwell, J. and Littler, M. (2012). *Why those who do God do good: Faithful citizens.* Demos report. Retrieved from www.demos.co.uk/publications/faithfulcitizens.

Bracken, P., Thomas, P., Timimi, S., Asen, E., Behr, G., Beuster, C. et al. (2012). Psychiatry beyond the current paradigm. *British Journal of Psychiatry, 201*, 430–434.

Campbell, D. (2012). Former NHS manager awarded £1m in racial discrimination case. *Guardian.* Retrieved from www.guardian.co.uk/society/2012/jan/09/nhs-manager-race-discrimination-case.

Campling, P. and Ballat, J. (2011). *Intelligent kindness: Reforming the culture of healthcare.* London: Royal College of Psychiatrists Press.

Cardozo, B. L., Bilukha, O. O., Crawford, C. A., Shaikh, I., Wolfe, M. I., Gerber, M. L. and Anderson, M. (2004). Mental health, social functioning, and disability in postwar Afghanistan. *JAMA, 292*(5), 575–584.

Chan, C. S., Rhodes, J. E. and Perez, J. E. (2012). A prospective study of religiousness and psychological distress among female survivors of Hurricanes Katrina and Rita. *American Journal of Community Psychology, 49*(1–2), 168–181.

Charter for Compassion. (2012). Retrieved from http://charterforcompassion.org.

Clark, R. (2004). Interethnic group and intra ethnic group racism: Perceptions and coping in Black university students. *Journal of Black Psychology, 30*(4), 506–526.

Cornah, D. (2006). *The impact of spirituality on mental health: A review of the literature.* Mental Health Foundation. Retrieved from www.mentalhealth.org.uk/content/assets/PDF/publications/impactspirituality.pdf?viewStandard.

Cornwell, J., Levenson, R., Sonola, L. and Poteliakhoff, E. (2012). *Continuity of care for older hospital patients: A call for action.* Retrieved from www.kingsfund.org.uk/sites/files/kf/field/field_publication_file/continuity-of-care-for-older-hospital-patients-mar-2012.pdf.

Cox, J. L. and Verhagen, P. J. (2011). Spirituality, religion and psychopathology: Towards an integrative psychiatry. *International Journal of Person Centred Medicine, 1*(1), 144–147.

Crabtree, S. and Pelham, B. (2009). *Religion provides emotional boost to world's poor.* World Gallup Poll. Retrieved from www.gallup.com/poll/116449/religion-provides-emotional-boost-world-poor.aspx.

Craddock, N., Antebi, D., Attenburrow, M.-J., Bailey, A., Carson, A., Cowen, P. *et al.* (2008). Wake-up call for British psychiatry. *British Journal of Psychiatry, 193*, 6–9.

De Marinis, V. (2008). The impact of postmodernization on existential health in Sweden: Psychology of religion's function in existential public health analysis. *Archive for the Psychology of Religion, 30*(1), 57–74.

Engel, G. L. (1977). The need for a new medical model: A challenge for biomedicine. *Science, 196*, 129–136.

Errihani, I. H., Mrabt, I. H., Boutayeb, S., El Ghissassi, I., El Mesbahi, O., Hammoudi, M. *et al.* (2008). Impact of cancer on Moslem patients in Morocco. *Psycho-oncology, 17*(1), 98–100.

Falkenberg, L. (2004, 13 December). Religiosity common among mothers who kill children. *San Antonio Express-News.* Retrieved from http://today.uchc.edu/headlines/2004/dec04/religiosity.html.

Fernando, S. J. (1978). Aspects of depression in a Jewish minority group. *Psychiatria Clinica, 11*, 23–33.

Fernando, S. J. (1975). A cross-cultural study of some familial and social factors in depressive illness. *British Journal of Psychiatry, 127*, 46–53.

Fernando, S. (1986). Depression and ethnic minorities. In J. L. Cox (Ed.), *Transcultural psychiatry.* London: Croom Helm.

Fiala, W. E., Bjorck, J. P. and Gorsuch, R. (2002). The religious support scale: Construction, validation, and cross-validation. *American Journal of Community Psychology, 30*(6), 761–786.

Francis, R. (2010). *Robert Francis Inquiry report into Mid-Staffordshire NHS foundation trust.* Retrieved from www.dh.gov.uk/en/Publicationsandstatistics/Publications/PublicationsPolicyAndGuidance/DH_113018.

Freeth, R. (2007). *Humanising psychiatry and mental health: The challenge of the person-centred approach.* London: Radcliffe.

Fukui, S., Starnino, V. R. and Nelson-Becker, H. B. (2011). Spiritual well-being of people with psychiatric disabilities: The role of religious attendance, social network size and sense of control. *Community Mental Health Journal, 48*(2), 202–211.

Fulford, K. W. M., Campbell, A. V. and Cox, J. (Eds.). (2007). *Medicine of the person: Faith, science and values in health care provision.* London: Jessica Kingsley.

Gallup. (2012). *Poll: In U.S., very religious have higher wellbeing across all faiths.* Retrieved from www.gallup.com/poll/152732/religious-higher-wellbeing-across-faiths.aspx.

Graham, J. R. and Roemer, L. (2012). A preliminary study of the moderating role of church-based social support in the relationship between racist experiences and general anxiety symptoms. *Cultural Diversity and Ethnic Minority Psychology, 18*, 268–276.

Gray, A. J. (2001). Attitudes to mental health issues in a church congregation. *Mental Health, Religion and Culture, 4*(1), 71–80.

Gray, A. J. (2011). Worldviews. *International Psychiatry, 8*(3), 58–60.

Hill, P. and Dwiwardani, C. (2010). Measurement at the interface of psychiatry and religion: Issues and existing measures. In P. Verhagen, H. M. Van Praag, J. J. López-Ibor, Jr., J. Cox and D. Moussaou (Eds.), *Religion and psychiatry: Beyond boundaries* (pp. 319–340). London: Wiley.

Hollifield, M. (2008). Symptoms and coping in Sri Lanka 20–21 months after the 2004 tsunami. *British Journal of Psychiatry, 192*(1), 39–44.

Hughes, R. (2004). The death of children by faith-based medical neglect. *Journal of Law and Religion, 20*(1), 2004–2005.

Inzlicht, M. and Kang, S. (2010). Stereotype threat spillover: How coping with threats to social identity affects, aggression, eating, decision-making, and attention. *Journal of Personality and Social Psychology, 99*, 467–481.

Khan, M. and Ecklund, K. (2012). Attitudes toward Muslim Americans post-9/11. *Journal of Muslim Mental Health, 7*(1). Retrieved from http://hdl.handle.net/2027/spo.10381607.0007.101.

Klocker, N., Trenerry, B. and Webster, K. (2011). *How does freedom of religion and belief affect health and wellbeing?* Retrieved from www.vichealth.vic.gov.au/Publications/Freedom-from-discrimination/Freedom-of-religion-and-belief.aspx.

Koenig, H. (2007). Religion and depression in older medical inpatients. *American Journal of Geriatric Psychiatry, 15*(4), 282–291.

Koenig, H. (2011). *Spirituality and health research: Methods, measurements, statistics, and resources.* West Conshohoken: Templeton Foundation Press.

Koenig, H., King, D. and Carson, V. (2012). *Handbook of religion and health* (2nd ed.). Oxford: Oxford University Press.

Koenig, H., McCullough, M. and Larson, D. (2001). *Handbook of religion and health.* Oxford: Oxford University Press.

La Cour, P. (2010). Research on meaning-making and health in secular society: Secular, spiritual and religious existential orientations. *Social Science & Medicine, 71*(7), 1292–1299.

Lauderdale, D. S. (2006). Birth outcomes for Arabic-named women in California before and after September 11. *Demography, 43*(1), 185–201.

Levin, J. (2012). Religion and positive well-being among Israeli and Diaspora Jews: Findings from the World Values Survey. *Mental Health, Religion & Culture, 15*(7), 70–20.

Lewis, V. A., Macgregor, C. and Putnam, R. D. (2013). Religion, networks, and neighborliness: The impact of religious social networks on civic engagement. *Social Science Research, 42*(2) 331–346. Retrieved from www.sciencedirect.com/science/article/pii/S0049089X12002141.

Longabaugh, R., Donovan, D. M., Karno, M. P., McCrady, B. S., Morgenstern, J. and Tonigan, J. S. (2005). Active ingredients: How and why evidence-based alcohol behavioral treatment interventions work. *Alcoholism: Clinical and Experimental Research, 29*(2), 235–247.

Nelson, S. (2001). *Say little, do much: Nurses, nuns, and hospitals in the nineteenth century.* Philadelphia: University of Pennsylvania Press.

Nisbet, P. A., Duberstein, P. R., Conwell, Y. and Seidlitz, L. (2000). The effect of participation in religious activities on suicide versus natural death in adults 50 and older. *Journal of Nervous and Mental Disease, 188*(8), 543–546.

Paloutzian, R. F. and Ellison, C. W. (1982). Loneliness, spiritual well-being and the quality of life. In L. A. Peplau and D. Perlman (Eds.), *Loneliness: A sourcebook of current theory, research and therapy* (pp. 224–237). London: Wiley-Interscience.

Pascoe, E. and Richman, L. S. (2009). Perceived discrimination and health: A meta-analytic review. *Psychological Bulletin, 135*, 531–554.

Payman, V. and Ryburn, B. (2010). Religiousness and recovery from inpatient geriatric depression: Findings from the PEJAMA Study. *Australian and New Zealand Journal of Psychiatry, 44*(6), 560–567.

Piedmont, R. L. (2001). Spiritual transcendence and the scientific study of spirituality. *Journal of Rehabilitation, 67*(1), 4–14.

Piedmont, R. L. and Leach, M. M. (2002). Cross-cultural generalizability of the spiritual transcendence scale in India: Spirituality as a universal aspect of human experience. *American Behavioral Scientist, 45*, 1888.

Poole, R. and Higgo, R. (2011). Spirituality and the threat to therapeutic boundaries in psychiatric practice. *Mental Health, Religion & Culture, 14*(1), 19–29.

Reese, A. M., Thorpe, R. J., Bell, C. N., Bowie, J. V. and Laveist, T. A. (2012). The effect of religious service attendance on race differences in depression: Findings from the EHDIC-SWB study. *Journal of Urban Health: Bulletin of the New York Academy of Medicine, 89*, 510–518.

Ringdal, G. (1996). Religiosity, quality of life and survival in cancer patients. *Social Indicators Research, 38*(2), 193–211.

Rosenthal, B. S. and Wilson, W. C. (2012). Race/ethnicity and mental health in the first decade of the 21st century. *Psychological Reports, 110*(2), 645.

Salander, P. (2006). Who needs the concept of 'spirituality'? *Psycho-oncology, 15*(7), 647–649.

Schumann, C., Stroppa, A. and Moreira-Almeida, A. (2011). The contribution of faith-based health organisations to public health. *International Psychiatry, 8*(3), 62–64.

Schuster, M. A., Stein, B. D., Jaycox, L. H., Collins, R. L., Marshall, G. N., Elliott, M. N. et al. (2001). A national survey of stress reactions after the September 11, 2001, terrorist attacks. *N Engl J Med, 345*(20), 1507–1512.

Skevington, S. M., Gunson, K. S. and O'Connell, K. A. (2012). Introducing the WHOQOL-SRPB BREF: Developing a short-form instrument for assessing spiritual, religious and personal beliefs within quality of life. *Quality of Life Research*. Retrieved from www.ncbi.nlm.nih.gov/pubmed/22836375.

Sokol, D. (2009). *The value of hospital chaplains*. Retrieved from http://news.bbc.co.uk/1/hi/health/7990099.stm.

Steele, C. M. and Aronson, J. (1995). Stereotype threat and the intellectual test performance of African Americans. *Journal of Personality and Social Psychology, 69*(5), 797–811.

Stoneham, E. (2012). *Why religions work: God's place in the world today*. Abingdon: Circle Books.

Strawbridge, W. J., Shema, S. J., Cohen, R. D. and Kaplan, G. A. (2001). Religious attendance increases survival by improving and maintaining good health behaviors, mental health, and social relationships. *Annals of Behavioral Medicine, 23*(1), 68–74.

Swaab, D. F. and Verweij, W. T. P. (2010). Neuro-theology: Demasque of religions. In P. Verhagen, H. M. Van Praag, J. J. López-Ibor, Jr., J. Cox and D. Moussaou (Eds.), *Religion and psychiatry: Beyond boundaries* (pp. 541–568). London: Wiley.

Swinton, J. and Pattison, S. (2010). Moving beyond clarity: Towards a thin, vague, and useful understanding of spirituality in nursing care. *Nursing Philosophy, 11*, 226–237.

Tepper, L., Rogers, S. A., Coleman, E. M. and Maloney, H. N. (2001). The prevalence of religious coping among persons with persistent mental illnesses. *Psychiatric services, 52*(5), 660–665.

Williams, D. R., Mohammed, S. A., Leavell, J. and Collins, C. (2010). Race, socio-economic status & health: Complexities, ongoing challenges & research opportunities. *Annals of the New York Academy of Sciences, 1186*, 69–101.

Woodbridge, K. and Fulford, B. (2004). *Whose value? A workbook for values-based practice in mental healthcare*. London: Sainsbury Centre for Mental Health.

Ysseldyk, R., Matheson, K. and Anisman, H. (2012). Religiosity as identity: Toward an understanding of religion from a social identity perspective. *Personality and Social Psychology Review, 14*(1), 60–71.

9 In the therapist's chair is Suman Fernando

Charmaine Williams

Introduction

Dr. Suman Fernando has spent decades dedicated to the cause of anti-racist mental health care. As a consultant psychiatrist in the United Kingdom's National Health Service, he became deeply concerned with the poor treatment of black and ethnic minority patients. That concern led him to a lifetime of work as an advocate for services and mental health policy that would address the misdiagnosis and mistreatment that he observed as a clinician. Dr. Fernando firmly asserts that race matters. He has spoken unflinchingly of the ways in which racism systemically influences the practice of psychiatry, and how psychiatry has been and continues to be a tool for racism and domination of racialized people. He is a prolific author, regularly contributing articles, editorials and blog postings in response to mental health policies affecting racial and ethnic minority people. He has published five books, most of which have multiple editions. He is probably best known for *Mental Health, Race and Culture*, a text that is used throughout the world to educate mental health professionals. He is also well-known for refusing to accept the honor of an OBE as a protest against what he described as a 'deeply flawed' mental health care system that disproportionately harmed black and ethnic minority patients. Recent work has taken him to Sri Lanka where he is building capacity in the mental health care system as part of an international Trauma Global Health Program.

Dr. Fernando joined us at the sixth Critical Multicultural Counselling & Psychotherapy Conference in Toronto as the honoured recipient of the 2011 OISE/University of Toronto Lifetime Achievement Award in Multicultural and Diversity Counselling. What follows is a transcript of the 'In the Therapist's Chair' interview held on the last day of the conference. The interviewer is Charmaine Williams, of the Factor-Inwentash Faculty of Social Work.

Charmaine Williams (CW) interviewing Suman Fernando (SF)

CW: *You were the first, or at least one of the first, to bring the discussion of race and racism into psychiatry. What drew you to take on this topic?*

SF: After qualifying as a doctor, I was attracted to psychiatry and so trained in this discipline. From very early on I was rather curious about its philosophical roots. And then in the 1970s, I became interested in how the practice impacted on new immigrants and the interplay between 'culture' and psychiatry. This was during the asylum days of course. I was then doing outpatient clinics at the London Jewish Hospital and the consultant I was working with suggested that I might study Jewish 'culture' in relation to mental illness. I explored the possibilities for funding such research (essentially to give me time off for research) and after a lot of hassle, struck lucky when the new professor appointed to the London Hospital (in East London) agreed to sponsor me for this research. I had difficulty finding time to write up, but finally, I presented what I think was the first MD thesis at Cambridge in the field of 'transcultural psychiatry' – on 'Depression among Jews'. That venture taught me a lot. I took the standard approach of comparing samples of Jewish and non-Jewish people controlled for age, gender, social class, etc. But, as I interviewed these subjects in the 1960s, I discovered that their backgrounds (which I thought had been 'controlled' to be similar) were strikingly different – mainly because of the anti-Semitism in East London during the first half of the 20th century. That got me interested in the importance of knowing people's stories in studying 'culture', and the lesson that stayed with me ever afterwards was that one could not study 'culture' ignoring racism.

But what really brought me to look closely at race and culture in psychiatry was when I discovered that psychiatry in the UK was often and quite consistently felt by people identified as 'black people' as oppressive and discriminatory. Basically I was appalled that a medical discipline could be felt as racist and oppressive and that I and many other psychiatric colleagues were actually operating a racist system. I decided to take a step back to look at how we had got here and that led me to study 'race' and 'culture' academically as it were in the context of the history of psychiatry and psychology, trying to connect this study with the experience of people who were caught up in the system. Naturally I got drawn into debates and struggles which I now see are largely political – the politics of psychiatry as much as that of the capitalist system we live in.

CW: *What did you think was possible when you started this work, what do you believe has been accomplished and where do you think things have fallen short?*

SF: Not really sure when the starting date was but I suppose it was the early 1980s when I began to make noises of dissent and work together with others to highlight the injustices inherent in the system of psychiatry that we practice, and then later agitating to bring about changes, both in the practice of psychiatry and the ways in which mental health services were delivered. The group I was attached to was the Transcultural Psychiatry Society (UK) that was started in the mid-1970s and was at its high point in terms of activity in the 1980s and early 1990s. I got to know some very thoughtful and genuine people there and the discussions at our meetings went a long way towards my books – the first coming out in 1988 – *Race and Culture in Psychiatry*.

In the 1980s, we thought – naively as it turns out – that once we had highlighted the deficiencies of psychiatry and worked out what changes were required, things would change, that the Department of Health and society at large would *want* changes that would lead to a more just society. I think many British people in the professions thought like that in the late 1970s and 1980s. The Race Relations Act had come into force indicating the way things should go and we thought that progress towards justice and fairness was bound to happen. As the riots of the 1980s showed this was far from the case. Justice required a struggle. The most political book I wrote was about this struggle – and that is still going on. The book is called *Cultural Diversity, Mental Health and Psychiatry: The Struggle against Racism* (2003).

What has been accomplished I think mainly by people at grass roots – not so much writers and psychiatrists like me – is that there are alternative ways of helping people with mental health problems, alternatives, that is, to the standard traditional mental health system, and that these are effective and credible. The work has been mainly in the voluntary (NGO) sector and not very much known except to those who use services; nor are they written about in peer-reviewed journals, so that when governments plan services which they claim to be 'evidence-based' the stories – experiences – of people who use these services do not qualify as worthy of consideration! With other people, I have tried to make known some of these services by editing (jointly with Frank Keating in one case) two books: namely, the two editions of *Mental Health in a Multi-ethnic Society* (1995 and 2009). Then among accomplishments, we can point to an impressive literature built up critiquing the theoretical models and practices of Western psychiatry and psychology from a race and culture perspective providing clear indications of how and why changes are required. Some of these critiques are not new but until the last 20 years they have been mainly in anthropological journals, often in a language not easily accessible to people working in mental health. If and when there is the political will to make the radical changes there is a now a body of information and thought to draw on. Most of all, I think, today, in comparison to the 1980s, there is some understanding among ordinary people, especially those who use – or are forced into using – mental health services that something different is possible and a gradual realization that the struggle to induce change is part of a wider struggle against injustice, especially racism.

Clearly we have a long way to go. Psychiatry is often considered by psychiatrists in the UK to be at a cross-roads or in crisis. As we know, times of crisis could well be when change is possible. I think that geo-political changes could also determine change. The power of 'the West' and Western ways are on the way down it seems. Perhaps we will gradually see Indian and Chinese cultures becoming respectable and influential as world power bases change. Even the dynamics of racism may well change radically. Finally, the gradual advent of new ideas from neurosciences – some people think that they are culturally more like 'Eastern psychology' than 'Western' – and these would eventually impinge on practices in psychiatry and psychology. In my view, current philosophy and theory in psychiatry and Western psychology is from the 19th century, so the changes we talk about are about modernizing these disciplines. The movement for racial and cultural justice in psychiatry could well be on the threshold of getting somewhere, but now it is for the new generations to take up the struggle. Clearly we have left a lot undone, our strategies on the whole did not work. New thinking on strategies for change has to be thought through.

CW: *Here in North America there are people that thought the election of Obama signaled we were living in a post-racial world. Do you think talking about race, racism and mental health could be losing its usefulness?*

SF: Electing a black person to be president and 'leader of the free world' was indeed an important signal and a significant point in the history of the West, but let's not get carried away. I believe that today under Obama there are more black African Americans in prison than there were black slaves 200 years ago; and more young African Americans are in custody than in education. As I often say about psychiatry, it's the system that has to change if change is to be sustainable – just changing the people at the top or even right throughout is not the answer. That said, yes, there is certainly a need to change language to suit the times. The language of 'equality' and 'human rights' may have to be used without – and that is the challenge – losing sight of the dynamics of inequality. For example, inequality stems often from people being seen 'racially' or as 'culturally' different. Institutional racism fades into conservatism of institutional practices. So we may have to voice our anti-racism as a struggle against conservatism, the resistance to change and modernization, but we have to do this without ignoring the fact that how people are seen – as 'racial beings' – matters. Yes, we have to adjust our language to suit the occasion and the times but do so without losing the plot.

CW: *How do you think intersectionality, diversity and other identity advocacy agendas have helped or undermined anti-racist mental health practice?*

SF: I am not sure that I understand what exactly you mean. Anti-racist practice to be effective has to be promoted in ways that are sensitive to context and the context we live in is that we identify on various dimensions – class, gender, 'race', etc. I believe that racial identity is only important because of racism – there is no biological importance, for example – and so it may well be unique with respect to other identities. This is a big subject and the whole issue of identity – and the dimensions along which identity is located – is one that will be discussed in this conference. It is difficult to give a short answer to our complex question I am afraid and I will be presenting some of my ideas later on.

CW: *Could you then, perhaps, comment on the extent to which you have been able to work with people seeking equity based on other categories of exclusion, for example, feminist or LGBT advocacy. Have there been opportunities to form strategic alliances with such groups in your work against institutional racism in the mental health care system?*

SF: I can now see what you were getting at in the main question. There has been a move recently to discuss various forms of discrimination oppressing people simultaneously resulting in an 'inequality agenda' that lumps together various 'isms' and discriminatory processes affecting groups of people identified in various ways. This approach argues for some sort of generalized 'equality' or 'equity' and not one focused on any one particular identity such as 'race'. At least that is how it plays out in practice. I do think that this approach does undermine the drive towards racial equality, just as it undermines the drive towards counteracting sexism and LGBT discrimination. Things like sexism and racism have to be named if they are to be addressed properly in practical ways that are effective. Not naming them and talking of a general 'equality' I think may be OK in an academic discussion of what they are about (after all, they are indeed different forms of inequality), but when it comes to addressing them in the sense of doing something about them, each type of inequality has to be named. Otherwise, instead of focusing on (say) 'race' – or rather anti-racist practice – the discourse moves into a sort of messy idealism – something we can all agree about no doubt, but need not really do anything about. How this happens is well illustrated by looking at schemes of equality training in the UK where a variety of inequalities and discriminations are listed without any specific focus. In fact, one training scheme specially commissioned by the Department of Health's strategy for 'Delivering Race Equality' specifies something like 8 or 10 'isms' that need addressing in the mental health field, including 'cronism' and 'heightism'.

So this brings me to the follow-up question. Indeed strategic alliances of the type you mention can be useful but, in the mental health field at least, we have not really developed these alliances adequately. In doing so I think the differences in how discrimination and exclusion affects people must be recognized and thrashed out for such alliances to work in a political sense; assuming that all types of discrimination are the same leads to problems in any movement. Yet, I think the future does lie in such alliances because otherwise there is a sort of divide and rule situation. So far the alliances for the anti-racist movement – in the UK at least – have been with people suffering oppression and exclusion as a result of being given a psychiatric diagnosis and identified as 'mental patients'. In other words, the alliance has been with survivor and service user movements and more recently some parts of the critical psychiatry movement (among psychiatrists). The link has been that both 'racism' and 'diagnosis' are unjustified, irrational and often oppressive, and they tend to affect people adversely in similar ways, up to a point. In fact, I think Fanon drew attention to the fact that racism and labeling as (say) 'schizophrenic' both de-humanize the person affected. But even this sort of alliance has not always been easy in practice. I know how black service users within predominantly white groups of service users often feel that white people dismiss the effects of racism by attributing oppressions they all feel (as service users) to labeling with diagnoses and not to racism, although of course both are involved. And the problems of alliances are even more difficult in the case of LGBT advocacy.

CW: *What do you think about work (by psychologists) that addresses racism as a type of psychopathology and racists as people who need to be treated and hopefully cured?*

SF: I would not want to go down the road of (as it were) medicalizing a social and ethical issue – racism. I am not totally against medicalizing human problems but only if by doing so we can be sure of being able to deal effectively with the problems. In other words, I think medicalizing problems must be critically examined and only pursued if doing so is shown to be – proved to be in practical terms of weighing up the pros and cons – shown to be definitely useful. That is my view about diagnoses and medicalized labeling of any sort. In the case of many very serious problems that human beings face, diagnosing medical illness has indeed been a very useful way of understanding and alleviating suffering. That may be why we have tolerated for so long the medicalizing of problems seen as being located in the 'mind' and constructing the massive number of psychiatric (or 'mental') 'illnesses' we have in DSM. In the case of nearly all so-called psychiatric 'illness' – nowadays called 'disorders' – medicalizing has not I think paid off. It is time I think to rethink the whole approach to 'mind'. As you know 'schizophrenia' as an illness is now more of a hindrance than a help in understanding certain types of human problems and, more importantly, of helping people who suffer from certain problems. In the case of racism, the practical problem of needing to eradicate racism is most unlikely to be taken forward by constructing it into an illness. In fact I think it will merely justify its continuation.

CW: *If racism was eliminated, do you think that there would be a decrease in the incidence of mental illness for racialized people?*

SF: The problem for me in answering this question is that it begs the more serious issue of what is 'illness'. The best I can do is to say that I think eliminating racism will not necessarily decrease 'mental illness' in the way it is constructed by psychiatry today but eliminating racism will certainly decrease human suffering. So if we construct all suffering as 'illness' – and I sometimes think the pharmaceutical industry will like to do just that – eliminating racism it will of course decrease 'illness'. But by then we will have a tablet – or more likely a long-acting injection – for that illness too. And then where will we be? This takes us back to the previous question.

CW: *Given what you have achieved with your work over so many years, what tasks do you feel you are handing over to an upcoming generation of mental health professionals?*

SF: A very difficult task indeed. Basically I think of making changes that would bring about justice and fair play in delivering mental health services in a multicultural society where racism will continue to be a major impediment for the foreseeable future. In the past I think we have struggled against racism, trying to make big changes. Obviously we should continue to do so, but perhaps more could be achieved if we focus on delivering services in spite of racism, minimizing its effects in the disciplines that are responsible for the professional inputs into services, minimizing its effect in the way services are organized and so on. I would suggest looking at the nitty-gritty of what goes on at the coal face of service delivery. Not ignoring the bigger issues (of racism and injustice in society at large and in the disciplines that underpin the services), but concentrating on making life better for the people concerned – the current service users. In the past, I think too little attention was paid to what service users said about what needs changing. The bigger issues I think are part and parcel of a larger struggle in society that I hope all people of goodwill takes part in and support, but your question was on what mental health professionals particularly should focus on, and that is what I have tried to voice an opinion on.

Conclusion

Talking to Dr. Fernando one cannot help be impressed with the span of time he has been grappling with these issues. From the asylum to hospitals and then the advent of community-based care, he has persisted in challenging the system to know better and do better for racialized people. In conversation with him, one can see how his gentle yet persistent assertions of the rights of patients, the link between justice and psychiatry, and the capacity of the system to deliver antiracist mental health care has made him so influential. Dr. Fernando is reflective and critical of his field, but also optimistic that awareness, new knowledge and the right kind of alliances can transform it. In all of his work, it is clear that he has never lost sight of the people who brought him to these issues, racial and ethnic minority patients who deserved the best care possible. He is a worthy recipient of this honor as he has truly spent a lifetime advocating for a system of care that can meet the needs of a multicultural population. It is clear that he has a further hope that while services become better equipped to meet the needs of racial and ethnic minority patients, society will also transform to decrease the need that racial and ethnic minorities have for services.

Part III
Training and development in mental health practice

10 Institutional racism as a seminal concept of cultural competency training

Jaswant Guzder

Introduction

Suman Fernando introduced the seminal concept of institutional racism into the mental health discourse, promoting a wider application and deconstruction of psycho-social, cultural, ideological and political dimensions in psychiatric care, inclusive of race, power, gender, psycho-historiography and social signifiers. Institutional racism was a key formulation that appeared in the 1999 report of the Stephen Lawrence Inquiry prepared by Sir William MacPherson for the UK Home Office, addressing the lack of police response to a 1993 hate crime targeting a Black British boy. The disquiet following the Stephen Lawrence murder trials in London and subsequent MacPherson Inquiry on the lack of police charges for this hate crime brought the concept of "institutional racism" into the public discourse of the United Kingdom (Dacre, 2012). Fernando (2002, p. 26) applied this concept to medical and mental health care, quoting the MacPherson Report's definition of institutional racism:

> The collective failure of an organization to provide an appropriate and professional service to people because of their colour, culture or ethnic origin. It can be seen or detected in processes, attitudes and behaviour that amount to discrimination through unwitting prejudice, ignorance, thoughtlessness and racist stereotyping that disadvantages minority ethnic people.
> (Home Office, 1999, p. 28)

Fernando has positioned this key concept as a bedrock issue for psychiatry building on the earlier key contributions of Fanon (1952, 1967, 1968), Said (1978) and Foucault (2006) on race, power and powerlessness. The colonial agendas of the Other remained relevant implicitly and explicitly as mental health practice positioned the tensions of primitive versus civilized or the powerful versus the powerless.

The understanding of projective identifications that are built on distorted or prejudiced views of Others remain as part of stigma encountered in mental health care and training (Kirmayer, 2011; Young-Bruehl, 1996). Fanon's (1952) formulations and distress as a black psychiatrist are evident in his explicit articulations relevant to the concept of institutional racism. He outlines the views of his European psychiatric colleagues who proposed a formulation of the Other (the Algerian subject during the French Algerian conflicts) as driven by undeveloped "primitivism". The Algerian savage was depicted as killing without civilized intent, as elaborated in the following passage quoting Professor Porot and cited by Edward Said (2003, p. 19):

> This primitivism is not merely a way of living which is the result of a special upbringing; it has much deeper roots.... The Algerian has no cortex; or, more precisely, he is dominated, like the inferior vertebrates, by the diencephalons.

Said elaborates that the post-modern world has a far more complex relationship with the Other or the non-European outsiders than the ethnographic subjects of Freud's explorations in *Totem and Taboo* (1955), which focused on Hannibal and Moses and presumed the reader's acquaintance with Greco-Roman and Hebrew antiquities. Otherness and the Diaspora have now expanded to a contemporary appreciation of the colonial subject and civilizations beyond Euro–North American boundaries. The challenges of post-modern ethnographic explorations of Otherness suggested by Fernando's conceptualization of institutional racism require us to cultivate a careful exploration of our subjectivities and understanding of psycho-historiographies (Hickling, 2007; Mbembe, 2001), especially in the context of diversity and hybridity of the post-modern subject.

Fernando understood that institutional racism provides a useful framework to formulate and promote equitable and dignified mental health care especially relevant to the Euro–North American multi-ethnic post-modern societies. This clinical and ethical discourse engages considerations of gaze, voice and agency at multiple levels that are intrinsic to clinical decision making and relationships as well as engagement with the interaction of a therapist's internalized and unconscious agendas (Fanon, 1952; Hickling and Hutchison, 1999; Said, 2003; Young-Bruehl, 1996). The original European mental health signifier of the Asylum (Foucault, 2006) may seem a distant memory in post-modern America, but the issues of invisibility, stigma, lack of agency, silencing, subaltern status and forced confinement remain as current challenges for the mentally ill despite policies of de-institutionalization (Fernando and Keating, 2009; Goffman, 1961; Hickling, 2007). The significant gaps and blind spots of applying Euro–North American agendas of Otherness have also missed the complexities and nuances of cultural context, mythologies and power reflected in a widening interdisciplinary literature that gives consideration to such issues as cultural specificity, caste, gender and tribalism (Chavan, Gupta, Arun, Sidana and Jadhav, 2012; Jain and Jadhav, 2008; Obeyesekere, 1990).

Fernando has contributed a legacy of writing exploring mental health advocacy with dimensions of access and cultural competencies, rooted in his UK experience with Black and Minority Ethnic (BME) groups. His conceptualization invites us to consider local, colonial and post-colonial history and contexts of institutional racism contributing to training agendas and to the creation of "cultural safety" (Hart-Waselkeesikaw, 2009) in patient care.

Institutional racism and public discourse

During the American Civil Rights Movement, Stokeley Carmichael and Charles Hamilton in their book *Black Power* (1967) had first proposed the term "institutional racism". The potent agendas of racism in the civil rights protests of the United States had implications for a widening discourse on power, invisibility and privilege affecting parallel emerging movements for promoting rights of women, homosexuals, mentally ill and ethnic minorities (Collins, 2005; Taylor, Trierweiler and Williams, 2004). Subaltern subjects, including those highly stigmatized within the Euro–American mental health system, benefited from the African American political struggles. Earlier documents such as the personal account, first published in 1831, of Mary Prince, the first black British woman to escape from slavery, "unconsciously reveals how much besides the legal and social exclusion of the African from society lay behind the expression of male Anglo-Saxon (European) dominance" (Ferguson, 1987, p. viii).

Fernando's explorations of the historical, ideological and socio-cultural underpinning and obstacles to equitable or competent health care for minorities (Fernando, 1988, 1993) have also noted a shift in a mental health discourse focused on bio-genetic agendas in psychiatry to more recent inclusion of psychosocial dimensions of wellness (Christopher, 1999), service providers, recovery (Anthony, 1993), social suffering (Kleinman, Das and Lock, 1997), cultural competence (Kirmayer, 2012), cultural responsiveness (Sue, Fujino, Hu, Takeuchi and Zane, 1991), cultural safety (Papps and Ramsden, 1996), resilience (Ungar, 2011) and spirituality (Obeyesekere, 1990). Institutional racism offers a helpful framework of analysis not only for unmasking enactments and the explicit agendas of racism but also the broader agendas of "inadvertent", unconscious, internalized, implicit and invisible racism (Young-Bruehl, 1996) that are part of these agendas of structural violence in mental health care delivery. This dynamic process of articulating and shaping social and cultural impingements on mental health care requires a kind of transitional phenomena and space (Winnicott, 1967) where institutional discourse may revise and reconsider the predicaments of power hierarchies, class barriers, systemic racism, limited diversity among staff or limited training in cultural competencies.

Training implications of institutional racism in mental health disciplines

The paucity of cultural competence skills training for mental health professionals across disciplines presumes a Euro–North American lens despite clinical realities of multi-ethnic societies. Fernando's work has explored institutional avoidance or resistance to a reflective discourse on these factors in provision of equitable care resonating with the writings of Fanon (1952), Said (1978, 2003), Foucault (2006) and Kareem and Littlewood (1992).

Fernando (1995) has often advocated for a "needs-thinking" rather than a "symptom-thinking" psychiatry orientation that faces more towards recovery or resilience promotion than an illness or psychopathology focus. He has promoted a need for cultural training of all levels of mental health care professionals. He has advocated for paradigm shifts towards the terms of "service users" rather than "patients" (Fernando, 1995), with less emphasis on diagnostic categories evident in his continued contestation of diagnostic nosologies. He has emphasized the need for greater diligence in reducing the application of "sectioning" or forced confinement, and advocates for community engagement to promote recovery rather than focusing only on developing hospital- or clinic-based care. Jaffar Kareem's advocacy for ethnic matching as a choice or option for service users and his emphasis on therapist supervision opportunities to promote cultural competency culminated in his creating the Nafisiyat Centre in London to increase accessible patient-centered care to minorities as an early initiative in the United Kingdom (Kareem and Littlewood, 1992; Thomas, 2009).

Fernando suggested that racism and minority identity were often absent in case discussion. The neutrality premises of psychoanalytic theory (Said, 2003; Kareem and Littlewood, 1992) further served to undermine a fuller examination or inclusion of psycho-social parameters operating in the consulting process. Kleinman *et al.* (1997) advocated that socio-cultural realities were crucial to understanding distress and shaped mental health outcomes. The silos created by pharmaceutical influences and bio-medically based psychiatric definitions of mental disorder tended to reinforce a bio-medical emphasis that diminished the acknowledgment of the strong evidence of epigenetic theory that situates environment as a crucial element in the genesis and outcome of mental illness. Horowitz (2007) has also underlined the dangers of failing to distinguish between distress and diagnosis of psychiatric disorders as crucial in generating mental health interventions.

Historical legacies of racism in mental health systems

Fernando (1991) carefully documented historical legacies of racism that were reflected in institutional scotomas. He suggested that an absence of self-reflection on these social agendas of psychiatry has been built on multiple historically embedded factors fostering cultural bias, barriers to access, ideological bias, colonial agendas, structural power issues and racism agendas in mental health institutions. He noted that BME communities lack confidence in the mental health services where "the focus is largely on community cohesion rather than counteracting discrimination" (Fernando and Keating, 2009, p. 3). "The mental health system continues to be experienced as racist by BME service users" (Fernando and Keating, 2009, p. 3). Though in fact there is an increasing BME visibility among mental health providers, he suggests paradoxically that this increase may not have resulted in increasing capacity of mental health teams to reflect on service access. Racism "expressed through cultural language" (Fernando and Keating, 2009, p. 18) can be complicated by the political agendas of right-wing groups or conflation of "race" and "culture" that erodes possibilities in many cases for service users defining their own positions, identities or needs as identities may be systemically assigned rather than allowed to emerge in the therapeutic encounter.

In the United Kingdom, the over-representation of black children in foster care (as well as expulsions from schooling), the disproportionate under-utilization of minorities in mental health referrals, over-representation of black citizens under compulsory detention, disproportionate numbers of black men diagnosed as schizophrenic under confinement and in prison systems, all point to complex agendas in equitable access and care (Fernando and Keating, 2009, p. 56). These issues of minorities versus the dominant host cultural groups are evident across the European and North American mental health care systems, generating distrust and under-utilization by minorities (Whaley and Davis, 2007; Whaley, 2011). The black UK citizen is still at least 10 times more likely to be diagnosed as schizophrenic and sectioned than his white counterpart. Nor is the black patient likely to be offered psychotherapy but rather he is likely to be treated only with medication (Hickling and Hutchison, 1999; Hickling and Paisley, 2012). African Caribbeans, including large numbers of women (Stanley, 2009), continue to be over-represented in psychiatric institutions at all levels. Predominant treatment does not take account of the impact of race and racism and there is no widespread acceptance of the importance of culturally diverse methods in working with black mental health service users and carers (Mental Health Task Force, 1994).

In the United States, which has the highest rates of incarceration in the world per capita, half of its prisoners are black. More than 8% of American black men are imprisoned, 25% of black children by age 18 will have experienced one parent in prison and 37% of incarcerated black men have not obtained a high-school level of education. In a recent book, *Invisible Men: Mass Incarceration and the Myth of Black Progress*, Pettit (2012) suggests these statistics indicate that the gains of the civil rights movements may be erased when the wider social realities of Black America are taken into account. Social realities reinforce the need for psychiatry to reconsider institutional agendas in our patient care and assumptions about cultural distrust of health care providers or institutions, and to question structural realities of stigma, access and models of care delivery that reinforce hierarchies of privilege or differentials of care (Jackson *et al.*, 2008).

"Working with Culture" seminar series: teaching institutional racism paradigms

Suman Fernando has, since the 1980s, been a visiting scholar to the McGill University Annual Transcultural Psychiatry Summer School seminar series "Working with Culture: Clinical Methods in Cultural Psychiatry" (Guzder and Rousseau, 2013), where he would present the concept of institutional racism as a bedrock issue in framing mental health intervention. The subsequent month-long clinically focused seminars at McGill University would build on the conceptual premises of both institutional racism (Fernando, 1991) and social suffering (Kleinman, Das and Lock, 1997) with explorations of the implicit intersections of individual, systemic, historical, legal, social, mythic and anthropologic elements relevant to cultural frameworks of patient care. Case discussions would amplify the contribution of the therapist's unique cultural imagination in therapeutic work. Since the McGill "Working with Culture" seminars included a large portion of international students, the implications of institutional racism were often applied beyond the Diaspora realities, emphasizing the need to encourage the developing world to speak and write authentically from their own perspectives. Institutional racism implies an understanding and appreciation of local contexts, histories and realities in deconstructing premises of equitable and ethical mental health care (Fernando and Keating, 2009; Hickling, 2007).

Despite the emergence of his work in multicultural London, Fernando's premise of institutional racism is relevant across cultures. Community health efforts in the regions of the Indian subcontinent, for example, have indicated that gender, caste and social exclusion are powerful agendas in delivering equitable care (Chavan *et al.*, 2012; Davar, 2001; Jain and Jadhav, 2008; Weerackody and Fernando, 2011), though socio-cultural training might be absent or limited in their mental health curricula. Similarly, Caribbean mental health agendas of both native-born and migrating populations within the emerging reality of de-institutionalization have included cultural competence as well as institutional racism issues interacting with powerful social agendas (Hickling, 2007; Hickling and Paisley, 2012; Hickling and Hutchison, 1999). While developing societies have been influenced by the scotomas of an ethnocentric literature and colonial shadows, there is an increasing awareness that their local contexts and socio-cultural contexts are crucial to building a culturally competent model of psychiatric care and addressing institutional racism. The use of a case study approach has been helpful to students employing this framework of institutional racism and a constructive process of engaging in advocacy or change.

Application of the conceptual framework of institutional racism to clinical care: unpacking clinical realities

Often in the "Working with Culture" seminars, case studies are presented and institutional racism issues are considered as possible aspects of the clinical predicaments, including cases from Fernando. A case example will also be presented that invokes aspects of Major Depressive Disorder, marital strain, systemic dynamics, war-related distress or dislocation, as well as some aspects linked with institution policies that fail to accommodate patients' needs, such as the following:

> A married 30-year-old South Asian Tamil-speaking woman was hospitalized repeatedly for suicide attempts and depression, over a 5-year period.

After multiple antidepressant trials the patient remained clinically depressed and at risk for suicide. A cultural consultation was requested by her medical clinic, who had diagnosed intractable depression, suggesting the woman was possibly "homesick" and should return to Sri Lanka. Both the emergency room and clinic had often interviewed her husband separately to explore the possibilities of spousal abuse and considered removal of the couple's two young children, though the patient had strongly denied this hypothesis.

Initially the patient was seen with an interpreter and the second consult was with her husband present. She was a survivor of the Sri Lankan civil war, socially isolated and had intense conflicts with the husband's extended family, which impacted her marital relationship and her parenting of her children. Her systemic family and cultural issues had not emerged in previous history with the husband present, as she had experienced intense shame and discomfort in revealing these issues in his presence. She was clear that she had no desire to return to her war-devastated region. Her migration was already a form of forced exile from a home that no longer existed. She was relieved to have become a Canadian citizen and did not see any future for her children or herself in a return to Sri Lanka. While there was no domestic violence, she was enraged that her husband was torn between his loyalties to her and to his extended family. Exploration of their complex systemic issues and addressing her social isolation were crucial to her alliance. She and her husband had also not understood that the antidepressant needed to be taken consistently to maintain a therapeutic blood level.

Without some understanding of the cultural predicament of the patient's life within her extended family, the clinic seemed to have based their assessment on cultural stereotyping of her husband as an oppressor and had not appreciated their struggles in the aftermath of the Sri Lankan civil war. While clinical issues were crucial to proper diagnosis and treatment planning, policy issues including the institution's lack of support for use of interpreters or culture brokers had impeded her assessment and treatment. The clinic had not considered culture-change issues, the family's social isolation and possible involvement of a primary care physician who spoke Tamil. Institutional policies to ban use of interpreters and encourage cultural competency training or dialogue were reviewed in the teaching seminar, as a significant portion of the clinic's service users were minorities without local language skills.

During his visiting lectures, Fernando invariably spoke to both subtle and obvious layers of institutional racism. He offered the example of Stephen Lawrence's murder as overt racism and the implications of police inaction as institutional racism. The accounts of several mental health inquiries (Fernando, Ndegwa and Wilson, 1998), including the Orville Blackwood Inquiry (named for one of three black men who died in seclusion rooms at Broadmoor Hospital), was discussed in the context of institutional perceptions of Afro-Caribbean men in the Euro–North American context. The Orville Blackwood Inquiry of 1993, for example, involved the death of an over-medicated black patient left in seclusion as a consequence of a sequence of events that began with his resistance to asylum routines of going to occupational therapy sessions. The historical legacy of slavery and post-slavery generations, linked with the current over-diagnosis or incarceration of blacks (Fernando, 1995), were reviewed in Fernando's lectures and writings as complex clinical vignettes relating his extensive experience in forensic and psychiatric cultural consultations. Colonialism exported the concept of the asylum with its multifaceted political, social and mental health aspects and remains not only the primary signifier of mental health but also a setting that was often used to suppress social defiance to colonial rule (Fernando, 2002; Fernando and Keating, 2009; Hickling, 2007).

Fernando presented a psychiatric consultation shown in a BBC 4 documentary, in which he had been asked by an African immigrant patient to challenge a forced treatment order:

> The patient was a Black man from Ghana diagnosed as a paranoid schizophrenic, who was maintaining his self care, mobility and physical health while living independently in the community but refusing medication. He had no thought disorder but had delusions that he was born white but his skin had changed to black, that he was related to the Queen, and that his mother was indeed an imposter who spread lies about him. Though he had been found near the Queen's palace and written her some letters as he described himself as her loyal Commonwealth subject and her distant relation, he presented no overt threat to society nor did his delusions indicate any dangerous intent.

After being sectioned and admitted in forcible confinement the patient was obliged to submit to accepting long-acting neuroleptic injections with considerable debilitating side effects. The institution was adamant that best practices involved medication and increased surveillance for the safety of the patient and society, though he had always cooperated with follow-up. Fernando suggested the patient had a right to refuse neuroleptics given his lack of danger to society, despite his delusions fixatated on his mother and the Queen. His role as a cultural consultant in this case supporting the patient's right of treatment refusal failed to change the outcome for the patient, who was forcibly confined. In the McGill seminars this case was often presented for discussion of the complex issues implicating both institutional, psychiatric and individual premises of clinical work. Cultural competency in some sense involved a dethroning of an expert position and making space for the service user's perspectives as well the internalized motivations or assumptions of the healer.

Cultural safety as a counterpoint to institutional racism

Institutional racism underlines the absence of a co-construction of therapeutic aims and an appreciation of the multiple parameters that define the therapeutic intent in mental health. Cultural safety (Hart-Waselkeesikaw, 2009; Papps and Ramsden, 1996; Syme and Browne, 2002) is one of the premises of cultural competence and therapeutic engagement that offers a counterpoint to the predicaments of institutional racism, as quoted by Kirmayer (2012, p. 157):

> Cultural safety focuses on the potential differences between health providers and patients that have an impact on care and aims to minimize any assault on the patient's cultural identity ... to educate students to examine their own realities and attitudes they bring to clinical care ... to not blame the victims of historical and social processes for current plight, and to produce a workforce ... who are culturally safe to practice as defined by the people they serve.
> (Crampton, Dowell, Parkin and Thompson, 2003, p. 596)

This concept arose from the Maori's demands for participation and co-construction of their health care. Unlike many global minorities, aboriginals or colonized peoples, the Maori in post-colonial New Zealand pursued an assertive and progressive involvement in sharing the power to define their mental health care.

Kirmayer (2012, p. 157) refers to the alternative notions of "cultural responsiveness" (Sue *et al.*, 1991), "cultural humility" (Tervalon and Murray-Garcia, 1998) and "cultural safety" as an engagement with the Other's life world. This active clinical negotiation engaged at many levels of meaning, rather than being a passive acquisition of cultural competency skill training approaches. Institutional racism similarly requires an open dialogue or sensitive response to the social, political, linguistic, ecological and spiritual realities of the minority group or individuals to shape the parameters of "safety". The elements of therapeutic safety are not easily acknowledged, defined or realized within mainstream institutions except through the feedback of the client or service users.

Institutional racism and cultural safety offer conceptual models that foster a shift to a discourse on resilience building, wellness, protective factors, spirituality or local metaphors of distress, and challenges models emphasizing psychopathology, diagnosis, medication, confinement or bio-medical models divorced from socio-cultural meaning systems. Fernando's pioneering work on the history of racism and mental health has offered us the option of examining our perspectives and scotomas within the framework of institutional racism. While paradigms such as cultural safety provide a response to diversity that are a counterpoint to services organized in a "one size fits all model" (Kirmayer, 2003), they are in constant tension with the forces that maintain institutional homeostasis.

Conclusion

Suman Fernando has offered us a conceptual model of institutional racism that engages both therapist and institutional responsibilities in working ethically and actively to develop models of healing, including ongoing exploration of unconscious, implicit and explicit factors that may impede or promote cultural safety. Institutional racism shapes both the external landscapes, including institutional rules of engagement, training or policy, and the internal positioning of the therapist in contemporary psychiatric practice. While an institution or professional organization can create a context that welcomes or suppresses a constructive critical dialogue of these multiple agendas of power, history, agency, voice and healing (Foucault, 2006), the more subtle territory of the therapist's transference and counter-transference issues (Young-Bruehl, 1996) remain crucial matters in training and role modeling. Institutional racism is as much an internalized project engaging our personal psycho-historiographies as an intentional examination of collective or group contexts in our public institutions including police, mental health, judicial or school settings.

References

Anthony, W. (1993). Recovery from mental illness: The guiding vision of mental health service systems in the 1990's. *Psychosocial Rehabilitation, 16*(4), 11–23.
Carmichael, S. and Hamilton, C. (1967). *Black power*. Harmondsworth: Penguin.
Chavan, B. S., Gupta, N., Arun, P., Sidana, A. and Jadhav, S. (Eds.). (2012). *Textbook of community mental health in India*. India: Jaypee Brothers Publishing.
Christopher, J. C. (1999). Situating psychological well-being: Exploring the cultural roots of its theory and research. *Counselling and Development, 77*(2), 141–152.
Collins, P. H. (2005). *Black sexual politics: African Americans, gender, and the new racism*. New York: Taylor & Francis.
Crampton, P., Dowell, A., Parkin, C. and Thompson, C. (2003). Combating effects of racism through a cultural immersion medical education program. *Acad. Med., 78*(6), 595–598.
Dacre, P. (2012, January 4). Statement: On the risks that he and the *Mail* ran to secure justice for Stephen Lawrence. *Daily Mail*. Retrieved from www.dailymail.co.uk/news/article-2081736/Stephen-Lawrence-trial-verdict-Paul-Dacre-Daily-Mail-editor-shares-views.html
Davar, B. V. (Ed.). (2001). *Mental health from a gender perspective*. New Delhi: Sage.
Fanon, F. (1952). *Black skins, white masks*. New York: Grove Press.
Fanon, F. (1967). *Towards the African revolution*. New York: Grove Press.
Fanon, F. (1968). *The wretched of the Earth*. New York: Grove Press.
Ferguson, M. (Ed.). (1987). Introduction. In Mary Prince (1831), *The History of Mary Prince, a West Indian Slave Related by Herself*. London: Pandora.
Fernando, S. (1988). *Race and culture in psychiatry*. New York: Brunner-Routledge.
Fernando, S. (1991). *Mental health, race and culture*. London: Macmillan.
Fernando, S. (1993). Racism and xenophobia. *Innovation, 6*(1), 9–19.
Fernando, S. (Ed.). (1995). *Mental health in a multi-ethnic society*. London: Routledge.
Fernando, S. (2002). *Mental health, race and culture* (2nd ed.). London: Croom Palgrave.
Fernando, S. (2003). *Cultural diversity, mental health and psychiatry: The struggle against racism*. Hove.
Fernando, S. and Keating, F. (Eds.). (2009). *Mental health in a multi-ethnic society: A multidisciplinary handbook* (2nd ed.). London: Routledge.
Fernando, S., Ndegwa, D. and Wilson, M. (1998). *Forensic psychiatry, race and culture*. London: Routledge.
Foucault, M. (2006). *History of madness* (Jean Khalfa, Trans.). London: Routledge.
Freud, S. (1955). *Moses and monotheism* (standard ed., Vol. 13) (James Strachey, Trans.). London: Hogarth Press.

Goffman, E. (1961). *Asylums: Essays on the social situation of mental patients and other inmates.* New York: Anchor Books.

Guzder, J. and Rousseau, C. (2013). A diversity of voices: The McGill "Working with Culture" seminars. *Culture, Medicine, and Psychiatry, 37*(2), 347–364.

Hart-Waselkeesikaw, F. (2009). *Cultural competence and cultural safety in nursing education: A framework for First Nations, Inuit and Metis nursing.* Ottawa: Aboriginal Nurses Association of Canada.

Hickling, F. W. (2007). *Psychohistoriography: A postcolonial psycho-analytic and psychotherapeutic model.* Kingston, Jamaica: CARIMENSA, University of the West Indies.

Hickling, F. W. and Hutchison, G. (1999). Roast breadfruit psychosis: Disturbed racial identifications in African-Caribbeans. *Psychiatric Bulletin, 23,* 132–134.

Hickling, F. W. and Paisley, V. (2012). Issues of clinical and cultural competence in Caribbean migrants. *Transcultural Psychiatry, 49,* 223–244.

Home Office. (1999). *The Stephen Lawrence inquiry. Report of an inquiry by Sir William Macpherson of Cluny.* London: Stationery Office.

Horowitz, A. V. (2007). Distinguishing distress from disorder as psychological outcomes of stressful social arrangements. *Health: An Interdisciplinary Journal for the Social Study of Health, Illness and Medicine, 2*(3), 273–289.

Jackson, J. S., Torres, M., Caldwell, C., Neighbors, H., Ness, R., Taylor, R. et al. (2008). Prevalence and correlates of conduct disorder and problem behaviour in Caribbean and Filipino immigrant adolescents. *Eur Child and Adolesc Psychiatry, 17*(5), 264–273.

Jain, S. and Jadhav, S. (2008). A cultural critique of community psychiatry in India. *Int. J of Health Services, 38*(3), 561–584.

Kareem, J. and Littlewood, R. (1992). *Intercultural therapy: Themes, interpretations and practice.* Oxford: Blackwell.

Kirmayer, L. J. (2003). Failures of imagination: The refugee's narrative in psychiatry. *Anthropology and Medicine, 10*(2), 167–185.

Kirmayer, L. J. (2011). Multicultural medicine and the politics of recogition. *J. Medicine and Philosophy, 36*(4), 410–423.

Kirmayer, L. (2012). Rethinking cultural competency. *Transcultural Psychiatry, 49*(2), 149–164.

Kleinman, A., Das, V. and Lock, M. M. (Eds.). (1997). *Social suffering.* Berkley: University of California Press.

Mbembe, A. (2001). *On the post colony.* Berkley: University of California.

Mental Health Task Force. (1994). *Black mental health: A dialogue for change.* London: Department of Health.

Obeyesekere, G. (1990). *The work of culture.* Chicago: University of Chicago Press.

Papps, E. and Ramsden, I. (1996). Cultural safety in nursing: The New Zealand experience. *Int. J of Quality of Health Care, 8*(5), 491–497.

Pettit, B. (2012). *Invisible men: Mass incarceration and the myth of black progress.* New York: Russell Sage Foundation.

Said, E. W. (1978). *Orientalism: Western conceptions of the Orient.* London: Routledge & Kegan Paul.

Said, E. W. (2003). *Freud and the non-European.* London: Verso.

Stanley, J. (2009). African and Caribbean mental health services in Manchester. In S. Fernando (Ed.), *Mental health in a multi-ethnic society.* London: Routledge.

Sue, S., Fujino, D. C., Hu, L. T., Takeuchi, D. T. and Zane, N. W. (1991). Community mental health services for ethnic minority groups: A test of the cultural responsiveness hypothesis. *Consulting and Clinical Psychology, 59*(4), 533–540.

Syme, V. and Browne, A. J. (2002). Cultural safety and the analysis of health policy affecting Aboriginal people. *Nursing Researcher: International Journal of Research Methodology, 9*(3), 42–56.

Taylor, R. J., Trierweiler, D. R. and Williams, D. (2004). The National Survey of American Life: A study of racial, ethnic and cultural influences on mental disorders and mental health. *Int. J of Methods in Psychiatric Research, 13*(4), 196–207.

Tervalon, M. and Murray-Garcia, J. (1998). Cultural humility versus cultural competence: A critical distinction in defining physician training outcomes in multicultural education. *Journal of Health Care for the Poor and Underserved, 9*(2), 117–125.

Thomas, L. (2009). Psychotherapy in the context of race and culture: An intercultural therapeutic approach. In S. Fernando (Ed.), *Mental health in a multi-ethnic society*. London: Routledge.

Ungar, M. (2011). The social ecology of resilience: Addressing contextual and cultural ambiguity of nascent construct. *Amer. J. Orthopychiatry, 81*(1), 1–17.

Weerackody, C. and Fernando, S. (Eds.). (2011). *Reflections on mental health and wellbeing: Learning from communities affected by conflict, dislocation and natural disaster in Sri Lanka*. Columbo: People's Rural Development Association.

Whaley, A. L. (2011). Clinicians' competence in assessing cultural mistrust among African American psychiatric patients. *Journal of Black Psychology, 37*(4), 387–406.

Whaley, A. L. and Davis, K. E. (2007). Cultural competence and evidence-based practice in mental health services: A complementary perspective. *American Psychologist, 62*(6), 563–574.

Whitley, R. (2007). Cultural competence, evidence-based medicine and evidence based practices. *Psychiatric Services, 58*(12), 1588–1590.

Winnicott, D. W. (1967). The location of cultural experience. *Int. J. of Psychanal, 48*, 368–372.

Young-Bruehl, E. (1996). *The anatomy of prejudice*. Cambridge, MA: Harvard University Press.

11 Race equality and cultural capability training in mental health

Peter Ferns

We have known for a very long time that mental health is not just about a person's inherent health issues but invariably encapsulates their social, economic and political context. Unfortunately mental health services in the United Kingdom continue to be restricted professionally and structurally to a narrow medical model, with some developments around social interventions, but little attention paid to wider economic and political influences on mental health. At a time of severe financial constraints on public services, mental health services must use their scant resources effectively and deliver outcomes that have significant impacts on the quality of service users' lives.

The challenges for mental health services in the United Kingdom are numerous and are of a long-standing nature. Services across the country are variable in quality and are often piecemeal and fragmented in nature and do not take a holistic view of the needs of service users. Multidisciplinary working is hampered by different professionals attempting to work together without a shared vision of the purpose of their services and without training that has reflective practice and promoting equality at its core. Government and professional bodies still do not engage in a cogent analysis of the covert but powerful political and economic forces that shape the mental health debate in the United Kingdom and thereby miss opportunities for sorely needed systemic and transformational change in services.

In this desultory context of service development, the dangers for marginalised groups and people vulnerable to institutional discrimination have become crystallised in statistics around compulsion, over-medication, use of forensic services and poor prevention in mental health and well-being. We have to start working in a different way in mental health services if we are going to address long-standing institutional racism in services and work positively and creatively with race and culture issues or indeed any form of inequality.

Multidisciplinary training is one step towards creating holistic mental health practice that promotes equality and establishes transcultural working as an ordinary part of good practice. We have much to learn from the past and Suman Fernando's historical analysis provides useful clues as to what the pitfalls are and how we can avoid them in the future. A central dichotomy that always arises in multidisciplinary mental health training is the juxtaposition of a holistic, social model approach to mental health with a 'narrow' medical approach. This theme recurs in Fernando's writing and informs his ideas about ways forward in formulating new approaches to service delivery. His discussion about the social context of mental health diagnosis has led to the development of a useful model in training materials that I have produced called 'Race Equality and Cultural Capability' (RECC). The model frames and structures discussion about the context for multidisciplinary working and has helped workers to find common ground in practice around 'diagnosis' and 'treatment' issues.

Fernando's writings have been inspirational because they have always been imbued with a sense of common humanity and a passionate concern for people in mental distress. His writings help to remind us that systems in mental health services are designed and operated by people, and although we may feel daunted by the complexity and scale of systems, individual mental health workers can and do make big differences to the lives of individual service users. We can fundamentally influence the way systems are operated to achieve meaningful outcomes for service users by shaping the behaviours of front-line staff and, crucially, to design systems that are fit for purpose to achieve those outcomes by establishing feedback loops for service development based on evidence from the interface between workers, service users, their families and communities. A huge amount of money is spent on bricks and mortar services and resources that may look good superficially but do not meaningfully achieve improvements in the quality of life of service users. The incalculable potential of service users, their families and communities remains untapped as empowerment, participation and social capital are seen as peripheral issues in professional training and development.

In this chapter, I will discuss some contextual issues around RECC training by highlighting the importance of social context for practice, taking diagnosis as an example, and then present some challenges from the current debate about racism and discrimination. Key themes and concepts in RECC training and some useful models for transcultural work will be outlined. Finally, the possible elements and principles of a future holistic approach to equality will be explored.

The social context of diagnosis

According to Fernando (2010), psychiatric diagnosis in a medical model of mental health is based on an assessment of 'what are perceived as symptoms and signs ... which are themselves evaluations – essentially comparisons of the patient's feelings, behaviours and beliefs set against values implicit in the discipline of psychiatry' (p. 32). The purpose of diagnosis being to help the practitioner determine the prescribed treatment, 'for it is assumed, in a medical model, that treatment is geared to diagnosis' (p. 32). The rise of the bio-medical approach to psychiatry has been reinforced by commercial interests in psychopharmacology and has in turn strengthened the need for clear diagnosis as specific drugs are marketed as being suitable for specific 'mental illnesses'. Fernando warns of the dangers of the 'reification' of diagnosis, 'promoting the idea of diagnosis as *fact*, rather than what it actually is – a social construction for describing human problems that may or may not be useful' (p. 32).

The bio-medical model of psychiatry is based on identifying signs of illness using 'objective data' to define a patient's psychopathology or 'abnormality of psyche' associated with a particular 'illness' and, moreover, the cause of this illness is biological in nature. Fernando (2010) points out that the judgements underpinning this process of diagnosis are based on 'the assumed correctness of values, philosophies of life and beliefs about the human condition that inform what is assumed to be normal, namely, western ideas of mind' (p. 32). Therefore, diagnosis is a value-driven process based on judgements about what is 'normal' or 'abnormal' and as such is essentially *culturally defined*.

Fernando concludes that

> First, psychiatry is ethnocentric and carries in it ideologies of western culture including racism; second, the practice of psychiatry, including its ways of diagnosing, is influenced by the social ethos and the political system in which it exists and works.
>
> (2010, p. 35)

In RECC we have extensively used Fernando's model of the 'social context of diagnosis' to introduce front-line workers to a broader social model of mental health rather than a narrow medical approach that increases the risk of discrimination and stigma in service delivery. In this model Fernando highlights the 'micro' and 'macro' forces that influence the process of diagnosis, rendering it essentially a non-scientific process.

The issues surrounding the personal values of practitioners are part of the 'micro' forces operating in the diagnostic process. Practitioners will be strongly influenced by their sense of 'what feels natural' to them or what feels like 'common sense' when faced with making judgements about social situations. Underlying these natural preferences are the practitioner's own cultural assumptions gained from a variety of sources, including their ethnic background and the cultural 'norms' of the society in which she or he operates. Racial stereotypes are liable to influence a society's cultural norms and so perceptions of 'racialised' people tend to be negative in Western societies.

The current political agenda will also have a big impact on the diagnostic process as part of the 'macro' forces in operation. For example, if there is a public panic about a specific group of people, such as those with a diagnostic label of 'personality disorder', there will be pressure on authorities to 'do something' about that group and the perceived threat 'they' present to the public. This group effectively constitutes an 'out-group' in society. The impact on diagnosis may then be to have a greater focus on 'dangerousness' and risk or the issue of 'treatability', all leading to the person's best interests being sidelined. Traditional views of mental distress will also influence the purpose, process and outcomes of diagnosis as it is essentially a value-based process.

Models such as this can help us understand and analyse the current debates about the direction of mental health service development in the United Kingdom in relation to race and culture issues and how this development has set a context for training in this area.

The context of RECC training

The pattern of change in relation to race and culture issues in mental health in the United Kingdom has been largely a reactive response to a litany of crises, moral panics and indefensibly poor examples of practice highlighted by research and statistical analysis. It has often been driven by tragic deaths of young black people as victims of racist violence or as a result of poor treatment within psychiatric and prison services. We have had a cycle of denial about institutional racism, grudging acknowledgement followed by a short-term and politically expedient reaction, leaving racialised groups feeling sceptical about any new initiative and a credibility gap that inexorably grows between Black and Minority Ethnic (BME) communities and mental health services. We are now in a situation where that gap has become hard to bridge, and intermittently throwing a little more government money at the problem does not address the underlying systemic and service culture problems created by institutional racism.

Other important 'macro' factors that have became more prominent under the current coalition government has been the concept of the 'Big Society', wherein people and local communities do more for themselves and become more 'self-sufficient', encouraged by a reduction in central government 'interference'. This has become the main way of sweetening the bitter pill of reduced finances for local authority services, leaving less powerful racialised groups trying to compete for shrinking resources with stronger voluntary sector and community organisations that have not seriously considered their needs in the past.

Fernando maintains that

> the discourse has again shifted away from 'race' (and the need to address racism) to 'diversity' ... while in society at large the focus is on promoting 'social cohesion' rather than counteracting discrimination – and the pressure is on BME communities to be good (*sic*) citizens.
> (Cantle, 2005, cited in Fernando and Keating, 2009, p. 3)

The primary responsibility for this change is covertly and powerfully shifted onto BME communities who are seen as 'alien' and a threat to social cohesion if they do not accommodate this change.

The Equality Act (2010) is likely to have a significant impact on the debate around race and culture in the coming years. This act introduces the concept of 'multiple discrimination' for the first time, which is potentially a step forward, along with changes in the way that Impact Assessments are done to evaluate how policies and procedures affect BME and other groups vulnerable to oppression. It introduces a 'Single Equality' approach but effectively reduces the nature and requirements for monitoring arising from Equality Impact Assessments, relying more on self-reporting and reducing the depth of equality data collected.

The effects of these developments on the debate on race and culture in mental health is likely to be profound but hard to predict, although there are already doubts about the disproportionate effects that cuts will have on targeted services for BME groups, the deepening of inequalities in service systems and increased danger of public authorities, service commissioners and providers manipulating the figures even more to comply with the law and government guidelines in a tokenistic way.

The culture of mental health services does not encompass promoting race equality as an ordinary part of mental health practice as yet and these issues are often considered to be doing something 'special' or 'different' by practitioners. Individual local authorities now have to make difficult decisions about where and how to cut services in the region of 25% initially, with more cuts likely in the years ahead. Many have resorted to altering the criteria for service eligibility in terms of social care and housing with health authorities doing the same in relation to health care. In a context of institutional racism, changes to procedures and systems that already have in-built biases makes it likely that racialised groups and communities will be most severely affected and denied further help at a time of economic hardship.

Delivering Race Equality

Fernando contends that in many ways *Delivering Race Equality* (DRE; Department of Health, 2005), a five-year national strategy to improve mental health services for BME people, was a missed opportunity. Instead of building on a more radical agenda set by *Inside Outside* (NIMHE, 2003), which called for changing statutory services to be more in line with what BME communities wanted, DRE focused on gathering yet more information about what people want and 'community engagement' rather than 'community development', as advocated by *Inside Outside* (Fernando, 2009a, p. 54). The strategy created was not informed by BME community consultation or any real participation by service users and their families. Attempts were made to rescue a fragmented strategy with more specific outcomes to concretise the DRE vision and aid monitoring of impacts and the setting up of focused implementation sites to try out changes in statutory services. Several Community Engagement projects were also set up and did foster a degree of local BME service user participation, but many of the projects did not result in any lasting practical changes in services. During the time of DRE, from 2005 to 2009, there was also a shift in the debate about BME mental health issues away from tackling institutional racism and differential treatment in services to a focus on the lack of 'engagement' with BME communities. The result was a superficial attempt to change the message about services without any substantive improvement in services, an approach that was doomed to failure with a further loss of credibility of mental health services within BME communities. Moreover, it could be argued that there were some backward steps taken with a denial of institutional racism in services altogether and the 'blaming' of communities as being 'hard to reach' and unreasonably distrustful of services.

'Race' and cultural capability

Fernando argues that 'race' is essentially a social concept with no creditable scientific merit, but it still profoundly influences the way that social, political and economic power is structured in society (Fernando, 2002, 2009a).

In RECC we define 'race' as a categorisation of people defined by colour of skin and physical appearance, which has developed from a falsely scientific way of thinking about human beings as arising from different 'species'. It has now become a social concept with negligible importance attached to its biological and/or scientific connotations, but it is influential in community relationships and the way we organise our institutions and power structures within society.

In RECC, we focused on cultural capability and not just competence. We perceive the difference as being that competence is related to knowledge, skills and to some extent values involved in performing tasks associated with a specific work role. Competence frameworks are usually constructed through a functional analysis of job roles, which are then broken down into work tasks with the requisite knowledge and skills. Capability is a broader and more complex concept that relates not just to present performance in a work role but also takes into account future performance through consideration of values, knowledge, skills, problem-solving ability, application of skills in practice and the ability to learn from experience. It implies the need for a flexible and responsive workforce with staff able to use their judgement more in their work, think and act creatively and reflect on their practice to achieve continuous improvement. This approach implies that cultural capability should not result in culture being reduced to a collection of superficial bits of knowledge about particular cultures or mere 'respect' for cultural differences, but requires mental health workers to consider culture in *every* interaction with *all* service users and view culture as a complex interaction between individuals and their cultural and social contexts that shape and influence them but do not define their unique characteristics and personalities.

Models of culture

The concept of culture underpinning the approach in RECC views culture as a dynamic and layered concept involving core beliefs, assumptions, values, behaviours and decisions and the more observable aspects of culture such as appearance, food, clothing, architecture and art – the tangible artefacts or products of culture. Most importantly, the 'iceberg' or layered model of culture emphasises the interaction between these layers of culture to help people understand the nature of cultural change and the dynamism present in every culture – the model is informed by the ideas of Suman Fernando as well as the work of Chris Argyris (1990) and Trompenaars and Hampden-Turner (1997).

Models of culture such as these are essential to help mental health practitioners understand why they make the decisions they do in everyday practice and reflect upon how their values and beliefs have shaped their decisions as well as recognising and respecting the values and decisions of service users who may have different cultural values and social contexts.

The 'iceberg' model in RECC represents culture as a series of layers and the deepest level of any culture consists of its 'unwritten rules' or core beliefs and assumptions. These core beliefs and assumptions are like a social 'glue' that holds a cultural group together and enables people in the group to see the world in similar ways as well as communicate more easily as they share many hidden cultural meanings that usually remain unspoken. Core beliefs and assumptions develop over a long period of time and are shaped by responses to familiar problems that continually have to be solved by a cultural group in order to survive in its physical, social and economic environment. The solutions for survival become more and more familiar to the extent that they become unspoken ways of relating to the environment. They eventually become embedded in the culture's traditions, spiritual beliefs, rituals and symbols.

The 'rainbow' model of cultural differences in RECC is a further development of the 'iceberg' model of culture. It helps front-line staff to avoid cultural stereotyping by presenting a set of core assumptions, beliefs and values that are common to all cultures, where any individual in a culture can take a position on a spectrum of values under each of seven key dimensions of cultural difference. While every culture will have values and norms held by a majority, there is always going to be a *range* of values held by people within that culture. To assume that people have a specific set of values because they come from a particular culture is dangerous and denies the person their uniqueness and individuality. The model of cultural difference proposed in RECC has been designed to avoid such cultural stereotyping by identifying individual and group cultural identities as fluid concepts and not as fixed sets of attributes. The model provides a useful framework to look at cultural differences across seven key dimensions that are important in every culture, and allows for an infinite number of variations of culture within this framework. The model is based on the premise that all cultures have elements within them of difference and similarity and these elements are functional or useful for the particular culture concerned. Thus it is meaningless to compare cultures with a view to judging which ones are 'better' in social or ethical terms. There are 'good' and 'bad' things in every culture and inclusive cultures are likely to take the best from all the cultures they incorporate.

The cultural 'rainbow' in RECC has been adapted from the work of Trompenaars and Hampden-Turner (1997). The 'seven dimensions' of culture – relating to how people express feelings, approach rules, view individuality, solve problems, perceive social status, relate to their environment, experience the passing of time – are represented by the seven colours of the rainbow. These dimensions represent fundamental aspects of living that are common to all cultures and thus offer a useful framework for looking at cultural differences in a more structured way. In reality culture is a lot more complex than it is represented in the rainbow model. There are an infinite number of 'colours' and 'tones' created in any culture as the process of mixing and merging of cultures has been going on since human beings began living together in larger social groups.

In his books, Fernando highlights several crucial cultural variations in understanding mental health and responding to distress. His use of the term 'liberation' is a direct challenge to the medical model of mental health and challenges services to 'liberate' people from mental distress working through interactive alliances between people and with their living environments rather than interventions or therapies that are objectified and separate from the people they are applied to. The 'rainbow' model in RECC helps to formulate a more inclusive culture that incorporates the 'best' of either end of the spectrum in each dimension of cultural difference, seeking to identify the strengths of each position and helping people to reflect upon and challenge the dysfunctional aspects of a person's or group's cultural context. This may require the person or group to gradually change assumptions and beliefs, values and behaviours or to change environmental factors shaping their cultural context.

A holistic approach to equality

The introduction of new legislation in the form of the Equality Act (2010) in the United Kingdom has highlighted a recent shift in thinking about the experience of discrimination as being a set of unique experiences for individuals rather than more homogeneous patterns of experiences based on membership of specific categories of people that are seen as being vulnerable to discrimination. The 'Single Equality' approach engendered by the new act covers nine 'protected characteristics', which cannot be used as a reason to treat people differentially. The protected characteristics in the act are age, disability, gender assignment, marriage and civil partnership, pregnancy and maternity, race, religion or belief, sex and sexual orientation.

The Equality Act (2010) sets out the different ways in which it is unlawful to treat someone, such as direct and indirect discrimination, harassment, victimisation and failing to make a 'reasonable adjustment' for a disabled person. There is currently a lot of debate about how effective this act will be in eradicating unfair discrimination and promoting equality. Fears such as loss of focus on specific forms of inequality, less clear Equality Impact Assessments, ineffectual data collection and monitoring and ineffective action plans are all problematic issues that are yet to be resolved.

Consideration of people's unique characteristics is valid as it reflects the complexities of people's lives in a dynamic and rapidly changing society. The recognition of 'multiple discrimination' in the act also reflects the multiple social identities that individuals hold at any point in time. A more comprehensive and holistic approach to equality itself can help service providers to deal with the complexity of people's lives and their experiences of oppression. Moreover, there are compelling arguments for a coherent ethical stance in tackling discrimination and promoting equality across all groups that are vulnerable to oppression. For example, it is not ethically defensible for someone to be anti-racist but then espouse sexist or homophobic views and for this to be tacitly accepted by others opposed to racism.

Identity is subject to a variety of sources of influences and sources and it must be recognised that individuals can have 'multiple identities' given different social contexts. Fernando identifies these sources of influences affecting identity viewing them under three main headings of community and family, individual and personal choice and contextual pressures in society. In relation to racial, cultural and ethnic identity, he lists community sources as relationships, religion, 'racial' background, historical background and allegiance to profession, workplace or family. Individual sources relate to religious and spiritual beliefs; sexuality; body-related issues such as illness, impairments, size or 'race'; loyalties to family, country and occupation; values and sense of belonging. Contextual influences are determined by forces in society at large such as racism; categorization by authorities such as class and disability; occupational allegiance and place of residence or birth (Fernando, 2010, p. 17).

Identity would be a key element in any new holistic model of equality, the 'social contexts' mentioned by Fernando would also have to be analysed and taken into account. All human societies inherit a legacy from their past collective experiences and an inherent part of this legacy would have been shaped by oppressive ideologies and actions. Social processes such as stigmatisation, labelling and stereotyping of specific groups would become embedded within a culture's core beliefs and assumptions and create an oppressive social context for the formation of individual identities.

For example, in relation to stigma, Fernando (2010) comments 'Stigma denotes a marker – visible or implied – that discredits a person or group of people (Goffman, 1968). But the marker itself carries a baggage of its own, in terms of feelings, attitudes and historical happenings' (p. 37). Stigma will be created and manifested in different ways within different cultures and with varying consequences for the individuals or groups concerned. For example, in Western societies psychiatric stigma may be associated with people who are not productive, a burden on society, unpredictable and dangerous or even feigning illness. Whereas in some societies such as Sri Lanka where 'mental illness' is seen as being caused by 'spirit possession', and psychiatric stigma is almost absent (Fernando, 2010, p. 39).

Social context is also influenced by institutional discrimination, which is transmitted through systems and structures in society that are inherently biased in the way they impact on the lives of specific groups of people. The design of discriminatory systems and structures reflect stereotypical ways of thinking about people who are vulnerable to oppression and the negative values assigned to them by dominant groups in society. Analysis of the mechanisms that deliver institutional discrimination and the community and societal processes involved would also need to be incorporated into any holistic model of equality. The resulting *life experiences* of people would have a significant effect upon the person's identity, their sense of self-worth and their self-confidence.

As societies and cultures become more fluid and complex, the creation of multiple identities becomes more commonplace. If we are to build an ethically coherent value base that binds all forms of equality together, we must formulate a new theoretical model of holistic equality that helps service providers to analyse the social contexts of people's lives and respond appropriately to their mental health needs. It is possible to identify common social processes and mechanisms involved in institutional discrimination and in the promotion of equality without losing sight of the different causations and consequences for the various groups who are vulnerable to oppression. It is useful to focus on *identity, legacy and life experiences* in building an understanding of a person's and group's unique experience of oppression and formulate ways of empowering people and eradicating discrimination in society.

Conclusion

An overarching set of principles for training about holistic equality could be derived from the writings of Suman Fernando and the principles of RECC. It is clear that issues of oppression and discrimination cannot be fully addressed merely by focusing on differences or diversity; themes such as power and systemic and structural inequalities must also be considered. When considering cultural diversity it is crucial to have an accurate understanding of the complexity of culture that does not lead to stereotyping.

Equality should be seen as an ordinary part of good practice and a 'whole systems' approach should be adopted in all equality strategies. Participation is a key issue in any equality initiative and service users, their families and communities must have an influence on decision making and use of resources. Clear communication and open acknowledgement of institutional discrimination will lead to greater credibility and trust in services and professionals. The professionals involved in service delivery need to be aware of their own cultural assumptions and values, including acknowledging prejudices and stereotypes that influence everyone in society. Finally, regardless of the improvements in scientific techniques and treatments we must never forget that values will always influence all decisions we make in mental health services.

The way forward for mental health services must include greater service user participation in the design and delivery of services and the training of staff at the front line. An important feature of RECC was its delivery through equal training partnerships between BME service users, carers and professional staff. This approach modelled empowerment and partnership working and demonstrated to staff how their work can become more creative, inspiring and effective through greater service user and family participation.

References

Argyris, C. (1990). *Overcoming organizational defenses.* Upper Saddle River, NJ: Prentice Hall.

Cantle, T. (2005). *Community cohesion: A new framework for race and diversity*. Basingstoke: Palgrave Macmillan.
Department of Health. (2005). *Delivering race equality in mental health care: An action plan for reform inside and outside services and the government's response to the death of David Bennett*. London: Department of Health.
Fernando, S. (2002). *Mental health, race and culture* (2nd ed.). Basingstoke: Palgrave.
Fernando, S. (2009a). Inequalities and the politics of 'race' in mental health. In S. Fernando and F. Keating (Eds.), *Mental health in a multi-ethnic society: A multidisciplinary handbook*. London: Routledge.
Fernando, S. (2009b). Meaning and realities. In S. Fernando and F. Keating (Eds.), *Mental health in a multi-ethnic society: A multidisciplinary handbook*. London: Routledge.
Fernando, S. (2010). *Mental health, race and culture* (3rd ed.). Basingstoke: Palgrave Macmillan.
Fernando, S. and Keating, F. (2009). Introduction. In S. Fernando and F. Keating (Eds.), *Mental health in a multi-ethnic society: A multidisciplinary handbook*. London: Routledge.
Goffman, E. (1968). *Stigma: Notes on the management of spoiled identity*. Harmondsworth: Penguin.
Great Britain. (2010). *Equality Act 2010: Elizabeth II. Chapter 15*. London: Stationery Office.
NIMHE (National Institute for Mental Health in England). (2003). *Inside outside: Improving mental health services for black and minority ethnic communities in England*. London: Department of Health.
Trompenaars, F. and Hampden-Turner, C. (1997). *Riding the waves of culture: Understanding cultural diversity in business*. Boston, MA: Nicholas Brealey Publishing.

12 Race and cultural diversity

The training of psychologists and psychiatrists

Rachel Tribe

Introduction

How issues of cultural diversity are dealt with, or not, in training psychiatrists, psychologists and mental health professionals is an important issue. This is noted in policy documents produced by the Royal College of Psychiatrists (2013) and the British Psychological Society (2013). It will determine to some degree if the psychiatric or psychological services these professionals offer, when qualified, are appropriate and accessible to all (James and Prilleltensky, 2002; Marsella, 2011; Newland et al., 2014). Making mental health professionals aware of the importance of these issues during training, and of the possible limitations of Western psychological theories sometimes generalised unthinkingly to other contexts, can only widen the applicability and relevance of psychological and psychiatric knowledge to the benefit of service users nationally and internationally (Bhugra and Gupta, 2011; Fernando, 2010; Lane and Tribe, 2010). Although many mental health professionals may state a desire to encourage criticality and to consider the limits of knowledge, this is not always easy in the face of long-established traditions, organising principles and models of working, let alone established or vested interests and power structures (Fernando, 2010; Howitt and Owusu-Bempah, 1994; Patel et al., 2000; Richards, 1997). Change of any sort is often difficult for an array of reasons (see Kuhn, 1962), as the discipline of organisational development shows (Handy, 1976).

Training of psychiatrists/psychologists in relation to issues of culture and race

The need for all clinicians to be fully cognisant of issues relating to race, culture and diversity within mental health and to use these in their daily clinical practice is a core skill and requirement. The issue of diversity and difference is one that affects all of us, every day of our lives and in many ways (Lane and Tribe, 2010). Diversity that is visible and invisible needs to be actively considered, not only in the clinical encounter but also in how these may impact upon the individual, societal constructs of diversity in all its forms and in how service provision is set up (Shankar, 2013). Every individual is unique and carries within him/

Race and cultural diversity 135

herself a personal culture and belief system. While there may be similarities across culture and/or religion, culture is multi-layered, individual, nuanced, complex and to some degree fluid (Tribe, 2011). Culture is not a monolithic or unitary entity that is dictated by one's place of birth, although place of birth and subsequent country of residence may play a role, as may ethnicity, race and religious or spiritual beliefs (Fernando, 2010; Lago, 2011). Fernando (2006) writes that cultures are never static, arguing that "They are dynamic living systems continually changing. So a culturally diverse society may (for convenience and shorthand) recognise 'cultural groups', but the reality is that the society as a whole is culturally hybrid or mixed" (p. 1). For example, culture changes over time as new ideas, values, technologies and influences develop, and as people have more influences upon them (Senior and Fleming, 2006). These changes may be further mediated by familial beliefs, individual experiences throughout our lives, and our interpretation of these.

The International Organisation for Migration (IOM) (2012) states that 1 in every 33 people in the world is classified as a migrant. The term "migrant" is itself highly politicised, as are some associated terms and definitions that may be used differently and on occasions rather loosely. The Migration Observatory at Oxford University states that, in 2011, 12.3% of the UK population consisted of residents who were born in other countries (up from 7.3% in 1993), with London hosting 2.6 million people who were born in other countries. Worldwide there are over 215 million international migrants (World Bank, 2011). Issues of diversity, race and culture are important regardless of place of birth, as racism and bad practice do not differentiate between recently arrived migrants and long-established British Black and Asian Minority Ethnic (BAME) individuals and communities, but these figures may provide some contextual information. Thus all clinicians need to be trained to think about how issues of diversity, race and culture are present in their work if they are to be effective practitioners who can work with the entire population. The best place for this to start is as a central part of their qualification training. The seminal work of Suman Fernando in bringing the specific issues of race, culture and accessible and appropriate services to the fore within mental health is to be commended, and the influence of his work will be considered throughout this chapter in relation to his practice and work.

All professional bodies operating within mental health state that they support equality of access and require competencies in working effectively across cultures. The Royal College of Psychiatrists has a Race Equality action plan (2004), which states the importance of

> Ensuring that psychiatric training equips psychiatrists to be culturally sensitive and culturally competent in their therapies ... ensuring equal access to services for all black and ethnic minority communities, continuing dialogue with all relevant user groups, including black user groups ... promoting racial equality.
>
> (p. 3)

The British Psychological Society (BPS), in their plan for equality and diversity (2008) (currently under review), states, "Our experience as psychologists who teach, research or practise shows that we must take account of factors such as people's ethnicity, gender and age" (BPS, 2008, p. 2). The BPS Division of Clinical Psychology's Race & Culture Faculty, one of whose aims is "To ensure that services are relevant and accessible to people from [BME] communities", has as its mission statement "Psychologists working to advance the development of inclusive and meaningful knowledge and practice with and for ethnically diverse communities" (BPS, n.d.). The importance of race and culture being foregrounded in training and service provision is therefore recognised at least in theory by professional bodies, even if the reality or experiences of this are sometimes less evident on the ground and in service provision in various areas (Fernando, 2010; Newland et al., 2014).

This chapter will next look at how some of the ideas developed in Western psychology and psychiatry may have limited utility when used by clinicians working in multi-ethnic societies or applied to varied cultural contexts as they fail to account for cultural and racial diversity adequately (Kleinman, 1988; Marsella, 2011; Patel et al., 2000; Tribe, 2007). The disciplines of psychology and psychiatry have often failed to consider the ethno-centricism of their theories, many of which were developed from research conducted in the West, or if in other cultures, the concepts and psychometrics used were those developed and located in Western psychiatry and psychology with little regard to diverse cultures and contexts (Fernando, 2010; Summerfield, 2012; Tribe, 2007). Marsella (2011) claims that

> Under the illusion of "good intentions" dominant populations in charge of mental health services see their goal as preparing the ethno-cultural patient to accept, adopt and live according to the dominant group's standards of normality and expectation … must be reconsidered since they seek to homogenize diversity and in doing so, destroy critical ethnic identity resources. Emphasis upon using dominant culture norms and expectations can distort, deny, hide or contribute to patient problems, and interfere with the service needs of minority and marginalized groups.
>
> (Section 12)

Usage of mental health services

Evidence of this may be found in the fact that the use of mental health services by people from BAME communities is reported to be less than the rest of the population (Bhugra and Gupta, 2011), which is a grave cause for concern. The reasons given for this discrepancy are many and have included racism, stigma, poor accessibility, attempts to standardise patients to fit a preconceived view based on Western "norms", lack of appropriateness, a failure to understand cultural diversity, and language differences (Fernando, 2010; Mental Health Foundation, 2012). Diverse explanatory health beliefs and idioms of distress also require consideration, if mental health services are going to be appropriate and accessible to everyone (Tribe, 2005). Bhui *et al.* (2003) in a systematic review found that black patients had more complex pathways to specialist care, and that there were a series of issues that require attention. Politics and media influences may also play a role, as will any prevailing current or historic discourses about mental health, as well as issues of culture and race. It was argued (Addley, Topkin, Donolis and Lewis, 2011) that some of the media coverage of the UK riots in 2010 took a particular perspective on race, and was presented in such a way as to give the impression that the rioters were mostly black, which was not the case.

The issues of culture, race and mental health or well-being have a developing literature. Suman Fernando has been a leading writer and theorist in this area. In addition to this he has been an erudite and critical voice of the global mental health movement, whom he accuses of using an inappropriate and contested Western framework that fails to account for local knowledge and perspectives, in addition to trying to medicalise distress around the world and to colonise other knowledge bases (Fernando, 2013).

Current training issues

Taking a holistic approach that considers the socio-cultural and historical context from which Western psychological theory emanates, and in which it is still embedded, is sometimes strangely absent from psychiatric and psychological training. Several theorists have claimed that psychological theory is Eurocentric (see Howitt and Owusu-Bempah, 1994; Richards, 1997), while others have claimed it can be racist (Newland *et al.*, 2014). Prilleltensky and Nelson (2002), among many other theorists, have argued for mental health professionals to consider the context and experience of service users. The recovery agenda has assisted with this and the importance of the context and experiences that frame and define an individual's life are being recognised by some mental health professionals and training programmes. The notion of globalisation in the literature and the media has been discussed, although this often means Western notions being dominant over others (Sacks, 2003). Also, mental health practitioners are likely to be influenced by their professional culture, thus adding another variable into how they conceptualise psychological distress and ways of addressing it. Thus culture and related conceptions of mental health may be multifaceted and complex.

That some service users have been subject to racism is worryingly absent from much of the literature (Newland *et al.*, 2014). The faculty of Race & Culture of the British Psychological Society were concerned about service provision for members of BAME communities and about the teaching on issues of race and culture in professional training for psychologists, and produced a book entitled *Clinical Psychology: "Race" and Culture – A Training Manual* (Patel *et al.*, 2000). A new edition is currently under discussion. The Royal College of Psychiatry's transcultural psychiatry special interest group has also undertaken a range of work and produced resources.

The connection between culture and psychological knowledge

Considering diversity and culture in relation to mental health and well-being has particular resonance as it will affect our worldview and influence our perceptions and views of good mental health and ways of dealing with difficulties (Bhugra and Gupta, 2011; Bhui and Black, 2011). For example, notions of individualism or collectivism, family values, views of the self and issues of heritage all need to be considered by clinicians and commissioners of mental health services (Lago, 2011). Also, race, culture and ethnicity should not be uncritically conflated. Self-definition is the most appropriate. People from a single ethnic group or country may have very different cultures, and the terms can be used in over-simplified ways or based on outdated and inaccurate stereotypes. For example, whereas ethnicity has often been taken as signifying an allegiance to the "culture of origin or heritage", in reality it can be highly individual, entailing issues of choice that may also have been mediated by other variables. In addition, it has sometimes been used in a pejorative way to define difference, in that ethnicity is seen as a "difference", assuming that "the other" is the norm (Fernando, 1991).

Critique of Western psychological theory

Western psychological and cultural theory contains a number of assumptions, which include an acceptance of Cartesian dualism (Foster, 1996; Paechter, 2004), which sees body and mind as separate and which leads to the division or specialisms of mental and physical health rather than an integration of the two as seen in many countries (Tribe, 2007; Watters, 2001). Psychologists and psychiatrists trained in the West may pay little attention to service users who present with physical manifestations of their distress, other than interpreting it as a form of somatisation and dealing with it accordingly. Krause (1994) favours a more nuanced consideration of this, and argues that existential, physical, psychological and social references all make up cultural understandings of illness and body–mind divisions. Maclachlan (2006) has written of the role of illness in conveying personal or social distress, while Fernando (2010) has repeatedly noted the over-medicalisation and social construction of distress or mental illness. He writes, "Complex human problems (dealt with in other cultural settings as issues of philosophy, spirituality, ethics and so on) were constructed in western culture as medical illnesses, and then elaborated through observations from the basic sciences etc." (Fernando, 2006, p. 1).

Perhaps of most importance is remembering that mental health should not be reified, and that there will be elements of cultural and social construction contained within any definition (Fernando, 2010; Kleinman and Kleinman, 1991). For example, psychological theories developed in the West tend to take the individual as the unit of analysis, emphasising individuality rather than collectivity. The transfer of Western psychological ideas uncritically and their generalisation to the wider world can unthinkingly undermine the rich traditions and cultural heritage of low- and middle-income countries.

The uncritical application of Western psychological theory can be further complicated by income and power differentials, when low- and middle-income countries are often offered Western psychiatric/psychological expertise or help, particularly following a natural or man-made disaster. People may wish to accept this help given the tragedy of the disaster or traumatic event that has befallen their country or region, but the content of this help, which they may on occasion feel powerless to question, may be entirely inappropriate (Ganesan, 2011). For example, after the South Asian tsunami, many people took it upon themselves to jet into the affected countries to "help", without attempting to work within the community or governmental structures that had been set up, thereby inadvertently undermining them rather than working in partnership and being accountable to local agencies and people (Tsunami Evaluation Coalition, 2006). These individuals sometimes ignored both the cultural frameworks and organisational systems for coordination that were in place, as well as uncritically bringing their own conceptual frameworks to people who had lived through a natural disaster. That is not to say that the help offered was not genuine, but that people or agencies offering it sometimes overlooked the limitations of their Western models or failed to recognise the local models and systems. This unthinking imposition of Western psychology and the assumptions that this is the best or only model to assist individuals and communities can be viewed as a form of neo-colonialism (Summerfield, 2012).

Differences in culture, language or religious or spiritual beliefs are often downplayed or ignored by those from high-income or powerful countries, and are often wrapped up in such comments as "being colour blind" or the assumptions that the models and ways of thinking, theory and practice are generalisable. This can be exacerbated by geo-politics, the Western media and the policies of some aid agencies, and may be detrimental and undermining to individuals, families and communities. After the tsunami, the Tsunami Evaluation Coalition (2006) stated that the current system

> produces an uneven and inequitable flow of funds for emergencies that encourages neither investment in capacity nor responses that are proportionate to need [and] [d]espite some donors' commitment to the principles of Good Humanitarian Donorship (GHD), donors often took funding decisions based on political calculation and media pressure.

There are a range of good practice guidelines and initiatives available for humanitarian agencies working in disasters in cultures very different from their own (IASC, 2007; NATO, 2008), although there are apparently inadequate sanctions for agencies or individuals that fail to adhere to these protocols (Cosgrave, 2007).

Some of the ideas developed in Western psychology and psychiatry may or may not be relevant and helpful but should be considered in conjunction with local practice and traditions (for a discussion of health pluralism, see Tribe, 2007). On occasions lip service is paid to culture, but it is seldom viewed as a central organising concept in any partnership. The notion of health pluralism, offering a diverse range of explanatory health beliefs, idioms of distress, varieties of coping strategies or help-seeking behaviours, may be most appropriate. Most cultures embody this multiplicity, though some perspectives may be viewed or valued as more powerful or dominant by different groups. There may be a varied range of designated healers or helpers (see, e.g., Somasundaram and Sivayokan, 2000; Fernando and Weerackody, (2011; Lawrence, 1997). Working in partnership with these systems and viewing them as important resources rather than a "necessary nuisance" or "add-ons" to a Western way of working is essential. This may well be more appropriate in assisting individuals and communities than Western models of individual trauma diagnosis and therapy. These systems often have long histories and are the preferred and familiar option for many people. They can be undermined by an uncritical reliance on Western methods and assumptions about shared explanatory health beliefs and idioms of distress, from which they may differ markedly. In addition, people identified as healers are not always those to whom this role would be ascribed in a Western context (Lawrence, 1997; Sax, Quack and Weinhold, 2010). Priests and indigenous healers, local rituals and traditions have an important role in assisting people to deal with psychological distress in most countries in the world, though the emphasis on this may vary.

Collaboration between service users and service providers

Research and best practice guidelines have begun to emerge to encourage service providers to develop services in collaboration and engagement with service users in the United Kingdom (Royal College of Psychiatrists, 2013), as well as the communities they serve (NICE, 2008). The National Institute for Health and Clinical Excellence (NICE) guideline on *Community Engagement to Improve Health* (2008) details the importance of community engagement and development. The community guidance is to be reviewed in 2014 following NIHR-funded research and the impact of community engagement approaches used in the New Deal for Communities. It is hoped that these guidelines might start to lead to more appropriate and accessible services, and to an improved sense of inclusivity and ownership, although, as stated earlier, guidelines and policy documents do not always lead to changes in practice. Real community engagement offers the opportunity to those commissioning services and service providers to develop in a dynamic way based on need, and in line with any changes in the population as well as the requirements of the complete community which will include a range of cultures and races.

Conclusion

We need to remain vigilant and reflective to ensure that issues of diversity, race and culture are foregrounded in our training institutions and in clinical practice if we are to ensure that mental health services are accessible and appropriate to the entire population in the future. There are a range of policy documents written by the major professional bodies (RCP and BPS) and at the national level (NICE guidelines) that stress the need to consider issues of diversity, race and culture and to listen to service users from BAME communities, but unfortunately trainees' experiences, clinical practice, pathways to care and service usage does not always reflect the requirements of these documents. The Western ethnocentricism of much of psychology and psychiatric theory is often taught uncritically, which can mean that the status quo remains and changes are not implemented that stress the importance of race, culture and diversity despite the work of Suman Fernando and others. The innovative work of Suman Fernando in raising these issues throughout his career in the United Kingdom and around the world is impressive. He has consistently raised these issues through his publications and talks to a wide range of audiences. He has also been an example of a consistent and dedicated academic and clinician writing about the importance of considering and valuing the rich sources of support and meaning in relation to well-being and health found in most cultures and how conventional cultural wisdom can be undermined by an insistence on applying Western ideas uncritically. Clearly, the work of Suman Fernando in the United Kingdom, Sri Lanka and around the world shows the enormous scope and influence of his work on both theory and practice within a range of domains within mental health. The impact of his most recent work may also be yet to be felt.

References

Addley, E., Topkin, M., Donolis, J. and Lewis, H. (2011, 10 August). UK riots: "Those who seek to racialise this problem are taking us backwards". *Guardian*. Retrieved 29 December 2011 from www.guardian.co.uk/uk/2011/aug/10/uk-riots-racial-dimension.
Amnesty International. (2008). Retrieved 29 December 2011 from www.amnesty.org.
Bhugra, D. and. Gupta, S. (Eds.). (2011). *Migration and mental health*. Cambridge: Cambridge University Press.
Bhui, K. and Black, T. (2011). Identity, idioms and inequalities: Providing psychotherapies for South Asian women. In D. Bhugra and S. Gupta (Eds.), *Migration and mental health*. Cambridge: Cambridge University Press.
Bhui, K., Stansfeld, S., Hull, S., Priebe, S., Mole, F. and Feder, G. (2003). Ethnic variations in pathways to and use of specialist mental health services in the UK: Systematic review. *British Journal of Psychiatry, 182*, 105–116.
BPS (British Psychological Society). (n.d.). Race and Culture Faculty: Aims of the Faculty. Retrieved from http://raceandculture.bps.org.uk.
Cosgrave, J. (2007). *Synthesis report: Expanded summary – Joint evaluation of the international response to the Indian Ocean tsunami*. London: Tsunami Evaluation Coalition.
Fernando, S. (1991). *Mental health, race and culture*. Basingstoke: Macmillan.
Fernando, S. (2003). *Cultural diversity, mental health and psychiatry: The struggle against racism*. Hove and New York: Brunner-Routledge.
Fernando, S. (2006). *Conference presentation Sri Lanka*. Retrieved 27 December 2012 from www.sumanfernando.com.
Fernando, S. (2010). *Mental health, race and culture* (3rd ed.). Basingstoke: Palgrave Macmillan.

Fernando, S. (2013). *Challenges for mental health development in low and middle-income countries.* Paper presented at McGill University.
Fernando, S. and Weerackody, C. (2011). *Aspects of mental health in Sri Lanka.* Colombo: People's Rural Development Association (PRDA). Retrieved from www.prdasrilanka.org.
Foster, J. (1996). *The immaterial Self: A defence of the Cartesian dualist conception of the mind.* London: Brunner-Routledge.
Ganesan, M. (2011). Building up mental health services from scratch: Experiences for East Sri Lanka. *Intervention, 9*(3), 359–363.
Handy, C. (1976). *Understanding organisations.* Oxford: Oxford University Press.
Howitt, D. and Owusu-Bempah, J. (1994). *The racism of psychology: Time for change.* Hemel Hempstead: Harvester Wheatsheaf.
Inter-Agency Standing Committee (IASC). (2007). *IASC guidelines on mental health and psychosocial support in emergency settings.* Geneva: IASC.
International Organisation for Migration. (n.d.). *Home.* Retrieved 11 December 2012 from www.iom.int.
James, S. and Prilleltensky, I. (2002). Cultural diversity and mental health: Towards integrative practice. *Clinical Psychology Review, 22*(8), 1133–1154.
Kleinman, A. (1988). *Rethinking psychiatry: From cultural category to personal experience.* New York: Free Press.
Kleinman, A. and Kleinman, J. (1991). Suffering and its professional transformation: Towards an ethnography of interpersonal experience. *Culture, Medicine and Psychiatry, 15*(3), 275–301.
Krause, I. B. (1989). Sinking heart: A Punjabi communication of distress. *Social Science in Medicine, 29*(4), 563–575.
Krause, I. B. (1994). Numbers and meaning: A dialogue in cross-cultural psychiatry. *Journal of the Royal Society in Medicine, 87,* 278–282.
Kuhn, T. (1962). *The structure of scientific revolutions.* Chicago: University of Chicago Press.
Lago, C. (Ed.). (2011). *The handbook of transcultural counselling and psychotherapy.* Milton Keynes: Open University Press.
Lane, P. and Tribe, R. (2010). Following NICE 2008: A practical guide for health professionals – Community engagement with local black and minority ethnic (BME) community groups. *Diversity, Health & Care, 7*(2), 105–114.
Lawrence, P. (1997). Violence, suffering Amman: The work of oracles in Sri Lanka Eastern War Zone. In V. Daas and A. Kleinman (Eds.), *Violence, agency and the self.* California: University of California Press.
Lerch, I. (1999). Letter from the Chair of the American Association of the Advancement of Scientific Freedom Committee responsible to Richard McCarty Executive Director of Scientific American Psychological association [reprinted Nov./Dec. 1999]. *Science Agenda, 12*(6), 2–3.
Maclachlan, M. (2006). *Culture and health.* Chichester: John Wiley.
Malan, R. (1990). *My traitor's heart.* New York: Grove Press.
Marsella, A. (2011). Twelve critical issues for mental health professionals working with ethno-culturally diverse populations. *Psychology international.* Retrieved 10 April 2012 from www.apa.org/international/pi/2011/10/critical-issues.aspx.
Mental Health Foundation. (2012). Retrieved 19 April 2012 from www.mentalhealth.org.uk.
National Institute for Health and Clinical Excellence (NICE). (2008). *Guideline no.*

PH9: Community engagement. Retrieved 29 December 2011 from www.nice.org.uk/ Search.do?keywords=community+engagement&newSearch=true&searchType=Guidance.
NATO. (2008). *Psychosocial care for people affected by disasters and major incidents: A model for designing, delivering and managing psychosocial services for people involved in major incidents, conflict, disasters and terrorism.* Retrieved from www.healthplanning.co.uk/nato.
Newland, J., Patel, N. and Senapati, M. (2014). Professional and ethical practice in a multi-ethnic society. In R. Tribe and M. J. Morrissey (Eds.), *Handbook of professional and ethical practice for psychologists, counsellors and psychotherapists.* London: Brunner-Routledge.
Owusu-Bempah, K. and Howitt, D. (2000). *Psychology beyond western perspectives.* Leicester: BPS books.
Patel, N., Bennett, E., Dennis, M., Dosanjh, N., Mahtani, A., Miller, A. and Nadirshaw, Z. (2000). *Clinical psychology: "Race" and culture – A training manual.* Leicester: BPS Books.
Paechter, C. (2004). "Mens Sana in Corpore Sano": Cartesian dualism and the marginalisation of sex education. *Discourse: Studies in the Cultural Politics of Education, 25*(3), 309–320.
Prilleltensky, I. and Nelson, G. (2002). *Doing psychology critically: making a difference in diverse settings.* New York: Palgrave Macmillan.
Richards, G. (1997). *"Race", racism and psychology: Towards a reflexive history.* London: Routledge.
Royal College of Psychiatrists. (2004). *Race equality plan.* Retrieved from www.rcpsych.ac.uk.
Royal College of Psychiatrists. (2013). Retrieved from www.rcpsych.ac.uk.
Sacks, J. (2003). *The dignity of difference.* New York: Continuum.
Sax, W., Quack, J. and Weinhold, J. (2010). *The problem of ritual efficacy.* Oxford: Oxford University.
Senior, B. and Fleming, J. (2006). *Organisational change.* Harlow: Pearson.
Shankar, R. (2013). Personal communication.
Somasundaram, D. (1998). *Scarred minds: The psychological impact of war on Sri Lankan Tamils.* Colombo: Vijitha Yapa.
Somasundaram, D. (2007). Collective trauma in northern Sri Lanka: A qualitative psychosocial-ecological study. *International Journal of Mental Health Systems, 1*(5).
Somasundaram, D. and Sivayokan, S. (2000). *Mental health in the Tamil community.* Jaffna: Transcultural Psychosocial Organization (sponsored by the World Health Organization).
Summerfield, D. (1999). A critique of seven assumptions behind psychological trauma programmes in war affected areas. *Social Science and Medicine, 48*, 1449–1462.
Summerfield, D. (2001). The invention of post-traumatic stress disorder and the social usefulness of a psychiatric category. *British Medical Journal, 322*, 95–98.
Summerfield, D. (2012). Afterword: Against "global mental health". *Transcultural Psychiatry, 49*(3), 1–12.
Tribe, R. (2002). Mental health and refugees. *Advances in Psychiatric Treatment, 8*(4), 240–248.
Tribe, R. (2005). The mental health needs of asylum seekers and refugees. *The Mental Health Review, 10*(4), 8–15.
Tribe, R. (2007). Health pluralism: A more appropriate alternative to western models of

therapy in the context of the conflict and natural disaster in Sri Lanka? *Journal of Refugee Studies, 20*(1), 21–36.

Tribe, R. (2011). Migrants and mental health: Working across culture and language. In D. Bhugra & S. Gupta (Eds.), *Migration and mental health.* Cambridge: Cambridge University Press.

Tsunami Evaluation Coalition. (2011). Retrieved 29 December 2011 from www.tsunami-evaluation.org.

UNHCR. (2009). Retrieved 29 December 2011 from www.unhcr.org/statistics.html.

US House of Representatives. (1999). July 12th Concurrent Resolution of the 106th Congress.

Watters, C. (2001). Emerging paradigms in the mental health care of refugees. *Social Science & Medicine, 52*(11), 1709–1718.

World Bank. (2011). Retrieved 12 April 2012 from www.worldbank.com.

World Health Organization (2001). *The world health report 2001: Mental health – New understanding, new hope.* Geneva: World Health Organization.

13 An anti-racist and anti-oppression framework in mental health practice

Martha Ocampo and Fritz Luther Pino

Introduction

Anti-racism is a social movement, a framework and a set of practices that seek to eliminate all areas and forms of racism – individual, systemic, institutional, textual, ideological and social relations, processes and practices (Bonnett, 2000). Anti-oppression, on the other hand, is an umbrella term for liberatory frameworks that include anti-racist and feminist practices (Massaquoi, 2011). Both anti-racist and anti-oppression frameworks (AR/AO) aim to continuously critique, resist, name and unmask systems of dominations that shape and constitute oppression, marginalization and forms of violence in order to foreground a social justice perspective. We argue that racist ideologies and practices continue to shape, constitute and inform the mental health care system in Canada.

Canada is a white settler society whose founding was based on the theft of Aboriginal lands (Razack, 2000). While white settler colonialism continues in the present, the discourse of multiculturalism conceals and silences such historical and contemporary racism and colonialism in Canada (Thobani, 1998, cited in Jiwani, 2006). Psychiatry and psychology is embedded with racist ideologies and epistemologies (Fernando, 2010). Darwin's theory of evolution, a legacy of the European Enlightenment, constructs the non-European, non-Western and non-white subject as non-human or as a lesser human being, thereby rendering the White Western Subject as the human, since he/she occupies the space where the evolutionary process culminates (Fernando, 2010). Such racist ideologies benefit the White Western Subject by making his identity, practices and ways of knowing as the universal understanding and standard in mainstream psychiatry (Fernando, 2010; Fernando, Ndegwa, and Wilson, 1998). As racism affects mental health care (Sarang *et al.*, 2009), mental health care in Canada does not serve all groups of people equitably, despite a universal form of health care system in the country (Durbin and Sondhu, 1992; MHCC, 2009; Nestel, 2012). AR/AO are necessary to address racism and oppression in the mental health care system and service delivery in Canada.

In this chapter, we foreground how the AR/AO framework can be applied in mental health care practices and delivery for racialized groups in Toronto, Canada.[1] We specifically illustrate how AR/AO constitutes a holistic model of mental healthcare. A holistic model of health recognizes and considers all aspects of human life – physical, mental, social, emotional, spiritual – as equally significant and interrelated. A holistic model of care informed by AR/AO reveals the inadequacy of the bio-medical model and therefore echoes with the struggles of racialized communities against systems of dominations – neo-liberalism, whiteness, patriarchy, sexism and classism – that shape mental health services. AR/AO provides a social justice framework that enables mental health agencies to integrate both the micro- and the macro-level practice of mental health care and service delivery.

Mental health care in Canada: barriers and access issues

Racialized communities cannot genuinely benefit from mainstream mental health services because these lack relevance to their needs, culture and ways of knowing (Fernando, 2010). Studies reveal that racialized communities continue to face barriers in the mental health care system (Fang, 2010; Li and Browne 2000; Nestel, 2012; Whitley, Kirmayer, and Groleau, 2006). These barriers include stigma, the use of the dominant language English in the system and socio-economic and immigration status. The struggles of a racialized individual with mental illness lie in both his/her mental illness and his/her racialized subjectivity and existence, thereby affecting his/her coping with mental illness.

For racialized individuals, the experience of stigma due to mental illness links to their racialized bodies. While seen as inferior races, racialized bodies are already imagined as 'dangerous', 'criminal' and 'irrational', as opposed to white Western bodies that are considered the epitome of reason and respectability. Psychiatry and psychology construct racialized bodies as symbols and signifiers of mental illness, including in the construction of diagnosis and classification of mental disorders (Fernando, 2010). Hence, when racialized individuals are beset by mental illness, they would no longer seek help and would feel disempowered. They would deny the presence of a mental health problem for fear of being automatically judged as carriers of mental illness. Such a situation fulfils the discourse of the mainstream bio-medical psychiatry: that it is just natural for racialized bodies to experience mental illness because they are genetically defective.

The usual response of the state in disrupting stigma is to produce and promote 'scientific' narratives and explanations that essentialize biological and genetic malfunctioning due to the belief that such narratives invite feelings of pity for an individual with mental illness; that such is not his/her own fault but is a result of 'natural' biological breakdown (Jiwani, 2006). In return, such scientific discourses maintain the legitimacy and superiority of medical institutions to 'fix' and 'correct' the defective racialized subject, leaving the 'non-biomedical' systems of health practices illegitimate. Medical institutions then emerge as benevolent because they have brought back the image of a healthy citizen, thereby re-narrating the national myth of Canada as a humanitarian and benevolent nation that is 'saving' a racialized and mentally ill subject. Such a response to stigma grounded in 'scientific' explanations and 'liberalist ideologies' are problematic since these continue to reproduce a disempowered, disabling, non-agentive subject who can only function with the help of a white hand. Unless intervention is carried out by means of critically interrogating the dominant ideologies – whiteness, patriarchy, masculinity, heterosexism, classism, racism – embedded in nationalist, liberal and bio-medical discourse, stigma continues to pose a barrier for racialized individuals with mental illness.

Language becomes another barrier to mental healthcare (MHCC, 2009; Li and Browne, 2000). Eurocentric assessment tools are produced in English, which fails to capture the nuance of non-English and non-French speakers. Such results in the de-contextualization, de-historization and de-politicization of the meanings of their experience of mental illness, and, therefore, contribute to misinterpretation and misdiagnosis (Fernando, 2010; Ong, 1995). They become frustrated, fearful and intimidated when communicating to a mental health care professional who does not speak their language (Simich, 2010). They are racialized as their incapacity to speak the dominant language English places them in the position of a less desirable or less preferred client or patient (Jiwani, 2006).

In such a Eurocentric mental health system, another type of barrier lies in the socio-economic and immigration status of individuals accessing the service. Refugees and foreign temporary workers, such as live-in caregivers and seasonal farm workers, are in a precarious health situation since their immigration status limits their access to mental healthcare (Hennebry, 2010; MHCC, 2009). Access to private insurance is not a viable option because of their low-income status. The majority of people occupying such immigration programmes are from countries in the global South whose racial and cultural background are non-Western. Their bodies are, therefore, 'disposable', let alone beset with mental health issues.[2]

While these aforementioned barriers exist, the mental health care system itself continues to become less accessible for racialized individuals with mental illness. Such access issues include the lack of culturally responsive models of care and programmes as well as the lack of information regarding services and knowledge of how the mental health system works (MHCC, 2009; Kafele, 2004; Williams, 2002). These access issues, therefore, depict the clash and 'mismatch' between the dominant ideological construct of the mental health care system and the social location and socio-cultural and political histories of racialized immigrants (Yee, Shahsiah, Janczur, Ocampo and Rahim, 2006). These induce risks and harm to racialized immigrants with mental illness. For example, mental health care professionals automatically resort to 'medicalized' interventions in addressing a mental illness (Jiwani, 2006), dismissing other options of care such as the use of alternative remedies and traditional healing practices utilized by many non-Western peoples. Such highly medicalized intervention programmes have been universalized, thereby promoting a culture of hegemony in which only the highly 'scientific' and the highly 'evidenced-based interventions' are seen as legitimate, while the health beliefs, practices and values of racialized immigrants are discounted, rejected and regarded as 'unscientific' and 'not modern' (Fernando, 2010).

Anti-racism and anti-oppressive framework

The barriers experienced by racialized communities when accessing the mental health care system enable the forging of solidarity and social antagonisms against racist and oppressive ideologies, conditions and practices (Fernando, 2010). Social movements, activism and alliances among racialized communities become spaces and tools for public education and voicing out of issues of marginalization and oppression. Ideas and knowledges grounded in the lived experience of racialized communities – experiences of racial violence, brutality and oppression – and then supplemented by the works of critical race and anti-racist scholars have contributed to the development of political ideas and frameworks critical of Eurocentric and racist knowledges and practices (Fernando, 2010). It is through them that the AR/AO framework emerges (Fernando, 2010). Generated by social justice and equity principles that recognize, question, reveal and name social injustice and forms of oppression, AR/AO counters and interrogates racist narratives and ideologies. To be clear, the primary focus of anti-racism practice is antagonizing and acting against racist practices in and from individual and systemic levels. Anti-oppression, on the other hand, coheres with anti-racism as it aims to remove all forms of oppressive norms and practices – heterosexism, homophobia, patriarchy, classism, sexism, ableism, ageism, mentalism – that hinder the growth, opportunities, quality of life and life chances of marginalized and racialized peoples.

The AR/AO framework applied in mental health is not a straightforward process. Such a framework creates tension with the dominant discourse within mental health care systems such as the medical model and the bio-psycho-social perspective (Larson, 2008). In addition, the market ideology in the health care system that enables the 'economy of care' by focusing merely on physiological and biological symptoms as the site of intervention through the use of pharmaceutical drugs (Jiwani, 2006), as opposed to engaging the client holistically, goes against the AR/AO practice principles. In particular, anti-racism is said to reinforce stereotypes because it emphasizes difference between groups (Macey and Moxon, 1996, as cited in Corneau and Stergiopoulos, 2012). Anti-oppressive practice, on the other hand, is too general in that it tends to conceal specific forms of oppression and discrimination (Williams, 1999, as cited in Corneau and Stergiopoulos, 2012). Indeed, these issues in implementing AR/AO models are important to consider in order to serve as a cautionary measure in how such a framework may be taken up by the hegemony of liberalism, patriarchy, capitalism, and even in the justification of violence. Nevertheless, as Williams (2002) suggests, anti-racism complements anti-oppression practices by serving as an entry point in being able to perform anti-oppressive practices.

While putting the AR/AO approach into practice is complex, Fernando (2010) illustrates the micro-level application of this framework, which is in terms of client engagement. The client is experiencing not only mental illness but also systemic oppression. In such a micro-level approach, naming the various issues, including whiteness, racism, sexism, classism, etc., is an important step. Service providers need to give close consideration to such social and structural factors that influence the well-being of the individual client/service users, thereby refraining from individualizing the problem of the client (Abrams and Moio, 2009). In addition, providing service users with wider options and choices, such as information about their rights and about their prescribed medications and diagnosis, enables an atmosphere of empowerment and possibilities that effect change.

Meanwhile, in a group- or meso-level approach, providing training and workshops for service providers on AR/AO approaches is also helpful. Group work for service providers may focus on sharing stories of their lived experiences of oppression to understand how systems of oppression work, thereby creating a community based on shared experiences of oppression. This enables them to become more aware of the impact of racism in health/mental health so that they are able to develop and increase their capacity to deal with individual, systemic and internalized racism. AR/AO practice, therefore, focuses on building up people's strengths and critical thinking to be able to change the power structures within the dominant system and institutions (Fernando, 2010).

In an organizational level, front-line and management people not only may possess the professional training, but also may share a similar life experience and social location with the clients they serve (Sarang *et al.*, 2009). Professional staff with lived experience of racism can integrate their personal experiences into their work that enables client support. This allows the racialized population to create a community that foregrounds their voices, issues and concerns and to put these into action so that they become designers of their own services and processes. In light of this, because racism manifests and implicates various bodies and systems including racialized people, AR/AO training for staff or service providers should continue. In other words, education on issues around racism and oppression and how these affect their day-to-day work and interaction with their clients must be part of the AR/AO practices of the organization (Larson, 2008; Sarang *et al.*, 2009). Education then must make racial issues visible and must take up race as a marker of difference with tangible material consequences. Such an understanding is an entry point to understand systems of oppression and dominations. In addition, the organization may also collaborate with other community agencies as partners in the continuous task of learning AR/AO practices. Such collaboration via training and education serve as a form of community development and forging of solidarities and alliances with various agencies. Training and workshops with other organizations also allow for feedback that is vital to the enrichment of the AR/AO framework.

Finally, AR/AO practice is highly relevant to policy and programme development in the organization. The AR/AO framework must also be reflected in the governance of the organization such as in developing the client's care plan and service delivery, which foregrounds the debilitating effects of racism. Clear actions and avenues to address racist issues and practices experienced by both staff and clients must be undertaken in developing the policies and programmes of the organization. This means further that service users and staff should be part of the decision-making process of the organization (Larson, 2008). Service users are seen not just as clients but as community partners who actively participate in developing the organization. Racialized service providers who experience racism in their work must not only be seen as mere performers/executors of top management's policy and guidelines but should be consulted and be part of the decision-making process. Such a strategic way for racialized bodies to own the organization signifies a strong critique of mainstream health care systems where racial hierarchy among the employees prevail: management functions are given to white bodies while front-line and service provision functions are designated to racialized people (Jiwani, 2006).

An example of the application of the AR/AO framework at an organizational/community level is at Across Boundaries.[3] Suman Fernando himself serves as one of its mentors and guides. Since the opening of its doors for services, Fernando has regularly visited the centre to show his support and has generously made himself available to the staff, clients and the community for consultation. Indeed, his support has not just been within and among staff and clients. He has accompanied community advocates to meet the Program Consultant of the Ontario Provincial Ministry of Health to advocate for policy change in the mental health system and to increase the funding for the centre.

Through a collaborative effort, Across Boundaries foregrounds the following principles in their practice. First, that racism, racial abuse and racial violence affect the health and mental health of individuals and their communities. Second, that individual and systemic racism is a barrier to the quality of health and mental health services. Third, that the way to multiculturalism is anti-racism. Fourth, that there is diversity among racialized people who, in addition to race, may also be discriminated against on account of their religion, language, ethnicity, class, gender, sexual orientation, disabilities, age, country of origin and citizenship status (Sarang et al., 2009).

The first principle considers racism as a distinct social determinant of mental health that simultaneously works with other systems of oppression resulting in and maintaining other social issues affecting health such as poverty or inadequate housing. The second principle is an explicit statement on barriers that include inappropriate use of interpreters, culturally inappropriate treatment methods and mental health providers who impose their own values and perspective on populations they know very little about. The third principle is a call to continually challenge the limits of multiculturalism that applies a 'culturally competent' approach, an approach that continues to produce racism. The fourth principle recognizes racism as part of other forms of oppression but is highly significant and particular to racialized bodies.

The emergence of such an agency with both anti-racism and anti-oppression practice signifies the possibility of challenging mainstream mental health care, which is traditionally governed by the bio-medical approach. Evidently, the application of AR/AO in all levels of the centre embodies the holistic approach to mental health care. In the next section, we provide a discussion of this holistic model of care that further illustrates how the AR/AO framework links with mental health in the context of client care.

A holistic model of care

The insistence of the Western bio-medical model of psychiatry and psychology on the universal standard of intervention for people with mental illness has produced what Fernando (2010) terms 'psychiatric imperialism'. In such a paradigm, non-Western types of medical practices and intervention for mental illness are constructed as inferior, ineffective, weak and full of dangers. Colonization, globalization and modernization has spread such notions of universality and superiority of Western psychiatry and psychology. By subjugating and destroying the 'Other', including their knowledges, cultures and subjectivities, enables the success of such universalist discourse (Fernando, 2010). The practical effects of this psychiatric imperialism, as Fernando notes, has been the 'underdevelopment of medical approaches to mental health and illness indigenous to Asian and African cultural traditions and the suppression of the indigenous ways of dealing human suffering, family problems, and social disturbance' (2010, p. 113).

Using the AR/AO framework to address issues in the mental health care system, racialized communities in Canada have pushed to foreground a holistic model of mental health care. By utilizing their indigenous healing practices and belief systems that facilitate the strengthening of their mind, body and spirit, racialized communities reveal and unveil the inadequacy of Western scientific medicine. However, this is not to say that they invoke a return to a 'nativist' position in order to denounce the Western scientific approach to mental illness. Instead, such utilization of traditional healing practices creates a model of care that is attentive not only to their physical bodies, but also to their mind, spirit and community. Thus, the integration of traditional healing practices into medical psychiatry fosters a holistic approach in understanding, analysing and intervening in mental illness.

Such a holistic approach is not one-sided; nor does it impose a universal standard of care. Rather, it is an integrative model of care in which various types of intervention co-exist. By focusing on the different aspects of the human body, such as the physical, emotional, mental and spiritual dimensions, as well as the individual's connection to his/her community, the holistic approach attains its goal of regarding the human as a human whose parts and dimensions are not compartmentalized but are interconnected. In other words, the holistic model of care involves the integration of alternative therapies, prescribed medications and social support for clients, which includes seeking out spiritual support from churches, mosques, temples or traditional healers (Fernando, 2010).

Holistic care is not divorced from the AR/AO framework. It is attentive to lived experiences, multiple knowledges, belief systems and practices, including the indigenous, communal and traditional approaches of racialized communities (Fernando, 2010). Racialized communities' health beliefs, traditional healing, caring practices and ways of knowing and meaning making are treated as equally significant in the development of the plan of care. However, as an approach that integrates AR/AO principles, holistic modality is cautious of being taken up as a token that operates through the logic of liberal multiculturalism and continues to conceal contemporary and historical oppressions. In so doing, the holistic care approach is grounded in community-based approaches; it is situated within the activism of racialized communities.

Across Boundaries, for example, is committed to such a holistic model of care. Music and dance therapy, expressive art therapy and other forms of non-Western healing practices such as acupuncture and yoga, are available for the members of the agency. These enable clients to engage in non-drug-related or non-medical-related types of intervention. This practice is not to advocate for the removal of medication in their treatment plans. Such forms of therapies serve as alternative form of treatment, thereby opening and widening clients' choices and options. What makes these therapies relevant is that they are grounded in clients' social locations and beliefs systems.

One unique type of holistic modality that is also available at Across Boundaries is the so-called community kitchen. Here, clients plan their own meals for the day that best fit with their religious beliefs and dietary requirements: clients prepare a nutritious meal that includes a halal and vegetarian menu. To be clear, the programme is not about knowing other people's culture via food as in the idea of multiculturalism. What the programme promotes is the spirit of solidarity, community, accountability and ownership in terms of sharing ideas and plans in the actual preparation of the food, as well as in sharing chores and tasks. For example, both men and women pair up in planning and preparing food for the day. Such a holistic model of care via 'food' illustrates that the holistic approach is not merely in terms of therapeutic intervention to mental illness, but also about keeping up one's everyday well-being.

In advocating for a holistic model of care, Fernando also reveals two important points for consideration as an ethical dilemma. Such a dilemma is rooted in thinking about how various traditional healing practices that originate in various socio-cultural and historical contexts can be realistically and pragmatically applied. For Fernando (2010), the problems are: first, in terms of defining the limits of the technique, and second, in terms of evaluating the effectiveness of the technique. He suggests that it is important that 'technology introduced into a culture fits into it and is absorbed by it; and such a transplanted technology should be given time to grow and become incorporated (or rejected)' (p. 173). If Western psychiatry, as Fernando (2010) contends, is to use techniques from non-Western cultural sources, 'it must move away from its present position on defining illness' (p. 173).

The existence of holistic models of care is politically telling. It signifies the ability of racialized groups to resist and assert a space to preserve and uphold their traditional ways of knowing. It illuminates and articulates the 'lack' of Western mainstream model in mental health care (Fernando, 2010). While dominant and oppressing forces (i.e. racism, colonialism, imperialism, whiteness) continue to displace individuals and communities with non-dominant beliefs and cultures, traditional healing practices become a movement of the non-dominant groups to emancipate and express their subjectivity and self-determination. Holistic modalities that integrate traditional healing practices, are, therefore, a mental health intervention of *possibility*: that how we know what we know is not only by way of applying Western/Eurocentric knowledge/s promoted by dominant institutions, but also by the knowledges rooted in non-Western/non-European spaces. Both West and non-West knowledges and ways of knowing and thinking must have a space to co-exist, thereby resulting in a holistic perspective that recognizes that the mind, body and spirit are altogether significant to a person's well-being.

Conclusion

Bio-medicalization as the dominant intervention of Western psychiatry and psychology that has become globalized and universalized cannot adequately address the mental health issues of racialized, non-Western subjects. Racialized individuals with mental illness are not only suffering from such a health problem but are also experiencing racism and other forms of oppression embedded in the historical construction of mental illness and its intervention. AR/AO in mental health practice restructures the very idea of mental illness and its intervention using a social justice framework. This enables racialized individuals to cope with mental illness with a clear recognition of racism and other forms of oppression as impediments to one's health and well-being. Interventions grounded in AR/AO target not only the bio-psycho-social factors of mental illness but also the political and historical configuration of a racialized individual's identity. Therefore, AR/AO enables the development of a holistic model of health since it allows marginalized knowledges and health beliefs and practices to be part of the health care intervention plans and goals. In such a holistic modality, racialized individuals have wider options in terms of caring for his/her mental health. AR/AO practice in mental health care continues to resist Western psychiatry and psychology's universal and imperial tendency. By genuinely applying and incorporating the AR/AO framework in mental health care and practice, mental health organizations participate in becoming culturally sensitive and mindful to the experiences of racialized bodies as well as to the ongoing white settler colonialism in Canada, without being paternalistic and tokenistic. Health must be continually understood as holistic and racism as ongoing and prevalent. The work of Suman Fernando, particularly his critique of mainstream psychiatry and psychology, provides the roadmap and intellectual grounding in the continual resistance and talking back to racist practices and epistemologies in mental health care.

Notes

1 'Racialized person or group' is preferred over racial minority, visible minority, person of colour or non-white, as it recognizes the dynamic and complex process by which racial categories are socially produced by dominant groups in ways that entrench social inequalities and marginalization (Ontario Human Rights Code, 2009).

2 Given that temporary foreign workers are on temporary permits, they are in a precarious working situation in that they can be easily be dismissed and returned to their countries of origin; hence the term disposable workforce (Canadian Council for Refugees, 2010).
3 Across Boundaries is a community-based mental health agency in Toronto with strong anti-racism values and principles.

References

Abrams, L. S. and Moio, J. A. (2009). Critical race theory and the cultural competence dilemma in social work education. *Journal of Social Work Education, 45*(2), 245–261.

Braun, K. L. and Browne, C. V. (1998). Perception of dementia, caregiving and help seeking among Asian and Pacific Islander Americans. *Health & Social Work, 23*(4), 262–271.

Bonnett, A. (2000*). Anti-racism*. London: Routledge.

Canadian Council for Refugees. (2010). Immigration policy shifts: From nation building to temporary migration. *Association of Canadian Studies (ACS): Canadian Issues, Temporary Foreign Workers*, 90–93. Spring Issue.

Corneau, S. and Stergiopoulous, V. (2012). More than being against it: Anti-racism and anti-oppression in mental health services. *Transcultural Psychiatry, 49*(2), 262–282.

Durbin, J. and Sondhu, R. (1992). *Improving mental health supports for diverse ethnoracial communities in Metro Toronto*. Project funded by the Ontario Anti-racism Secretariat, the Ontario Ministry of Health and the City of Toronto Department of Public Health.

Fang, L. (2010). Mental health service utilization by Chinese immigrants: Barriers and opportunities. *Association of Canadian Studies (ACS): Canadian Issues, Immigrant Mental Health*, 70–74. Summer Issue.

Fernando, S. (2010). *Mental health, race, and culture* (3rd ed.). Basingstoke: Palgrave Macmillan.

Fernando, S., Ndegwa, D. and Wilson, M. (1998). *Forensic psychiatry, race and culture*. London: Routledge.

Hennebry, J. L. (2010). Not just a few bad apples: Vulnerability, health, and temporary migration in Canada. *Canadian Issues: Temporary Foreign Workers*, 73–77.

Jiwani, Y. (2006). *Discourses of denial: Mediations of race, gender, and violence*. Vancouver: University of British Columbia Press.

Kafele, K. (2004). *Racial discrimination and mental health: Racialized and Aboriginal communities*. Retrieved January 2013 from www.ohrc.on.ca/en/race-policy-dialogue-papers/racial-discrimination-and-mental-health-racialized-and-aboriginal-communities.

Larson, G. (2008). Anti-oppressive practice in mental health. *Journal of Progressive Human Services, 19*(1), 39–54.

Li, H. Z. and Browne, A. J. (2000). Defining mental illness and access mental health service perspectives of Asian Canadians. *Canadian Journal of Community Mental Health, 19*(1), 143–160.

Massaquoi, N. (20011). Crossing boundaries to radicalize social work practice and education. In D. Baines (Ed.), *Doing anti-oppressive practice: Building transformative politicized social work*. Halifax, NS: Fernwood.

MHCC (Mental Health Commission of Canada), Diversity Task Group. (2009). *Improving mental health services for immigrant, refugee, ethno-cultural and racialized groups: Issues and options for service improvement*. Retrieved from www.mentalhealthcommission.ca/SiteCollectionDocuments/Key_Documents/en/20 10/Issues_Options_FINAL_English%2012Nov09.pdf.

Nestel, S., (2012). *Colour coded health care: The impact of race and racism on Canadians' health*. Toronto: Wellesley Institute.

Ong, A. Y. M. (1995). *Text of address: Launching of Across Boundaries*. Toronto: Across Boundaries.

Ontario Human Rights Code. (2009). Ontario Human Rights Commission's Policy and Guidelines on Racism and Discrimination.

Razack, S. (2000). Simple logic: Race, the identity documents rule and the story of a nation besieged and betrayed. *Journal of Law and Social Policy, 15*, 181–209.

Sarang, A., Ocampo, M., Durbin, J., Strike, C., Chandler, C., Connelly, J. et al. (2009). *How we do it: Across Boundaries' anti-racist, holistic, service delivery model*. Retrieved 5 January 2013 from www.acrossboundaries.ca.

Simich, L. (2010). Health literacy, immigrants and mental health. *Association of Canadian Studies (ACS): Canadian Issues Immigrant Mental Health*, 17–22, Spring Issue.

Whitley, R., Kirmayer, L. J. and Groleau, D. (2006). Understanding immigrants' reluctance to use mental health services: A qualitative study from Montreal. *Canadian Journal of Psychiatry, 51*(4), 205–209.

Williams, C. (2002). A rationale for an anti-racist entry point to anti-oppressive social work in mental health services. *Critical Social Work, 2*(2), 20–31.

Yee, J. Y., Shahsiah, S., Janczur, A., Ocampo, M. and Rahim, C. (2006). *Striving for best practices and equitable mental health care access for racialized communities in Toronto: A research report*. Canadian Institutes of Health Research, Institute of Health Services and Policy Research and Institute of Neurosciences, Mental Health & Addiction. Retrieved from http://accessalliance.ca/sites/accessalliance/files/documents/EquitableMentalHealthCareAccessResearchReport.pdf.

Part IV
Transnational contexts
Engaging the work of Suman Fernando

14 Developing mental health services

The myth of 'global' mental health

Suman Fernando

Introduction

In the immediate post-colonial era when the Cold War was in full swing, the term 'Third World' was given to countries that did not fall into one or other power bloc. Then, as industrial development was seen as the way forward for all countries, the world was roughly divided into 'developed' and 'under-developed'/'developing' nations. More recently, it has become customary, for example in the *World Mental Health Casebook* (Cohen, Kleinman and Saraceno, 2002), to adopt the World Bank categorization of economies based on gross national income (GNI) per capita, whereby countries are classified as low-income, middle-income (subdivided into lower middle and upper middle) and high-income countries.

Many countries that fall into the low- and middle-income group (referred to henceforth as LMICs) have suffered from colonialism, with its associated exploitation of resources and people for the benefit of the (now) high-income countries – the original colonizing countries of Europe plus countries such as Australia, Canada and the United States, where there was massive settlement by migrants from Europe, with land-grabbing from its inhabitants, often accompanied by genocide. Most LMICs are culturally 'non-Western' but the past few decades have seen major changes both economically and culturally across the world giving rise to cultural mixtures, so-called 'hybrid' cultures and cultural diaspora (see Kirmayer, 2006; Pieterse, 2007, 2009; Baumann, 2011).

In many LMICs, general health and welfare services are under-developed and under-resourced; often there is a rudimentary or no welfare system to support people facing misfortune or hardship. Whatever mental health systems that exist within the state sector are largely based on Western models of mainly institutional care, a carry-over of the asylums introduced by colonialists. Indigenous medical and religious systems for promoting mental health, having suffered many years of under-development, are generally badly organized and unregulated. It should be noted, however, that what mental health professionals may call 'mental health problems' requiring individual treatment and care are often seen in many LMICs as problems of living or existence, personal misfortune that is the result of unknown (perhaps supernatural) forces, or problems of relationships and communality.

However, with globalization and (more recently) aggressive marketing by pharmaceutical companies (see later) the picture is changing quite dramatically in some places. The low priority given to developing mental health services by governments of many LMICs means that specific services for mental health care is left to non-governmental agencies (NGOs) which are poorly regulated and often provide piecemeal development based on agendas set by their funders which are nearly always based in the West.

In this chapter, I will review briefly some of the published literature that informs mental health development in LMICs; the role of the World Health Organization (WHO) in setting the priorities for development; the current context that development has to address; and future prospects in LMICs; ending with some conclusions.

Background literature

Interest in examining cross-national differences in mental health as a prelude to promoting mental health services in LMICs dates to research studies carried out by WHO in the 1960s and 1970s, exemplified by its International Pilot Study of Schizophrenia (IPSS) (WHO, 1973, 1975, 1979) and the Determinants of Outcome of Severe Mental Disorder (DOSMeD) (Jablensky et al., 1992). Being based on traditional epidemiological approaches with ethnocentric assumptions, the methodology of the IPSS was criticized (at the time it was carried out) because it failed to take on board 'category fallacy' (Kleinman, 1977), namely imposing the 'schizophrenia' diagnosis as a measure of ill health. Yet it is worth noting that apparent outcomes for people seen as seriously mentally ill (in psychiatric terms) were actually *better* in non-Western settings where (at that time anyway) the bio-medical model for mental health problems was not very popular and psychotropic drugs were used sparingly if at all. More recently, this better outcome has been questioned (see Cohen, Patel, Thara and Gureje, 2008; Haro, Novick, Bertsch, Karagianis and Dossenbach, 2011), possibly because now, three decades later, psychotropic drugs are used more extensively than they used to be, and the model of 'schizophrenia' with its stigma and its image of genetic lifelong disability has spread in many LMICs with 'psycho-education' programmes and other means of imposing psychiatric thinking in their populations.

Some recent papers in international journals too point to some interesting possibilities that systems currently active for 'mental 'illness' in LMICs may be as effective as those derived from psychiatry. The paper by Raguram and colleagues (2002), published in the *British Medical Journal*, was a study of healing at a Hindu temple in Tami Nadu (South India) known for helping people with mental health problems. The authors had elicited the views of both the patients and their carers about their experiences and also made psychiatric assessments (of the patients) on a standard scale before and after their stay at the temple. They found that most of the patients studied (1) suffered from psychotic illness (as per psychiatry) and (2) showed a degree of improvement (judged by reduction of psychiatric symptoms and their own expressed views), improvement that matched the sort of result that may be expected through bio-medical therapy. There are many healing centres in South Asia like the one referred to – and the same is true for many other LMICs; so there may be something to learn from these places, if they are studied sensitively. A paper by Halliburton (2004) in *Transcultural Psychiatry* documented experiences of 100 people who had accessed treatment in three forms of therapy in Kerala (South India) – Ayurvedic (an Indian medical system), bio-medical psychiatry and religious healing at one or other of three locations, namely a Hindu temple, a Muslin mosque and a Christian church, all of which had reputations for healing people who suffer from mental illness. All the patients had mixtures of symptoms that would give the diagnosis 'schizophrenia' or other severe mental disorder. Similar proportions of patients benefited from each form of therapy, and several had changed from one to another until they derived benefit. This shopping around by clients and their families had resulted in a very high overall improvement rate.

Role of the World Health Organization

LMICs tend to look to WHO for guidance and sources of funding for developing mental health services, and WHO helps these countries by providing support for individual projects and advice to governments both in policy and service development (see WHO, 2002). The broad guidelines for health care enunciated at the Alma Ata Conference in 1978 (WHO/UNICEF, 1978) and reconfirmed at Riga in 1988 (WHO, 1988) defined health as 'a state of complete physical, mental and social well-being' (1988, p. 7). *The World Health Report 2001* (WHO, 2001) pointed to the following principles for good systems of mental health care: continuity of care, wide range of services, partnerships with patients and families, involvement of the local community and integration into primary health care. The report supported the importance of understanding and integrating local knowledge and, in the case of African and Asian countries, 'working with traditional healers' (WHO, 2001, p. 58). The strategy for South-East Asia (WHO Regional Office for South-East Asia, 2008) emphasized the need for community-based mental health programmes that are 'culturally and gender appropriate and reach out to all segments of the population, including marginalized groups' (p. 1). In other words, WHO seemed to advocate moving away from formal mental health services on traditional psychiatric models of treating 'illness', towards a public health and welfare model.

However, while advocating for community care and a public health model for LMICs, it was never made clear (by WHO) how this should be converted into policies and practical service development. There may well have been a division of opinion at WHO on where exactly *mental health care* as a category should fall – that is, on whether it should be an extension of a mental illness service or one within a broader framework of welfare and psycho-social care. For example, a paper from WHO quoting Benedetto Saraceno (2004) (who was then Director of the Department of Health and Substance Abuse at WHO) pointed out that, if medical care is separated from psycho-social care, '*mental health* care services may inadvertently promote exclusively biological care for the severely mentally ill by drawing human resources skilled in non-biological interventions away from formal mental health services' (van Ommeren, Saxena and Saraceno, 2005, p. 71; italics in original). Also, there was an apparent reluctance of WHO to move too far away from the traditional psychiatric approach to mental health as the absence of 'illness', reflecting political forces within the organization itself; for example, there were reported issues around funding from the pharmaceutical industry being funnelled to WHO through patient organizations (Day, 2007) – and this industry has a vested interest in promoting bio-medical psychiatry.

Recent publications of WHO suggest a trend going even further towards the approach of traditional bio-medical psychiatry – miles away from its stance in the 1980s at the time of Riga (see above). The Mental Health Gap *Interventions Guide* (WHO, 2010), launched in 2010, aimed at 'scaling up services' for mental health in LMICs, promoting what WHO calls 'evidence-based interventions to identify and manage a number of priority conditions'; these conditions include 'depression, psychosis, bipolar disorders, epilepsy, developmental and behavioural disorders in children and adolescents, dementia, alcohol use disorders, drug use disorders, self-harm/suicide and other significant emotional or medically unexplained complaints' (2010, p. 1). Clearly, WHO argue in this document for spreading psychiatry in LMICs in order to reduce what it calls 'the burden in terms of mortality, morbidity or disability' and promote 'human rights' (2010, p. 2). Together with this shift in approach by WHO has come the Movement for Global Mental Health (MGMH) with its detailed website. MGMH has collaborated with the US National Institute for Mental Health (NIMH) to identify 'challenges' that need to be faced (Collins *et al.*, 2011). These challenges, meant to attract funding for research and development, were devised by a process of consulting people identified by NIMH as 'experts' with little or no consultation with people living in the countries concerned. Strong opposition to the MGMH was voiced recently at a meeting in Montreal of professionals and academics in the field of transcultural/cultural psychiatry (Bemme and D'souza, 2012). Articles critical of the movement have appeared in journals (e.g. Shukla *et al.*, 2012; Summerfield, 2012) and magazines (e.g. Fernando, 2011), and more such articles are likely to appear during the next few years.

Realities on the ground

Dependence on WHO means that LMICs are subject to the geo-political and economic forces that may determine the policies followed by WHO. A problem noticeable on the ground is that consultants sent by WHO do not often implement the sort of changes that WHO itself advocates in its reports. Quite often, experts (nearly always from Western countries) tend to impose models and ideologies derived from their own experiences in the West without much sensitivity to local cultures and customs (personal observations). Local politics and local vested interests too play a part in this: for example, local professional elites often favour services that imitate those in the West that they have been taught to regard as scientific and modern; and local professionals are usually unfamiliar with service users playing a role in mental health development. But in spite of all this, there are agencies and community workers in many countries striving hard to provide culturally sensitive services – people who tend to be in local NGOs whose voices are seldom heard in the corridors of power.

The dependence of many LMICs on the work of NGOs sometimes raises problems. In many places, services provided by NGOs are not coordinated, and they often compete with one another and do not share information and know-how, either between themselves or with government agencies. Many NGOs are dependent to a large extent on funding from Western countries and their work tends to be geared to interests and priorities set by funding agencies that usually favour promoting particular philosophies and approaches that reflect needs or attitudes in donor countries rather than the needs of the receiving countries. So anti-stigma campaigns, individual rights and de-institutionalization (see Scull, 1984) are pushed as the main thrust of some NGO work or even that of WHO, ignoring (1) the connection of stigma with the bio-medical model (Angermeyer, Holzinger, Carla and Scholerus, 2011; Read, Haslam, Sayce and Davies, 2006); (2) the tendency for community rights (to have their cultures and ways of living respected) to be as important as individual rights for people in developing countries; and (3) the lack of welfare systems in many developing countries that would militate against people unable to lead productive lives – for example, because of disabilities – in their own community. Other systems that are sometimes promoted without proper regard to local conditions, all of which the author has seen happening, include: General Practitioner (GP) centred treatment – ignoring the fact that in many LMICs GP services are fee-paying while hospital services are free; day-hospital-based group therapy – even though group therapy may not be culturally appropriate; and Cognitive Behaviour Therapy (CBT) – in settings where individualized focus on challenging beliefs may contradict religious convictions. Moreover, systems derived from a bio-medical, diagnosis-based approach to mental health care clash with local non-Western cultural patterns (see Fernando, 2010).

Current scene

Most LMICs suffered from oppression and under-development between the mid 18th and mid 20th centuries and little is known today of what may well have been thriving health and social care systems that existed in the pre-colonial era, addressing (what psychiatrists today may call) 'mental illness'. For example, Field (then working for the British colonial government) described Ashanti shrines in Ghana where people with 'fear and guilt frenzies' and people who 'are indistinguishable from classical schizophrenics' benefited from attending (Field, 1960, p. 1045). The author is aware of a service carried out for many years well into the 20th century at a Buddhist temple near Colombo, Sri Lanka, where treatment based on Ayurveda (Obeyesekere, 1977) was administered by a priest-doctor, while the clients, usually with their carers, were accommodated in a local village. Even today there are numerous centres – usually around a temple, mosque or church – in Asian and African countries where people designated as 'mad' are taken for cures, although there are hardly any recent reports on these services in medical or psychiatric journals except for the two papers (Halliburton, 2004; Raguram et al., 2002) referred to earlier.

In most of South Asia, people with mental health problems, if they obtain any help at all, obtain this through informal family networks; attending statutory services, usually run on psychiatric lines; therapy from indigenous physicians; centres of healing; religious institutions where they can consult priests or other religious leaders; and help of healers of various types. The reality today in many African and Asian countries is that systems of religion and indigenous medicine (closely related if not co-incident) form the main sources for the alleviation of suffering that psychiatry would refer to as mental health problems or 'mental illness'; and bio-medical psychiatry is only accessed by a small minority of people who suffer from mental health problems. Although the efficacy of any of the systems accessed by people in LMICs is not known, it should be noted that the imposition of bio-medical psychiatry in non-Western cultural settings is fraught with problems and dangers to the societies concerned (see Fernando, 2010; Watters, 2011).

However, it is important not to idealize what happens in LMICs. The situation today is far from satisfactory, especially for that small number of people who become very disturbed mentally – 'psychotic' in the language of psychiatry. In many LMICs such people may well get tied up, sometimes for long periods, in order to prevent damage to themselves or other people (Gilbert, 2002; and personal communications to the author from various sources), at least until they can be transported to a mental hospital, if one is available. Conditions at healing centres too may be inhumane; on a visit in January 1998 the author observed mentally disturbed people being housed in cages in the grounds of a religious institution, cared for by relatives sitting outside the cages. But we have to remember that physical abuse within psychiatric hospitals is not unusual; in many developed countries people are known to be locked in solitary confinement away from contact with other human beings sometimes for prolonged periods – and one could argue that being tied up but in contact with others may be preferable to isolation from human contact.

The future

Currently, the ground appears to be shifting significantly in the field of mental health development in LMICs. The advent of the MGMH, as discussed above, presents a serious danger to LMICs. According to the article in *Nature* (Collins et al., 2011), MGMH starts by lumping together 'mental illnesses' categorized by Western nosology that may have little relevance in non-Western settings and 'neurological and substance-use disorders'; and then US NIMH has derived 25 challenges from opinions provided by the so-called 'Delphi panel' of people nominated by US NIMH – as far as one can see, *excluding* stakeholders among community workers and service users in LMICs. What is even more worrying is that the pharmaceutical industry seems to be supporting its activities and thus is likely to determine the direction they take. The Gates Foundation (2010) states on its website that it has chosen not to fund *mental* health because the US NIMH and the pharmaceutical industry already do so. Clearly, the paradigm that MGMH is built on seems to assume that (1) bio-medical approaches (defined as 'evidence-based') alone – with cultural tweaking, no doubt – has all the answers; and (2) local people – apart from selected professional elites – in LMICs should have little say in what type of models (of mental health and illness) and systems (of mental health and social care) are developed in their countries. If implemented, the MGMH programme opens the door in LMICs to intrusive marketing by the pharmaceutical industry. The danger for LMICs is that the (all too real) argument that conditions in LMICs for people (seen as) suffering from mental health problems or 'mental illness' should be improved may blind us to the fact that some types of change may well turn out to be for the worse.

We know that the imposition in colonial times of Western-type asylums did not really do much good and possibly helped towards under-development, if not actual suppression, of indigenous systems of mental health care. The asylum approach has been abandoned in the West and we have seen considerable progress in the West towards addressing human rights violations in mental health facilities, although not much progress in combating stigma. Perhaps asylums should never have been introduced in LMICs, but many still function in these countries and require urgent attention, not least to prevent human rights violations. But in planning more general services, we need to be careful not to make the same mistake we made about asylums – assuming that what seems appropriate for the West must be the best for everyone. The assumption that there are global remedies for mental health problems – indeed that there is something called '*global*' mental health that can be applied worldwide – is on the whole misconceived.

Moreover, it is worth noting that serious doubts are being voiced today about the effectiveness of predominantly bio-medical psychiatry in Britain and North America (Carlat, 2010; Ramon and Williams, 2005; Tew, 2002; Whittaker, 2010), especially for ethnic minorities of Asian and African backgrounds in the United Kingdom (e.g. Bhui and Olajide, 1999; Fernando and Keating, 2009; Ingleby, 2004). Also, there are questions being asked in the United States (for example) about the way medications are used in a frame of psychiatric models of 'illnesses' and theories of chemical imbalance of neurotransmitters in the brain (see Angell, 2005; Bentall, 2010; Carlat, 2010; Fernando, 2010; Kirsch, 2009; Whittaker, 2010). They are still minority voices (in terms of their power), but are increasingly persuasive, as exemplified by articles in the *New York Review of Books* (see Angell, 2011a, 2011b) and *New York Times* (Allen Frances, 2012, who led the DSM Task Force for *DSM IV*). And today's minority opinion could well be established wisdom tomorrow. Like the asylum era, the current era of rigid diagnosis linked to early and prolonged medication may well be regretted before too long. So we have to be very wary indeed about promoting narrow, rigid systems of diagnosis that would promote the marketing of psychotropic drugs by the pharmaceutical industry.

Conclusion

There is little doubt that people with psychological and emotional needs in LMICs, especially those who are severely disturbed in behaviour, require better services or systems of help and support than are presently available. LMICs need help to bring this about and 'development' is what they look to for improving systems of mental health care and promotion. People looking for evidence on how best mental health development may take place would find very little that is of use in publications in peer-reviewed journals because most research reported there has been carried out within a framework that is not applicable to non-Western settings. Further, there is very little hard data available about the efficacy of systems of mental health indigenous to LMICs – i.e. those derived from (say) Ayurveda or African ways of dealing with illness (mainly seen from a holistic standpoint), or from systems of social care and support. But that does not mean that the mental health of people in LMICs is not helped by these seemingly 'non-scientific' therapies and care. Some recent studies published in prestigious journals suggest that the opposite may well be the case. Developing mental health systems in LMICs is not a simple matter of transferring strategies commonly used in high-income countries. The idea that a 'global' system exists, and that it is justified to impose this in all locations, negates the human rights of *local* people who deserve something that is locally relevant – fit for *their* purposes and *their* needs. For mental health is not just a technical matter but is tied up with ways of life, values and worldviews that vary significantly across cultures and societies.

Mental health services in non-Western LMICs should be 'home-grown', suited to the cultural context and needs of the communities themselves. They need to be developed against a background of knowledge about the culturally determined meaning of 'mental health' in the countries concerned and care should be taken to avoid imposing unmodified models derived from psychiatry and Western psychology – because they are branded as 'scientific' and 'modern' – something that is now highly questionable anyway. However, approaches developed in the West may indeed have some relevance, particularly when they are rethought from the perspectives of transcultural psychiatry, and they should not be automatically excluded during service development. An approach that may be useful is to make community consultation the starting point of all development; then, Western expertise could be brought in in an advisory role rather than a decision-making or determining role.

References

Angell, M. (2005). *The truth about drug companies: How they deceive us and what to do about it.* New York: Random House.

Angell, M. (2011a). The epidemic of mental illness: Why? *New York Review of Books*, 23 June 2011.

Angell, M. (2011b). The illusions of psychiatry. *New York Review of Books*, 14 July 2011.

Angermeyer, M. C., Holzinger, A., Carla, M. G. and Scholerus, G. (2011). Biogenetic explanations and public acceptance of mental illness: Systematic review of population studies. *British Journal of Psychiatry, 199*, 367–372.

Baumann, Z. (2011). *Culture in a liquid modern world.* Cambridge: Polity Press.

Bemme, D. and D'souza, N. (2012). Global mental health and its discontents. *Somatosphere.* Retrieved 26 April 2013 from http://somatosphere.net/2012/07/global-mental-health-and-its-discontents.html.

Bentall, R. P. (2010). *Doctoring the mind: Why psychiatric treatments fail.* London: Penguin.

Bhui, K. and Olajide, D. (1999). *Mental health service provision for a multi-cultural society.* London: Saunders.

Carlat, D. (2010). *Unhinged: The trouble with psychiatry – A doctor's revelation about a profession in crisis.* New York: Free Press.

Cohen, A., Kleinman, A. and Saraceno, B. (Eds.). (2002). *World mental health casebook: Social and mental programs in low-income countries.* New York: Kluwer Academic/Plenum Publishers.

Cohen, A., Patel, V., Thara, R. and Gureje, O. (2008). Questioning an axiom: Better prognosis for schizophrenia in the developing world? *Schizophrenia Bulletin, 34*(2), 229–244.

Collins, P. Y., Patel, V., Joestl, S. S., March, D., Insel, T. R. and Dar, A. (2011). Grand challenges in global mental health. *Nature, 475*, 27–30.

Day, M. (2007). Who's funding WHO? *British Medical Journal, 334*, 338–339.

Fernando, S. (2010). *Mental health, race and culture* (3rd ed.). Basingstoke: Palgrave.

Fernando, S. (2011). A global mental health program or markets for Big Pharma? *Openmind, 168*, 22.

Fernando, S. and Keating, F. (2009). *Mental health in a multi-ethnic society. A multidisciplinary handbook* (2nd ed.). London and New York: Routledge.

Field, M. J. (1960). *Search for security: An ethnocentric study of rural Ghana.* Evanston, IL: Northwestern University Press.

Frances, A. (2012, 11 May). Disgnosing the DSM. *New York Times.* Retrieved from www.nytimes.com/2012/05/12/opinion/break-up-the-psychiatric-monopoly.html?_r=0.

Gates Foundation. (2010). Global Health Strategy Overview. *Bill and Melinda Gates Foundation.* Retrieved 20 April 2012 from www.gatesfoundation.org/global-health/Documents/global-health-strategy-overview.pdf.

Gilbert, J. (2002). Responding to mental stress in the Third World: Cultural imperialism or the struggle for synthesis. In D. Eade (Ed.), *Development and culture: Selected essays from development in practice* (pp. 155–167). Oxford: Oxfam in association with World Faiths Development Dialogue.

Halliburton, M. (2004). Finding a fit: Psychiatric pluralism in South India and its implications for WHO studies of mental disorder. *Transcultural Psychiatry, 41*(1), 80–89.

Haro, J. M., Novick, D., Bertsch, J., Karagianis, J. and Dossenbach, M. (2011). Cross-national clinical and functional remission rates: Worldwide Schizophrenia Outpatient Health Outcomes (W-SOHO) study. *British Journal of Psychiatry, 199*, 194–201.

Ingleby, D. (2004). *Critical psychiatry: The politics of mental health.* London: Free Association Books.

Jablensky, A., Sartorius, N., Ernberg, G., Anker, M., Korten, A., Cooper, J. E. *et al.* (1992). *Schizophrenia: Manifestations, incidence and course in different cultures.* Psychological Medicine (Monographs Supplement 20). Cambridge: Cambridge University Press.

Kirmayer, L. J. (2006). Beyond the 'new cross-cultural psychiatry': Cultural biology, discursive psychology and the ironies of globalisation. *Transcultural Psychiatry, 43*(1), 126–144.

Kirsch, I. (2009). *The emperor's new drugs: Exploding the antidepressant myth.* London: The Bodley Head.

Kleinman, A. (1977). Depression, somatization and the 'new cross cultural psychiatry'. *Social Science and Medicine, 11*, 3–10.

Obeyesekere, G. (1977). The theory and practice of psychological medicine in the Ayurvedic tradition. *Culture, Medicine and Psychiatry, 1*, 155–181.

Pieterse, J. N. (2007). *Ethnicities and global multiculture: Pants for an octopus.* Plymouth, New York and Toronto: Rowman & Littlefield.

Pieterse, J. N. (2009). *Globalisation and culture: Global mélange.* Plymouth, New York and Toronto: Rowman & Littlefield.

Raguram, R., Venkateswaram, A., Ramakrishna, J. and Weiss, M. (2002). Traditional community resources for mental health: A report of temple healing from India. *British Medical Journal, 325*, 38–40.

Ramon, S. and Williams, J. E. (Eds.). (2005). *Mental health at the crossroads. The promise of the psychosocial approach.* Aldershot: Ashgate.

Read, J., Haslam, N., Sayce, L. and Davies, F. (2006). Prejudice and schizophrenia: A review of the 'mental illness like any other' approach. *Acta Psychiatrica Scandinavica, 114*, 303–318.

Saraceno, B. (2004). Mental health: Scarce resources need new paradigms. *World Psychiatry, 3*, 3–6.

Scull, A. (1984). *Decarceration: Community treatment and the deviant – A radical view* (2nd ed.). Cambridge: Polity Press.

Shukla, A., Philip, A., Zachariah, A., Phadke, A., Suneetha, A., Davar, B. *et al.* (2012). Critical perspectives on the NIMH initiative 'Grand Challenges to Global Mental Health'. *Indian Journal of Medical Ethics, 9*(4), 292–293.

Summerfield, D. (2012). Afterword: Against 'global mental health'. *Transcultural Psychiatry, 49*(3), 1–12.

Tew, J. (2002). *Social perspectives in mental health: Developing social models to understand and work with mental distress.* London: Jessica Kingsley.

van Ommeren, M., Saxena, S. and Saraceno, B. (2005). Mental and social health during and after acute emergencies: Emerging consensus? *Bulletin of the World Health Organization, 83*(1), 71–75.

Watters, E. (2011). *Crazy like us: The globalization of the Western mind.* London: Constable & Robinson.

Whittaker, R. (2010). *Anatomy of an epidemic: Magic bullets, psychiatric drugs, and the astonishing rise of mental illness in America.* New York: Broadway.

WHO (World Health Organization). (1973). *Report of the International Pilot Study of Schizophrenia*, vol. 1. Geneva: WHO.

WHO. (1975). *Schizophrenia: A multinational study – A summary of the initial evaluation phase of the International Pilot Study of Schizophrenia.* Geneva: WHO.

WHO. (1979). *Schizophrenia: An international follow-up study.* Chichester, New York, Brisbane & Toronto: John Wiley.

WHO. (1988). *From Alma-Ata to the year 2000: Reflections at the midpoint.* Geneva: WHO.
WHO. (2001). *The world health report 2001: Mental health – New understanding, new hope.* Geneva: World Health Organisation.
WHO. (2002). *Working with countries: Mental health policy and service.* Geneva: WHO.
WHO. (2010). *mhGap Interventions Guide.* Geneva: WHO.
WHO Regional Office for South-East Asia. (2008). *Broad regional strategy for non-communicable diseases and mental health: Mental health and substance abuse.* New Delhi: WHO Regional Office for South-East Asia. Retrieved from www.searo.who.int on 15 September 2008.
WHO/UNICEF. (1978). *Primary health care: The Alma Ata conference.* Geneva: WHO.

15 Critical psychiatry in Canada

Laurence J. Kirmayer

Introduction

The work of Suman Fernando has been an inspiration for many in Canada striving to address a long and complex legacy of social exclusion, marginalization and institutionalized racism and discrimination in psychiatry and health services. His writing and advocacy have served to unmask inequities in mental health care in the United Kingdom, and through his visits and teaching, he has provided a spur to similar critical analyses and service development in Canada. Attention to these issues has been complicated by a distinctive Canadian tradition of deference to authority (Friedenberg, 1980) and an overly benign self-image that has contributed to complacency within the field of mental health.

In raising awareness of issues of racism and oppression, Fernando's work has served a vital function of breaking through this complacency, ethnocentric "colour-blindness" and "repressive tolerance". At the same time, it has made it clear that the situation in Canada is not the same as that in the United Kingdom, United States or other major centers where versions of critical psychiatry have been advanced. Distinctive features of the Canadian context include very high levels of diversity in large cities, policies of integration that explicitly value the maintenance of cultural heritage among newcomers and a benign self-image as a tolerant society. These realities make it comfortable for people to identify themselves as "hyphenated Canadians" with a mixed identity or heritage, and research and clinical practice in cultural psychiatry has emphasized the impact of ethnicity on illness explanations, help-seeking and coping. The struggle of Aboriginal peoples in Canada for political recognition is also central to issues of equity in health. We thus need our own analysis of the nature of racism, marginalization, oppression and social exclusion, even though we have been and continue to be heavily influenced by the cultural values, policies and political agendas of the United Kingdom and United States, both historically and now through new media and the forces of globalization. Finding the right conceptual vocabulary and stance toward the inequalities in our society and their impact on mental health is a major challenge.

In this chapter, I outline some of the distinctive features of the Canadian context to show how attention to issues of migration, racialization and marginalization have influenced approaches to diversity in psychiatry and mental health. This has relevance for the development of critical psychiatry not only in Canada but also in the United States and United Kingdom and other places where models and approaches tend to be presented as universally applicable rather than as a response to unique local circumstances. More broadly, I will try to show how cultural perspectives can inform our understanding of social inequality and the struggle for equity in mental health services.

Thinking about difference in Canada

Fernando has done much to draw attention to the importance of racialized identities for psychiatry (Fernando, 2002, 2003, 2005). Indeed, in the United Kingdom cultural psychiatry was for a long time more or less synonymous with anti-racist psychiatry (Kareem and Littlewood, 1992; Lipsedge and Littlewood, 1982). Compared to the United Kingdom, in Canada the development of cultural psychiatry has paid less attention to issues of racism and discrimination. Uncovering the reasons for this inattention and redressing the problems it has evaded are ongoing issues for a critically engaged cultural psychiatry.

Much of the discussion of racism in psychiatry has been driven by the scenarios in the United Kingdom and United States, both of which differ in important ways from Canada. Although the ideologies and institutional systems of racism are rooted in global historical processes of colonization and the slave trade (Fredrickson, 2002), the particular racialized categories at play in a given society reflect local histories and politics. Just as there are different versions of multiculturalism and multi-ethnic societies, "[t]he multi has to also apply to our analysis of racism: there is not a singular racism but multiple racisms" (Modood, 2007, p. 44). The forms that racism takes in each society reflect local politics, and addressing these practices requires attention to historical and current social contexts and dynamics (Elliot and Fleras, 1992).[1]

In Canada, the Constitution of 1867 defined Canadian identity in terms of the identities of the two charter groups who were descendants of English and French settlers. Aboriginal peoples, who were the original inhabitants of the Americas and made it possible for the early settlers to survive, were marginalized in this process of nation building. A broader Canadian identity emerged in the 1940s with the rise of the welfare state, focused on the notion of a community of citizens. Medicare, the universal system of health insurance which aims to insure equitable access to health care, has been viewed as a key expression of this notion of community. In Canada, overt discussion of race, class and other divisions have been largely subordinated to considerations of language and ethnicity. Canadians have tended to view their society as lacking major divisions and disparities and as being essentially classless (Comeau and Allahar, 2001). Both at home and abroad, Canada's history has been viewed as more tolerant and less racist or exclusionary than that of Australia, the United Kingdom or the United States (Mackey, 1999). However, this portrait ignores the discriminatory practices that have been central to immigration policy, dominant institutions and collective self-definition. The effect has been an ideological tendency to deny various forms of inequality in the society, including gender, race and class.

Unlike the United States and United Kingdom, Canada did not build an empire or extensive network of colonies. Colonialism in Canada has been largely internal, directed to the subjugation of indigenous peoples. Canada had a smaller slave industry than the United States and was the end of the underground railroad that slaves followed to escape the United States. However, Canada has had its own system of discriminatory and exclusionary practices, founded on similar racist ideologies and anxieties.

From its inception, Canada had an immigration policy that aimed to protect the "white" identity of the nation (Ward, 2005).[2] The 1910 Immigration Act officially designated race as a legal category and imposed head taxes on Chinese immigrants (Jakubowski, 1997, p. 16). Security concerns were repeatedly used to justify harsh discriminatory measures. During World War II, Japanese Canadians were interned in camps and lost their property. The *St. Louis*, a ship carrying Jews fleeing Nazi Germany, tried to dock in Canada and was turned away (Abella, 2000). Discriminatory laws and practices persisted for a long time. Chinese Canadians could vote in elections only after 1947, when the government also rescinded the Continuous Journey Act and allowed Indo-Canadians to vote. Attitudes toward non-white immigrants started to change more substantially in the 1950s and 1960s, but it was not until 1962 that the government officially set aside the "white Canada" policies of the past and ended explicit racial discrimination in immigration law (Kivisto, 2002, p. 97).

Psychiatrists have played a role in these practices of exclusion, in particular in immigrant screening and deportation. North American psychiatrists generally supported the medical inspection of immigrants (Dowbiggin, 1995). "Immigration entry restrictions on the basis of 'lunacy and idiocy' were present as early as 1869 in Canada's first Immigration Act" (Comeau and Allahar, 2001, p. 149). "The belief was that immigrants were more prone to violent crime, insanity, moral degeneracy, and subversive activities created fears of race suicide, whereby the pure Canadian would stop reproducing in the face of this onslaught of degeneracy" (Comeau and Allahar, 2001, p. 151). Institutional racism influences the treatment of minorities in Canada in complex ways. There is some evidence that Afro-Canadian patients receive differential treatment in the mental health care system; they may be less likely to be referred to outpatient mental health services for common mental health problems and, when suffering from psychosis, may be more likely to receive coercive treatment (Jarvis, Kirmayer, Jarvis and Whitley, 2005; Kirmayer *et al.*, 2007). Much of the complicity of psychiatry in racist discourse and discriminatory practices, however, has been expressed on a micro-social scale through biased assessment and public comments on specific cases (Knowles, 1996). In many cases, these biases may be unconscious, expressed in common stereotypes, or hidden by a focus on social structural issues like poverty, without adequate consideration of the ways in which economic disadvantage itself is racialized.

Of course, psychiatrists and other mental health practitioners have also been advocates for individuals and communities facing discrimination. There have been efforts to address racialized inequalities in the policy reports for government commissions (Federal Task Force on Mental Health Issues Affecting Immigrants and Refugees, 1988; McKenzie, Hansson, Tuck and Lurie, 2010). Most recently, many psychiatrists have been active in efforts to protect refugee rights and promote social inclusion and better services for minorities (e.g., Rousseau *et al.*, 2008; Rousseau, Hassan, Moreau and Thombs, 2011).

The view of Canada as relatively benign – as having less overt racism and discrimination than the United States, with a smaller-scale history of slavery and little external colonialism – has allowed Canadians to sidestep our own history of racism and inequality, including discriminatory immigration policies and institutionalized racism in many public and private organizations (including the university) (Dowbiggin, 1995; Gunew, 2003; Satzewich, 2011). The relative lack of ongoing discussion of these issues makes it difficult to raise concerns in clinical settings.

Multiculturalism and the politics of diversity

Despite the stark examples of racism and discrimination recounted above, Canada has provided a comparatively welcoming space for newcomers (Heath and Cheung, 2007). In large part, this reflects cultural values that have been reinforced by the official policy of multiculturalism which represents a political commitment to some form of unity in diversity.

Canada was the first country to have an official policy of multiculturalism. Although multiculturalism was devised in part to address the tensions between the English and French, it has its roots in long-standing demographic facts. Over the last 100 years almost one in five Canadians at any given time have immigrated from other countries. Rather than the large ethnoracial blocs in the United States, Canada has been a patchwork quilt of many smaller ethnic groups. Newcomers and long-standing ethnocultural communities have tended to congregate in cities and form enclaves where they can live out aspects of their cultural life through local institutions. This diversity is the basic fabric of Canadian society from which many draw a sense of collective identity. For many, to be a Canadian is to be a hyphenated Canadian, comfortable with a bicultural identity.

Multiculturalism as a term simply describing the fact of cultural diversity in a society must be distinguished from multiculturalism as a political process, aimed at "managing" that diversity, guided and regulated by a set of government policies. Multiculturalism as policy makes cultural diversity an explicit norm or virtue by supporting the maintenance of distinct ethnocultural identities and establishing overarching forms of recognition that include diverse groups within a pluralistic civil society (Guttman, 1992).

In Canada, approaches to multiculturalism have reflected the politics of two founding settler peoples, and this factors into the definition of culture itself. Not all forms of diversity are recognized as cultures in theories of multiculturalism, which generally adopt some version based on existing distinctive ethnocultural groups worthy of formal political recognition. For example, Kymlicka (1995), a major theorist of multiculturalism, approaches culture as synonymous with community. But this definition may not fully address the hybrid cultures that arise from the inter-mixing of peoples, the transnational identities of diasporic peoples or the emergent cultures of the Internet that weave together communities of interest who congregate in virtual places of games and social media. These communities lack conventional "territorial concentration" – or even geographic location – and institutional completeness, yet may be central to individuals' identities and ways of life.

Critiques of multiculturalism must be understood against the backdrop of the local history and political uses of the construct (Ryan, 2010). The basic claims against multiculturalism are that (1) it undermines collective identity and solidarity and (2) it limits cultural identity and assigns people to bounded, homogenizing groups that do not respect the complexity and fluidity of their actual identities and commitments. In the popular media, the arguments against multiculturalism include many contradictory claims. Multiculturalism is said to harm people by fostering moral relativism or moral absolutism, excessive individualism or conformity and generally by fostering unrealistic expectations concerning society's obligations to members of minority groups and resentment when those expectations are not met. At the same time, critics argue that multiculturalism also harms cultures, by promoting stereotypes and reducing the rich dynamics of community to "objects for display", or to "festivals and food fairs". More conservative critics worry that multiculturalism harms society by offering a poisoned view of history, obsessed with various alleged sins of our past. The result will be a loss of our coherence as a society and the exchange of collective solidarity for mere coexistence of divergent groups separated by cultural walls or boundaries (Ryan, 2010, pp. 41–42).

In fact, there is evidence that Canadian multiculturalism has had positive effects. For example, Bloemraad (2006) argues that multiculturalism contributes to immigrant integration in several ways: legitimating immigrants' sense of belonging to both Canadian society and their homeland; providing resources to community organizations that ultimately promote citizenship and participation; orienting ethnic community leaders toward engagement with political processes of inclusion and citizenship; and changing the symbolic landscape of public discourse to include ethnocultural minorities.

A further challenge to the ideals of multiculturalism comes from the dynamics of Canada as a consociation of peoples. Descendants of French settlers may see themselves as a minority in the context of predominately English-speaking Canada or North America and hence invoke some of the same rights to protection of identity accorded minorities. At the same time, in reality, they are the dominant cultural group, and gets to define the social matrix into which newcomers must integrate. This dilemma has been expressed through a preference for social integration through interculturalism rather than multiculturalism (Bouchard and Taylor, 2008). The metaphor of interculturalism implies a dialogical encounter or exchange between two cultures as the basic structure of social institutions. In practice, however, interculturalism often expresses a fundamental asymmetry in which French culture is contrasted with that of ethnic minorities and questions about the limits of "reasonable accommodation" to the other become paramount (Bouchard and Taylor, 2008).

The deployment of multiculturalism and interculturalism as policy and practice is still in its early phases. Hence, reports of the "death of multiculturalism" are premature and represent a failure of commitment rather than a reasoned response to obstacles. The rejection of multiculturalism has been fueled by anxieties about terrorism that are out of proportion to its impact (Appadurai, 2006), and do not give sufficient weight to all the positive effects of policies of inclusion that have manifest effects on mental health and well-being (Kirmayer, 2011).

The predicament of Aboriginal peoples

Although official history and the myths of nation building emphasized the role settlers, North America was populated by indigenous peoples for millennia before the European colonization. Recent acknowledgment of the primacy of indigenous peoples has exerted much influence on contemporary debates about cultural diversity in Canada. Following the Oka Crisis of 1990, the Royal Commission on Aboriginal Peoples (1996) collected much testimony that laid bare the long history of policies of marginalization, oppression and forced assimilation. These have resulted in great disparities in health, with high suicide rates among young people in many communities and over-representation of Aboriginal peoples in the social welfare and criminal justice systems (Kirmayer and Valaskakis, 2008; King, Smith and Gracey, 2009).

From the earliest times of contact, church and government worked hand-in-hand to undermine and prohibit traditional religious and cultural practices. Aboriginal peoples living near settlements were repeatedly displaced from their traditional lands and pushed to progressively less desirable land. Nomadic peoples were sedentarized to provide them with education and medical care but along with this came radical changes in lifestyle and increasing bureaucratic surveillance and control. Among the most violent and disruptive policies involved the elaborate system of over 100 residential schools, which operated from the late 1800s into the 1980s and through which more than 150,000 Aboriginal children were schooled in Euro–Canadian ways. The schools resulted in early and prolonged separation of children from family and community and immersion in institutional regimes that included the deliberate denigration and extirpation of language, culture and tradition. Whole generations of children endured these oppressive policies that have wreaked havoc among Aboriginal communities. In the 1960s, child welfare organizations adopted a strategy of systematic out-adoption for Aboriginal children from troubled homes. The destructive effects of these policies were recognized in a formal apology by the Canadian government on June 11, 2008. This was followed by the establishment of a Truth and Reconciliation Commission, which has crossed the country witnessing stories of survivors to build an archive so that this history can be documented and become more widely known.

For Aboriginal peoples, reciprocity and renewal were at the basis of the encounter with Europeans. The treaties represented not only binding political agreements but also sacred agreements, with profound moral import. The political structures that emerged from the struggles of two European founding peoples and the encounter with indigenous peoples gave Canada its distinctive political language of "fairness" (Saul, 2008). Indeed, the philosopher and cultural critic John Ralston Saul has argued that Canada should understand itself as a "Metis Nation" founded on values of fairness, sharing and exchange central to indigenous communities.

While some progress has been made to redressing the wrongs of the past, much work remains and this involves transforming attitudes of the society as a whole. The Royal Commission on Aboriginal Peoples (1996) argued that four principles should guide the renewed relationship with the state: mutual recognition, mutual respect, sharing and mutual responsibility. Mutual recognition has three major facets: equality, co-existence and self-government. These principles can govern a renewal of civil society that is inclusive of indigenous peoples and, when framed in terms of a larger multiculturalism, can be extended to consider the communities of newcomers as well. As Saul notes, "the missing conversation, which is desperately needed, is between Aboriginals and new Canadians" (p. 282).

Implications for psychiatry

The history outlined above shapes the distinctive ways that diversity and disparities are addressed in mental health policy and practice in Canada. In particular, it influences the ways that cultural identity is defined, the kinds of difference to which mental health services are expected to respond and the strategies adopted in mental health training and service delivery.

The Mental Health Commission of Canada (2012) identified responding to the diversity of society and redressing the health disparities of Aboriginal peoples as priorities in its strategy for a reformed mental health care system. Diversity in this context is framed broadly to include immigrants, refugees, ethnocultural communities as well as racialized groups. In this broad view, everyone has a distinctive culture and contributes to society not despite this difference but precisely through its public expression. Hence, attention to culture and ethnicity must be a concern of mainstream institutions and services. One model of service consistent with these values is cultural consultation, which provides resources and expertise to address relevant social and cultural issues in mental health through case-based consultations to primary care providers and other front-line clinicians (Kirmayer, Guzder and Rousseau, 2013).

The First Nations, Inuit and Métis advisory committee of the Mental Health Commission of Canada emphasized the importance of addressing the long-standing inequities in mental health that derive from colonization and subsequent policies of forced assimilation. The advisory committee advocated developing strategies to ensure cultural safety in the health care system (Smye, Josewski and

Kendall, 2010). The concept of cultural safety, derived from work by Maori nurses, aims to address the structural inequalities and institutionalized racism that beset indigenous peoples in their efforts to seek care. The Indigenous Physicians Association of Canada (2009) has developed a curriculum for family physicians and medical students to present basic material for cultural competence. This includes awareness of collective history and its impact on identity, well-being and perceptions of health care services.

Addressing the inequities that arose from colonization is one basic component of cultural safety but it frames cultural difference in largely negative terms, as structures of disadvantage. The deliberate attempt to suppress indigenous ways of life has made the notion of culture salient for Aboriginal peoples and reclaiming and revitalizing cultural traditions is widely seen as an important component of personal and collective healing (Kirmayer and Valaskakis, 2008). Focusing on culture as intrinsic to collective identity and both individual and community well-being leads to consideration of distinctive sources of resilience among Aboriginal peoples that reside in their stories, connection to family and the land, and political activism (Kirmayer, Dandeneau, Marshall, Phillips and Williamson, 2011). Principles of cultural safety and attention to the cultural sources of resilience and well-being are equally relevant to the experience of immigrants, refugees and ethnocultural minorities as well as those from dominant cultural communities.

The clinical alliance has a complex historical and political background that includes histories of colonialism, racialized identities and systems of power and oppression that precede clinicians into the consulting room and that, inevitably, frame the therapeutic alliance. Approaches to training must therefore focus not simply on distinctive ethnocultural communities, minorities or racialized groups but on the cultural assumptions and practices of mental health professionals and institutions of the dominant society (Kirmayer *et al.*, 2012). However, forms of tacit individual and institutional racism that arise from ignorance, passivity, neglect or ethnocentrism rather than conscious animosity or deliberate exclusion may be harder to identify, and the person who raises these issues may be perceived as the source of the problem. This dilemma can be addressed in part in training through modeling a stance of self-reflexivity, critical awareness and advocacy. It is here that the work of Suman Fernando has made a signal contribution, and he has been immensely helpful in our own pedagogical efforts in this direction at McGill (Guzder and Rousseau, 2013).

Conclusion

The ways that nations frame cultural difference and respond to diversity vary according to their ideologies of identity, histories of migration, and citizenship policies. These responses, in turn, shape the delivery of mental health services. In Canada, the approach to diversity in mental health policy and practice reflects the history of two "founding peoples", official bilingualism and policies of multiculturalism. Behind this official history is a legacy of internal colonialism, discrimination and marginalization that has resulted in marked disparities in mental health and access to services for Aboriginal peoples as well as for many ethnocultural minorities.

The politics of alterity in clinical settings is determined by larger political attitudes toward the cultural "Other" but health care also constitutes a potential site of resistance and social transformation (Kirmayer, 2011). Recent acknowledgment of the cultural oppression of Aboriginal peoples has influenced ongoing discussions of transformation of the mental health care system and led to an emphasis on notions of "cultural safety". These concerns must be extended to other marginalized groups. In seeking to address these histories of inequality and exclusion, however, it is important that we always keep in mind the strengths and resilience of cultural communities. Anti-discrimination efforts are not simply a matter of resisting and rejecting racialized categories but require the active re-appropriation, affirmation and creative elaboration of collective identity.

Recognition of cultural specificity poses real challenges in health care, where clinicians face extraordinarily high levels of diversity. One response is to shift attention away from culture toward structural inequalities that contribute directly to health disparities and difficulties in access. The idea that social structural factors external to a group are more important determinants of behavior than internal cultural features ignores the extent to which these structures themselves depend on cultural arrangements both within the larger society and within and between groups (Modood, 2007). Although anthropologists have criticized the utility of the notion of culture in recent years, noting the ways in which it leads to reification and stereotyping when applied to clinical thinking, the term culture remains a useful placeholder for many important dimensions of social life and experience, notably, the collective strengths, communal practices and modes of identity, experience and communication that provide patients and clinicians with some of their deepest understandings and strongest commitments. Multicultural mental health can be an arena for building a pluralistic and inclusive civil society. Understanding the histories and cultural frameworks of the dominant social institutions is an essential step to revealing the ideologies that underwrite the politics of difference in mental health.

Notes

1 More generally, as Appadurai notes,

> minorities do not come preformed. They are produced in the specific circumstances of every nation and every nationalism. They are often the carriers of the unwanted memories of the acts of violence that produced existing states.... They are embarrassments to any state-sponsored image of national purity and state fairness.
>
> (Appadurai, 2006, p. 42)

2 Despite the claims of the Commonwealth to allow free circulation among constituent countries, practices developed to limit immigration. From 1904 to 1908, about 5,000 immigrants from India settled in Canada (mainly in British Columbia). The government feared this influx was the start of increasing immigration and constructed

arguments about how ill-suited South Asians were to the climate of Canada. This culminated in the crisis of the Komagata Maru in May 1914 in which 376 people were held in Vancouver harbor, refused entry to Canada and eventually forced to return to India on the technicality of the Continuous Journey law (Johnson, 1989). They were denied entry on the grounds of the Continuous Ship Journey Act of 1908, which was a calculated attempt to block migration from East India and the Middle East to Canada by insisting that journeys had to be made without stopping for refueling – an impossibility at the time (Jakubowski, 1997, p. 14).

References

Abella, I. (2000). *None is too many: Canada and the Jews of Europe, 1933–1948*. Toronto: Key Porter.
Appadurai, A. (2006). *Fear of small numbers: An essay on the geography of anger*. Durham, NC: Duke University Press.
Bloemraad, I. (2006). *Becoming a citizen: Incorporating immigrants and refugees in the United States and Canada*. Berkeley: University of California Press.
Bouchard, G. and Taylor C. (2008). *Building the future: A time for reconciliation* [abridged report]. Quebec: Commission de consultation sur les pratiques d'accommodement relies aux differences cultural, Gouvernment du Quebec.
Comeau, T. D. and Allahar, A. L. (2001). Forming Canada's ethnoracial identity: Psychiatry and the history of immigration practices. *Identity: An International Journal of Theory and Research, 1*(2), 143–160.
Dowbiggin, I. (1995). Keeping this country sane: C. K. Clarke, immigration restriction, and Canadian psychiatry, 1890–1925. *Canadian Historical Review, 76*(4), 598–627.
Elliot, J. L. and Fleras, A. (1992). *Unequal relations: An introduction to race and ethnic dynamics in Canada*. Toronto: Prentice Hall.
Federal Task Force on Mental Health Issues Affecting Immigrants and Refugees. (1988). *After the door has been opened: Mental health issues affecting immigrants and refugees in Canada*. Ottawa: Health and Welfare Canada.
Fernando, S. (2002). *Mental health, race and culture* (2nd ed.). New York: Palgrave.
Fernando, S. (2003). *Cultural diversity, mental health and psychiatry: The struggle against racism*. New York: Routledge.
Fernando, S. (2005). Multicultural mental health services: Projects for minority ethnic communities in England. *Transcultural Psychiatry, 42*(3), 420–436.
Fredrickson, G. M. (2002). *Racism: A short history*. Princeton, NJ: Princeton University Press.
Friedenberg, E. Z. (1980). *Deference to authority: The case of Canada*. New York: Random House.
Gunew, S. M. (2003). *Haunted nations: The colonial dimensions of multiculturalisms*. New York: Routledge.
Gutmann, A. (Ed.). (1992). *Multiculturalism and "the politics of recognition": An essay by Charles Taylor*. Princeton, NJ: Princeton University Press.
Guzder, J. and Rousseau, C. (2013). A diversity of voices: The McGill "Working with Culture" seminars. *Culture, Medicine & Psychiatry, 37*(2), 347–364.
Heath, A. and Cheung, S. Y. (2007). *Unequal chances: Ethnic minorities in Western labour markets*. Oxford: Oxford University Press.
Indigenous Physicians Association of Canada & The Royal College of Physicians & Surgeons of Canada. (2009). *Cultural safety in practice: A curriculum for family medicine*

residents and physicians. Winnipeg and Ottawa: IPAC-RCPSC Family Medicine Curriculum Development Working Group.

Jakubowski, L. M. (1997). *Immigration and the legalization of racism.* Halifax, NS: Fernwood Publishing.

Jarvis, G. E., Kirmayer, L. J., Jarvis, G. K. and Whitley, R. (2005). The role of Afro-Canadian status in police or ambulance referral to emergency psychiatric services. *Psychiatric Services, 56*(6), 705–710.

Johnson, H. (1989). *The voyage of the Komagata Maru: The Sikh challenge to Canada's colour bar.* Vancouver: University of British Columbia Press.

Kareem, J. and Littlewood, R. (Eds.). (1992). *Intercultural therapy: Themes, interpretations and practice.* Oxford: Blackwell Scientific Publications.

King, M., Smith, A. and Gracey, M. (2009). Indigenous health part 2: the underlying causes of the health gap. *Lancet, 374*(9683), 76–85.

Kirmayer, L. J. (2011). Multicultural medicine and the politics of recognition. *Journal of Medicine and Philosophy, 36*(4), 410–423.

Kirmayer, L. J., Dandeneau, S., Marshall, E., Phillips, M. K. and Williamson, K. J. (2011). Rethinking resilience from indigenous perspectives. *Canadian Journal of Psychiatry, 56*(2), 84–91.

Kirmayer, L. J., Fung, K., Rousseau, C., Lo, H. T., Menzies, P., Guzder, J. *et al.* (2012). Guidelines for training in cultural psychiatry. *Canadian Journal of Psychiatry, 57*(3), Insert 1–16.

Kirmayer, L. J., Guzder, J. and Rousseau, C. (Eds.). (2013). *Cultural consultation: Encountering the Other in mental health care.* New York: Springer.

Kirmayer, L. J. and Valaskakis, G. (Eds.). (2008). *Healing traditions: The mental health of Aboriginal peoples in Canada.* Vancouver: University of British Columbia Press.

Kirmayer, L. J., Weinfeld, M., Burgos, G., du Fort, G. G., Lasry, J. C. and Young, A. (2007). Use of health care services for psychological distress by immigrants in an urban multicultural milieu. *Canadian Journal of Psychiatry, 52*(5), 295–304.

Kivisto, P. (2002). *Multiculturalism in a global society.* Oxford: Blackwell.

Knowles, C. (1996). Racism and psychiatry. *Transcultural Psychiatric Research Review, 33*(3), 297–318.

Kymlicka, W. (1995). *Multicultural citizenship.* Oxford: Oxford University Press.

Lipsedge, M. and Littlewood, R. (1982). *Aliens and alienists: Ethnic minorities and psychiatry.* London: Penguin.

Mackey, E. (1999). *The house of difference: Cultural politics and national identity in Canada.* London, New York: Routledge.

McKenzie, K., Hansson, E., Tuck, A. and Lurie, S. (2010). Improving mental health services for immigrant, refugee, ethnocultural and racialized groups. *Canadian Issues* (Summer), 65–69.

Mental Health Commission of Canada. (2012). *Changing directions, changing lives: The mental health strategy for Canada.* Ottawa: Mental Health Commission of Canada.

Modood, T. (2007). *Multiculturalism.* Cambridge: Polity.

Phillips, A. (2007). *Multiculturalism without culture.* Princeton, NJ: Princeton University Press.

Rousseau, C., Hassan, G., Moreau, N. and Thombs, B. D. (2011). Perceived discrimination and its association with psychological distress among newly arrived immigrants before and after September 11, 2001. *American Journal of Public Health, 101*(5), 909–915.

Rousseau, C., ter Kuile, S., Munoz, M., Nadeau, L., Ouimet, M. J., Kirmayer, L. and Crepeau, F. (2008). Health care access for refugees and immigrants with precarious status: Public health and human right challenges. *Canadian Journal of Public Health,* *99*(4), 290–292.

Royal Commission on Aboriginal Peoples. (1996). *Report of the Royal Commission on Aboriginal Peoples.* Ottawa: The Commission.

Ryan, P. (2010). *Multicultiphobia.* Toronto: University of Toronto Press.

Satzewich, V. (2011). *Racism in Canada.* Don Mills, Ont.: Oxford University Press.

Saul, J. R. (2008). *A fair country: Telling truths about Canada.* Toronto: Viking Canada.

Smye, V., Josewski, V. and Kendall, E. (2010). *Cultural safety: An overview.* Ottawa: Mental Health Commission of Canada.

Ward, W. P. (2005). *White Canada forever: Popular attitudes and public policy toward Orientals in British Columbia.* Montreal: McGill Queen's University Press.

16 Culture, race and ethnicity in US psychiatry

Carl C. Bell and Dominica F. McBride

Introduction

People of color make up the majority of the world's population. Despite this fact, European–American, Western psychology and psychiatry have a prominent history of disregarding the cultural variation that goes along with culture, race and ethnicity and context. This historical irreverence has been destructive for many "people of color" in the United States and because of Suman Fernando's work, we see that it has been equally noxious for those outside the United States, supporting the view that this is a more universal fact rather than a contextual happening. It is because of people like Fernando that European–American, Western psychiatry has gone from a dark place of racial degradation to an era of working toward cultural sensitivity.

Over the years, American psychiatry has managed culture, race and ethnicity in various ways. From the beginning, cultural, racial and ethnic precepts in American psychiatry have been virtually ignored. Even now, there is significant confusion about how these three issues influence mental health and wellness. Currently, from meaningless to mundane to manipulative, culture, race and ethnicity are being used alternatively as a genetic, social-situational, an ethnic and/or meaningless variable, or even a political tool (Bell, 1994b). Fortunately, American psychiatry has progressed in this area from a time of cultural destructiveness to attempted cultural integration, although there is still significant room for growth.

The purpose of this chapter is to review the history of addressing issues of culture, race and ethnicity in American psychiatry. It will also be shown, where applicable, how Fernando's work illustrates the universality of racism, prejudice and cultural influences on mental health and how it validates people of color's experience in the United States by showing that it happens around the world.

History of culture, race and ethnicity in US psychiatry

The history of mental health, culture, race and ethnicity in the United States goes back to times of slavery, where disorders were identified particularly for people who were enslaved, to the present where culture, race and ethnicity are more valued and integrated into mainstream mental health services and diagnostic tools, like the *Diagnostic and Statistical Manual for Mental Disorders*. This section describes this difficult but hopeful story.

Slavery

During times of enslavement, diagnosis was used to try to keep control and a certain perspective on and for those who were enslaved. In 1851, Samuel A. Cartwright proposed two disorders that "affected" slaves: Drapetomania and Dysaethesia Aethopica. He identified Drapetomania as a disorder where slaves would run away and seek their freedom. Cartwright asserted that equal treatment was the cause of this disorder and the treatment was punishment designed to enforce submissiveness. The preventive mechanism was treating them like children (Cartwright, 2004). Dysaethesia Aethopica was characterized by laziness. This disorder was supposedly due to a partial insensitivity of the skin. Treatment consisted of stimulating the skin by washing it, covering it with oil and then slapping it with a leather strap, followed by hard work in the sun (Cartwright, 2004). Furthermore, there were few psychiatric facilities in which they were allowed to be treated, regardless of the mental disorder (Washington, 2006).

Pre- and post-civil rights era

Pinderhughes (1973) outlined two themes in US psychiatry – one prior to and another following the Civil Rights Movement. Prior to the Civil Rights Movement, US psychiatry was based in ethnocentric monoculturalism (Sue, 2004), and much of the psychiatric literature and practice was racist in nature and content. Racist science, such as eugenics, ruled the day, as shown in books like Kardiner and Ovesey's (1951) *The Mark of Oppression*; the thesis for the book was essentially that because of slavery and Jim Crow policies, American Negroes had a permanent mark of oppression on them. As a result, they were essentially hopeless, and such a history would permanently prevent Negroes from ever having any self-esteem.

After the Civil Rights Movement began to take hold, psychiatry began to open up and become more reflective about its past and present as it relates to culture, race and ethnicity. Thomas and Sillen (1972) published *Racism and Psychiatry*, which catalogued various aspects of racism in psychiatry and highlighted pitfalls of early psychiatric epidemiology that suggested, for example, that African Americans were too primitive to be depressed. Psychiatrists of Color especially began to take steps forward, identifying then current racist patterns in psychiatry, like what Pierce (1973) labeled in 1970 as microaggressions (Sue *et al.*, 2007) and Pinderhughes' (1979) identification of the human propensity to stereotype. In 1978, Bell (1978, 1980) proposed that racism might be related to narcissistic psychodynamics in bigots. In *Mental Health and People of Color* (1983), Chunn and colleagues called for more research and training in African American, Asian, Hispanic and Native American populations from the perspectives of psychiatrists, psychologists, nurses and social workers.

A year later, Fernando proposed that racism may contribute to depression (Fernando, 1984). In his seminal book, *Mental Health, Race and Culture*, he stated that "Racism is an integral part of Western culture" (Fernando, 1991, p. 26) and outlined the notion that European and European–American Western culture attempted to acculturate people of color and, thus, was destructive to them (Fernando, 1991, pp. 24–50). Still today, Western cultures destroy.

European–American, Western culture destroys

There are various examples that show the continued destructiveness of European–American, Western culture toward people of color. Despite equal rates of drug use (Alexander, 2010) and levels of violence (US Public Health Service, 2001) between African American and European American males, men of color constitute the majority in prisons (Alexander, 2010). US history reveals that law enforcement traditionally "hunted" runaway slaves and returned them to their owners. Although Jon Burge was sent to prison for lying about beating murder confessions from innocent black men (with the result that they were placed on "Death Row", only to be released decades later thanks to DNA evidence), though not imprisoned for the actual beatings (Federal Court Transcript, 2011), in Chicago the black community has a saying "The police hunt black men!" The reality is that there is a saying in Chicago that "The police hunt black men!" and the first person I heard that from was a retired Chicago police officer.

Here again Fernando's work comes into play by supporting US psychiatrists' observation of the destructive nature of European–American, Western culture. Unfortunately, due to America's tradition of monocultural ethnocentrism (Sue, 2004), Fernando's work, which parallels observations of US Psychiatrists of Color, has not been widely respected by American psychiatry. However, it has been of great support to Psychiatrists of Color in the United States. The experience of people of color is often invalidated (e.g., with of microaggression) and denigrated; thus, it is enormously helpful when someone in another country validates the human experience of prejudice and in-group out-group behavior, such as racism. Fernando's work clearly highlights the universality of racism, prejudice and cultural influences on mental health.

Era of cultural sensitivity

In the 1980s, America's cultural landscape began to shift from a bi-racial context (European American and African American) to a multicultural context. With the publication and translation of *DSM-III* (American Psychiatric Association, 1980) into 30 languages (Alarcon, 2009), more scientists began to wonder whether a US psychiatry nosology fit non-Western cultures. In 1980 and 1981, researchers in Chicago started a line of investigation that highlighted the misdiagnosis of black patients with manic depressive illness (Bell and Mehta, 1980, 1981). These articles led to a series of research investigations on the misdiagnosis of people of color (Adebimpe, 1994; Jones, Gray and Parson, 1981; Jones and Gray, 1986;

Mukherjee et al., 1983; Strakowski et al., 1996, 2003). During this time, black psychiatrists were busy addressing issues of racism (Brantly, 1983). Most notable was Chester Pierce (Pierce, 1988, 1992, 1995; Bell, 1994a), who began to emphasize the issues of microinsults, microaggressions and racism's analogy to torture and terrorism.

On the other side of the Atlantic, Fernando addressed the issue of misdiagnosis in ethnic minorities in Britain (Fernando, 1989). It was also Fernando who published the extraordinary *Mental Health, Race, and Culture* (1991), which addressed the issues of culture and racism in psychiatry in Britain, wellness in non-Western cultures, other cultures' healing techniques (e.g., acupuncture, yoga) and mental health promotion. Much of the information contained in this tome presaged many of the current mental health initiatives that are being developed in the United States, which will be discussed later.

Psychiatrists of Color in the United States also placed concentrated focus on how culture influenced diagnostic issues (Lu, Lim and Mezzich, 1995). Due to significant criticism about the lack of cultural sensitivity in *DSM-III* (Lewis-Fernandez and Diaz, 2002), cultural issues were addressed in *DSM-IV* (American Psychiatric Association, 1994). Although only two pages, the Cultural Formulation provided guidelines regarding how to consider patients' culture as a factor in diagnosis (Alcarnon, 2009). The Cultural Formulation discussed how to assess the cultural identity of the patient, explore the patient's cultural explanations of their illness, consider cultural factors related to the patient's psychosocial environment and levels of functioning, and account for cultural elements of the relationship between the patient and clinician (American Psychiatric Association, 1994). Thus, the idea was that by taking these steps, the diagnostician could obtain a relatively complete overall cultural assessment of the patient useful for diagnosis and care.

Culture-bound syndromes

In addition, *DSM-IV* included an incomplete glossary of "culture-bound syndromes". Unfortunately, the idea of capturing the influence of culture on psychiatric diagnosis by cataloguing "culture-bound syndromes" did not get much traction in the International Classification of Diseases (Alacron, 2009). Alacron (2009) proposed that this lack of traction is predominately due to the lack of research in issues of race and culture that shape psychiatric practice such as diagnosis and treatment. Fernando also wrote about the paradox of "culture-bound disorders" (1991, pp. 79–81); although "culture-bound" disorders might have some utility, this categorization may be conducive to further racism, as a "culture-bound" illness is often marginalized. Alacron's tacit suggestion may address this issue through further research on culture-bound syndromes and use in diagnosis (Alacron, 2009).

In the 21st century, the 16th Surgeon General of the United States began releasing extremely influential mental health reports and the *Culture, Race, and Ethnicity* report called for more research on culture, race and ethnicity (US

Public Health Service, 2001). This report consisted of several chapters on Asian, Black, Hispanic and Native American mental health issues and made the significant point that "culture counts". The report bemoans the reality that there is a dearth of empirical literature and research on people of color's psychiatric issues and health care disparities (Bell, 2003), including the problem of their absence in research investigations (Bell and Williamson, 2002). As a result, there has been an explosion of interest in mental health issues in people of color within the United States. A year after the Surgeon General's *Culture, Race, and Ethnicity* report was published, the American Psychiatric Association published *A Research Agenda for DSM-V* (Kupfer, First and Regier, 2002). This agenda contained a proposed research agenda to explore the influence of culture and psychiatric diagnosis, and also considered issues of culture, race and ethnicity in conceptualizing and assessing relational disorders.

More scientists started to explore cultural, racial and ethnic dynamics in US psychiatry and more psychiatrists made efforts to promote the use of the Cultural Formulation in *DSM-IV* (American Psychiatric Association, 2006a). In 2006, the American Psychiatric Association released its position statement entitled "Resolution against Racism and Racial Discrimination and Their Adverse Impacts on Mental Health", in which it stated that "The American Psychiatric Association recognizes that racism and racial discrimination adversely affect mental health by diminishing the victim's self-image, confidence, and optimal mental functioning" (American Psychiatric Association, 2006b). The statement also suggested, as Fernando had done (Fernando, 1984), that racism causes impairments in physical functioning (Carroll *et al.*, 2001; Faegin and Sikes, 1994; Karlsen and Nazroo, 2002).

The 21st century heralded many other advances in the issues of culture, race and ethnicity in US psychiatry. In the first decade of the new century, Carter (2007) published a seminal article that sought to highlight the issue of "race-based traumatic stress". In this thoughtful exposition, he appropriately noted that the issue of race-based trauma was poorly defined in US psychiatry. Thus, Carter (2007) proposed developing an objective-based measure of race-based trauma. However, such an assessment has not yet been developed, due in part to funding for "Researchers of Color" being more difficult to obtain (Ginther *et al.*, 2011); unfortunately it is mostly "Researchers of Color" who are by and large interested in such investigations.

Current status of the consideration of culture, race and ethnicity in American psychiatry

Research in the area of culture, race and ethnicity and mental health is still lacking today. Due to the dearth in this area, suggestions for mental health professionals from Bell (1996) are still relevant and need to be reiterated. Therapists should: (1) self-reflect around ethnicity, culture, race, class, family structure, education and social issues; (2) understand the barriers to promotion, access and employment that African Americans face and the frustration that ensues; (3)

gain knowledge of the importance of social cohesion and group identity; (4) be responsive to and direct with patients when appropriate; (5) be open to learning about the distrust, and reasons for it, around authority and the health care system; (6) understand the social issues that are conducive to African Americans feeling inferior and vulnerable and the ways this manifests in behavior; (7) be open to exploring the issues around self-image related to the biologic fallacy of race (e.g., hair texture, skin color); (8) understand the importance of establishing rapport; (9) be willing to explore potential problems of anger/hostility, self-esteem, confidence, assertiveness, initiative and the need for external approbation; (10) understand that some African Americans are confused about racism and have a continuous, torturous struggle with self-identity and self-determination; and (11) understand the initial and possible persistent difficulties in bi-racial therapist–client dyads.

Although in 2008, the American Medical Association apologized for its participation in racist behaviors (many counter to the aforementioned suggestions) toward African American physicians (Baker et al., 2008; Davis, 2008), there still is a great need to address the issues of cultural bias within American psychiatry. Regarding the need for cultural sensitivity in diagnostic criteria, more than half (N=74, or 55%) of the American Association of Community Psychiatry respondents noted that *DSM-IV* was difficult to apply across cultures, whereas 38% (N=51) noted that *DSM-IV* was useful and reliable in their practice regardless of ethnicity and culture. In addition, nearly one-third (N=41, or 31%) of the social psychiatry group felt that *DSM-IV* was over-embedded in concepts or values derived from European culture, and 27% (N=36) responded that *DSM-IV* was "too often unreliable or inappropriate where clinician and service user were from different cultures" (Bell, Sowers and Thompson, 2008). Toward this end, the *DSM-V* Research Agenda also proposed that research be done to determine the degree of cultural bias associated with various measures used in US psychiatry to determine its effect on the measure's validity (Kupfer et al., 2002). A perfect example of this problem was highlighted when Pinkham et al. (2008) discovered that the recent research on face-processing among African American and European American individuals with schizophrenia was fundamentally flawed due to a lack of cultural sensitivity (Bell, 2008). Prior to Pinkham's research (Pinkham et al., 2008) most face-processing research illustrated that African Americans with schizophrenia had greater impairment in recognizing and remembering emotions in faces compared with European American schizophrenia patients (Brekke, Nakagami, Kee and Green, 2005; Habel, 2000). Of course, these studies showed research subjects only European American faces. When shown both European American and African American faces, Pinkham et al. (2008) found that there was no appreciable difference between African American and European American schizophrenic patients when shown both African American and European American faces. As a greater appreciation of cultural sensitivity has been developing, there has been more investigation into the appropriate use of culturally sensitive measures and processes creeping into American psychiatry (Bell and McBride, 2011).

However, the research in this area is still lacking. Under the current paradigm of neuroscience, neuroscientists are now able to consider racism as a viable area of scientific study. Racism, for example, has been linked to anxiety disorders, which has in turn been examined in terms of amygdala abnormalities (Etkin, Prater, Schatzberg, Menon and Greicius, 2009), and oxytocin has also been found to mediate amygdala responsivity to emotional facial expressions (Domes et al., 2007). Less activity in the amygdala in relation to positive and negative stimuli may reflect a reduced uncertainty around social stimuli and, thereby, facilitate social approach behavior (Kirsch et al., 2005). Thus, as Bell and Dunbar (2012) note, the issue of racism is extremely complex, but investigations in this area of American psychiatry are gradually gaining ground. Dunbar and colleagues (Dunbar, 1997, 2003, 2004; Dunbar, Krop and Sullaway, 2000; Dunbar, Blanco, Sullaway and Horcajo, 2004; Dunbar and Simonova, 2003; Dunbar, Sullaway, Blanco, Horcajo and de la Corte, 2007) have been developing objective measures to tease out the dynamics of racism that stem from learned behavior and/or psychopathology.

Conclusion

Despite the efforts of mostly "Researchers of Color" and a few European American researchers, the issues of culture, race and ethnicity continue to elude research by American psychiatry. However, there is hope. Slowly but surely, research on whether or not some forms of racism are the product of a mental illness, neuropsychiatry or learned behavior is being published. Researchers are beginning to understand that they need to use culturally sensitive procedures and measures to obtain valid research results. Professional associations are beginning to decry racist practices within their professions. A Medline search on psychotherapy and various ethnic, racial and cultural groups reveals far more articles published in Britain since Fernando wrote his seminal work on *Mental Health, Race, and Culture* and Dr. Satcher published his seminal work on *Culture, Race, and Ethnicity*. With more sophisticated research tools, there is even a developing scientific literature on how culture, race and ethnicity impact mental health and wellness, an issue Fernando raised in the late 1970s.

Unfortunately, we still have a long way to go before people are actually judged by the content of their character and not the color of their skin or culture. As Fernando has long advocated, we need to not only honestly and fairly study issues around the psychopathology of culture, race and ethnicity, but we also need to study strength and resilience in various groups, as we can all learn from one another. Clearly, he has been a guiding light for the profession of psychiatry and we are lucky he has passed our way.

References

Adebimpe, V. R. (1994). Race, racism, and epidemiological surveys. *Hospital and Community Psychiatry*, 45(1), 27–31.

Alarcon, R. D. (2009). Culture, cultural factors and psychiatric diagnosis: Review and projections. *World Psychiatry, 8*(3), 131–139.
Alexander, M. (2010). *The new Jim Crow: Mass incarceration in the age of colorblindness.* New York: The New York Press.
American Psychiatric Association. (1980). *Diagnostic and Statistical Manual of Mental Disorders* (3rd ed.). Washington, DC: American Psychiatric Press, Inc.
American Psychiatric Association. (1994). *Diagnostic and Statistical Manual of Mental Disorders* (4th ed.). Washington, DC: American Psychiatric Press, Inc.
American Psychiatric Association. (2006a). Cultural formulation: From the APA Practice Guideline for the Psychiatric Evaluation of Adults, 2nd edition. *Focus, 4*(1), 11.
American Psychiatric Association. (2006b). *Resolution against racism and racial discrimination and their adverse impacts on mental health.* Washington, DC: American Psychiatric Association. Retrieved from www.psych.org/edu/other_res/lib_archives/archives/200603.pdf.
Baker, R. B., Washington, H. A., Olakanmi, O., Savitt, T. L., Jacobs, E. A., Hoover, E. and Wynia, M. K. (2008). African American physicians and organized medicine 1846–1968: Origins of a racial divide. *Journal of the American Medical Association, 300*(3), 306–313.
Bell, C. C. (1978). Racism, narcissism and integrity. *Journal of the National Medical Association, 70*(2), 89–92.
Bell, C. C. (1980). Racism: A symptom of the narcissistic personality disorder. *Journal of the National Medical Association, 72*(7), 661–665.
Bell, C. C. (1994a). Finding a way through the maze of racism. *Emerge, 5*(11), 80.
Bell, C. C. (1994b). Race as a variable in research: Being specific and fair. *Hospital and Community Psychiatry, 45*(1), 3.
Bell, C. C. (1996). Treatment issues for African-American men. *Psychiatric Annals, 26*(1), 33–36.
Bell, C. C. (2003). The making of the Surgeon General's Supplement to Mental Health: A brief commentary. *Culture, Medicine, and Ethnicity, 27,* 499–503.
Bell, C. C. (2004). Racism: a mental illness? *Psychiatric Services, 55*(12), 1343.
Bell, C. C. (2008). Recognizing each other and the effects of racial differences. *American Journal of Psychiatry, 165*(5), 560–561.
Bell, C. C. and Dunbar, E. (2012). Racism and psychopathology. In T. A. Widiger (Ed.). *The Oxford handbook of personality disorders* (pp. 694–709). New York: Oxford University Press.
Bell, C. C. and McBride, D. F. (2011). A commentary for furthering cultural sensitivity within research in geriatric psychiatry. *American Journal of Geriatric Psychiatry, 19*(5), 397–402.
Bell, C. C. and Mehta, H. (1980). The misdiagnosis of black patients with manic depressive illness. *Journal of the National Medical Association, 72*(2), 141–145.
Bell, C. C. and Mehta, H. (1981). The misdiagnosis of black patients with manic depressive illness: II. *Journal of the National Medical Association, 73*(2), 101–107.
Bell, C. C., Sowers, W. and Thompson, K. S. (2008). American Association of Community Psychiatrists' views on global features of DSM-IV. *Psychiatric Services, 59*(6), 687–689.
Bell, C. C. and Williamson, J. (2002). Psychiatric services across the millennium: A celebration of 50 years of *Psychiatric Services* journal – special populations. *Psychiatric Services, 53*(4), 419–424.
Brantly, T. (1983). Racism and its impact on psychotherapy. *American Journal of Psychiatry, 140,* 1605–1608.

Brekke, J. S., Nakagami, E., Kee, K. S. and Green, M. F. (2005). Cross-ethnic differences in perception of emotion in schizophrenia. *Schizophrenia Research, 77,* 289–298.

Carroll, D., Smith, G. D., Shipley, M. J., Steptoe, A., Brunner, E. F. and Marmot, M. G. (2001). Blood pressure reactions to acute psychological stress and future blood pressure status: A 10-year follow-up of men in the Whitehall II Study. *Psychosomatic Medicine, 63,* 737–743.

Carter, R. T. (2007). Racism and psychological and emotional injury: Recognizing and assessing race-based traumatic stress. *Counseling Psychology, 35,* 1–93.

Cartwright, S. A. (2004). Report on the disease and physical peculiarities of the Negro race. In A. L. Caplan, J. J. McCartney and D. A. Sisti (Eds.), *Health, disease and illness: Concepts in medicine* (pp. 28–39). Washington, DC: Georgetown University Press.

Chunn, J., Dunston, P. and Ross-Sheriff, F. (Eds.). (1983). *Mental health and people of color: Curriculum development and change.* Washington, DC: Howard University Press.

Davis, R. M. (2008). Achieving racial harmony for the benefit of patients and communities: Contrition, reconciliation, and collaboration. *Journal of the American Medical Association, 300*(3), 323–325.

Domes, G., Heinrichs, M., Gläscher, J., Büchel, C., Braus, D. F. and Herpertz, S. C. (2007). Oxytocin attenuates Amygdala responses to emotional faces regardless of valence. *Biological Psychiatry, 62*(10), 1187–1190.

Dunbar, E. (1997). The relationship of DSM diagnostic criteria and Gough's Prejudice Scale: Exploring the clinical manifestations of the prejudiced personality. *Cultural Diversity and Mental Health, 3*(4), 247–257.

Dunbar, E. (2003). Psycho-legal defense arguments of hate crime perpetrators. *Journal of Contemporary Criminal Justice, 15*(1), 64–78.

Dunbar, E. (2004). Reconsidering the clinical utility of bias as a mental health problem: Intervention strategies for psychotherapy practice. *Psychotherapy: Theory/Research/Practice/Training, 41*(2), 97–111.

Dunbar, E., Blanco, A., Sullaway, M. E. and Horcajo, J. (2004). Human rights and ethnic attitudes in Spain: The role of cognitive, social status and individual difference factors. *International Journal of Psychology, 39*(2), 106–117.

Dunbar, E., Krop, H. and Sullaway, M. E. (2000). *Behavioral, psychometric, and diagnostic characteristics of bias-motivated homicide offenders.* Unpublished manuscript.

Dunbar, E. and Simonova, L. (2003). Individual difference and social status predictors of anti-Semitism and racism: U.S. and Czech findings with the Prejudice/Tolerance and Right Wing Authoritarianism Scales. *International Journal of Intercultural Relations, 27,* 507–523.

Dunbar, E., Sullaway M., Blanco, A., Horcajo, J. and de la Corte L. (2007). Human rights attitudes and peer influence: The role of explicit bias, gender, and salience. *International Journal of Intercultural Relations, 31*(1), 51–66.

Etkin, A., Prater, K. E., Schatzberg, A. F., Menon, V. and Greicius, M. D. (2009). Disrupted amygdalar subregion functional connectivity and evidence of a compensatory network in generalized anxiety disorder. *Archives of General Psychiatry, 66*(12), 1361–1372.

Faegin, J. and Sikes, M. (1994). *Living with racism: The black middle class experience.* Boston, MA: Beacon Press.

Federal Court. (2011, January 21). The sentencing of Jon Burge [transcript, posted by Michael Miner]. Retrieved from www.chicagoreader.com/Bleader/archives/2011/01/24/the-sentencing-of-jon-burge.

Fernando, S. (1984). Racism as a cause of depression. *International Journal of Social Psychiatry, 30,* 41–49.
Fernando, S. (1989). Schizophrenia in ethnic minorities. *Psychiatric Bulletin, 13,* 573–574.
Fernando, S. (1991). *Mental health, race, and culture.* London: National Association for Mental Health (MIND).
Ginther, D. K., Schaffer, W. T., Schnell, J., Masimore, B., Liu, F., Haak, L. L. and Kington, R. (2011). Race, ethnicity, and NIH research awards. *Science, 333*(6045), 1015–1019.
Habel, U., Gur, R. C., Mandal, M. K., Salloum, J. B., Gur, R. E. and Schneider, F. (2000). Emotional processing in schizophrenia across cultures: Standardized measures of discrimination and experience. *Schizophrenia Research, 42,* 57–66.
Jones, B. E. and Gray, B. A. (1986). Problems in diagnosing schizophrenia and affective disorders among blacks. *Hospital and Community Psychiatry, 37*(1), 61–65.
Jones, B. E., Gray, B. A. and Parson, E. B. (1981). Manic-depressive illness among poor urban blacks. *American Journal of Psychiatry, 138*(5), 654–657.
Kardiner, A. and Ovesey, L. (1951). *The mark of oppression.* New York: Norton.
Karlsen, S. and Nazroo, J. Y. (2002). Relation between racial discrimination, social class, and health among ethnic minority groups. *American Journal of Public Health, 92,* 624–631.
Kirsch, P., Esslinger, C., Chen, Q., Mier, D., Lis, S., Siddhanti, S. *et al.* (2005). Oxytocin modulates neural circuitry for social cognition and fear in humans. *Journal of Neuroscience, 25*(49), 11489–11493.
Kupfer, D. J., First, M. B. and Regier, D. A. (eds). (2002). *A research agenda for DSM-V.* Washington, D.C.: American Psychiatric Association.
Lewis-Fernandez, R. and Diaz, N. (2002). The cultural formulation: A method for assessing cultural factors affecting the clinical encounter. *Psychiatric Quarterly, 73*(4), 271–295.
Lu, F., Lim, R. and Mezzich, J. (1995). Issues in the assessment and diagnosis of culturally diverse individuals. In J. Oldham and M. Riba (Eds.), *American Psychiatric Press review of psychiatry* (Vol. 14, pp. 477–510). Washington, DC: American Psychiatric Press.
Pierce, C. (1973). The formation of the Black Psychiatrists of America. In C. V. Willie, B. M. Kramer and B. S. Brown (Eds.), *Racism and mental health* (pp. 525–554). Pittsburgh, PA: University of Pittsburgh Press.
Pierce, C. (1992). *Public health and human rights: Racism, torture and terrorism.* Presented at American Psychiatric Association Annual Meeting, May 4, 1992, Washington, DC.
Pierce, C. (1995). Stress analogs of racism and sexism: Terrorism, torture, and disaster. In C. Willie, P. Rieker, B. Kramer and B. Brown (Eds.), *Mental health, racism, and sexism* (pp. 277–293). Pittsburgh, PA: University of Pittsburgh Press.
Pierce, C. (1998). Stress in the workplace. In A. F. Conner-Edwards and J. Spurlock (Eds.), *Black families in crisis* (pp. 27–33). New York: Brunner/Mazel.
Pinderhughes, C. (1973). Racism and psychotherapy. In C. V. Willie, B. M. Kramer and B. S. Brown (Eds.), *Racism and mental health* (pp. 61–121). Pittsburgh, PA: University of Pittsburgh Press.
Pinderhughes, C. (1979). Differential bonding: Toward a psychophysiological theory of stereotyping. *American Journal of Psychiatry, 136*(1), 33–37.
Pinkham, A. E., Sasson, N. J., Calkins, M. E., Richard, J., Hughett, P., Gur, R. E. and Gur, R. C. (2008). The other-race effect in face processing among African American and Caucasian individuals with schizophrenia. *American Journal of Psychiatry, 165*(5), 639–645.

Strakowski, S. M., Flaum, M., Amador, X., Bracha, H. S., Pandurangi, A. K., Robinson, D. and Tohen, M. (1996). Racial differences in the diagnosis of psychosis. *Schizophrenia Research, 21,* 117–124.

Strakowski, S. M., Keck, P. E., Arnold, L. M., Collins, J., Wilson, R. M., Fleck, D. E. *et al.* (2003). Ethnicity and diagnosis in patients with affective disorders. *Journal of Clinical Psychiatry, 64*(7), 747–754.

Sue, D. (2004). Whiteness and ethnocentric monoculturalism: Making the "invisible" visible. *American Psychologist, 59*(8), 761–769.

Sue, D. W., Capodilupo, C. M., Torino, G. C., Bucceri, J. M., Holder, A. M. B., Nadal, K. L. and Esquilin, M. (2007). Racial microaggressions in everyday life: Implications for clinical practice. *American Psychologist, 62*(4), 271–286.

Thomas, A. and Sillen, S. (1972). *Racism and psychiatry.* New York: Brunner/Mazel.

US Public Health Service. (2001). *Mental health: Culture, race and ethnicity – A Supplement to Mental Health: A Report of the Surgeon General.* Rockville, MD: US Public Health Service. Retrieved January 28, 2008 from: www.surgeongeneral.gov/library/mentalhealth/cre.

Washington, H. A. (2006). *Medical apartheid: The dark history of medical experimentation on black Americans from colonial times to the present.* New York: Doubleday.

17 Race, culture and psychiatry in South Africa

Nkokone Tema and Tholene Sodi

Introduction

The concepts of race and culture often raise emotions whenever they are debated. According to Fernando (2012), although the idea of "race" (based on physical characteristics of human beings, more especially skin colour and appearance) is no longer useful in the biological sciences, it has, however, continued to persist as a social reality. With a history that is inextricably tied to slavery and colonialism, the concept of race has continued to be mobilized as a useful tool by the proponents of racism – an ideology suggesting that human beings can be divided into groups or races that share some distinct features that will make these groups either desirable or less desirable, superior or less superior, or even intelligent or less intelligent. Culture, on the other hand, refers to a mixture of behaviour and cognition arising from shared patterns of belief that people carry in their minds (Fernando, 2010b). It is a flexible system of values and worldviews that people live by, a system by which we define aspects of our identities and negotiate our lives (Fernando, 2010b). In other words, culture is a kind of roadmap that guides human beings in shaping their identities and how they live their lives. The implication here is that the various cultural realities that people have created will influence their behaviour, including how they conceptualize and respond to conditions of ill health. In his publications, Fernando (1988) has identified race and culture as very critical in the field of psychiatry.

In South Africa, the twin concepts of racism and culture have played a significant role in shaping the provision of (mental) health services to communities. In this chapter, we explore the problematic nature of race and culture in South Africa using the work of Suman Fernando as a tool of analysis. We start by presenting the history of psychiatry in South Africa and demonstrate how racism was perpetuated through the different stages that this mental health discipline went through. We move on to illustrate how the colonial ideology of apartheid has negatively affected the provision of mental health services in South Africa. The second part of the chapter looks at how democratic South Africa has attempted to deal with the legacy of apartheid to address the mental health needs of all the people in the country. In this regard, some of the challenges that were created by the apartheid legacy are identified and highlighted while the legislative and policy interventions that were developed by the post-apartheid government are critically reviewed and presented. The unique challenges of a dual mental health care system (i.e. the Western-oriented and indigenous health care systems) that has been accentuated by the apartheid legacy are highlighted. In the third part of the chapter, we look critically at the role of culture in the training of mental health workers, including the associated challenges. In the last part, we focus on the role of indigenous healing in South Africa and move on to highlight some of the prospects and challenges associated with calls for the integration of this alternative health care system and the Western mental health care system in the treatment of mental illness and other conditions of ill health. We conclude the chapter by highlighting the potential contributions that Suman Fernando's work could make in deepening our understanding of the theory and practice of psychiatry in South Africa. We argue that such an understanding could also help to shape the training agenda for psychiatrists and other mental health professionals in the country.

The history of mental health/psychiatry in South Africa

The development of psychiatry in South Africa has been influenced by a number of historically significant events. As Fernando has pointed out in a number of his publications, the origin of psychiatry is deeply rooted in European culture. Similarly, from the time when it was introduced during the colonial period, psychiatry was deeply influenced by European culture (Minde, 1974a, 1974b). It did not accommodate and in fact displaced the traditional mental health approaches that were practised by the indigenous people. In his analysis of mental health services in South Africa, Minde (1977a, 1977b) has described how psychiatry evolved from a period of colonialism through to the apartheid era. He described four stages, which largely guided knowledge and practice of psychiatry in that time.

The first, which Minde (1977a) called "the demonic stage", was marked by the belief that mental illness was caused by possession by demons. These views prevailed from the time of the first colonization by the Dutch in 1652 up to the mid 18th century. The second stage, which he referred to as the "custodial" period, was characterized by treatment approaches that were largely limited to keeping the patients safely in the asylum to protect the community. Treatment of patients was purely symptomatic with the use of sedatives to calm the patients, hypnotics to quieten the noisy ones and laxatives for the constipated. This stage dominated most of the 19th century until the middle of the 1930s, which saw the arrival of physical therapy. The third stage was marked by the use of insulin coma for the treatment of schizophrenia, and cardiozol and electric shock for bipolar disorder and schizophrenia. This was also a time when prefrontal leucotomy made a brief appearance and was abandoned. This stage lasted until the mid-1950s. The fourth stage was the period of psychotropic drugs, which has prevailed to date. The introduction of chlorpromazine and imipramine hydrochloride is said to have revolutionized psychiatry the world over. These drugs facilitated de-institutionalization in the Western countries around that time.

In South Africa, de-institutionalization as a mental health care strategy was introduced in the 1990s (Stein, Allwood and Emsley, 1999; Thom, 2004; Uys, 1991). The aim of this strategy was to release psychiatric patients from the hospitals and to plant them in the community to ensure continuity of care. To effectively implement the de-institutionalization strategy, there was a need to develop community residential care facilities and ambulatory services in order to reduce the possibility of relapse, homelessness and high re-admission rates among de-institutionalized patients (Mkhize and Kometsi, 2008; Stein et al., 1999). However, this has not been the case in South Africa. The mental health services remain under-developed and poorly resourced with the worst affected in the poor rural African communities. Several studies have suggested that in the provinces, where downscaling of patient beds occurred in line with de-institutionalization, the motivation had been financial constraints rather than the development of ambulatory or residential community care (e.g. Mkhize and Kometsi, 2008; Petersen and Lund, 2011). This then led to a "revolving door" pattern of care in which service users who were discharged from hospitals were soon re-admitted due to lack of adequate services to support them in the community (Mkhize and Kometsi, 2008).

The apartheid laws that were implemented in South Africa in the early 1950s compounded this pattern of repeated re-admissions. As indicated earlier, apartheid was a peculiar form of colonialism in South Africa that perpetuated the myth of white supremacy and black inferiority. Based on this ideology, the successive apartheid governments continued to implement policies that sought to oppress black people while continuing to protect white privilege. Consequently, a number of segregationist laws that deeply entrenched white privilege were passed by parliament. For example, the Population Registration Act 1950 required that all South Africans be classified and registered according to their racial characteristics as Blacks, Whites, Coloured and Indian. Consequently, any individual's social rights and political rights including educational opportunities were determined by this classification. This piece of legislation, together with many other segregationist policies of the apartheid regime at the time, tended to fit into what Fernando (1988) viewed as colonial projects that sought to project black people as a species with small brain sizes and low IQ.

The consequence of the above pieces of legislation, together with many other apartheid laws, was social disintegration and the fragmentation of the lives of the majority of people in South Africa. According to Kaliski (1998), it is these kinds of oppressive actions by the apartheid government that led to the high levels of social ills like poverty, violence and alcohol and drug abuse in the African communities. These social ills, in turn, increased levels of mental health problems in these oppressed communities. On the other hand, access to the mental health services that were available earlier in South Africa was largely marked by discrimination based on race (Minde, 1974a, 1974b). Psychiatric institutions were established centrally in more urban areas where whites were better able to access them.

In the mid–late 1970s as criticism of the apartheid government and its discriminatory practices gained momentum, the World Health Organization (WHO) appointed a committee to inspect private and state mental health services in South Africa. The WHO report pointed to the many deficiencies of the mental health services, and also to the discrimination in the provision of psychiatric services based on race. The main findings of WHO were as follows: undue higher death rates among black patients that resulted from grossly inadequate care; substandard care in private facilities that housed psychiatric patients; professional staff was grossly inadequate with black staff paid much lower wages than whites; and that apartheid had destructive implications for the mental health of black South Africans, with specific mention of the migrant labour policies that disrupted black families (Gillis, 1979; Stone, Pinderhughes, Spurlock, Weinberg and APA, 1979). Given the findings, a number of recommendations were proposed to address the identified problems.

Democratic South Africa and mental health

With the dawn of democracy in South Africa in 1994, most of the recommendations by WHO were implemented. One such intervention that was informed by the WHO recommendations was the White Paper on the Transformation of the Health System, which was drafted with a view to re-engineering South African health services that had hitherto been fragmented along racial lines (WHO, 2007). The main purpose of this draft piece of legislation was to chart a vision for a health system that would, for the first time, be accessible to all South Africans. The White Paper on the Transformation of the Health System was intended to integrate primary health care at the district level (Petersen *et al.*, 2009). This move was also motivated by the fact that mental health services had been skewed in favour of the wealthier urban areas, and therefore not readily available to the majority of the people in South Africa. The White Paper put emphasis on prevention and health promotion, when compared to the previous racially based health care system that was more curative and hospital-based (Petersen *et al.*, 2009; WHO, 2007).

One other important development that was proposed in the White Paper was the inclusion of mental health services into the primary health care system. While considered a positive move, the proposed inclusion of mental health services into the primary health care system was unfortunately perceived as having the potential to burden a health care system that was already under serious strain in terms of financial and human resources (Thom, 2004). According to Petersen *et al.* (2009), the inclusion of the mental health service was not preceded by proper preparations. The other challenges associated with the integration of mental health into general health care and the development of primary mental health care, among others, included prejudicial attitudes by primary care staff towards mental health service users, work overload and burn-out among primary care staff (Thom, 2004; WHO, 2007). It was these challenges, together with some disagreements among the stakeholders, that resulted in the White Paper not being adopted and implemented as a policy in South Africa. As a result of this situation, there was no national health policy that was put in place. This led to variable mental health service provision from one province to another (WHO, 2007). Related to this problem was the lack of nationally agreed indicators for mental health information systems, with the result that information on current service resources (budgets, staff, facilities) and provision (admissions, outpatient visits) was extremely sparse (Lund and Flisher, 2006).

Taking into account the challenges associated with the White Paper on the Transformation of the Health Care System, the Mental Health Care Act (Act 17 of 2002) was developed with a view to introducing mental health care that would be in keeping with international standards of human rights. The Mental Health Care Act advocates for a rehabilitative, community-based model of health care (Republic of South Africa, 2002; Ramlall, 2012). This approach was meant to reduce the stigma attached to mental illness. Since its implementation, there are a number of provinces in South Africa that have used the Mental Health Care Act to draft their mental health policies. It has also emerged that there is wide variability between provinces in the implementation of the Mental Health Care Act, including the availability of assessment and treatment protocols for key mental health conditions. For example, Ramlall (2012) stated that there had been isolated reports from other provinces in South Africa confirming that accessibility of mental health services and quality of care had been enhanced.

Fernando has pointed out that the inequality associated with access to resources in rich and poor countries makes it difficult to adopt same strategies in providing mental health services in different parts of the world (Fernando, 2005; Fernando and Weerackody, 2009). In his view, mental health services should be "homegrown" and suited to the cultural context and needs of the communities themselves (Fernando, 2005). He pointed out that Western constructs of illness and health should not be rejected. Instead, these constructs should be adapted and modelled to suit the local context with respect to culture and needs. There are countries that have successfully implemented services that are in keeping with cultural norms, and as such can serve as examples to others (Fernando, 2006). According to Fernando (2012), it has proven difficult to make changes that will combat racism in psychiatry and mental health systems. Fernando (1988) proposed some answers, and at times very radical suggestions on how to deal with these problems that beset psychiatry. He proposed that the institution of psychiatry should implement deliberate anti-racist strategies in as many platforms as there are available (Fernando, 1988). These include research and publications that include all professionals from different racial and cultural backgrounds, so as to address misconceptions. With regard to diagnostic approaches, he is of the view that the current traditional diagnostic approaches used in psychiatry and psychology are not culturally sensitive. Instead, they could be regarded as similar to those used in the diagnosis of medical illness. To deal with this challenge, Fernando proposes that mental health experts should adopt a dimensional approach that would also capture the patient's context. As he puts it:

> once the diagnostic process is loosened in this way, the practice of psychiatry will change: instead of looking for illness in individuals, psychiatrists

will concentrate on the needs and the problems of the patients; a problem-oriented approach will emerge.

(Fernando, 1988, p. 183)

It is, however, apparent that there has been a lot of resistance to implementing these suggestions that Fernando and a number of other scholars have proposed. There is a lack of political will within the fraternity of psychiatry to advocate for these changes. It does seem that the profession is content with the status quo.

Culture and training

One of the major changes that Fernando has proposed as a necessary vehicle in the transformation of psychiatry is the introduction of culture in the training of mental health care workers. In order to ensure cultural sensitivity, Fernando (2008) suggested that training must involve the study of cultural variation in mental health. Elaborating on this further, he said that the content of the curriculum in the training of health professionals would be guided by local practices. He further suggested that the curriculum should cover a wide range of topics that could include, among others, the following: the concepts of illness and health, socio-political constructions of illness categories, and idioms of distress.

It is this kind of training that could equip mental health professionals to acquire the necessary cultural competence that will enable them to work with clients from different contexts. Anderson et al. (2003) describes cultural competence as having the capacity to function effectively as an individual and as an organization within the context of the cultural beliefs, behaviours and needs presented by customers and their communities. Such a setting should include the following: a culturally diverse staff that reflects the communities served; providers or translators who speak the clients' language(s); training for providers about the culture and language of the people they serve; signage and instructional literature in the clients' language(s) and consistent with their cultural norms; and culturally specific healthcare settings. According to Fernando (2008), it is these kinds of skills that could improve the provision of appropriate services and reduce the incidence of clinical errors resulting from misunderstandings caused by differences in language or culture. This ensures that information given and received is clearly understood by both parties, i.e. the client and the health care provider.

Despite the emphasis placed on the significance of cultural competence in mental health service provision, there has been very little done with regard to adding this dimension to the training of mental health professionals in South Africa (Anderson et al., 2003; Fernando, 2008). Though this is not a problem unique to South Africa, one would have thought given our past history of apartheid this training would have been imperative. The big challenge is the diverse cultures that are present in the country. A good place to start, though, would have been to learn about the predominant culture. Some countries have included this in their training protocols of undergraduate training of health care workers

(Purdie, Dudgeon and Walker, 2010). In other countries this component of training is even enforced by legislation (see Brach and Fraser, 2000).

The other option to meet this challenge would be to upscale the training of health care workers according to the demographic profile of the particular community, which would go some distance in influencing access to a culturally sensitive health care. It is encouraging to see that since the dawn of democracy in South Africa, some of the institutions training undergraduate health care workers have responded to the call to increase the intake of previously disadvantaged populations, to some degree (Khan, Thomas and Naidoo, 2013; Lehman, Andrews and Sanders, 2000). According to Lehman *et al.* (2000), this effort is particularly undermined by the inferior education that was provided for blacks under apartheid.

Integrating Western and African indigenous healing traditions: challenges and opportunities

Several studies have suggested that up to 70% of African people in South Africa consult traditional healers at some point in their lives (Mkhize and Kometsi, 2008; Muelelwa, Sodi and Maake, 1998; Thom, 2004; WHO, 2007). Studies have shown that in clinical practice, patients can seek help from different sources whose frameworks and treatments contradict each other (see, e.g., Arnault, 2009; Awanbor, 1982; Straker, 1994). Provided that each does not claim exclusivity, this may not lead to conflict. As Johnson, Sathyaseelan, Charles and Jeyaseelan (2012) suggested, patients from non-Western cultures may hold multiple and contradictory models of illness, and these would serve different purposes within a patient. In this kind of situation, it does appear that the Western understanding of illness seems to facilitate some interpretation of why a non-Western patient would accept and take the psychiatric medication. On the other hand, non-medical supernatural and external explanatory models seem to facilitate coping strategies in those who suffered from debilitating and chronic illnesses. Despite the reality of patients seeking help from the two health care systems, there has been very little attempt made to integrate the two health care systems in South Africa. According to Swartz (1998), failure to integrate the two health care systems could be attributed to a number of factors that include the different worldviews and the uneven power relationships between the Western-trained health professionals and indigenous healers.

In order to improve the services rendered to communities, Fernando (2006, 2010a) suggested that there is a need to integrate Western forms of counselling and psychotherapy with other healing traditions that are found in Asia and Africa. Though integration of the two healing traditions is desirable, Fernando (2010b) was cognizant of the many challenges associated with such a move.

First, the issue of cultural arrogance, which amounts to racism, was identified as one of the major stumbling blocks that hinder integration. In this case, a mental health practitioner, in particular Western-trained would belittle the traditional healing system. This is generally because government sponsors and promotes bio-medical psychiatry. In essence, what is seen as the superior culture with financial backing will dictate the way mental health systems operate. Sodi and Bojuwoye (2011) also made reference to the notion of cultural arrogance when they suggested that it is often the attitudinal problem of the Western-oriented health care practitioners who tend to perceive indigenous healing as harmful, unhygienic, unscientific and inferior.

Second, Fernando (2010a) argued that the worldviews on which the various healing traditions are based also pose a challenge when it comes to efforts aimed at integration. Sodi and Bojuwoye (2011) made the same observation by suggesting that the divergent epistemological origins of the two systems also make it difficult for them to be integrated. Fernando pointed out that these different worldviews are also complicated by value judgements linked to perceptions of what is scientific and what is not. Finally, there is an inherent contradiction in collaboration because of the assumption that both cultural relativity (where very different are seen as equivalent) and psychological universalism (where a universally applicable basis for human psychology is assumed) can be worked with simultaneously.

According to Fernando (2010a), it becomes imperative to have mutual respect for each other if any form of collaboration, including integration of the two healing systems, is expected to be effective. He recommended further that there should also be some sort of evaluation, albeit at a very basic level, with genuine understanding of the political forces that usually tend to keep Western approaches on top. Fernando (2010a) warns that if these measures are not put in place, collaborative efforts will become tools for the imposition of Western thinking. The hesitancy about the integration of traditional healers into the mainstream health care system could also be due to lack of knowledge about traditional healing, a point that is also emphasized by Sodi and Bojuwoye (2011). Based on Fernando's analysis, it could therefore be suggested that efforts aimed at integrating Western psychotherapy and indigenous healing systems in South Africa are bound to fail if challenges like the cultural arrogance of Western psychiatry are not addressed.

Conclusion

As we have pointed out throughout this chapter, Suman Fernando has consistently argued that race and culture are inextricably linked to psychiatry. In other words, the practice of psychiatry cannot be divorced from these critical social constructs. In South Africa, the philosophy of apartheid was premised on the false notion that white people are intellectually superior to black people. Consequently, the architects of this colonial project introduced laws that were meant to entrench segregation based on race and culture. While the democratic dispensation brought an end to this oppressive system, it is evident that its consequences continued to be felt in many areas of South African life, including the uneven provision of mental health care services. Furthermore, these segregationist policies have resulted in the continued existence of two parallel healing traditions, with Western medicine being the official health care system, while indigenous healing continues to be sidelined. Suman Fernando's work helps us to understand these racial and cultural dichotomies in health delivery in South Africa and other developing countries. It is only through the understanding of these challenges that we will be in a better position to shape the training agenda for psychiatrists and other mental health professionals in the country.

References

Anderson, L. M., Scrimshaw, S. C., Fullilove, M. T., Fielding, J. E., Normand, J. and the Task Force. (2003). Culturally competent healthcare systems: A systematic review. *American Journal of Preventive Medicine, 24*(3), 68–78.

Arnault, D. S. (2009). Cultural determinants of help seeking: A model for research and practice. *Research and Theory for Nursing Practice, 23*(4), 259–278.

Awanbor, D. (1982). The healing process in African psychotherapy. *American Journal of Psychotherapy, 34*(2), 206–212.

Bojuwoye, O. and Edwards, S. (2011). Integrating ancestral consciousness into conventional counseling. *Journal of Psychology in Africa, 21*(3), 375–381.

Brach, C. and Fraser, I. (2000). Can cultural competency reduce racial and ethnic health disparities? A review and conceptual model. *Medical Care Research and Review, 57*(1), 181–217.

Fernando, S. (1988). *Race and culture in psychiatry.* London and New York: Tavistock/Routledge.

Fernando, S. (2005). Mental health in low-income countries: Challenges and innovations. *International Journal of Migration, Health and Social Care, 1*(1), 13–18.

Fernando, S. (2006). Working with communities. *Openmind, 139* (May/June), 12–13.

Fernando, S. (2008). Cultural competence. *Openmind, 151* (May/June), 24.

Fernando, S. (2010a). Multicultural counselling. *Openmind, 161* (Jan./Feb.), 25.

Fernando, S. (2010b). *Mental health, race and culture* (3rd ed.). Basingstoke: Palgrave Macmillan.

Fernando, S. (2012). Race and culture issues in mental health and some thoughts on ethnic identity. *Counselling Psychology Quarterly, 25*(2), 113–123.

Fernando, S. and Weerackody, C. (2009). Challenges in developing community mental health services in Sri Lanka. *Journal of Health Management, 11*(1), 195–208.

Gillis, L. S. (1979). Mental health care in South Africa. Letters to the editor. *The Lancet,* 920–921.

Group Areas Act No. 41 of 1950. Retrieved from www.historicalpapers.wits.ac.za/.../AD1812-Em3-1-2-011-jpeg.pdf.

Johnson, S., Sathyaseelan, M., Charles, H., Jeyaseelan, V. and Jacob, K. S. (2012). Insight, psychopathology, explanatory models and outcome of schizophrenia in India: a prospective 5-year cohort study. *BMC Psychiatry, 12*(159), 1–12.

Kaliski, S. (1998). The South African context. In S. E. Bauman (Ed.), *Psychiatry and primary health care: A practical guide for health care workers in Southern Africa* (pp. 29–35). Kenwyn, SA: Juta & Company.

Khan, T., Thomas, L. S. and Naidoo, S. (2013). Analysing post-apartheid gender and racial transformation in medical education in South Africa province. *Global Health Action, 6,* 75–81.

Lehman, U., Andrews, G. and Sanders, D. (2000). *Change and innovation at South African medical schools: An investigation of student demographics, student support and curriculum innovation.* Health Systems Trust.

Lund, C. and Flisher, A. J. (2006). Norms for mental health services in South Africa. *Social Psychiatry and Psychiatric Epidemiology, 41*(7), 587–594.

Minde, M. (1974a). The history of mental health services in South Africa: In the days of the Dutch East India company. *South African Medical Journal – Suid-Afrikaanse Tydskrif Vir Geneeskunde, 48*(29), 1270–1272.

Minde, M. (1974b). History of mental health services in South Africa, Part II: During the British occupation. *South African Medical Journal – Suid-Afrikaanse Tydskrif Vir Geneeskunde, 48*(38), 1629–1632.

Minde, M. (1977a). History of mental health services in South Africa, Part XIV: Psychiatric education. *South African Medical Journal – Suid-Afrikaanse Tydskrif Vir Geneeskunde, 51*(7), 210–214.

Minde, M. (1977b). History of mental health services in South Africa, Part XV: The future of mental health services. *South African Medical Journal – Suid-Afrikaanse Tydskrif Vir Geneeskunde, 51*(16), 549–553.

Mkhize, N. and Kometsi, M. (2008). Community access to mental health services: Lessons and recommendations. In P. Barron & J. Roma-Reardon (Eds.), *South African Health Review* (pp. 103–113). Durban: Health Systems Trust.

Muelelwa, E., Sodi, T. and Maake, M. J. (1998). Attitudes of patients in a rural hospital towards traditional healers. In L. Schlebusch (Ed.), *South Africa beyond transition: Psychological well-being.* Durban: University of Natal.

Petersen, I., Bhana, A., Campbell-Hall, V., Mjadu, S., Lund, C., Kleintjies, S. and Mental Health and Poverty Research Programme Consortium. (2009). Planning for district mental health services in South Africa: A situational analysis of a rural district site. *Health Policy and Planning, 24*(2), 140–150.

Petersen, I. and Lund, C. (2011). Mental health service delivery in South Africa from 2000 to 2010: One step forward, one step back. *South African Medical Journal – Suid-Afrikaanse Tydskrif Vir Geneeskunde, 101*(10), 751–757.

Purdie, N., Dudgeon, P. and Walker, R. (2010). Working as a culturally competent mental health practitioner. In *Working together: Aboriginal and Torres Strait Islander mental health and wellbeing principles and practice.* Canberra: Department of Health and Ageing. Retrieved 17 May 2013 from www.childhealthresearch.org.au/media/54895/chapter12.pdf.

Ramlall, S. (2012). The Mental Health Care Act Number 17 – South Africa. Trials and triumphs: 2002–2012. *African Journal of Psychiatry, 15*(6), 407–410.

Republic of South Africa. (1950). Population Registration Act of 1950. Retrieved from http://upload.wikimedia.org/wikipedia/commons/9/90/Population_Registration_Act_1950.pdf.

Republic of South Africa. (2002). Mental Health Care Act (Act 17 of 2002). Retrieved from http://info.gov.za/view/DownloadFileAction?id=68051.

Sodi, T. and Bojuwoye, O. (2011). Cultural embeddedness of health, illness, and healing: Prospects for integrating indigenous and western healing practices. *Journal of Psychology in Africa, 21*(3), 349–356.

Stein, D. J., Allwood, C. and Emsley, R. A. (1999). Community care of psychiatric disorders in South Africa: Lessons from research on deinstitutionalization. *South African Medical Journal – Suid-Afrikaanse Tydskrif Vir Geneeskunde, 89*(9), 942–943.

Stone, A. A., Pinderhughes, C., Spurlock, J., Weinberg, J. and American Psychiatric

Association. Committee to Visit South Africa. (1979). Report of the committee to visit South Africa. *American Journal of Psychiatry, 136*(11), 1498–1506.

Straker, G. (1994). Integrating African and Western healing practices in South Africa. *American Journal of Psychotherapy, 8*(3), 455–467.

Swartz, L. (1998). *Culture and mental health: A Southern African view*. Cape Town: Oxford University Press.

Thom, R. (2004). Mental health service policy, implementation and research in South Africa: Are we making progress? *South African Journal of Psychiatry, 10*(2), 32–37.

Uys, L. R. (1991). A theoretical framework for psychiatric rehabilitation. *Curationis, 14*(3), 1–5.

WHO (World Health Organization). (2007). WHO AIMS report on mental health systems in South Africa. Retrieved 23 March 2013 from www.who.int/mental_health/evidence/south_africa_who_aims_report.pdf.

18 Mental health services in Sri Lanka

Chamindra Weerackody and Suman Fernando

Introduction

The understanding of mental health is largely determined by the meanings given by people to their experiences and feelings and the worldviews they hold about the nature of the human condition. In pursuing a universal definition of mental health, Sudhir Kakar (1984), a European-trained psychoanalyst who has worked in India for decades, uses the term as 'a rubric, a label which covers different perspectives and concerns, such as the absence of incapacitating symptoms, integration of psychological functioning, effective conduct or personal and social life, feelings of ethical and spiritual well-being and so on' (p. 3). There are no reliable studies reported in the English-language literature of what mental health may mean to people in Sri Lanka. So, the nearest we can get to such an understanding is by exploring how the people in the island deal with (what they see as) mental health problems – what sorts of help or 'therapy' they seek and/or benefit from, considered against their social and political background.

As in many countries of South Asia, Sri Lankan people use multiple medical and healing systems for personal problems they regarded as 'illness' (see Nichter, 1980; Sachs, 1989; Waxler-Morrison, 1988). In the case of (what in the West are called) 'mental health problems' these would include allopathic (Western) medical systems (i.e. psychiatry), indigenous medical systems and non-medical healing of various types (see Amarasingham, 1980; Obeyesekere, 1981; Waxler, 1984). The traditional words for madness are *pissu* (in Sinhala) and *paithiyam, mananoi* and *ulanoi* (in Tamil); but there has been an increasing tendency in the past decade to use the literal translations of the English 'mental illness', namely *mānasikaroga* (in Sinhala) and *mananoi* (in Tamil).

The Trauma and Global Health (TGH) Program,[1] a programme of research, capacity building and knowledge transfer coordinated by staff at McGill University in Montreal, was implemented between 2007 and 2011. The work in Sri Lanka was led by one of us (CW), and the other author (SF) was consultant to the programme. In this chapter we report on the lessons derived about mental health development during our work on the programme, set against the background of 'mental health' in Sri Lanka.[2]

Colonization, independence and mental health

Sri Lanka's geographical location at the centre of trading routes and its abundant natural resources have resulted in the island being at the centre of movement of people from very early times. Western influence came with colonization by European powers from the early 16th century. First, the Portuguese occupied the maritime regions of the West and North; then the Dutch replaced them in the mid 17th century; and finally the British colonization of what they called 'Ceylon' began in 1796 when their forces defeated the Dutch to occupy the maritime regions held by the latter. The British conquered the whole country in 1815 to establish a crown colony. During the 133 years of British colonization, Ceylon underwent enormous social, cultural and political changes. By 1850, plantation capitalism had replaced traditional landholding in all parts of Ceylon, and the economic pattern had changed from subsistence agriculture to plantation economy (Bandarage, 2009; Jayawardena, 2010; Ludowyk, 1962).

The population doubled between 1900 and 1948, and an extensive system of medical provision based on Western medicine was established, superior to that in most other British colonies, including British India (Jones, 2004). This consisted of a hospital system, a network of free 'dispensaries' offering outpatient treatment in rural areas and a system of estate hospitals and dispensaries. Although state expenditure in health was mainly devoted to services offering Western medicine, 'there was [by 1947] a highly developed indigenous system of medicine' (Jones, 2004, p. 102), with an Ayurvedic Research Institute and College and some Ayurvedic hospitals and dispensaries. In 1945, a system of universal free education from kindergarten to university was established; this was extended after independence in 1948 so that by the 1960s, the population was highly educated with a high level of literacy equivalent to that in many developed countries, and a health service for general medical services that was superior to most neighbouring countries.

Mental health care based on Western psychiatry was first introduced to Sri Lanka when the first small lunatic asylum was opened in 1847 (Uragoda, 1987). This was later replaced with a larger asylum and observation units (for lunatics) were established in Colombo, Kandy, Galle and Jaffna (Principle Medical Officer, 1896). Angoda Asylum just outside Colombo (which is still operational) was opened in 1926 to house 1,830 patients (Uragoda, 1987).

Soon after Ceylon became politically independent in 1948, a second mental hospital was planned at Mulleriyawa (close to Angoda), but this did not open until 1957 (Carpenter, 1988). The cadre of psychiatrists was expanded from four in 1952 to 20 in 1967 and a 25-bed psychiatric unit was opened at Colombo General Hospital about that time. Inpatient and outpatient psychiatric facilities attached to general hospitals were opened in Galle, Kandy, Jaffna, Ratnapura and Kalutara, and university departments of psychiatry were established in Colombo, Peradeniya and Jaffna in the late 1960s (Carpenter, 1988). Graduate training in psychiatry in Sri Lanka began in 1981 with the establishment of the Post-Graduate Institute of Medicine.

Social disruption, civil war and natural disaster

From the early 1970s the country was torn by political violence, at first in the South led by a Marxist organization and later in the North and East led by various Tamil militant groups. While the violence in the South was contained by the state apparatus, the troubles in the North developed into a military insurrection against the state led by the Liberation Tigers of Tamil Eelam (LTTE), seeking to establish a separate Tamil state in the North and East. After the breakdown of several abortive ceasefires, government forces gained control of the whole country in May 2009 (Bandarage, 2009; Gokhale, 2009). Much of the North and East was devastated by the conflict and the (mainly) Tamil people living in that area suffered extensively (Somasundaram, 1998). In addition to the devastation caused by conflict that lasted 26 years, Sri Lanka was faced in December 2004 by a tsunami affecting the north-east and southern coasts, resulting in loss of life and displacement of people. The conflict and tsunami resulted in many people losing their livelihoods and homes but most had by November 2012 been rehoused either in new settlements or in their original villages, except for Muslims expelled from the North in 1990 (when the LTTE occupied the area), who continue to live as 'internally displaced people' in the north-central and north-western regions of the country.

Psycho-social trauma to individuals and communities in Sri Lanka resulting from prolonged conflict and the 2004 tsunami cannot be overstated. Many questions have been raised about the sort of psychological interventions directed at helping tsunami survivors in Sri Lanka. For example, Galappatti (2005) observed that while the dominant impulse among helping agencies was to provide 'counselling' for survivors of the tsunami, there was little understanding of what this meant: 'There was a widely held assumption that speaking about their experiences and feelings with "counsellors" would be emotionally beneficial for people who had faced the loss of their families, houses, livelihoods' (p. 66). Samarasinghe (2006), a psychiatrist, questioned the practice (of psychiatrists and psychologists) of enabling victims 'to ventilate and work through unhealthy suppressed emotions' (p. 9), observing that they faced (primarily) the loss of 'anchors and normal routines' (p. 10). Mattock (2005) concluded from her own research that loss of family, home and livelihood engendered personal (psychological) losses, and that the idea of 'loss-spirals' could help in working out what sort of help victims of disasters like the tsunami needed most: 'These people are not "dependent" – if they had resources with which to instigate gain spirals, they have attempted to do so' (p. 149).

There is very little recorded information on mental health work carried out in areas of conflict during the conflict, although many NGOs, usually subsumed under the category of 'humanitarian organisations', claimed to have carried out 'psychosocial interventions' (personal communication from the Confederation of Humanitarian Organisations), a category that included a variety of interventions (Galappatti, 2003). For example, models of 'trauma therapy' and 'counselling' derived from Western cultural sources and usually supplied by professionals visiting the country for very short periods from various European and North American countries, sometimes with little knowledge of the cultures within Sri Lanka (personal observation, 2007). The psycho-social and social sequelae of a 'man-made' civil war may be very different in some ways from that resulting from a natural disaster. Somasundaram (1998), a psychiatrist who lived in Jaffna during most of the conflict, speaks of the 'scarred minds' of Tamil people who lived through the conflict in the North. Atrocities against civilians allegedly committed by both sides in the last days of the conflict (Weiss, 2011) are likely to have left psychological and social effects that may well require long-term interventions to promote personal healing and reconciliation between communities (Somasundaram, 2010).

In 2005, soon after the tsunami of December 2004, the World Health Organization (WHO) became involved in developing mental health services in the country, leading to a Mental Health Policy for Sri Lanka 2005–2015 (Mental Health Directorate, 2006). However, progress in implementing its recommendations has been slow and community mental health services are non-existent at present (2012), except for some follow-up programmes in a few places such as Batticaloa, Kalmunai and occasionally from the National Institute of Mental Health (NIMH) (formerly Angoda Hospital), where social workers or nurses visit the homes of ex-patients to provide consultations or supervise medication (personal observation, November 2012). A recent report (Pedersen et al., 2012) quoting official statistics provided by the mental health directorate stated that there are 60 consultant psychiatrists in the country, half being located in the Western Province, 60 medical officers with a diploma in psychiatry and another 130 medical officers in mental health. There are 21 acute inpatient units in 19 districts (out of 25 districts in the island), and there are some medium–long stay units attached to hospitals in nine towns or cities. Officially, around 40,000 persons diagnosed for psychiatric illnesses are discharged annually from government hospitals; and a few private organizations house some people described as 'stabilized persons'. Meanwhile, innovative local community-based mental health services in the East of the country originally based at Batticaloa have now been replicated (with similar ways of working as those at Batticaloa) at two other eastern towns, Kalmunai and Valachenai.

It should be noted that Western psychiatric care in the Sri Lankan statutory sector in most parts of the country are limited to psychotropic medication and Electro Convulsion Therapy. Multidisciplinary team work is rare; there are very few occupational therapists or clinical psychologists in the statutory sector (De Silva, 2002). Formal psychotherapies and counselling derived from (Western) psychology are rarely available except in the private sector and are difficult to access. There is no training available for clinical psychology (in the Western style). In the past decade or two, training in counselling has been available in some universities and private institutions but otherwise most people who practise as 'counsellors' are trained in Christian (usually Roman Catholic) settings. Treatment is provided at one of two mental hospitals near Colombo, at psychiatric units attached to general hospitals and outpatient clinics. Home treatment is available in a few regions through visits by community workers (but not nurses since they are limited to working from hospital settings).

Indigenous mental health

It should be noted that in Sri Lanka, as in most of South Asia, people with mental health problems (usually accompanied by their carers) tend to consult and obtain help from a variety of professionals apart from physicians practising Ayurveda or Western (allopathic) medicine; they include specialists in exorcism and other forms of healing (see Amarasingham, 1980; Kusumaratne, 2005; Pertold, 1930; Vogt, 1999; Wijesekera, 1989; Wirz, 1954) as well as astrologers who provide what Pugh (1983) calls 'astrological counselling'. The use of healing rituals, including exorcism rituals, pre-date Ayurveda in the Indian tradition; these and other ways of dealing with *unmada* (madness) due to spirit possession 'stand out as an uneasy meeting between medical and priestly concerns' (Kakar, 1984, p. 248), although in practical terms there is no conflict between them, with one merging into the other. And, neither Ayurveda nor healing is secular in the way that Western psychiatry and psychotherapy are secular. Neither recognize an absolute distinction between mind and body (as Western psychiatry does), thus taking a holistic approach to health and illness. Spirituality is important in all forms of healing – often central.

Some types of healing practised in Sri Lanka have been described in the English literature (Kapferer, 1991; Obeyesekere, 1981; Pertold, 1930; Wirz, 1954). The ceremonies usually involve dancing, where masked actors depict demonic figures; they are conducted by a specialist exorcist (*kattadiya*) and referred to as sorcery cutting (*huniyamkapima*). The ceremonies themselves are commonly called 'devil dancing' in English and *kovil/thovil/kalippu* in Sinhala and Tamil; a typical ceremony is described, with photographs, by Pate (2005) and analysed as a form of psychotherapy by Vogt (1999). The efficacy of these ceremonies in relieving or curing illness has not been studied using Western terms of reference.

Ayurvedic treatment involves herbal remedies, together with advice on diet that is carefully matched to the temperament of the patient and geared to an assessment of the manner in which the *dosas* (humours) are affected. Ayurvedic treatment is given in association with the patient's relatives or other helpers. Ayurveda in Sri Lanka became institutionalized during the 1920s and indigenous medical systems were officially recognized, professionalized and subsidized by 1941 (Jones, 2004). Ayurvedic Institutes with standardized systems of training were established under the 1961 Ayurvedic Act (Higuchi, 2002; Kusumaratne, 2005). A recent review of the state of Ayurvedic practice in Sri Lanka (Kusumaratne, 2005) suggests that (what the author calls) the 'Indigenous Medical System' (IMS) is widely used by many people across the country. However, it is true to say that although many indigenous medical practitioners (IMPs) are officially recognized as such, there are other medical practitioners using variations of traditional Ayurveda usually practising out of their own homes (Nordstrom,

1988). The registration of IMS in Sri Lanka currently recognizes nine branches, including *mãnasikarogavedakama*, which may be translated as 'psychiatry' (Kusumaratne, 2005). Yet, for conditions resembling (if not identical with) 'psychosis', people may access healers who practise healing rituals like *thovil* (in Sinhala) or *kalippu* in Tamil (pejoratively referred to as 'devil dancing' by the British) – see above.

Developing mental health services in Sri Lanka

Three points should be noted about developing mental health services in settings such as those in Sri Lanka: (1) the understanding of what is 'mental' and what is 'illness' being culturally determined (see Fernando, 2010; Gaines, 1992), merely transferring uncritically mental health systems developed in Western cultural settings may be inappropriate; (2) evidence from WHO studies of the 1970s and 1980s (Jablensky *et al.*, 1992; WHO, 1973, 1979) indicates that developing countries may provide a therapeutic context for recovery from 'mental illness' (as defined in psychiatric terms) that is lacking in developed 'Western' countries (Hopper and Wanderling, 2000; Myers, 2010) and so merely applying Western models of care may be self-defeating; and (3) compared to developed countries, resources available for health care are very limited and many – and this applies to Sri Lanka – suffer from coincident social problems such as varying degrees of poverty in a context of virtually absent social welfare networks and high levels of social disruption and political violence, all of which impact on mental health. Thus, it is essential in considering service development to (1) address fundamental issues of definition (of mental health and illness); (2) take on board the likely importance of traditional and indigenous social and cultural aspects of the countries concerned that may promote mental health and counteract mental ill health; and (3) consider carefully wider social and environmental issues that affect mental health, and the sustainability of services in the face of resource limitation.

The TGH programme implemented between 2007 and 2011 in Guatemala, Nepal, Peru and Sri Lanka had three major components, namely, Information Generation (IG), Capacity Building (CB) and Knowledge Transfer (KT). The programme is described fully elsewhere (Pedersen *et al.*, 2012). The programme in Sri Lanka was administered by the People's Rural Development Association (PRDA). As lead and consultant to the Sri Lanka programme, the authors worked with colleagues in Montreal in developing a design for the Sri Lankan programme. Although focused on the 'mental health' of people in areas affected by conflict and disaster, the programme had the flexibility to look more broadly at mental health needs in general and to interpret what was meant by mental health and well-being in line with perceptions of people in the country as a whole.

Lessons learned from the TGH programme in Sri Lanka

The first part of the programme in Sri Lanka was to explore the effects on Sri Lankan communities and people of the political violence and displacement resulting from the recent conflict that ended in May 2009 (Gokhale, 2009) and the major disaster of the Indian Ocean tsunami of December 2004 (de Alwis and Hedman, 2009). The methods we used for research were drawn from participatory rural appraisal (PRA) (Chambers, 1994, 1997) and have been described elsewhere (Weerackody and Fernando, 2011). During the research, communities affected by the conflict and the 2004 Asian tsunami were consulted to identify their perceptions and experiences of well-being, factors that increased/decreased their state of well-being, and their perceptions of the work of agencies that tried to help them in times of need. Our findings enabled us to understand how mental health services should be designed, planned and implemented in such communities. The capacity-building work of the programme consisted mainly of 'training programmes', where we used participatory approaches designed to create space for interaction between participants and 'trainers', and maximized sharing of experience and learning from one another. In both the community research and 'training', the TGH programme took a broad, open-ended approach to what 'mental health' may mean to people in the country, rather than imposing a particular way of thinking or merely reflecting the dominant bio-medical approach that local psychiatrists are still trained to practise. Helped by visiting teams from McGill University (in 2008 and 2010), we introduced to Sri Lankan colleagues in social work, psychology and psychiatry the basic tenets of transcultural psychiatry and the value of adopting social approaches in understanding and planning interventions for mental health related problems. And we emphasized the importance of striking a fair balance between the bio-medical and social approaches in service provision for mental health and the need to take on board fully the nature of social determinants of health and illness (see Blas, Sommerfeld and Kurup, 2011). As part of the programme, a multidisciplinary team from the United Kingdom made two visits to Sri Lanka (in 2008 and 2009) to help in the training of nurses and social workers. When the visiting teams from Canada and the United Kingdom carried out training, we ensured that they worked alongside counterparts from Sri Lanka and that in many of the sessions, local people were on hand to translate terms and concepts and to discuss different uses of words that may cause confusion. Thereby a process was put in place for facilitating the sharing of perspectives and mutual learning; a dialogue on how matters around mental health, healing, etc. are seen in the Northern and the Southern countries; and evaluation of what aspects of practices in Western countries could be usefully applied and/or adapted for use in Sri Lanka.

The capacity-building part of our programme allowed us to visit many locations and meet many people involved in providing health and social care as well as people in the community who were concerned at the lack of sufficient care. We heard that many Sri Lankan people access indigenous healers for (what mental health workers would call) 'mental health problems'; of the valuable roles being played by local institutions such as places of religious worship – Buddhist, Hindu and Christian – that often acted as healing centres; that some community-based organizations had won the trust and confidence of people for helping them in times of trouble (including emotional problems); and that most people value the availability of many systems they can choose from. We noted the tremendous problems – mainly of a social, institutional and political nature – that presented barriers to improvements in the care of patients in the main mental health institution in the country, NIMH, that used up much of the resources available for mental health care. We were impressed by innovative developments in the eastern part of Sri Lanka that had taken place at a time when that area was relatively cut off from the rest of the country as a result of the conflict. Our observations during the programme led us to advocate for a 'home-grown' model for mental health care in Sri Lanka that is culturally and socially sensitive and take on board the plurality of healing and medical systems that people wish to access. Also, we initiated some pilot studies to indicate the sort of research that is required if locally relevant and sustainable community-based mental health care are to be developed. And we came to the conclusion that the best model for mental health care in Sri Lanka may well be a hybrid of Western allopathic medicine and the indigenous systems of care, but that systems should be built up through community consultation and/or community development that involves people on the ground.

Conclusion

Sri Lanka inherited from its colonial days under the British a medical system based on allopathic (Western) medicine superior to many other ex-colonial countries in Asia, but mental health care (based on psychiatry) was neglected, being based during colonial times in just one mental hospital near Colombo. During the latter part of British colonial rule, indigenous medicine, which had once been neglected, was allowed to develop fairly well and a 'plural medical system' developed whereby bio-medicine and Ayurvedic systems flourished side by side (Waxler, 1984). Since independence in 1948 some improvements have been made in the (allopathic) mental health system, especially since mental health needs were highlighted after the tsunami of 2004.

The TGH programme in Sri Lanka (Pedersen *et al.*, 2012) was implemented between 2007 and 2011. Although primarily aimed at contributing to a better understanding of the effects of conflict and natural disaster on mental health and well-being of ordinary people in the country, the programme provided policy guidelines for promoting mental health and well-being more generally in the country as a whole and derived some fundamental lessons for ways and means of building mental health services in Sri Lanka that may well be applicable to many non-Western ex-colonial countries. Essentially, these lessons are about strengthening the inherent resilience of local communities and ordinary people by promoting available local resources and indigenous institutions, and about a 'home-grown' model for mental health service provision.

Notes

1 The Trauma and Global Health (TGH) Program was carried out with support from the Global Health Research Initiative (GHRI), a collaborative research funding partnership of the Canadian International Development Agency, Health Canada, the International Development Research Centre and the Public Health Agency of Canada.
2 Based on 'Background to Mental Health in Sri Lanka' in S. Fernando and C. Weerackody (Eds.), *Aspects of mental health in Sri Lanka* (2011). Colombo: People's Rural Development Association, used with permission from the publishers and editors.

References

Amarasingham, L. R. (1980). Movement among traditional healers in Sri Lanka: A case study of a Sinhalese patient. *Culture, Medicine and Psychiatry, 4*, 71–92.
Bandarage, A. (2009). *The separatist conflict in Sri Lanka: Terrorism, ethnicity, political economy.* Colombo: Vijitha Yapa.
Blas, E., Sommerfeld, J. and Kurup, A. S. (Eds.). (2011). *Social determinants approaches to public health: From concept to practice.* Geneva: World Health Organization. Retrieved 13 January 2013 from http://whqlibdoc.who.int/publications/2010/9789241563970_eng.pdf.
Carpenter, J. (1988). *The history of mental health care in Sri Lanka.* Colombo: Marga Publications.
Chambers, R. (1994). The origins and practice of participatory rural appraisal. *World Development, 22*(7), 953–969.
Chambers, R. (1997). *Whose reality counts? Putting the first last.* London: ITDG (Intermediate Technology Development Group) Publishing.
De Alwis, M. and Hedman, E.-L. (2009). *Tsunami in a time of war: Aid, activism and reconstruction in Sri Lanka and Aceh.* Colombo: ICES (International Centre for Ethnic Studies).
De Silva, D. (2002). Psychiatric service delivery on an Asian country: The experience of Sri Lanka. *International Review of Psychiatry, 14*, 66–70.
Fernando, S. (2010). *Mental health, race and culture* (3rd ed.). Basingstoke and New York: Palgrave Macmillan.
Gaines, A. D. (1992). *Ethnopsychiatry: The cultural construction of professional and folk psychiatries.* New York: State University of New York Press.
Galappatti, A. (2003). What is a psychosocial intervention? Mapping the field in Sri Lanka. *Intervention: International Journal of Mental Health, Psychosocial Work and Counselling in Areas of Armed Conflict, 1*(2), 3–17.
Galappatti, A. (2005). Psychosocial work in the aftermath of the tsunami: Challenges for service provision in Batticaloa, Eastern Sri Lanka. *Intervention, 3*(1), 65–69.
Gokhale, N. A. (2009). *Sri Lanka: From war to peace.* New Delhi: Har-Anand Publications.
Higuchi, M. (2002). *Traditional health practices in Sri Lanka.* Amsterdam: VU University Press.
Hopper, K. J. and Wanderling, J. (2000). Revisiting the developed vs developing country distinction in course and outcome in schizophrenia: Results from IsoS, the WHO-collaborative follow-up project. *Schizophrenia Bulletin, 26*, 835–846.
Jablensky, A., Sartorius, N., Ernberg, G., Anker, M., Korten, A., Cooper, J. E. et al. (1992). Schizophrenia: Manifestations, incidence and course in different cultures. *Psychological Medicine Monograph Supplement, 20*, 1–97.

Jayawardena, K. (2010). *Perpetual ferment: Popular revolts in Sri Lanka in the 18th and 19th centuries.* Colombo: Social Scientists' Association.

Jones, M. (2004). *Health policy in Britain's model colony: Ceylon (1900–1948).* New Delhi: Orient Longman.

Kakar, S. (1984). *Shamans, mystics and doctors: A psychological inquiry into India and its healing tradition.* New York: Knopf [republished by Unwin, London (1984), University of Chicago Press, Chicago (1991)].

Kapferer, B. (1991). *A celebration of demons: Exorcism and the aesthetics of healing in Sri Lanka* (2nd ed.). Washington, DC: Berg Publishers and Smithsonian Institute Press.

Kusumaratne, S. (2005). *Indigenous medicine in Sri Lanka: A sociological analysis.* Nugegoda, Sri Lanka: Sarasavi Publishers.

Ludowyke, E. F. C. (1962). *The story of Ceylon.* London: Faber & Faber.

Mattock, J. L. (2005). *Resource loss and psychological distress: An application of the Conservation of Resources (COR) model to the 2004 Asian Tsunami in Sri Lanka.* MSc Thesis, Northumbria University, Newcastle-upon-Tyne. Retrieved 13 January 2013 from www.alnap.org/pool/files/mattlock_psychosocial_distress_tsunami_nov_2005.pdf.

Mental Health Directorate. (2006). *The mental health policy of Sri Lanka 2005–2015.* Colombo: Ministry of Healthcare and Nutrition.

Myers, N. L. (2010). Culture, stress and recovery from schizophrenia: Lessons from the field for global mental health. *Culture, Medicine, Psychiatry, 34,* 500–528.

Nichter, M. (1980). The lay person's perception of medicine as perspective into the utilization of multiple therapy systems in the Indian context. *Social Science and Medicine, 14,* 225–233.

Nordstrom, C. R. (1988). Exploring pluralism: The many faces of Ayurveda. *Social Science and Medicine, 27*(5), 479–489.

Obeyesekere, G. (1981). *Medusa's hair: An essay on personal symbols and religious experience.* Chicago: University of Chicago Press.

Pate, A. (2005). *The yakunnatima: Devil dance ritual of Sri Lanka.* Retrieved 13 January 2013 from www.lankalibrary.com/rit/yakun%20natuma.htm.

Pedersen, D., Errazuriz, C., Kienzler, H., Lopez, V., Sharma, B. Bustamente, I. et al. (2012). *Political violence, natural disasters, and mental health outcomes: Devloping innovative health policies and interventions.* Final Technical Report of Trauma and Global Health (TGH) Program. Retrieved 3 February 2013 from www.mcgill.ca/trauma-globalhealth/reports.

Pertold, O. (1930). *The ceremonial dances of the Sinhalese: An inquiry into Sinhalese folk religion.* Dehiwala, Sri Lanka: Tisara Prakasakayo.

Principle Medical Officer. (1896). Report of Superintendent A. B. Spence. *Sessional Paper 1896.* Colombo: Government Printer.

Pugh, J. F. (1983). Astrological counseling in contemporary India. *Culture, Medicine and Psychiatry, 7,* 279–299.

Sachs, L. (1989). Misunderstanding as therapy: Doctors, patients and medicines in a rural clinic in Sri Lanka. *Culture, Medicine and Psychiatry, 13,* 335–349.

Samarasinghe, D. (2006). Different disasters, different needs. *International Psychiatry, 3*(3), 8–11.

Somasundaram, D. (1998). *Scarred minds: The psychological impact of war on Sri Lankan Tamils.* Colombo: Vijitha Yapa.

Somasundaram, D. (2010). Collective trauma in the Vanni: A qualitative inquiry into the mental health of the internally displaced due to the civil war in Sri Lanka. *International Journal of Mental Health Systems, 4,* 22. Doi: 10.1186/1752-4458-4-22.

Uragoda, C. G. (1987). *A history of medicine in Sri Lanka: From the earliest times to 1948.* Colombo: Sri Lanka Medical Association.

Vogt, B. (1999). *Skill and trust: The Tovil healing ritual of Sri Lanka as culture-specific psychotherapy,* Sri Lanka Studies 6 (M. H. Kohn, Trans.). Amsterdam: VU University Press.

Waxler, N. E. (1977). Is mental illness cured in traditional societies? A theoretical analysis. *Culture, Medicine and Psychiatry, 1,* 233–253.

Waxler, N. E. (1984). Behavioural convergence and institutional separation: An analysis of plural medicine in Sri Lanka. *Culture, Medicine and Psychiatry, 8,* 187–205.

Waxler-Morrison, N. (1988). Plural medicine in Sri Lanka. *Social Science and Medicine, 27*(5), 543.

Weerackody, C. and Fernando, S. (2011). *Reflections on mental health and wellbeing: Learning from communities affected by conflict, dislocation and natural disaster.* Colombo: People's Rural Development Association (PRDA).

Weiss, G. (2011). *The cage: The fight for Sri Lanka and the last days of the Tamil Tigers.* London: Bodley Head.

WHO (World Health Organization). (1973). *Report of the International Pilot Study of Schizophrenia,* vol. 1. Geneva: WHO.

WHO. (1979). *Schizophrenia: An international follow-up study.* London: Wiley.

Wijesekera, N. (1989). *Deities and demons, magic and masks,* part 2. Colombo: Gunasena.

Wirz, P. (1954). *Exorcism and the art of healing in Ceylon.* Leiden: E. J. Brill.

19 Transcultural psychiatry, psychology and social entrepreneurship in Denmark

Rashmi Singla

Introduction

Denmark is characterised by a state "cradle to grave" tax, supported welfare system, relative gender and economic egalitarianism and ethnic diversity (Jenkins, 2011).[1] The ethnic diversity of its population now presents a number of challenges, including mental health service provision.[2] A brief look at its recent immigration history reveals a relatively large number of migrants from Turkey, ex-Yugoslavians who arrived in Denmark in the early 1970s, and refugees from countries such as Iran, Lebanon and Sri Lanka who got asylum in Denmark in the 1980s. There have been some efforts to meet the psychiatric and psychological challenges presented by increasing diversity (Singla, 2012), yet a doctoral thesis about psychiatry and culture concludes that there have been limited systematic change, adjustment or targeting of care and treatment offers (Johansen, 2007). A number of studies indicate that there are several mental health problems and a relatively low mental health related quality of life among migrants (Carlsson, 2005; Matthiessen, 2000). There are also some paradoxes – while Amnesty International criticises the government policies that result in imprisoning vulnerable torture survivors, the Red Cross opened a clinic for undocumented immigrants in 2011, which is being used by increasing numbers of persons (Rasmussen, 2013). It seems that restrictive services coexist in Denmark with innovative services that attempt to fill the gaps for meeting the needs of the diverse populations.

This chapter describes mental health in relation to ethnic minorities in Denmark. It reviews the critical attitudes towards psychiatry and psychology currently being voiced; the information available that points to special needs of ethnic minorities; an overall description of transcultural psychiatry and psychology; and conclusions on the future directions for critical psychiatry and psychology in Denmark.

Critical psychiatry and psychology in Denmark

The mainstream psychiatry and psychology services in Denmark are primarily supported by the state and local authorities and are rather conventional (Møhl and Simonsen, 2010). However, changes are taking place due to the efforts of some professionals, service users and their relatives. There are non-governmental organisations (NGOs) such as the Danish Mental Health Fund, that encourage people to "dare to care" about mental illness to seek treatment at an early stage and prevent treatment non-compliance, fighting stigmatisation prevalent in all sectors of society (Psykiatrifonden, 2004). We can also mention the radical LAP-national organisation for former and current users of psychiatry and the less radical SIND – the sister organisation to the British MIND (LAP, 2013).

At an academic level, German–Danish *critical psychology* challenges institutional power structures that control the emancipatory potential in people's everyday lives (Schraube and Osterkamp, 2013). Meanwhile a critical voice that directly influences the mental health scenario in Denmark is that of psychologist Brinkmann (2010), who questions the exaggerated focus on psychiatric diagnosis and medicalisation of psycho-social problems.[3] He suggests that there is a diagnostic epidemic, with 15% of Danish people being treated with antidepressants, anxiety-reducing drugs or anti-psychotic medicine, and that these numbers are increasing. Brinkmann (2010) questions the pathologisation of human suffering and argues convincingly that human beings should be allowed to have problems of living without being considered psychologically ill. A model of four types of pathologisation – stigmatising, self-pathologising, risk pathologising and de-pathologising – is presented, inspired by Rose's (2006) critique of treating disease susceptibilities rather than disease. This evokes the concept of "personal resilience" (Fernando, 2010, p. 87) that challenges the conventional wisdom that adverse experiences invariably damages people. Citing Walsh, Fernando argues that 'when faced with adversity, trauma, and so on most people bounce back "strengthened and more resourceful"' (Walsh, 2006, in Fernando, 2010, p. 88).

Progressive development in mainstream psychiatry is exemplified by a project where a system of *integrated treatment* includes protocols for medication, family involvement and social skills training (Nordentoft *et al.*, 2006). This scheme postpones or inhibits the onset of psychosis in many cases. However, even here diagnostic systems as such are seldom questioned by Danish psychiatrists and psychologists.

In Danish psychiatry there are a few experts and practitioners who are critical, questioning the very bases of these diagnoses. One of the crucial, critical voices in the field of psychiatry is that of Hertz (2008, 2010), for whom symptoms are a communication form leading to *unfathomed potentials*. Hertz advocates an *actor perspective* instead of victim perspective as being decisive for challenging the problematic aspects of health. Fernando (2010) suggests a similar perspective in his nuanced discussion of the service user movement being promoted as "recovery" in the United Kingdom. However, he differentiates between the interpretation of the concept by service users, sometimes called survivors or consumers outside the United Kingdom, and the psychiatric establishment in the country. At this point it is worth adding that the international Hearing Voices Network has now become quite prominent in Denmark too, headed by the ex-service user Ranchman, who often makes critical contributions in the media on issues related to psychiatry (Stemmehørernetværket, 2012).

Mental health and ethnic minority communities

The Danish healthcare system is based on free access to the system, with equal access for all citizens under universal health care, and with ethnic minorities included in the generic services. Although services for ethnic minorities, primarily for traumatised refugees, were established in the 1980s (Matthiessen, 2000), there is no national strategy in Denmark aimed at ensuring that ethnic minorities receive appropriate and culturally sensitive health care. General practitioners form the general gateway to health care in Denmark with the patient list system ensuring a continuous relationship with a general practitioner. There are indications that immigrants in general use general practitioners more often than do ethnic Danes.

The Danish Research Center for Migration, Ethnicity and Health (MESU, 2013) documents that ethnic minorities have disease patterns and often experience barriers in access to health care that differ from the majority. Overall, immigrants judge their own state of health as being worse than that of ethnic Danes and experience stress more frequently. When compared to ethnic Danes, mental health is *worse* among ethnic minorities, with more immigrants than ethnic Danes experiencing chronic anxiety and depression (Holmberg, Ahlmark and Curtis, 2009).

Refugees, compared to native Danes, show higher overall risk of having a first-time psychiatric contact for mental disorders entailing that health care services need to target mental health issues from arrival in the receiving country (Nørredam, Garcia-Lopez, Keiding and Krasnik, 2009), while the same authors (2010) also demonstrate that migrant psychiatric patients are admitted involuntarily more often than Danish psychiatric patients. Some local health centres in districts with many immigrants have paid special attention to ethnic minorities, and the National Board of Health has initiated a number of activities during recent years in order to cope with problems relating to immigrant patients (Nørredam, Singla and Krasnik, 2008).

But, generally, initiatives to support immigrants' access to health care are limited and dependent on local and individual activities generated by a few health care professionals with an interest in migrant health. The question of providing an adequate health care system for all citizens with a special focus on the needs of migrants is primarily a political question – a conclusion that reflects Fernando's overall critical perspective regarding the mental health of ethnic minorities. Ethnic minorities in Denmark officially enjoy formal rights to health care, yet there are many informal barriers obstructing access to high-quality health services related to issues of *language*, a lack of knowledge regarding the healthcare system, *stigmatisation*, and doctors' *passive* approach (Dyhr, 1996). A special problem is evident in relation to immigrant psychiatric patients who tend to experience more enforced admissions than similar ethnic Danish patients

– interpreted as a result of barriers to seeking early treatment and experiences of societal exclusion. Non-Danish-speaking ethnic minorities have the right to free assistance of an interpreter in health care; however, the use of interpreters is unsystematic and most interpreters are not professionally trained (Jensen, Smith-Nielsen and Krasnik, 2010).

Transcultural psychiatry and psychology

A seminal work taking a critical approach to mental health in Denmark is *Transkulturelt Psykiatri* (Alberdi, Nørregaard, Kastrup and Kristensen, 2002). Transcultural psychiatry is perceived in Denmark as a compromise between two basic approaches: the *etic*, looking at problems from the outside, and the *emic*, understanding problems from the client's perspective. Although Fernando (2010) hardly uses the terms *etic* and *emic* directly, his contextualisation of psychiatry as a medical speciality concerned with disorder of mind as distinct from body – the system developed in the Western scientific tradition and its use with ethnic minorities and in diverse geographical contexts other than Western – implies *etic*, looking at problems from an outside perspective.

Transcultural psychiatry has so far had a limited role in Denmark, being primarily focused on traumatised refugees. This may be because Denmark, compared to other West European countries, has relatively fewer migrants from primarily low-income non-Western countries. However, the Health Ministry established a knowledge centre for transcultural psychiatry in 2002 (Videnscenter for Transkulturelt psykiatri, 2012) that aims to collect information from psychiatric practice settings around the country. Johansen (2007) criticises the system for considering ethnic minority patients' different ethnic backgrounds as a possible explanation for their difficult relations with the system. Invoking a relational culture concept on both sides, the *culture of the psychiatry workplace* is also explored. Similarly, Fernando emphasises accessibility, cultural appropriateness, anti-discrimination and sensitivity to cultural differences among the users in his delineation of the culture of the psychiatry service. Denmark still has a long way to go to reach these ideals, though some ground has been made up by a co-existence of "generic" and specific services for different groups, as also recommended by Fernando (1995). There are some civil society voluntary support groups such as Grandparents for Asylum and Refugee Contact (Seibæk, 2011) aimed at strengthening the marginalised in vulnerable situations. The specific ethnic minority health organisations discussed in this chapter are divided into two categories – *etic* and *emic*, based on the criterion of the initiative-taker being either *outside* or *within* the ethnic minority group. Two *etic* services providing ethnic minority mental health care are presented below.

Dignity and Oasis were established in the 1980s by ethnic majority professionals to provide services for the treatment of refugees who have been subjected to torture and trauma (Dignity, 2012; Oasis, 2012). They are government funded. The treatment assumption is that traumatised refugees suffer from a combination of complex PTSD (post-traumatic stress disorder) and depression, both psychological and neurobiological. While patients often have significant limitations in their physical, mental and social functioning (Oasis, 2012), the cross-cultural therapy provided involves therapists with intercultural competence.

Fernando (2010) has appealed for a reconceptualising of "problems" faced by ethnic minorities towards considering their resilience and resources. In the case of refugees, resilience implies their ability to deal with pre-migration experiences, often construed as trauma, journeys of migration and the stress-related implications of resettling. He invokes Muecke (1992, in Fernando, 2010, p. 156) while criticising the practice in refugee mental health care for using the *paradigm of pathology* and calls for another paradigm where refugee health is 'primarily concerned with refugees as *extraordinarily resilient human beings*'. These organisations are primarily pathology focused, almost overlooking post-migration experiences of exclusion and often fail to structure support in terms of refugees' needs within an overarching awareness and acknowledgement of their resilience. Dignity is an important organisation in the field, yet it is dominated by a preconceived focus on traumas related to torture, often without explicitly addressing the structural inequalities and institutional racism that the users face in Denmark. Also, spirituality is hardly addressed within the work of these two *etic* organisations, in contrast to the position taken by Fernando (2010) that spirituality is an important component of Asian and African cultures and central to human experience. Thus such organisations insufficiently reflect the diversity of worldviews and epistemologies (Santos, 2007). The resources of refugees are barely used in the *etic*-oriented organisations, as seen in their employment practices. People with ethnic minority backgrounds are mostly employed as interpreters and in cleaning jobs, and rarely employed as professionals even after three decades of presence in the country, which also reflects the lack of symmetrical inclusion. However, in the *emic*-oriented organisations presented below, the situation is different with a resource focus.

The *Transcultural Therapeutic Team* (TTT) for ethnic minority youth and families was established in 1991 by two psychologists, a refugee from Chile and the current author, a member of Indian diaspora in Denmark (Arenas and Singla, 1995). TTT receives partial state funding and is run by part-time volunteers. The ethos of TTT's work is based on principles of intercultural therapy practised at the Nafsiyat Centre (Kareem, 1992) and inspired by Fernando's (1991, 2010) work. TTT's staff is multi-ethnic and adheres to the following principles.

A major principle is to consider youth's identities as multidimensional. The ethnic minority psychologists provide probable *models* for identification for the young people. This *ethnic matching* – where a cultural framework and common language is shared by client and therapist, as well as a shared understanding of identity issues – has become more complex and nuanced over the decades. Inspired by Fernando's (2010) emphasis on integrating holistic understandings with spirituality from Asian psychology (Moodley, 2011), TTT has developed greater acceptance of flexible approaches. Also, TTT has introduced psycho-spiritual practices such as yoga, Buddhism-based meditation practices – mindfulness – for personal transformation and alleviation of suffering (Rao and Paranjpe, 2008; Singla, 2011).

Another TTT principle is to seek to involve the family, perceived as the psycho-social unit of operations because continuity of interdependence between family members is still an ideal in many users' countries of origin (Arenas and Singla, 1995). Efforts are made to establish/re-establish dialogue between generations, either directly by inviting family members into the therapy room or "indirectly" through therapeutic focus (Singla, 2004). The increasingly transnational character of migrants' lives (for example, as a result of easier travel and communication) has led to the perception of ethnic minorities as members of diasporas (transnational communities of people dispersed from their country of origin) rather than just migrants (Kalra, Kaur and Hutnyk, 2005; Singla, 2005). Thus, it is of increasing importance that identity with multiple dimensions and relationships in the country of origin and other relevant countries are addressed in the psycho-social work (Bloch and Solomos, 2010; Singla, 2008).

TTT's third principle addresses the broader social context: the state and society. Institutional racism and racial discrimination influence ethnic minority youth's everyday experience in European countries (Fernando, 2001). TTT tries to function as a bridge builder between youth and society in general, by establishing contact across sectors and encouraging participation in the wider society, while at the same time minimising exclusion processes at various levels including diverse worldviews.[4] The principles of TTT reaffirm Fernando's critical mental health framework (2010) by emphasising both macro-level and micro-level engagement. At the macro level, human, financial and material resources need to be mobilised, ensuring political commitment to *social equity*. Mental health promotion at a micro level cannot and must not ignore the overall social, economic and political aspects of the society in which the person lives.

Fernando's writings (1995, 2001, 2010) on the topic of diversity in the United Kingdom and Europe have helped in the difficult task of dealing with implicit historical discrimination in the specific Danish context with an alternative usage of the social stratification terms "race" and "ethnicity" compared to how they are used in the United Kingdom. In 1996–1997, in an exchange between Danish and British health professionals, Fernando introduced the term *multi-ethnic* in Denmark, when the dominant political rhetoric overlooked increasing diversity.

Ethnic Resource Team (ERT) multi-faith chaplaincy is a mental health service founded in 2003 by the Islamic–Christian Study Centre (IKS). The overall purpose is to secure access and optimal care for ethnic minorities in hospitals, especially for seriously ill and terminal patients and their relatives, bridge building between them and the hospital staff, along with teaching and supervision of the staff and patient counselling. The services are provided by volunteers with different ethnic and religious backgrounds. Five hospitals in the greater Copenhagen area support and utilise ERT,[5] which began to receive "permanent" financial support for the team coordinator in 2011, albeit after eight years of uncertainty. The coordinator and initiative-taker is a hospital chaplain with a Pakistani background, who aimed to close the gap between the spiritual and religious needs of ethnic minority patients for the sacred room, where chaplaincy services were only available for Lutheran Christian church members (Baig, 2011).

The theoretical basis of ERT is Clinebell's pain theory (Baig, 2011), with four domains for dealing with pain: the physical, psychological, social and existential, the last of the four covering needs relating to meaning, giving and receiving love, hope and creativity. Muslims are the single largest group among all minority faiths; thus Quaranic ideals, including sound health and physical well-being and the peace of heart (*qlbum saleem*)/spiritual well-being, are also included (Baig, 2011).[6] We can conclude that these *emic* organisations respond to the special needs of ethnic minorities related to identity with multiple dimensions, family interdependence, transnationalism, discrimination and spirituality.

Social entrepreneurship: Fernando's pragmatism

It will be evident from earlier discussions that the provision of specialised services to meet the mental health needs of ethnic minorities requires not only professional understandings but also pragmatic, realistic ways to establish and ensure the continued existence of such services, especially the *emic* ones. Fernando's contribution to this field also includes explicit attention to societal, structural and economic factors to ensure appropriate policies and resources for establishing and sustaining such organisations. The recommendation by the Danish European Commission against Racism and Intolerance (ECRI, 2012) emphasised the need for sufficient funding for such civil society organisations, as they still suffer from lack of funding. Therefore sustaining *emic* NGOs *along with* relevant changes in the statutory systems is vital for the positive mental health of ethnic minorities.

TTT and ERT as *emic*-based organisations illustrate that services initiated by ethnic minority professionals and their continued survival meet a challenge in Denmark. Fernando emphasised the sustainability of *emic* services by arguing against ethno/eurocentrism and advocating partnership between statutory and voluntary services (Fernando, 2001). He underlined that many projects that were started by black people for black people in the United Kingdom foundered on the question of finance, as the conditions proved too restrictive and the period of support for private agencies is limited to a few years.[7] Despite differences in structural aspects between the United Kingdom and Denmark, his pragmatism has contributed to the sustainability of emic services. With this appeal for a strong organisational base, we find that the issue of social entrepreneurship is emphasised in Denmark by Hulgård (2011), Danish professor of social entrepreneurship. Underlining social entrepreneurship in modern society as a distinct type of social practice, he argues that NGOs set up as social enterprises mirror the new trend witnessed in the welfare state of restructuring in times of decreased health budget. This reorientation generates a new role for NGOs, highlighting an adequate financial and legal structure for sustaining such enterprises (Hulgård, 2010).

Both TTT and ERT are *bottom-up* initiatives launched by ethnic minority professionals for the creation of social value, to further access to high-quality counselling and to meet mental well-being and spiritual needs. This was done in the face of informal barriers, contributing to ethnic minority's mental health through critical practices. Additionally, Fernando's (2001) practice of *mentoring* professionals, such as the current author, across national borders has been invaluable in establishing and sustaining critical psychological practices in Denmark. The critical issues related to ethnicity and culture were brought to the fore by the (in)famous Mohammad Cartoon crisis in 2006, revealing that ethnic minorities, especially Muslims, have been stigmatised by society including the Danish press (Hussain, 2011). Through both his work and mentoring, Fernando has contributed to transcultural psychiatry and psychology in Denmark. The present chapter documents this marginalised field, contributing to intervention in line with Appadurai (2004)'s emancipatory conceptualisation *documentation is intervention*.

Conclusion

Danish mental health services have been varied, complex and under transformation in the past decades. There has been a recent political prioritising of mental health issues and nuanced comprehension of mental illness dynamics, along with criticism of privatisation of psychological suffering (Krogh, 2012). This political vision, currently gaining support, fits with the path shown by Fernando (2012) emphasising the resilience of service users, appropriate policies and resources. However, these changes are fluid and vulnerable; there is a risk of neo-liberal ideas emphasising an individualised approach to mental health, including that of ethnic minorities.

The changing demography of Danish society has led to some changes in the current state of psychiatry and psychology, but there are still many barriers to overcome for ethnic minorities to experience fully the principles of equity and access. Critical psychiatry and psychology in Denmark are characterised by a mixed and paradoxical situation. There are critical voices of some professionals and questioning of the use of medication in psychiatry (e.g. Nye-veje, 2012). Regarding ethnic minority services, there are mental health organisations, mostly *etic* in orientation, but also some *emic*. Although the former are predominantly problem-oriented, the latter reflect an inclusive approach to mental health problems of the ethnic minorities, reflecting the critical psychiatry and psychology advocated by Fernando. Currently, there are some signs of positive transformations in the overall Danish policy, despite the economic crisis in Denmark. Academically, some approaches and criticisms bring hope. At the same time there is not much basis for predicting that inequity in the provision of mental health services for ethnic minorities in Denmark will be fully countered in the near future.

We can conclude that Fernando's writing and support for professionals have to some extent influenced work done in Denmark to improve ethnic minorities' mental health services. The continued way forward in Denmark can be through Fernando's two-fold vision: a critical, inclusive approach including a mega, macro-level of national policies as well as a micro-level engagement of the needs of people and the mentoring of professionals in this salient field. There is therefore a need for a further developing of transcultural psychology and psychiatry with critical perspectives, also through international collaboration and inspiration.

Acknowledgement

Thanks to Psychiatrist Soeren Hertz, Psychiatrist Suman Fernando, Dr. Spencer Hazel and Dr. Agnes Ringer for their valuable comments on earlier drafts of this chapter.

Notes

1 Denmark has seen a five-fold increase in the number of non-Western migrants since 1980, challenging the ethnic "homogeneity" discourse. There have been migrants and refugees in the past few centuries from other European countries such as Sweden, Poland and Germany (Matthiessen, 2000). But the recent immigration history between 1968 and 1971, when the labour market opened up, resulted in migration primarily from Turkey, the former Yugoslavia and Pakistan. The first immigrants were mostly 20–30-year-old young men, who came without families, later on supporting the migration of their relatives and friends, known as chain migration. The resulting transplanted communities, which provided security and comfort to their members, were also the targets of marginalisation and isolation from the receiving societies (Singla, 2008). Paradoxically, the laws that resulted in "Migration Stop" in 1972 led to the beginning of family reunifications with spouses and children. In the mid-1980s and 1990s a number of refugees arrived from Iran, Sri Lanka, Somalia and Iraq. At present non-Danish people can only enter Denmark as tourists, asylum seekers, refugees, temporary students, workers with special skills, or through family reunification.
2 Denmark has a population of 5.6 million, of which 10% are immigrants and their descendants, 6.7% are from so-called non-Western countries and 3.6% with a Muslim background (Danmarks Statistiks, 2012).
3 Professor Svend Brinkmann is currently carrying out a research project at the national level: *Diagnostic culture: The experience, history and social representation of depression and ADHD*.
4 Just as European culture retains a worldview that incorporates a sense of *power*, Asian, African and Native American cultures retain the scars of *imperial domination and persecution* during the era in which *genocide, slavery and colonialism* flourished, as well as the effects of current economic oppression and indirect political control, i.e. *neo-colonialism* (Fernando, 2010, p. 96).
5 The five hospitals in greater Copenhagen are: Rigshospitalet, Herlev-, Bispebjerg-, Glostrup- and Hvidovre hospital.
6 The Quranic ideals of patience (*sabr*), thankfulness (*shukr*), steadfastness in tribulation (*istiqamah*), self-purification (*tazkiyyah*) and reflection (*fikr*).
7 The impression is that, when government funding is available, the conditions attached to its use are often too *restrictive*, and private agencies (charities) are often reluctant to finance projects for more than 2 or 3 years, thereby placing too heavy a burden on the goodwill of people (Fernando, 1995, p. 212).

References

Alberdi, F. (2002). Tendenser i den transkulturelle psykiatris historie. In F. Alberdi, C. Nørregaard, M. Kastrup and M. Kristensen (Eds.), *Transkulturelt Psykiatri*. Copenhagen: Hans Reitzels.

Alberdi, F. Nørregaard, C., Kastrup, M. and Kristensen, M. (Eds.). (2002). *Transkulturelt Psykiatri*. Copenhagen: Hans Reitzels.
Appadurai, A. (2004). The right to research. *Globalisation, Societies and Education*, 4(2), 167–177.
Arenas, J. and Singla, R. (1995). *Etnisk minoritetsungdom i Danmark: om deres psykosociale situation* [Ethnic minority youth in Denmark: About their psychosocial situation]. Copenhagen: Dansk psykologisk forlag.
Baig, N. (2011). *Identity and spirituality amongst Muslims at Danish hospitals: The case of Ethnic Resource Team Hospital*. Retrieved 8 August 2012 from http://ebookbrowse.com/universitypaper-on-ert-work-doc-d111870640.
Bloch, A. and Solomos, J. (Eds.). (2010). *Race and ethnicity in the 21st century*. Basingstoke: Palgrave Macmillan.
Brinkmann, S. (Ed.). (2010). *Det Diagnosticerede liv; sygdom uden grænser* [The diagnosed life: diseases without borders]. Århus: Klim.
Carlsson, J. (2005). *Mental health and health-related quality of life in tortured refugees*. PhD dissertation, Faculty of Health Sciences, Copenhagen University.
Danmarks Statistiks. (2012). Retrieved from www.dst.dk.
Dignity. (2012). Danish Institute against Torture. Retrieved 1 February 2013 from www.dignityinstitute.dk.
Dyhr, L. (1996). *Det almene i det anderledes* [The ordinary in the different]. PhD thesis, Forskingsenhed for Almen Praksis, Copenhagen.
ECRI (European Commission against Racism and Intolerance). (2012). *Report on Denmark*. Retrieved 8 August 2012 from www.coe.int/t/dghl/monitoring/ecri/Country-by-country/Denmark/DNK-CBC-IV-2012-025-ENG.pdf.
Fernando, S. (Ed.). (1995). *Mental health in a multi-ethnic society: A multi-disciplinary handbook*. London: Routledge.
Fernando, S. (2001). *Mental health and power: Minorities' own service initiatives – An international overview*. A report about TTTs 10th Jubilee Conference, 1991–2001. Retrieved from www.tttdenmark.dk.
Fernando, S. (2010). *Mental health, race and culture* (3rd ed.). Basingstoke: Palgrave Macmillan.
Fernando, S. (2012). Global Mental Health: Bridging the Perspectives of Cultural Psychiatry and Public Health, Conference and Workshop, 5–7 July, Montreal, Québec. Retrieved 1 July 2013 from www.mcgill.ca/tcpsych/training/advanced/previous/2012-asi.
Hertz, S. (2008). *Børne – og ungdomspsykiatri – ny perspektiver og uanede muligheder* [Children and youth psychiatry: New perspectives and unfathomed potentials]. Copenhagen: Akademisk Forlag.
Hertz, S. (2010). There is a crack in everthing, that's how the light gets in. In S. Brinkmann, *Det Diagnosticerede liv: sygdom uden grænser* [The diagnosed life: Disease without borders]. Århus: Klim.
Holmberg, T., Ahlmark, N. and Curtis T. (2009). *"State of the art report" Etniske minoriteters sundhed*. Danmark: Statens Institut for Folkesundhed, Syddansk Universitet.
Hulgård, L. (2010). *Discourses of social entrepreneurship: Variations of the same theme?* Retrieved 8 May 2012 from www.emes.net/fileadmin/emes/PDF_files/Working_Papers/WP_10-01_Hulg_rd__web_.pdf.
Hulgård, L. (2011). *Socialt entreprenørskab TTT's 20 year's Jubilee Report 1991–2011*. Retrieved from www.tttdenmark.dk.
Hussain, M. (2011). *Muslims in Copenhagen*. London: Open society Foundation.

Jenkins, R. (2011). *Being Danish: Paradoxes of identity in everyday life*. Copenhagen: Museum Tusculanum Press.

Jensen, N., Smith-Nielsen, S. and Krasnik, A. (2010). Expert opinions on "best practices" in delivery of healthcare services to immigrants in Denmark. *Danish Medical Bulletin*, 57(8), 1–5.

Johansen, K. (2007). Der er to i et møde – perspektiver på kulturmøde fra psykiateren [There are two parties in an encounter]. *Antropologi*, 56, 27–45.

Kalra, V., Kaur, R. and Hutnyk, J. (2005). *Diaspora & hybridity*. New Delhi: Sage.

Kareem, J. (1992). The Nafsiyat Intercultural Therapy Centre: Ideas and experience in intercultural therapy. In J. Kareem and R. Littlewood (Eds.), *Intercultural therapy: Themes, interpretations and practice*. London: Blackwell.

Kragh, A. (2012, 7 August). Det er ikke din skyld [It is not your fault]. Feature article in *Politiken*.

LAP. (2013). Retrieved 13 March 2013 from www.lap.dk.

Matthiessen, P. (2000). Sundhedssystemet og indvandrere [Health System and immigrants]. In P. Mogensen and Matheiessen (Eds.), *Mislykket Integration* [Failed integration?]. Viborg: Spektrum.

MESU. (2013). Retrieved 8 January 2013 from http://mesu.ku.dk.

Møhl, B. and Simonsen, E. (2010). *Grundbog i psykiatri* [Psychiatry textbook]. Copenhagen: Hans Reitzels.

Moodley, R. (2011). *Outside the sentence: Readings in critical multicultural counseling & psychotherapy*. Toronto: CDCP (Centre for Diversity in Counseling & Psychotherapy).

Nordentoft, M., Thorup A., Petersen L., Øhlenschlæger J., Melau, M., Christensen T. et al. (2006). Transition rates from schizotypal disorder to psychotic disorder for first-contact patients included in the OPUS trial: A randomized clinical trial of integrated treatment and standard treatment. *Schizophrenia Research*, 83, 29–40.

Nyidanmark. (2012). Retrieved 8 August 2012 from www.nyidanmark.dk/en-us.

Nye-veje. (2012). Retrieved 13 March 2013 from www.eksistentielpsykologi.dk/afholdte-arrangementer/nye-veje-i-psykiatrien.

Nørredam, M., Garcia-Lopez, A., Kidding, N. and Krasnik. A. (2009). Risk of mental disorders in refugees and native Danes. *International Journal for Research in Social and Genetic Epidemiology and Mental Health Service*. Retrieved from http://link.springer.com/article/10.1007/s00127-009-0024-6/fulltext.html#Sec7.

Nørredam, M., Garcia-Lopez, A., Keiding, N. and Krasnik, A. (2010). Excess use of coercive measures in psychiatry among migrants compared with native Danes. *Acta Psychiatrica Scandinavica*, 121, 143–151.

Nørredam, M., Singla, R. and Krasnik, A. (2008). *Denmark country report: Health care and ethnic minorities*. Retrieved from www.ttdanmark.dk.

Oasis. (2012). Retrieved 8 August 2012 from www.oasis-rehab.dk.

PsykiatriFonden. (2004). *A politically-neutral advocacy organization for mental illness*. Retrieved from www.psykiatrifonden.dk.

Rao, K. and Paranjpe, A. (2008). Yoga psychology: Theory and application. In K. Ramakrishna Rao, A. C. Paranjpe and A. K. Dalai (Eds.), *Handbook of Indian psychology*. New Delhi: Cambridge University Press.

Rasmussen, L. (2013). *Amnesty: Danmark frihedsberøver torturofre* [Denmark detains torture victims]. Retrieved 4 March 2013 from www.vftp.dk/produkter/information_om_transkulturel_psykiatri/documents/januar2013000.pdf.

Rose, N. (2006). *The politics of life itself: Biomedicine, power, and subjectivity in the twenty-first century*. Princeton, NJ: Princeton University Press.

Santos, B. S. (Ed.). (2007). *Another knowledge is possible: Beyond northern epistemologies*. London: Verso.

Schraube, E. and Osterkamp, U. (Eds.). (2013). *Psychology from the standpoint of the subject: Selected writings of Klaus Holzkamp*. Basingstoke: Palgrave Macmillan.

Seibæk, G. (2011). En historie om irakiske flygtninge og deres danske bedsteforældre [A story about Iraqi refugees and their Danish grandparents]. *Fred & Frihed, 2,* 18–21.

Singla, R. (2004). *Youth relationships, ethnicity and psychosocial intervention*. New Delhi: Books Plus.

Singla, R. (2005). South Asian diaspora in Scandinavia: Youth, interethnic and intergenerational. *Journal of Psychology and Developing Societies, 17*(2), 215–223.

Singla, R. (2008). *Now and then: Life trajectories, family relationships and diasporic identities – A follow-up study of young adults*. Copenhagen: Copenhagen Studies in Bilingualism.

Singla, R. (2011). Origins of mindfulness & meditation: Interplay of Eastern & Western psychology. *Psyke & Logos, 32*(1).

Singla, R. (2012). Migration, etnisk diversitet og sundhedsfremme [Migration, Ethnic Diversity and Health Promotion]. In B. Dybbroe, B. Land and S. Baagøe Nielsen (Eds.), *Sundhedsfremme- Et Kritisk Perspektiv* [*Health promotion: A critical perspective*]. Samfundslitteratur: Frederiksberg.

Stemmehørernetværket. (2012). Retrieved 13 March 2013 from www.stemmehoerer.dk.

Videnscenter for Transkulturelt psykiatri. (2012). Retrieved 1 July 2013 from www.psykiatri-regionh.dk/NR/exeres/034D90DB-B372-4F3A-A7BB-AF559C7D960B.htm.

20 Culture and mental heath in Aotearoa, New Zealand

Judi Clements and Wayne Blissett

Introduction

As with many indigenous people across the world, the Maori people are significantly over-represented negatively in all the statistics for health, employment and social well-being. Aotearoa New Zealand as a diverse nation continues to debate the place and status of the Treaty of Waitangi and race-based policies in the country. While Aotearoa New Zealand has a history of strong race relations, the patterns in mental health data suggest that there are barriers of cultural bias and discrimination that continue within the mental health system. The impact of colonisation and disenfranchisement is possibly not understood by the mental health diagnostic system that is still applied largely by non-Maori practitioners. This upward trend in the admission and seclusion data for Maori can be traced to the 1970s, and in spite of some significant attempts to address these, the rates continue to be an ongoing concern and focus for Maori in Aotearoa New Zealand.

The struggles of the power and culture of the past 150 years or so, though, continue to oppress and impact on Maori. The ongoing impact of colonisation is salient in the data that continue to show Maori over-representation in the criminal justice statistics and in the "heavy end" of the mental health system. Salient examples of this include: Maori men and women, when inpatients, are more likely to be placed in seclusion than non-Maori and, although ethnic monitoring is very limited, are more likely to be placed under Compulsory Treatment Orders. There is less likelihood that Maori will be offered talking therapies and it is more likely that a diagnosis of schizophrenia will be the one applied. Maori are often described as "presenting late" to services and then ending up with more "severe disorders". It could be argued that the power relations that enabled colonisation are still at work in creating this situation. As Durie (2001) says, "The individual is part of an ethnic history and where colonisation has occurred the scars of oppression and humiliation may become intolerable" (cited in Beautrais and Ferguson, 2006, p. 165).

This chapter explores the historical context of race relations in Aotearoa New Zealand and discusses the issues and concerns related to the negative statistics for Maori people. The chapter also provides an overview of how Suman Fernando's work has relevance in advocating and advancing indigenous approaches to working with Maori within the mental health system in Aotearoa. The significant work of Fernando and others in the international community has assisted in providing a body of knowledge that supports advocacy and practice development to challenge the structures and systems that continue to oppress Maori as a minority group in Aotearoa New Zealand. Fernando's work in particular has provided important perspectives on the power dynamics of both the systems and the individual within those systems to effect better outcomes for ethnic diversity.

It is impossible to consider the situation regarding approaches to mental health and mental health services without setting the context of colonisation and attempts at cultural supremacy.

Colonialism and Maori freedom

The first attempt to establish an international presence by Maori in the Western world was formalised in 1835 with the Declaration of Independence, which was the first assertion of Maori sovereignty recognisable within the international community (King, 2003). The following influx of settlers created social upheaval in Aotearoa New Zealand as the cultural differences resulted in misunderstandings and exploitation on both sides of the cultural divide. The signing of the Treaty of Waitangi in 1840 countered the Declaration and removed the possibility of a Maori-led state with the agreement that the nation would be governed by British Law, while Maori retained their sovereignty – or the ability to self-determine their taonga/treasures, lands and resources. Debate over the translations between texts and whether sovereignty was ceded or not still continue (Durie, 1998). The New Zealand Constitution Act of 1852 provided the basis for New Zealand government. The right to vote and representation under this Act was based on individual land title, which virtually disenfranchised Maori as Maori own land as collectives not individuals, negating the promised equality in art. 3 of the Treaty.[1] A succession of Acts of Parliament continued to disenfranchise Maori from their tribal lands. This impacted not only the Maori economic base but also the social and demographic fabric of Maori society.[2]

With land acquisition under control, the focus of the colonial government moved to undermining the cultural social system that was still surviving. An important example of this was the Tohunga Suppression Act of 1907, which was a significant blow to Maori culture and social order (Durie and King 1997; King, 2003). The Tohunga Suppression Act deemed it illegal to practise Maori spiritual and cultural practices and provided the platform for forbidding the speaking of Te Reo in schools and public places. It saw the closure and destruction of Wananga, traditional Maori learning institutions and the traditional cultural practices of Maori becoming confined to Marae.

At the same time, psychiatry and psychology were establishing themselves as legitimate bodies of knowledge in Aotearoa. Sir Thomas Hunter, considered a pioneering figure in psychology in Aotearoa, established Australasia's first laboratory in experimental psychology in 1908 (Hunter, 1952; Shouksmith, 1990). Both psychiatry and psychology followed overseas trends as part of the Western inclination to construct psychiatry and psychology in scientific terms. Psychology and psychiatry had little influence on Maori communities, who were struggling to keep what little land and social fabric were left (Beaglehole, 1953; Brown and Fuchs, 1971). This minimal interface between Western psychology and Maori communities meant that there was little recognition or contribution by Maori to the development of psychology or psychiatry, leaving them both to develop as purely Western sciences with no indigenous influence.

Infusing Maori culture into health care

In 2000, the Treaty of Waitangi was included in the Health and Disability Act requiring hospitals and health services to adhere to the principles of the Treaty of Waitangi and include Iwi, Tribes, in their governance and consultative practices. This piece of legislation has provided further scope for the culture and identity of Maori to be central to the care and treatment of them and their whanau (Maori Family). The power imbalance of colonisation has meant that Maori realities have not been supported in the same way as dominant Pakeha realities. This has resulted in many Maori struggling to have a sense of belonging to their traditional lands and Maori institutions, and struggling to maintain or create a Maori identity, which in itself is a powerful determinant of health (Lawson-Te Aho, 1998).

The noticeable emergence of Maori-led initiatives began in the late 1970s when there were moves by Maori working in the mental health system to try to link tangata whaiora (people seeking wellness, i.e. service users/consumers) back to their whanau. There had been Maori in the workforce of the long-stay hospitals, albeit more usually at the unskilled level of nursing assistants or domestic staff rather than practising clinicians. It is possible that reflecting back on that era Maori would describe many of those working in the system as being colonised, and not always bringing a Maori perspective or Maori worldview. However, Durie notes that

> incorporating Maori cultural beliefs and values into counselling and healing has been an active goal since the early 1980s; at least three approaches have been used. First, there has been an increase in the use of traditional healing services, sometimes as an alternative to mainstream services though more often as a supplementary activity. Second, several mainstream services have added Maori values and customary practices to treatment programmes, creating a bicultural formula; and third, a number of Maori-centred techniques have been developed either independently of other processes or alongside them. Usually they aim to strengthen cultural identity.
>
> (Durie, 2003, p. 47)

There is a clear similarity in the approaches advocated by Suman Fernando in *Mental Health, Race and Culture* when he compares the differences in cultural traditions and contrasts holistic and non-holistic approaches to mental health and ill health. "A holistic tradition promotes a sense of health as a harmonious balance between various forces in the person and social context as opposed to seeing health as individualised sense of wellbeing" (Fernando, 2010, p. 42). Fernando's work on the analyses of the complex relationships between the dominant culture and the "Other", the power of the state, the role of professionals and clinicians and institutional and individual racism provide pertinent lessons in Aotearoa New Zealand. The racism experienced through the colonisation process continues to present itself through the structures and systems of the mental health system, although advances have been made.

In Aotearoa New Zealand, the 1990s began to see some major changes in views about and organisation of mental health services. Although the need for Maori influence in services had been recognised, a major inquiry into mental health services (Mason Inquiry under s 47 of the Health and Disability Services Act 1993–1996) found that there had been "no recognisable improvement in Maori being involved in planning services, at national level, in a meaningful way" (p. 140). The same inquiry found that "Pacific Island people appear to have become the forgotten group by those who plan mental health services" (p. 141). The inquiry resulted in the establishment of the Mental Health Commission, which in 1998 produced a Blueprint for Mental Health Services that recognised, among many other issues, that "Maori health is a priority for improvement for the health sector" (p. 11) and that as well as "within mainstream" there was a need for "separate kaupapa Maori Services, delivered by Iwi and/or other Maori providers" (p. 11). Emphasis was given to the aspiration that "Maori must be able to access mental health services which are aligned to Maori cultural expectations" (p. 66).

Making a difference

Suman Fernando's analysis of the background to racism in mental health is as relevant in New Zealand as it is in the United Kingdom or North America. The notions developed and promulgated by Western researchers and psychiatrists and cloaked in scientific language were that non-Western/European communities were primitive compared to white Europeans. Fernando draws attention to the review by Benedict and Jacks (1954) of studies on Maori in New Zealand, indigenous Fijians, Hawaiians and people described as "Negro Africa". This study, entitled "Mental Illness in Primitive Societies," was later seen as largely responsible for the acceptance of the universality of schizophrenia by mainstream psychiatry (Fernando, 1995).

The racist attribution of primitiveness and assumption of European superiority has been a persistent strand of thinking in (Western) psychiatry, which Fernando's work has persistently and explicitly referenced and exposed despite often drawing criticism and hostility from "mainstream" psychiatry. This history includes the views of Freud who saw similarities between "the mental lives of savages and (European) neurotics" in *Totem and Taboo* (1913/1918) and the anthropologist Devereux (1939) who viewed non-Western healers as neurotics or psychotics. As late as the 1970s a psychiatrist at the elite Institute of Psychiatry in London observed that people from industrially developed countries showed a superior level of emotional differentiation when compared to those from "developing" countries and black Americans (see Leff, 1973).

"The ways in which power is exercised in any society is complicated, but it seems to me that identifying one or more groups that need control is always a feature of the exercise of power" (Fernando, 2006, p. 26). The negative effects on the Maori population and way of life were huge but the resilience shown by Maori people was also remarkable. New skills were developed and Maori utilised the colonial system to support them in their fight for protection of their resources both physical and spiritual.

Fernando's work from the 1980s onwards draw attention to the assumptions made by professionals trained in a Western setting that a Western style of expression, behaviour and emotional differentiation is the norm against which "other" people are to be judged. In challenging this and recounting the history and development of psychiatry and mental health service responses, Fernando exposes the inherent racism and institutional racism that has and still does influence practice. The reaction from psychiatrists in leadership positions has often been less than benign. One of the authors of this chapter clearly recalls being strongly advised in the 1990s by the president of the Royal College of Psychiatrists to ignore the views of Fernando as he was "a trouble maker".

Fernando's analyses have mainly been undertaken from his UK or North American experience but his findings and observations have equal relevance and applicability in New Zealand. There are many forms of racial discrimination that can affect health, including mental health, in different ways. In New Zealand there is direct evidence linking self-reported experience of interpersonal racial discrimination to poorer health outcomes (Harris *et al.*, 2006; as quoted in Hauora: Maori Standards of Health IV, November 2007). Results from national surveys showed that Maori reported the highest prevalence of "ever" experiencing racial discrimination compared to other ethnic groups. This included ethnically motivated physical attack, verbal attack, unfair treatment by health professionals or at work or when buying a house. It is in this context that we must consider the attitudes, behaviours and experiences of mental health and mental distress. Good mental health depends on many factors, but among indigenous people the world over, cultural identity is considered a critical prerequisite. There have been developments that contribute to the potential but the journey of change is by no means concluded and sometimes the destination seems to recede over the horizon.

Te Whare Tapa Wha

In New Zealand Professor Sir Mason Durie (then Dr Mason Durie) was the main developer of the Te Whare Tapa Wha Model in 1982. To reflect the reality that the Maori philosophy towards health is based on holistic health and wellness approach, the four cornerstones (or sides) of Maori health are whanau (family health), tinana (physical health), hinengaro (psychological/mental health) and wairua (spiritual health). The model emphasises that mind and body are inseparable, that spirituality is an essential, physical wellness needs equal nurturing and that whanau is the most fundamental unit of Maori society. The difference between Western/Eurocentric individualistic thinking and holistic thinking is clearly defined by Fernando (2003) when he says:

> Holistic thinking is different to unconnected thinking in being characterised by "connectedness" ... the primary characteristic of holistic thinking is an all-pervasive connectedness; a sort of "connectedness thinking", that links together all happenings and experiences with feelings and instils "feeling" of connections between all human beings, indeed between all beings and possibly between all beings and inanimate objects in the environment.
> (pp. 124–125)

A very similar explanation of the holistic approach is explored by Durie (2003).

Another Maori model of health that emphasises the holistic approach was developed by Rose Pere in the concept of Te Wheke, the octopus, to define family health (see Durie, 1998). The head of the octopus represents the whanau (the family), the eyes of the octopus represent waiora (total well-being for the individual and family) and each of the eight tentacles represent a specific dimension of health. The dimensions cover such aspects as breathing life from ancestors, life force in people and objects, the extended family and spirituality (Durie, 1998).

Since their development these models have become accepted as essential in the approach to mental health and well-being for Maori and can now be found on the website and documentation of most New Zealand government departments and in training and professional development for clinicians and other mental health workers as well as social workers and psychologists.

Similar models have developed also for understanding a holistic approach to health from a Pacific Island perspective, in particular Fonofale, developed by Karl Poluto Enderman (Culbertson, Agee and Makasiale, 2007).

Maori cultural beliefs and perspectives on counselling have also evolved because of the lack of satisfaction with many (Western) psychological therapists and their focus on acquisition of skills or overcoming behavioural problems to the relative exclusion of the wider world and often inadequate recognition of culture as a force for change (Durie, 1998).

There were developments in the 2000s with the first national strategic plan developed for Maori, entitled *Te Puawaitanga: Maori National Strategic Framework*. Of particular note was Hua Oranga, developed to measure treatment outcomes for Maori by seeking views, not only from clinicians, but tangata whaiora (service users) and whanau (family) in relation to the cornerstones of health in Te Whare Tapa Wha. The need for a Maori workforce in mental health was clearly recognised by the late 1990s and led in 2002 to the establishment of Te Rau Matatini – the National Maori workforce development organisation. Now 10 years later a Maori workforce exists across different disciplines and is growing.

Much could be written about the discrimination and racism, individual and institutionalised, that are undeniable features of New Zealand life and detrimentally affect Maori, Pacific Island and Asian communities. As the indigenous people of Aotearoa New Zealand and Treaty partners under the Treaty of Waitangi, Maori have a unique position and rights but the journey towards achieving those fully has been arduous and continues. In mental health services, despite the changes and improvements already mentioned, the facts and statistics reflect that Maori are poorly served.

There are similarities between the experiences of African and Afro-Caribbean men in the United Kingdom and Maori men in Aotearoa New Zealand. Maori men are more likely to receive a diagnosis of schizophrenia and less likely to be offered talking therapies, and more likely to be placed in locked wards and in seclusion. An analysis of available statistics shows that Maori are statistically more likely to be secluded than any other ethnic group. Maori women are more likely to be placed in seclusion than non-Maori men. The over-representation of Maori in the criminal justice system bears similarity with the over-representation of black men in similar systems in the United Kingdom and United States. The most recent suicide statistics (2010) contain the shocking fact that while youth suicide overall is declining, the rate for Maori youth is not sharing the downward trend. Across all ages, 20% of those who die by suicide are Maori (16 per 100,000, compared to 11.5 deaths per 100,000 overall).

Despite these realities, or perhaps because of them, there are positive developments emerging. The current National Party-led government has, with the influence of the Maori Party, which has a governing arrangement with National, introduced a policy of Whanau Ora to drive government services and other agencies to work differently with Maori. Whanau Ora is a Maori concept of family well-being and the collective realising of whanau potential. "Whanau Ora is about empowering whanau to take control of their future. What we want for our whanau is to be self-determining, to be living healthy lifestyles, to be participating fully in society and to be economically secure" (Hon. Tariana Turia, Co-leader of Maori Party, Minister responsible for Whanau Ora. As quoted by Te Puni Kokiri – www.tpk.govt.nz).

A Whanau Ora fund was established and a competitive process resulted in a number of Whanau Ora providers around Aotearoa New Zealand. Whanau Ora has the potential to make deep and far-reaching changes and improvements for Maori whanau and these should impact positively on mental health and well-being. The approach to Whanau Ora implicitly, and where necessary explicitly, takes a strengths-based approach, avoiding the deficit approach non-Maori, including mass media and government agencies, so often take. The emphasis on strengths and potential is reminiscent of the well-being for all approach advocated by Suman Fernando. As he says,

> Wellbeing may be a better approach to get us away from the medicalization of human problems – not least in the light of its apparent universal appeal across cultural boundaries. Wellbeing while taking on the past, emphasises

positive liberation from past misfortunes, including being diagnosed, stigmatised and oppressed by institutional racism, while facing up to current realities and struggling against impediments to a fulfilling life.

(Fernando, 2009, p. 14)

Conclusion

There are achievements to be recognised and equally the determination to challenge and maintain progress remains essential. Suman Fernando's work over more than 4 decades demonstrates both and exemplifies the latter. The words of a Maori elder from the 20th century are poignantly relevant: "He tino nui rawa o tatau mahi, kia kore o matu nui.... We have come too far not to go further, you have done too much not to do more" (whakatauki spoken by Ta Himi Tau Henare, Ngati Hine, 1989).[3]

Notes

1 Maori leadership responses to the breaches of the Treaty and the assimilation attempts by the colonial government were wide and varied. What emerged was the advent of Maori nationalism, embodied in the Kingitanga movement where Te Wherowhero, later to become known as Potatou, was elected as the first Maori King in 1858. This was further built on by the second Maori King Te Tawhio, who established the Kauhanganui, "Great Council", as a political forum for the Waikato, Hauraki and Maniapoto Confederation of Tribes. As Maori opposition to land acquisition grew it was met by British armed troops and the core punishment for opposition was confiscation of tribal lands. This was legalised through two significant Acts of Parliament, the New Zealand Settlements Act and the Suppression of Rebellion Act, both passed in 1863. Tribes who actively or passively resisted surveyors or sales were regarded as rebels and their lands were confiscated. Twenty-five years later after the sovereignty wars tribes were left in little doubt that whatever else the Treaty promised it had excluded them from active roles in the governance of their own country and their own tribal territories.
2 The Native Land Act 1865 largely did away with customary land titles, freeing up land for sale and in the process undermining the social links between whanau and within tribes. This was followed by another Native Land Act in 1887 that allowed for the alienation of Maori reserves by putting them in the control of colonial rule. Maori society had been based on shared interests in land for interconnectedness and development. Out of nearly 66.5 million acres, by 1896 only 11 million acres remained in Maori ownership. At the same time, in parallel the Maori population had declined from an estimated 200,000 in 1840 to less than 43,000.
3 Ta Himi (James Clendon) Tau Henare (1911–1989), descended from a number of famous northern warrior chiefs. Having enrolled in the 28th New Zealand (Maori) Battalion to serve in the Second World War, he rose to the rank of Lieutenant Colonel and received the Distinguished Service Order in 1946. After the war he devoted himself to public service and the leadership of his people. He was made a Commander of the British Empire (CBE) in 1966, was knighted in 1978 and is widely regarded as one of Maoridom's finest leaders.

References

Beaglehole, E. (1953). Obituary: Sir Thomas Hunter. *Bulletin of the British Psychological Society, 4*(21), 1–2.

Beautrais, A. L. and Fergusson, D. M. (2006). Indigenous suicide in New Zealand. *Archives of Suicide Research, 10*(2), 159–168.

Benedict, P. K. and Jacks, I. (1954). Mental illness in primitive societies. *Psychiatry: Journal for the Study of Interpersonal Processes, 17*, 377–389.

Brown, L. B. and Fuchs, A. H. (1971). Early experimental psychology in New Zealand: The Hunter-Titchener letters. *Journal of the History of the Behavioural Sciences, 7*, 10–22.

Culbertson, P., Agee, M. N. and Makasiale, C. (2007). *Penina uliuli: Contemporary challenges in mental health for Pacific peoples*. Honolulu: University of Hawai'i Press.

Devereux, G. (1939). Mohave culture and personality. *Character & Personality: A Quarterly for Psychodiagnostic & Allied Studies, 8*, 91–109.

Durie, M. (1998). *Whaiora: Maori health development* (2nd ed.). Auckland: Oxford Press.

Durie, M. (2003). *Ngā kāhui pou: Launching Māori futures*. Wellington: Huia Publishers.

Durie, M. and Kingi, T. K. R. (1997). *A framework for measuring Māori mental health outcomes*. Research report TPH 97/5. Ministry of Health.

Fernando, S. (1995). *Mental health in a multi-ethnic society: A multi-disciplinary handbook*. London: Routledge.

Fernando, S. (2003). *Cultural diversity, mental health and psychiatry: The struggle against racism*. London: Routledge.

Fernando, S. (2006). Stigma, racism & power. *Aotearoa Ethnic Network Journal, 1*(1), 24–28.

Fernando, S. (2009). Wellbeing for all. *Open Mind*, September/October.

Fernando, S. (2010). *Mental health, race and culture* (3rd ed.). New York: St Martins Press.

Freud, S. (1913/1918). *Totem and taboo: Resemblances between the psychic lives of savages and neurotics*. New York: Moffatt, Yard & Company.

Harris, R., Tobias, M., Jeffreys, M., Waldegrave, K., Karlsen, S. and Nazroo, J. (2006). Racism and health: The relationship between experience of racial discrimination and health in New Zealand. *Social Science & Medicine, 63*(6), 1428–1441.

Hunter, T. A. (1952). The development of psychology in New Zealand: A report. *Bulletin of the British Psychological Society, 18*, 17–24.

King, M. (2003). *The Penguin history of New Zealand*. New Zealand: Penguin.

Lawson-Te Aho, K. (1998). *A review of evidence: A background document to support Kia Piki Te Ora O Te Taitamariki*. Wellington: Te Puni Kōkiri.

Leff, J. (1973). Culture and the differentiation of emotional states. *British Journal of Psychiatry, 123*, 299–306.

Mason, K. (1996). *Inquiry under section 47 of the Health and Disability Services Act 1993 in respect of certain mental health services: Report of the Ministerial Inquiry to the Minister of Health Hon. Jenny Shipley*. Wellington, New Zealand: Ministry of Health.

Mental Health Commission (1998). *Blueprint for mental health services in New Zealand: how things need to be*. Wellington, New Zealand: Mental Health Commission.

Ministry of Health. (2012). *Suicide facts: Deaths and intentional self-harm hospitalisations 2010*. Wellington, New Zealand: Ministry of Health.

Shouksmith, G. (1990). New Zealand. In G. Shouksmith and E. Shouksmith (Eds.), *Psychology in Asia and the Pacific: Status reports on teaching and research in eleven countries*. Bangkok: Unesco.

Te Puni Kokiri (n.d.). *Whanau ora factsheet*. Retrieved from www.tpk.govt.nz/en/in-print/our-publications/fact-sheets/whanau-ora-factsheet/page/1.

Part V

Personal reflections on Suman Fernando's life and work

The life and times of Suman Fernando

Ted Lo

At the suggestion of the editors of this book, I interviewed Dr Suman Fernando, a long-time friend and colleague. In the spring of 2012, I arrived in the United Kingdom from Toronto and made my way along a quiet street in north-west London towards an old Victorian house; the home of Suman and his wife Frances. Outside the house, the crabapple tree was the first one to bloom on the whole street. After tea and biscuits, we settled into his study, filled with books and artefacts from all over the world, and talked about his life in England and in Sri Lanka, and his passion and commitment to working in the field of health and mental health. In this piece, I offer you Suman Fernando, reflecting on some aspects of his life, as he says: 'I have been thinking about the past. I guess when one cannot remember the present, one thinks of the past.'

Suman Fernando: I have been always interested in people's cultures, their backgrounds.... Even as a child, I can remember reading about African tribes and missionaries like Schweitzer; an interest in the exotic I suppose. We didn't use the term 'multicultural' then but my early life was exactly that I think – very multicultural. Although from a Christian Sri Lankan Sinhalese background (my father was a Methodist and my mother an Anglican) the family was not religious. My father often went to sleep in church. He was a doctor but also a politician of a somewhat left-wing party – a sort of armchair left-winger. There were all sorts of visitors in the house from different religious backgrounds. I remember my mother covering a chair with a white sheet because a Buddhist monk was coming in. When a Muslim came, she had to keep the dogs away, I don't know why. I was baptized, and 'recognized' (a kind of confirmation when you are 14 or 15). Methodists formed a small group of a few thousand members, mainly from the middle class. They were descended from converts of early colonial days.

The primary school I attended was a girl's school (which took in a few boys until aged 12) called Lady's College, run by missionaries. The secondary school was Royal College, the only major state school in Colombo that was modelled on the 'public school' in Britain; and the principal and some of the teachers were imported. It was started for the sons of British people in 1835 (just 20 years after Britain subjugated the country) but soon became one of the best schools catering for the growing local middle class. Every morning, there was an assembly where there were readings from different scriptures. It could be Muslim or Buddhist, or even some reading from other non-religious literature followed by a brief discussion among the boys after returning to class. The school was very multicultural, but with hardly any white boys. Education was all in English. If a boy was heard speaking in Sinhalese or Tamil he would be admonished. Sinhalese and Tamil were the languages one used with servants. This upbringing bred a lot of resentment. My father instigated some of this resentment. He was critical of how we were expected to look down on local languages and habits but he himself dressed like what the British called a 'westernized oriental gentleman' – the origin of the word 'Wog', I believe, that became a term of abuse for black people in Britain. In a way, the British encouraged locals ('natives') to imitate them but at the same time despised the people who imitated them.

I grew up in a very class-conscious society, but multicultural. I recall going to Muslim and Buddhist functions and there were many Parsi boys at school, some of my best friends in fact. Lunch was brought from home and we all ate together, sometimes sharing things. What I am describing is the Colombo middle-class setting of the early and mid 20th century. As soon as you moved out to the villages it was very different, and probably was somewhat different even in other town and cities of Ceylon (as it was then called). Many villages were quite unicultural but there were some that were mixed. Sri Lankans are drawn from a variety of backgrounds – Sinhalese, Tamil, Burgher (mixed local–Dutch or Portuguese), Arab, Chinese and so on. There was even an African village, I believe – descendants of people brought in by the Portuguese as slaves; and of course the indigenous – first nations – called the Veddahs; now only a few thousand left.

My father studied medicine in England; in fact, his father did medicine in Edinburgh, in the late 19th century. He too became a politician and in fact died from a heart attack sustained after delivering a political speech. My father was educated at Cambridge and UCH [University College Hospital, London], just like I was. I came to England to do medicine at 17. I had to do the first MB examination in London to get my place. I attended a 'cram school' where there were all these foreign students 'cramming' to get into the British colleges. It was then difficult getting accommodation: there were notices saying 'No coloured, No Irish' and sometimes 'No dogs', although discrimination against dogs was not that common. I stayed for a while at a hostel run by Methodist ex-missionaries from China. Cambridge was of course different. You were protected and looked after. When you got there, the porter carried your suitcase to your room. Students stayed in college accommodation for the first year, but most had to find accommodation outside in the second year. In my case the tutor let me stay in College knowing that I would not be able to get accommodation outside. But then in the third year, I stayed in a vicarage because the vicar said he would take black students. People were not hostile openly, but there was always an undercurrent. The students were very well-behaved towards other students, but ill-behaved towards town people. Students always wore gowns when outside the College and looked down on the town people. That was in the 1950s.

For clinical studies, I came to London. Things were getting better but it was still not easy. I didn't like it in London, but now I see Cambridge was kind of a non-place. To learn about life, you have to be outside of the older residential universities like Cambridge and Oxford, I think. Clinical studies were interesting but most of the consultants who taught us were very snotty. At that time, there was a lot of antagonism to people from the newly independent ex-colonial countries – India, Sri Lanka, Burma, etc. At one of the ward rounds, an Australian instructor asked me a question, and I answered, 'I am not sure', to which he retorted, 'Of course, you people always sit on the fence'; referring no doubt to the non-alignment movement led by India and Indonesia. That was the beginning of the 'Third World', the alternative to the West and the communist world. The other students laughed but I cried inside and just smiled weakly. I dodged sessions when I could; just felt I did not want to face these people. I missed a lot of sessions on anaesthetics, something I regretted very much later. Now the world of medical education is very different. Much of the overt racism has been dealt with – at least, in London and the big cities. That is why I get really upset that the world of psychiatry has not changed that much, while everything else has changed. The psychiatric system has not been able to adapt to the multicultural nature of British society and continues to be racist I think – especially in its ways of working in the statutory system.

Once I qualified as a doctor, I found that I did not like surgery or medicine very much. I thought that if I had had a choice, I would not have gone into medicine at all. My grandfather was a doctor and my father was a doctor and I was expected to follow suit and just went along with it. I am curious about people and I like writing. If I had a choice I would probably have read English at university and, like a friend of mine at school, we both wrote very well when we were students. He became a journalist.

Once I decided to go into psychiatry I found I had to do the DPM and that the mental hospital in Sri Lanka at Angoda (near Colombo) was recognized as a site for experience before doing the exam in the UK. So I went back to Sri Lanka in 1960 and managed to get there only to find that the conditions were horrible and corrupt. Still I learned a lot while there. For example, I worked with a neuro-psychiatrist who had come from Vienna. He did not speak a word of Sinhalese or Tamil, but would sit by his patients and place his arm round them and speak quietly. None of the local psychiatrists did that! And the Viennese doctor's patients got better. I always think of this anecdote when ethnic matching is discussed. Sometimes mismatching is a good thing. Eventually, I left and came back to England six months later. Of course I had already met my future wife, Frances, before I went back to Sri Lanka in 1960 and that was a big pull factor to my returning so quickly.

I got married in 1961. I was not accepted initially by Frances' family, who are Jewish. I think it was more about my being a gentile than being brown-skinned. Reconciliation with my mother-in-law took place after the birth of our daughter and she never mentioned anything again. But, when my daughter married a gentile, her aunt (Frances' sister) said she could not come to her wedding because it was not a Jewish wedding.

In 1960s England, racism was more overt than it is now. I remember going to a hotel with Frances. They said there was no room when we appeared together, but when Frances called on the phone they said there were lots of rooms. So we went back there and confronted the owner, who claimed that his other guests would object if he gave us a room. I wrote to the AA, of which I was a member and after an inquiry, the AA told the owner of the hotel concerned that it would be de-listed unless they changed their discriminatory practice. The situation in the country changed a lot after race relations legislation was passed in the 1970s.

When I returned from Sri Lanka to England, I worked at several asylums. I did not want to go to the Maudsley, which was considered a 'centre of excellence', because of what I had heard about the practices there – very institutional and inhumane. As a 'coloured' person, I would not have been accepted anyway. However, in some of the asylums, it was the beginning of the therapeutic community movement and later de-institutionalization.

It was while working in east London doing clinics at the London Jewish Hospital that I got interested in research into 'culture' and mental health. That led to my first research project looking at depression among Jewish people in the East End of London.

Once I became a consultant I became more outspoken about the type of psychiatry I wanted to practise. And I began to see how unjust the whole system was, especially towards racial minorities. I was particularly unhappy about using so much medication and also about 'sectioning' (enforcing admission to hospital and compulsory treatment). Also I was against using ECT unless as a life-saving treatment, and later found one could as easily not use ECT at all. Later I got involved in supporting organizations in the voluntary sector. Something that upset me a lot was when I found I had to deal with poor practice and what I recognized as dishonesty at a voluntary organization for (what we now call) Black and Minority Ethnic (BME) people, run by BME people. I was accused of being racist because I was largely responsible for sacking the black person running it.

In 2007, when they offered me an OBE, I felt insulted. It was actually past experience that I was reacting to, as well as the fact that the government had recently brought in legislation that worsened discrimination in the mental health system, rejecting what some of us had been saying. So this OBE offer seemed like a consolation prize and I resented that.

Ever since the early 1980s, I have been involved with like-minded people to try to change ways of working in the mental health system, especially to change psychiatric practice. My feeling is that from time to time there has been interest at high levels – even at government level – in bringing about change, but it does not go beyond a certain point. In the 1980s, we thought things would be different in five or six years. But when we got to 2000, it was still the same. I think one of the sticking points is the psychiatric system itself. We have to get beyond the psychiatric diagnosis, which is so constraining. I doubt that effective change could come about without fundamental change in psychiatry. The current model that we are stuck with is open to racism. The most recent project I have been involved in is to inquire into the 'schizophrenia' label (and diagnosis) hoping that we can gather enough evidence to lobby for change.

Over the years, I have been looking out for opportunities to work to improve conditions in mental health care in Sri Lanka, and I have been privileged for the past 4 years to have been a consultant to a programme of work in collaboration with McGill University. This experience has made me rethink ideas about cultural division and cultural differences, about what is 'East' and what is 'West'. As a Sri Lankan who has become British – or a British Sri Lankan – I have found this experience of working with Canadians, British and current Sri Lankans a most edifying experience. Culture is not in one place any more. I suddenly realized how much 'culture' has changed in both Sri Lanka and the UK. I had this conception of how people in Sri Lanka see mental health and illness but that too had changed a lot in the 50 years I had been away. One thing that saddened me was the realization that while Britain has been getting more tolerant Sri Lanka appears sometimes to have been going backwards.

Another of my recent concerns has been the Global Mental Health movement which is gaining strength. I see this as another potential imperialism being visited upon Asian and African countries – the developing world.

***

But this is a big topic, and as we saw the night falling around us; we concluded our discussion, although Dr Fernando did not appear at all tired. He is equally tireless at 80, in his advocacy and his writing, as he was when I first met him many years ago. I realized that it had been a privilege for me to have this conversation, and I hope this record will allow this wonderful experience to be shared by more.

Suman Fernando's roots in Sri Lanka

Chamindra Weerackody

Born in 1932 to a middle-class family in Sri Lanka (formerly Ceylon), Dr Suman Fernando is the second eldest in a family of three. He had his primary and secondary education in one of the elite schools in Colombo, namely Royal College. After completing his school education, he proceeded to England and entered Cambridge University in 1950. At Cambridge he read Natural Sciences and medical subjects for his BA, MA and MBBChir obtained between 1953 and 1957, in spite of an enforced break in his career when his father died suddenly in 1953. As a qualified doctor, he was soon drawn to work in psychiatry where he developed an interest in the social dimensions of mental health. Having worked as a junior doctor at Fulbourn (Mental) Hospital in Cambridge for a short while, Dr Fernando returned to serve his motherland in 1959 intending to work as a psychiatrist.

In Sri Lanka (still called by its colonial name Ceylon at the time), Dr Fernando found that the medical system was highly bureaucratic and inflexible. He was initially told that he could not be posted to work in psychiatry, although it was not a popular field and there was a shortage of doctors at the only psychiatric institution in the country, the mental hospital at Angoda just outside Colombo, established by the British in 1927. However, when he decided to return to England the authorities in Sri Lanka agreed to give him a position as a junior doctor at Angoda. He was told that this hospital housed over 5,000 patients at the time, although originally built for 1,500; it was understaffed, severely overcrowded and unhygienic. He described it as

> an old fashioned asylum run like a prison with few doctors and very few nurses, patients being largely kept in custodial care under unqualified people called 'attendants'. Corruption was rife and abuse of the patients was common with people in authority seeming not to care. I found the conditions at Angoda too difficult to work in and certainly not conducive to the practice of any sort of therapy.
>
> (Personal communication)

Being blocked in his attempts to improve conditions for patients and being met with comments from people in authority at the institution that he had to learn to put up with what he found there, Dr Fernando decided to resign from Angoda six months after taking up his post and he returned to England in mid-1960. In 1971, Dr Fernando was awarded MRCPsych and FRCPsych by the Royal College of Psychiatrists, and in 1975 he also received an MD from the University of Cambridge for the thesis he wrote that compared Jewish and non-Jewish patients in East London on socio-cultural factors that impacted on depression. His thesis was one of the earliest studies in transcultural psychiatry and possibly the first such study presented to Cambridge for an MD degree.

Despite his being away from Sri Lanka almost continuously since mid-1960, Dr Fernando continued to maintain his links with the country of his birth with short visits to family members and regular communications with professional colleagues and schoolmates, although he found that many of his childhood friends who had become doctors began to emigrate during the 1970s and 1980s because of rising levels of ethnic hostilities and political strife in the country. He was dismayed during those years to see that, while racism resulting in personal discrimination was being tackled in the United Kingdom, levels of racism and personal discrimination seemed to worsen in Sri Lanka as social and political tensions increased. During his visits to Sri Lanka in the late 1980s and 1990s, Dr Fernando gave occasional talks on mental health related issues and visited places of religious and spiritual importance where people with mental health problems sought redress. In the early 2000s, he made informal approaches to the World Health Organization (WHO) (where he was recognized as someone with expert knowledge and innovative ideas about mental health) in an effort to induce the organization to focus on mental health work in Sri Lanka, providing informal assessments on how best WHO may be able to help in developing mental health services in the country. Then, when WHO did become involved in pursuing mental health work after the 2004 tsunami, Dr Fernando was in close contact with the staff at the local WHO office (whom he knew from the United Kingdom) advising informally on various matters. Furthermore, he supported *Nest*, one of the leading non-government organizations in Sri Lanka that has an island-wide network of community services that respond to the needs of people confronted with mental health problems (see www.nestsrilanka.org), and was appointed as a vice-patron of the organization. I had the privilege of associating with Dr Fernando over a period of four or five years in connection with the Trauma and Global Health (TGH) programme, learning and drawing insights from his expertise and experience in the mental health field.

The first time I met Dr Fernando was in 2007 when I was introduced to him by his brother, with whom I have had a long-standing professional relationship since the 1980s. When Dr Fernando invited me to be the Sri Lankan coordinator for the TGH programme I was eager to accept the position, but a little hesitant since I did not have much knowledge in the area of psychiatry or mental health, though I studied psychology as part of my undergraduate sociology programme. Dr Fernando spent long hours with me during his visits to Colombo and our annual meetings at McGill University in Montreal, trying to help me to understand the basic tenets of psychiatry and its different branches. During such discussions, he would point to the importance and relevance of social and cultural dimensions in understanding mental health problems and making relevant interventions. For a sociologist, this was quite motivating and I soon began to read and explore more and more on the subject. He shared with me several of his own writings as well as other materials useful for my learning. After I was formally appointed as the TGH programme lead for Sri Lanka, we maintained regular contact via email and skype calls almost daily for over a period of four to five years, sometimes even during his holidays. Dr Fernando was a great mentor for me in my planning and implementing the TGH programme in Sri Lanka. Whenever I requested help or advice for my programme-related work, he would respond to me within a few hours or overnight. In instances where I had difficulty dealing with certain matters, he would even intervene personally and communicate with relevant people to put things in order. He would never consider his age or other family obligations when it comes to work and would spend long nights working hard, tirelessly and efficiently to reach the targets. When he visited Sri Lanka to conduct training programmes he would even step beyond his training role and would shoulder part of my burden of dealing with the logistical arrangements of such programmes. Despite being a renowned academic and an erudite scholar, Dr Fernando never compromised his humane qualities of tolerance, patience, generosity and his empathy with people.

During visits to Sri Lanka in connection with the TGH programme (2007–2011), Dr Fernando participated in several awareness and capacity building training programmes for various professional groups working in the mental health field. Indeed the personal and professional networks and contacts he had in the country and in the United Kingdom, together with his recognition at international level, made a significant impact on the achievements of the TGH programme in Sri Lanka. His yearning and commitment to help the Sri Lankan institutions responsible for mental health service provision was evident from his largesse, even using his own personal resources at times when project funds did not permit spending on certain interventions that were considered important for the improvement of the capacities of the service sector. When the need arose, he would place long-distance international calls from London to coordinate with relevant authorities in Sri Lanka; he bought and donated rare and expensive books that he found useful for the knowledge enhancement and training of young medical officers or nursing staff; he complemented the resources available for young medical professionals to pursue foreign training. At his own expense, he sometimes travelled to conflict-affected areas to see for himself how mental health services have been organized and delivered in such areas. He always tried to ensure that resources and programme interventions were distributed with equity among different communities and regions irrespective of their ethnicity, language and gender.

Dr Suman Fernando's childhood and subsequently his professional career and worldview would have been influenced by the socialist and patriotic ideologies held by his father, a medical doctor and founder member of the Ceylon Labour Party – a political party formed in the 1930s modelled on the lines of the British

Labour Movement. (This party was active at a time when the political left was just developing in Ceylon and became well known for organizing the first strike by workers in Colombo pursuing better conditions of work.) Much of Dr Fernando's writing reflects his background and childhood experiences in Sri Lanka and his continuing involvement in Sri Lankan life after emigrating. This may be evident in his writings on issues around culture and mental health and on the importance of personal commitment to equity and non-discrimination in the provision of mental health services. Also, his interest in systems of help derived from indigenous Asian medicine and spiritual approaches practised through religious healing is likely to have derived from learning about the importance of indigenous healing and medicine in a Sri Lankan context.

Dr Fernando is a critical observer and analyst. In an international context, he was extremely critical of the developed countries in the global North trying to impose their dominant ideologies and practices on developing countries in the South. Also, he was very critical of the role of drug companies in the mental health field – as evidenced by his 2011 article in the British magazine *Openmind* (Fernando, 2011). And this critical perspective gave me a good framework and an approach to design and conduct several research programmes that I later directed under the TGH programme. Dr Fernando is also a brilliant writer and editor. Many Sri Lankan medical professionals were amused by his style of writing, especially his critical approach to institutional practices and people holding powerful positions. I was very fortunate to associate with him in bringing out several joint publications and in this process my own writing skills too improved remarkably. The joint publications include two significant books on mental health in Sri Lanka (Fernando and Weerackody, 2011; Weerackody and Fernando, 2011) and two papers in international journals (Fernando and Weerackody, 2009; Weerackody and Fernando, 2008).

References

Fernando, S. (2011). A 'global' mental health program or markets for Big Pharma? *Openmind, 168*, 22.

Fernando, S. and Weerackody, C. (2009). Challenges in developing community mental health services in Sri Lanka. *Journal of Health Management, 11*(1), 195–208.

Fernando, S. and Weerackody, C. (2011). *Aspects of mental health in Sri Lanka.* Colombo: People's Rural Development Association (PRDA).

Weerackody, C. and Fernando, S. (2008). Field report: Perceptions of social stratification and wellbeing in refugee communities in North-Western Sri Lanka. *International Journal of Migration, Health and Social Care, 4*(2), 47–56.

Weerackody, C. and Fernando, S. (2011). *Reflections on Mental Health and Wellbeing: Learning from communities affected by conflict, dislocation and natural disaster.* Colombo: People's Rural Development Association (PRDA).

Suman Fernando's contribution to British psychiatry

John Cox

Suman Fernando's influence on my academic and clinical career has been considerable; and I am delighted to have the opportunity to acknowledge how this came to be. When a 1st-year trainee at the London Hospital, without Suman Fernando as my first Senior Registrar I might not have continued training in psychiatry. Several years later we were again working together in the early days of the Transcultural Psychiatry Society (UK) – known at the time as 'TCPS'. In fact, TCPS had developed out of the Edinburgh Transcultural Psychiatry Society that I had collaborated with Sashi Sashidharan to launch in the 1970s.

As the (national) TCPS took shape and established itself as a foremost body highlighting issues of culture and 'race' in British mental health services, I was fortunate to be its first secretary; and when Aggrey Burke was elected chair in 1984, Suman succeeded me. Interestingly, other South Asian psychiatrists have also had an impact on my professional and personal life. For example, Channi Kumar's research at the Institute of Psychiatry stimulated my own interest in perinatal studies in Uganda and so encouraged the development of the Edinburgh Postnatal Depression Scale; and without the support of Dinesh Bhugra and Pearl Hettiarachy my election as Dean and College President might have had less support.

Suman's compact energy, agility of mind and body and his loyalty to the humanistic values of Desmond Pond were each noticed at a time when I was indeed uncommitted about the direction of speciality training. I was searching for a humanistic psychiatry exemplified by the therapeutic community movement, which had inspired me as a medical student at Claybury Hospital. My decision to apply for a lecturer post at Makerere University in Kampala was also in part a response to these faith-based humanistic values and motivations. On return to the London Hospital with my family in 1974, Suman was a consultant at Claybury Hospital, actively involved in promoting therapeutic community approaches in the field of old-age psychiatry (at that time called 'psychogeriatrics'). The two years in Uganda shaped most of my subsequent medical career, as well as my priorities at the College, and when Secretary General of the World Psychiatric Association. It was in Uganda that I was first personally exposed to racism and to its impact on mental health. The scapegoating of expatriates, the disappearance of African colleagues, the media critique of colonialism and of missionaries (this affected me personally, as my grandfather was a missionary in Cuzco, where my mother was born) and the humiliation of the Ugandan Asians left an indelible mark.

Suman Fernando's commitment to human rights and his burning advocacy for an anti-racist psychiatry was influenced also by a narrative that, as Suman recently reminded me, paralleled my own. Suman was ambivalent about aspects of religiosity (Methodists in Colombo and at Cambridge) but admired Mahatma Gandhi and, as a student, was greatly influenced by the wide-based religious teaching of Krishnamurthy, who used to hold his sessions in London under the aegis of the Quakers. He experienced racism ('No Coloured' notices) and knew the push and pull factors of migration and the tensions of acculturation.

In the 1960s in Britain, transcultural psychiatry as a discipline existed only in the minds of a few pioneers such as Lambo, Carstairs, Rawnsley and Murphy; yet a decade later it was developing a more firm conceptual base in medical anthropology, international psychopathology and cultural history. Pioneering psychiatric services for South Asian and Polish people was promoted by Philip Rack and his colleagues at the Transcultural Unit in Bradford. Later, transcultural research was also prompted by other organisations and lobbying groups (such as people in the service user movement), policy directives from government and by the increasingly obvious problems associated with high rates of mental disorder in African Caribbean people and their over-representation in medium-secure psychiatric units. This is something that Suman has written about for many years, beginning with the book *Race and Culture in Psychiatry* coming soon after the first British text on transcultural psychiatry edited by myself. Transcultural research was also undertaken at that time in the perinatal field, which was less politically driven, but advanced knowledge in this key area.

The Royal College of Psychiatrists, as an institution, also became more international and more sensitive to issues of race and ethnicity. The Transcultural Psychiatry Special Interest Group was established, postgraduate training for psychiatrists improved and transcultural psychiatry was included in the postgraduate curricula and in the list of competencies. South Asian psychiatrists (Parimala Moodley, Pearl Hettiarachy) became College Officers. Meanwhile, outside the College, the TCPS flourished under the leadership of Aggrey Burke and Suman Fernando, with the impact of Sashidharan's writings acting as an agent provocateur – and yet, crucially, maintaining dialogue with the College.

The Royal College of Psychiatrists and international psychiatry

The College, since its royal foundation in 1971, has always had a specific concern to improve the training of foreign medical graduates, assist with their adjustment to a different culture, overcome language difficulties and increase their chances of passing the professional examinations. It had gained from the migration of scholars and clinicians to Britain from post-war Europe – and in later decades particularly from the Asian-born and Afro-Caribbean psychiatrists, some of whom are in this book. In the 1960s the United Kingdom had become more overtly multi-racial and multi-faith, so that issues of the provision of services for minorities and the effects of racism were impinging abruptly on College members; up to a third of psychiatrists were from non-UK medical schools. There was also a renewed interest in transcultural psychiatry, not only as a research discipline, but also as a clinical approach to improving services for Black and Minority Ethnic (BME) people/communities; and gradually the cultural assumptions of Western psychiatry (individualistic, materialistic and biomedical), were increasingly acknowledged and appropriately challenged.

In 1993, I chaired a Working Party to review the 1987 Rawnsley report *Psychiatric Practice and Training in a Multi-Ethnic Society (CR 10)*. Other members included Suman Fernando, Aggrey Burke, Roland Littlewood, Parimala Moodley and Sashi Sashidharan. We noted in our report that the College had already been urged by Kenneth Rawnsley to introduce ethnic monitoring of appointments to Staff Grade posts; to counter racial discrimination against staff; and to discipline members who manifested racial discrimination in a professional context. Our task was to review the extent to which these recommendations had been implemented, and to consider recent issues within the field of training and practice with regard to the provision of services for a multi-ethnic society.

In 2001, because of the persisting importance of these matters, a second Ethnic Issues Project Group was convened to consider whether or not these issues should be reconsidered in the light of changed circumstances. At the outset we agreed that although there were emerging concerns of gender discrimination, our report would be restricted to issues concerned with BME people. The first of the 10 recommendations of this Working Party was historic and without precedent in medical professional organisations at that time. We recommended that a systematic review of College structures be undertaken to determine whether or not there was evidence of institutional racism, and with particular reference to the conduct of appointment committees. Other recommendations were that all psychiatrists should be trained in cultural competence, and should be specifically aware of possible discrimination when applying the mental health legislation to black and other ethnic minorities; that epidemiological studies should include BME communities, unless there was a specific reason for excluding them; and that an Ethnic Issues Committee should be established to raise awareness of cultural sensitivity and to promote ethnic monitoring throughout the College.

Thus in 2002 an audit with full access to College personnel and documents was commissioned by Council, to be carried out by Kamlesh Patel and colleagues from the Centre for Ethnicity and Health at the University of Central Lancashire. They would work closely with College staff and report to Council in 2002. The College thus became more transparent in its nomination and electoral processes and more open to serious dialogue with black user groups. The Transcultural Psychiatry Special Interest Group grew in size and influence; but regrettably an Ethnic Issues Committee was not established, and the curriculum for mandatory training in cultural competence was never agreed.

Transcultural psychiatry and the World Psychiatric Association (WPA)

In 2002, I was elected Secretary General of WPA – only the second British Executive office holder since its foundation in 1947. Somewhat to my surprise, however, my new responsibilities in WPA (an Association of associations), which included membership of the Review Committee, were deemed by some British colleagues to represent a conflict of interest. The College, as a WPA member society, appeared to have become more isolationist and tended to regard WPA as a rival organisation rather than as the only world organisation that could legitimise its international aspirations and enhance the optimal use of its enviable human and financial resources. Nevertheless the Patel Report has had a substantial effect on the College membership and increased its international credibility. It was emboldened, for example, to resource International Divisions in four regions of the world and to establish a high-profile International Committee under the leadership of Hamid Ghodse and later Rachel Jenkins. The election of Dinesh Bhugra, while College President, as President Elect of WPA in 2011, Afzal Javed as Secretary for Sections and Linda Gask as Zonal Representative for Western Europe, was therefore a culmination of the advocacy and leadership that energises this book.

However, despite all these positive institutional international developments, the specialist field of transcultural psychiatry appeared to lose its academic, institutional and clinical momentum. There are several possible explanations:

1. Cultural psychiatry had become politicised with regard to the counteracting of racial discrimination with the possible neglect of other aspects of the discipline. It then became a no-go area for some white academics and clinicians.
2. Issues of gender equality had become a greater institutional priority.
3. The writings of philosophers (such as Thornton and Fulford), rather than of anthropologists or social scientists (like Littlewood and Fernando), provided new conceptual insights into the nature of value differences across cultures, and shifted the debate to a less politicised discourse about the nature of scientific knowledge, the place for personal narrative and the attributes of selfhood. Furthermore, the philosophical ideas of the 'embodied self', of 'intentionality' and of the 'I–Thou relationship' from the continental philosophy tradition were influencing postgraduate courses in the philosophy of mental health; these Masters programmes, however, less commonly included the mental health perspectives from the social sciences and anthropology, as this was not their remit. Nevertheless, the existential understandings of persons (central to psychiatry) as having a fact/value nature became a bastion of the person-centred approach to medicine as a whole, and to psychiatry in particular.
4. Cultural psychiatry, with its roots in anthropology and understanding of cultural differences and discrimination, may have become a victim of its own

success. The cultural approach had become a part of good practice – to be considered alongside other socio-cultural approaches that were considered within a bio-psycho-social approach to health care.
5. Furthermore, these integrative models were being implemented by a new generation of younger psychiatrists born and trained in Britain and without the personal experience of discrimination. Racial discrimination, including institutional discrimination, had become unlawful.
6. The Spirituality, Religion and Psychiatry Special Interest Group, which attracted over 1,500 members, was thriving partly because of its multi-faith assumptions; and because psychiatrists with an interest in cultural psychiatry were finding a home in other college structures preoccupied with the political critique of transcultural psychiatry.
7. The contribution of cultural psychiatry to the vigorous debate about the boundaries of religious belief and psychiatric practice was, alas, less audible.

Nevertheless, despite the developments described above, the Transcultural Psychiatry Section of the World Psychiatric Association has continued to flourish and facilitated the establishment of a World Association of Transcultural Psychiatry.

The Transcultural Psychiatry Society (UK) (TCPS) led increasingly by service users and by an inclusive multi-disciplinary team, continued with its work of public advocacy until 2008 when it was, formally and by consent, disbanded. The issues that sparked its birth, however, have not gone away and its true legacy is for all who read this book is to be mindful of its history, to be watchful about the future of psychiatry and resistant to a thoughtless scientific physicalism. The target-driven internal market, which characterises much of the present day National Health Service with its enshrined contracts and industrial competition, may have improved accessibility to health services for black and ethnic minorities in the UK, but may have lost 'intelligent kindness' and needs to re-discover compassion and to listen to whistle-blowers. The radical voice of the 'outsider' still needs to be heard as when Suman Fernando and his colleagues first voiced their concerns over three decades ago, and still continue to do so. See, for example: *Intelligent Kindness: Reforming the Culture of Healthcare* (J. Ballatt and P. Campling, RCPsych Publications, 2011); John L. Cox's 1977 article 'Aspects of Transcultural Psychiatry', *British Journal of Psychiatry* (130), pp. 211–221; Suman Fernando's chapter 'Depression in Ethnic Minorities', in *Transcultural Psychiatry* (edited by John L. Cox, Croom Helm, 1986); and *Anthropological Approaches to Psychological Medicine: Crossing Bridges* (edited by V. Skultans and John L. Cox, 2000, Jessica Kingsley).

Satisfy my soul
Suman Fernando's work in mental health

Kamaldeep Bhui

Suman Fernando's writings on race, culture and ethnicity reveal some gross injustices visible in care pathways for minorities, but not noticed much by the professionals or the provider organisations. Suman, along with Parimala Moodley and Deenesh Khoosal, established the Transcultural Special Interest Group of the Royal College of Psychiatrists in the early 1990s, and it was this forum that gave momentum to psychiatrists in the United Kingdom to become more familiar with the ethnic inequalities in care experiences, outcomes and service users' dissatisfaction with the approaches to care that overlooked their opinions and preferences. In the United Kingdom, Transcultural Psychiatry has never been seen as a separate speciality or faculty, or a separate career track. Indeed, the crowded undergraduate and postgraduate curricula rarely included issues of culture in the 1990s, perhaps referring only to the International Pilot Study of Schizophrenia (IPSS) and the culture-bound syndromes. Ironically, these have frequently been under critical scrutiny by both psychiatrists and social scientists. Culture-bound syndromes are now regarded as exotic descriptions of behavioural patterns and expressions of distress that were unfamiliar to the observer, who felt obliged to categorise according to diagnostic trends of the time, or create a new exotic category that overstated the coherence or authenticity of these syndromes. Similarly, the use of diagnostic categories in IPSS was oversimplified to suggest that schizophrenia as a diagnostic category existed all over the globe, rather than consider what constituted this diagnosis and how the components vary across continents and cultural groups, and indeed how each component may vary in meaning and relevance to different world societies.

These central criticisms have been at the heart of Suman Fernando's work, to emphasise that diagnoses are working hypotheses that are only as good as the use to which they are put, and if they serve the patient well. That Black and Minority Ethnic groups in the United Kingdom did not seem to benefit raised questions about whether these diagnoses were helpful or just a further method of justifying existing practice, and overlooking a more complex challenge – that the disease categories of psychiatry do not lead to a precise course of action or intervention as might be expected, for example, in surgical removal of diseased or cancerous tissue, or as an ECG indicates which type of anti-arrhythmic drug might eradicate abnormal conduction patterns. This simple but profound challenge to the use of diagnosis has been a persistent narrative in Suman Fernando's writings, reminding scientists and the public of this neglected problem in care practices. And so Suman Fernando has championed taking an indigenous perspective, an insider's view, an experience-near approach to assessment and diagnosis, to understand the patient's symptoms and experiences in the context of their history, their personal narratives and biography, as well as the influence of the history of relations between their heritage group and other heritage groups the world over. The discourse challenged and provoked by Suman Fernando related closely to the work of others like Aggrey Burke and Roland Littlewood, all taking a critical look at the experience on the ground of patients from culturally diverse backgrounds, encountering a relatively inflexible and 'colour- and culture-blind' approach to mental health care. Indeed, although this sounds historical, this is the current dominant in the United Kingdom today.

The presence of power dynamics and relations between doctor and patient, between societies and organisations, and between government and the professions are a constant source of material for Fernando's analysis, which spans some 50 years of experience as a clinician, a Mental Health Act commissioner and an academic. The recent policy developments around delivering race equality and cultural competence training (between 2005 and 2010) also enlisted frank statements about them lacking impact.

Social action practice

Suman Fernando has never been an armchair critic, and his often public prose is informed by decades of clinical work in the United Kingdom. He has worked closely with charities and the NGO sector that provide services that are not formally commissioned but are valued by the public and patients; so he has worked with MIND, the FANON project in London and also with NGOs in Sri Lanka. The work in Sri Lanka has been especially powerful in challenging the over-diagnosis of PTSD, a practice that offers medical or psychological interventions which then breed complacency around understanding the needs of people as people and members of a society, of the need for human compassion and understanding and, most importantly, for interventions owned, developed and delivered by local people rather than parachuting in experts from the higher-income countries. This closeness to real causes and organisations that the public support is the reason that Suman Fernando is so well known and appreciated, by friends and even by his critics, as his voice and opinions carry the weight of truth and justice, and it is accepted that his insights are formed from the experience of patients and the public rather than relying solely on experts. So when the differential rates of admission and detention by ethnic group were not affected by government policy or equality actions were to be silenced and the regulator decided not to collect the data any more as nothing worked, he and his network of advocates and NGOs continued to encourage patients, the public and the NGO sector to keep this issue alive and not to look the other way as government seemed to advocate. The argument that 'nothing has changed therefore let's stop collecting the data' seemed negligent and itself fuelled by a racist lens, albeit in the service of business efficiency and economy, of what is worth bothering with and who is not worthy of effort. Clearly, ethnic inequalities of hospital admissions and detentions are complex to understand and remedy, as there is a higher incidence but also poor prognostic factors influenced by ethnicity and race. The issue here was that the need for remedy was being challenged and charges of institutional racism within provider organisations were considered unhelpful and so policy and plans were often rephrased, removing the words 'race' and 'racism' from the discourse.

Suman Fernando's desire to ensure authentic and honest debate on today's issues is often understood as yet another vicissitude of the legacy of colonialism and enslavement. He recently established an inquiry into the diagnosis of schizophrenia at the same time as an official inquiry was established without adequate representation from ethnic minority or public and patient groups. Suman Fernando questioned the ability of the members of the official inquiry to do justice or even to be sufficiently committed to address the power issue in diagnostic practice; his alternative inquiry carries great respect and, more importantly, grassroots support as it represents an account of experiences of mental health care that are just not to be found in official documents of governments, regulators or providers.

Much has changed in mental health care, including new legislation, better training, new standards of care, regulation of the professions and an expansion of psychological therapies. Suman Fernando has also contributed to modifications of curricula for training psychiatrists in the United Kingdom, a challenge that requires constant efforts as the training is changing all the time and there is pressure on the curriculum to include more new perspectives. Suman Fernando's approach here is helpful, as he stands for a psychiatry that serves the patient and the public, irrespective of their ethnic origins; but he recognises that where difference abounds and socio-economic inequalities are evident, power dynamics will become important to consider, and power is linked to knowledge and determines the official story that is told about a care experience, the official record that becomes part of the medical record, and this account becomes the truth.

Mental illness among ethnic minorities is linked with their experiences of discrimination and social adversity, but must also take account of histories of enslavement and colonisation; service users are disempowered by professional and managerial responses that tend to negate their experience or contribution to decision making; professional practices can be inflexible and pathologising. This is true in general adult and forensic settings. However, in forensic settings there is the added powerful influence of ideologies around crime and justice, and the awareness the black people are over-represented in the criminal justice system, and that many black people come to the attention of psychiatric services through the criminal justice system.

Alongside the forensic front of psychiatric practice, Suman Fernando has also encouraged learning from low-income countries and from Eastern philosophies in order to approach recovery from a spiritual and non-pharmacological perspective. Specifically, taking up social perspectives and accommodating different notions of self, each requiring an approach constructed around the person.

These persistent but fundamental concerns have led to Suman Fernando's reputation as a controversial figure who asserts the centrality of race and racism, rather than culture and ethnicity. Controversy continues with his recent refusal of an OBE, and most recently in the debate about global mental health being a further colonialising influence. The global mental health movment seems to remove local autonomy and power and imposes a pharmaceutically driven approach by reifying categories like depression to be universal disembodied diseases rather than a product of individual and group experience, both current and historical.

One of the repeated experiences of services users, policy makers, providers and professionals is negation of the issues encountered by Black and Minority Ethnic people in society in general and then in contact with mental health services. For example, there are active political interventions to remove the words 'race' and 'racism' as relevant factors to communities. Community champions like Fernando have to remind these very authorities of the history of the care of migrants and ethnic minorities, and he does this successfully.

The controversy reflects his remarkable ability to overcome 'the organisation without a memory', to name the violence against service users and failed human rights protections, to connect the heritage of colonisation and enslavement and its vicissitudes in modern life, to overcome polarisation of debate and still to assert the position of the service user-patient-victim. Policy makers shift positions not on the basis of evidence but on their own narrative or story influenced by political precedents, and service users notice this manufactured narrative, but professionals mostly follow the diktats of employers and the governing authorities. Fernando has consistently named the contradictions and duplicity to overcome a binary or psychologically split approach to debate. Such an approach often emerges when dealing with histories of violence and hostility. Powerful emotional contexts are always generated when issues of race, culture, ethnicity and coercion are involved. And so the emotional group response is often to negate, silence or split the experience of the oppressed. In essence, Suman Fernando is remarkable because he sustains the interests and protections sought by patients and the public, he understands that patients and the public who challenge existing care are 'just looking for a way to get through life', to recover with minimum fuss; they are not seeking to be difficult or obstructive but seek only to find a peaceful existence; to them Suman Fernando satisfies their soul when he speaks to their interests. When professionals, governments, policy makers, managers, etc. seem to exist in emotional contexts that prioritise the latest and most pressing operational issues, or latest fashion in policy and practice, the latest standard or requirement of the regulator, they seem to overlook the patient as a person in emotional pain and seeking only to recover, seeking another to help them do this. Suman Fernando has kept this in mind and continues to remind us of injustices and oversights. He continues to actively teach and write, and champion the cause of the patient. He continues to teach on the Masters programmes I established and to shape thinking and leadership marked by critical analysis, and by respectful but robust challenge. Such people are rare.

Suman Fernando and university mental health systems

Sharon Mier

In this personal statement I will speak to a number of Dr. Fernando's key tenets and describe how these tenets influenced my work developing a successful outreach program within a university counseling service in the United States.

I first met Dr. Suman Fernando in 1999 while working in community mental health in Leeds, UK. At that time I was supervising young clinicians who were providing counseling to men and women from the Black British, Pakistani and Indian communities. These young clinicians and their clients were struggling with the institutional racism and cultural biases inherent in the mental health service delivery system. Young black men were being diagnosed as violent and schizophrenic. Young Pakistani women, who spoke little English, were being overmedicated. They found some psychiatrists had a lack of willingness to listen to them. Some women reported waiting for weeks for a two to three minute appointment. Other women felt the situation to be impossible, as without the availability of interpreters, they would be required to bring their husbands to each appointment to speak for them.

One day as I was driving home from work, I heard Suman being interviewed by the BBC on my car radio. I did not know of him then, but was riveted, listening to him address so many of the key issues in community mental health. At that time, another colleague and I were organizing the first National Health Service Conference on Race, Culture and Mental Health, to be held in April 2000. We approached Suman with an invitation to become the keynote speaker, which he graciously accepted.

The conference drew over 400 mental health clinicians of color from across the country. Nationally, the conference was considered a resounding success. A few months later I left the United Kingdom and returned to the United States, with my colleague in Leeds continuing the work we had begun. In 2001, I started to work as a clinical psychologist at Cornell University in upstate New York. My remit was to develop a mental health outreach program that would reach students in distress who, for whatever reason, could not access existing mental health services. The university created the program in response to a decade in which multiple suicides on campus had caused great alarm.

While much had been written in the university mental health literature about outreach services, few programs existed that extended beyond traditional educational programs. My colleagues and I at Cornell began to build a clinical outreach program that reflected many of the key tenets highlighted by Suman in his writings and in his presentations. I believe that the program we created over the last decade provides an informative example of the applicability of Suman's ideas. This outreach program also suggests that Suman's ideas are as relevant in university mental health systems as they are in the provision of mental health care in communities around the globe. Below, I will touch briefly on the application of three of the key tenets from Suman's seminal work, *Mental Health, Race and Culture*, these being:

- the need to reduce the medicalization of mental health services;
- the need to allow individuals a voice in their care;
- the need to become change agents for social justice.

First, Suman speaks about the necessity of reducing the medicalization of mental health services. In one of the first developments of the new outreach program at Cornell, my colleagues and I began to introduce the language of 'support' into our outreach efforts. Historically, as in many other college settings, if students were seen by faculty or staff to be struggling, they were given the advice to 'see a counselor'. This approach could be off-putting, particularly to disenfranchised students, who were then required to ask for help, to get themselves to the counseling service, to share personal confidences and to possibly be given a diagnosis implying mental illness. In reality, some students were under much duress due to an acute environmental stress, such as institutional or personal racism, sexism, homophobia, financial crisis, etc. that was not actually diagnosable. It was our belief that if these students could get support, in an effort to lift these kinds of stressors, then their functioning would improve. We thus began to strengthen existing partnerships across campus, to meet students where they were in the community, to problem solve and to actively address the environmental factors (and isms) affecting the students' lives. We also successfully argued for equating the value of supportive clinical work provided within the larger campus community with traditional counseling provided within the counseling service. We also argued successfully for the resources to provide this community clinical work.

Second, Suman calls for individuals to have a voice in their mental health care. Another innovation at Cornell (which has now been replicated in over a dozen other universities) came from setting up multiple walk-in sites across campus, where hesitant students can drop by and meet with a counselor anonymously as a way to seek help. Importantly, the program's website provides helpful information about the counselors, including their biographical information, interests, philosophy and photo. It lists locations and hours of operation at each site. In this way, students can use their own agency to try to find the counselor and the setting where they might be the most comfortable, perhaps in their community, perhaps away from their community. It was our experience, after 8 years of this program, that many students in distress who had been unable to overcome the barriers to traditional counseling services have been much more likely initially to seek help through programs such as this one.

Third, Suman calls for those working in mental health to be change agents when social justice issues are at stake. Implementing such a change agent role for clinicians within the university was the most controversial aspect of this new program. As our outreach efforts grew, more students came forward with issues relating to racism, sexism, etc. There were those on campus who disputed the activist/advocate role that outreach counselors began to take, as they navigated and partnered with students through disciplinary hearings, faculty code violation investigations and fraternity sanction cases, etc. However, those of us doing the work began to believe that NOT to take on such a role and NOT to intervene when confronted with such stark injustices was, in fact, unethical.

My friendship with Suman has been more than inspiring in my work in the United Kingdom and here in the United States. His willingness to speak out, to shout out the truth, which rings loudly beyond his gentle voice, has energized so many of us around the world to continue to work for, and to fight for, equality and mental well-being for all.

Suman Fernando foraging a place for disenfranchised populations in mental health

Oliver Treacy

I first met Suman Fernando in 1986 when I came to work as a senior nurse manager at Chase Farm Hospital. My abiding memory at this time was of a man in a hurry, with apparent boundless energy, foraging a place for the disenfranchised populations of the seriously mentally ill. Suman was a consultant psychiatrist then and I learnt later from his followers, and he did have many, of his concerns about the impact of Eurocentric psychiatry on the mentally ill who were being treated both at the hospital and within the United Kingdom as a whole, and particularly on those who were not born in the country.

Race and culture and the impression that interacting with non-indigenous people made on the primary indigenous workforce was a theme he exposed from a perspective of how the non-British worker was perceived, and the feeling that psychosis leading to a diagnosis of schizophrenia for black people in contact with the mental illness system seemed inevitable. This struck me at the time as odd but I also remember reflecting on the notion of naming the last great taboo, the "elephant in the room" so to speak, in exploring this topic so openly – it almost felt like permission had been granted to think about it, never mind say it.

Suman was also the first non-white consultant psychiatrist I had met that had influence and authority. As the years went by, national and international perspectives of my own personal journey within the United Kingdom as a non-British person were furthered by seeing this experience as an impetus to examine what had happened to the other ethnic groups that were invisible within the United Kingdom, namely the Irish, and to come to terms with the past and arrive at a point in time that I now reflect on as "no longer sucking the proverbial colonial lemon".

My greatest awareness and interest in Suman's work arose when he had retired from the NHS and left Chase Farm. I frequently encountered his writings and opinions and learnt of his strident views on race and culture on hearing him speak about these issues, though he was resolutely charming in putting his point across. He and others might have described this time as his campaigning years and, I would say, perhaps some of his most productive.

In 2009, I encountered Suman again following a somewhat impromptu telephone call in which he asked my opinion and views of writing up teaching aids and materials for mental health workers in his own country, Sri Lanka. My own preference for a face-to-face interview rather than a telephone conversation led to an extended invitation to him to return to Chase Farm for tea to discuss the matter further.

This encounter led to a commitment on my part to visit Sri Lanka in 2009 to see how we might best help him, and led further to a return visit in 2010 with a small UK team under the sponsorship of PRDA and McGill University for the purpose of what we called at the time "building capacity". His work with PRDA in Sri Lanka revealed to me a side of Suman that one rarely sees in the individual – a sense of "not having enough time" and consequently making best use of the time left. The programme organised would be punishing to a man half his age and his openness to address the challenges facing the provision of mental health services within Sri Lanka was impressive. He clearly did not make claims, nor did we set out to lecture hector, address or comment on what might have been, given what we learned and what he knew; moreover, he created opportunities for doing things differently when it came to offering alternative services to the mentally ill in Colombo as they were developing, and other challenging environments in Sri Lanka.

Suman Fernando is best reflected on in my view as the man who accepted that being mentally ill, from an ethnic background and disenfranchised needs to be talked about openly.

A 'race' against time
Suman Fernando's contribution to clinical psychology

Zenobia Nadirshaw

The following is a personal reflection on Suman Fernando's thinking and how it shaped and formalised the field of clinical psychology within the Division of Clinical Psychology (DCP) of the British Psychological Society (BPS). I met Suman Fernando in the early 1980s under the aegis of the Transcultural Psychiatry Society (UK) and was suitably impressed with his discourse on psychiatry, mental health and mental illness for Black and Minority Ethnic (BME) communities in Britain.

The formation of the 'Race' and Culture Special Interest Group in 1981 (now the Faculty of Race and Culture of the DCP) came about after a national conference organised by the Transcultural Psychiatry Society (UK) chaired by Suman Fernando, who highlighted the deficiencies that existed in the psychiatric and psychological services within the mainstream mental health sector.

It was important that psychologists examine their own beliefs and highlight the limitations of the helping professionals, their stereotyped prejudiced attitudes and feelings when faced with somebody different from them. The principles of equity of access, equal opportunity in service delivery and staffing, and anti-discriminatory practice had to be incorporated within professional practice so that BME people feel confident to use psychological services and challenge its historical foundation and knowledge-base with its bias towards Eurocentric and ethnocentric thinking. We needed to show that mainstream clinical psychology services were failing to meet the needs of the BME communities both on a professional and on a clinical level.

As suggested by Suman through his writing, we took a critical view of psychology in that we posed questions relating to psychology and psychiatry being neutral sciences, and the range of Westernised assumptions and beliefs regarding diagnosing, labelling and working with mental health and mental ill health was questioned. We looked at Suman Fernando's writing about the racist practices in the mental health care system towards African Caribbean people born in the United Kingdom, with a high incidence of diagnoses of schizophrenia for this group. They were more likely to be detained under the Mental Health Act, have a 'non-standard' pathway into care (that is, greater police involvement, fewer direct referrals from GPs to psychology and psychotherapy, have a higher dosage of narcoleptic medication given intramuscularly and were more likely to receive electroconvulsive therapy).

In addition, Suman cautioned us of the differences within the discourse of Race, Culture and Ethnicity. Yet the everyday language used 'race' as the predominant characteristic to define the other two. We were concerned that, although 'race' was a concept that had been largely discredited in biological science, it continued to be used frequently to divide populations based on distinct hierarchical biological characteristics with consequent notions of inferiority and superiority and experience of socially disadvantaged status within a dominant white socio-political economic structures.

As emphasised by Suman, the psychological and mental health needs of BME people could no longer be ignored or devalued by the professions. The needs of these people needed to fit into standard service provision rather than being seen as 'special' and segregated from mainstream provision. It was imperative that the standard service provision incorporated the client's religious and other related cultural contexts and that the psychology profession needed to acknowledge this issue within service provision, service planning and service delivery.

There was widespread agreement with Suman that psychology has been affected by racism and that the dynamics of it were not seen as a result of neutral, objective and dispassionate intentions, but that they were influenced by the professional's experience and vested interests to maintain the status quo. That is, psychologists wittingly or unwittingly were part of the problem of racism, theorising about the issues of race and difference at an intra-pyschic level, to the exclusion of inter-group, ideological and social-structural factors. We needed to challenge the assumption that the teaching and learning of academic psychology and clinical interventions was culture-free and that it had universal applicability. We needed to move psychology away from being the domain of the economic and political positions of the white professional group, with its invidious form of imperialism, and to move it to a position where the profession could no longer ignore the psychology and the mental health needs of the BME population in the United Kingdom. We needed to look at psychology beyond Western perspectives, and get psychologists to be aware of and understand the social, political and professional issues that underpin health, education and social care settings.

Against such thinking the Special Interest Group was set up and subsumed under the DCP. We needed to alert the DCP that the value base of clinical psychology was not neutral and that we needed to challenge the inequalities that justified the gap in service provision and usage and downplayed the overemphasis on phenomenology as a function of individual pathology as opposed to environmental, social and interactional determinants.

In keeping with Suman's thinking about medical/psychiatric training I felt we needed to alert the academicians as to what is thought about, what is studied, what is taught and how it is taught and to review the primary functions of Western social research and theory within the dominance of white European culture and to re-examine the issues of 'race', culture and ethnicity. We needed to ensure that the DCP and the BPS address issues of race and culture not as a discrete topic but one that is mainstreamed into an overall agenda; treat BME communities not as a homogeneous group but acknowledge the extensive diversity that exists within these communities; and move from consulting with community groups to taking a collaborative approach with service users, community groups and voluntary organisations to shape and monitor services.

For me, the principles of equity of access, equal opportunity in service delivery and staffing and anti-discriminatory practice had to be incorporated within professional practice so that BME people can feel confident of using psychological services and challenge its historical foundation and knowledge-base with its bias towards Eurocentric and ethnocentric thinking. We needed to show that mainstream clinical psychology services were failing to meet the needs of the BME communities both on a professional and on a clinical level. It was important to move away from the 'culture-is-the-problem' aspect for these 'hard-to-reach clients'. In my view, these 'hard-to-reach clients' could be reached following better partnership working between health, education, housing and social services departments so as to prevent people getting 'lost along the way'.

With Suman's emphasis on service user participation and representation, the Faculty has been fortunate enough to be the first Faculty to have a carer representative from the DCP's Service User and Carer Liaison Committee. In the author's view, community psychology principles need to be working alongside the traditionalist viewpoint and move away from the tribe-like behaviour of psychologists, psychiatrists, GPs, social workers and educationalists.

I am happy to report that our individual Faculty members have produced models of good practice within their local psychology services and psychology establishments as well as in individual academic departments. For example, the Leicestershire course in doctoral training of clinical psychologists has a Diversity group chaired by the head of the course that includes academics, clinicians, service users and participants from the local community volunteer organisations. This group takes lead responsibility for developing and instilling 'race', culture and difference perspectives throughout the three-year teaching programme. The module is not seen as a specialist module given in a 'one-off' manner.

Thanks to Suman Fernando's influence in the inception of the 'Race' and Culture Special Interest Group several years ago, the Faculty has gone from strength to strength in highlighting the problems associated with the prevailing culture of the profession as well as the psychological service provision.

In my view, the profession of psychology and the psychologists within it need to have a collective as well as individual responsibility to reduce and eliminate the impact of social inequalities based on 'race' and culture, gender, class, sexual preference and age. The Faculty has moved this agenda from the world of rhetoric to real actions, and limited solutions have replaced myths and old adages. The members of the Faculty have presented themselves as part of the solution. The DCP needs to continue to take overall responsibility for monitoring and maintaining change. If it is not done, psychologists are doomed to continue the boring trudge towards professional credibility and political neutrality at the expense of our humanity.

Concluding remarks
Future directions of psychiatry and mental health

Suman Fernando

Suffering and illness are recognized as part of the human condition the world over. Also, there is no doubt that individuals affected by misfortunes require care, help and (if possible) treatment and/or support for illness or for the alleviation of suffering. And psychiatry and its co-disciplines in clinical psychology, counselling and psychotherapy have developed systems that attempt to address these realities. I think it is now obvious – and this book reiterates this fact – that fundamental changes are required if these disciplines are to be fit for purpose in the future. The field I have been involved in over a lifetime is mental health; and psychiatry is the professional discipline I was trained in. But before considering the future directions of psychiatry and mental health, it is necessary to recognize – and take on board wherever possible – changes of context that are occurring currently and likely to characterize the future.

First, the world, as it affects people everywhere, is getting smaller; and by this I mean that travel is easier and quicker and communication between distant parts now almost instantaneous. As a result of migration following de-colonization after the Second World War, Western societies have become culturally mixed, not just culturally 'hybrid' with many individuals of mixed heritage, but often composed of culturally defined diasporas connecting with people in far-away places living side by side and interacting with locally produced cultural groups. This is the nature of the multicultural world in Western societies today. And the non-Western world too has changed during the past four decades; the changes that are often seen (at least through Western eyes) as 'Westernization' are in reality no more than the mixing of cultures that has always been a feature of many parts of Asia and Africa, especially along the trade routes and then as a result of colonization.

Second, in spite of increasing familiarity about foreign parts and previously 'exotic' people – or perhaps partly *because* of these – antagonisms between peoples, suspicion and even rejection of 'the Other' (see Kapuscinski, 2008) do not appear to be diminishing. Moreover, old conflicts appear to have been revived in a post-colonial context and the breakdown of the European empires. Today, globalization appears to be accompanied by equally strong forces that predicate localization. World wars appear to have been replaced by numerous local wars. People all over the world seem to identify with both the local *and* the global (see Pieterse, 2009).

Third, there are geo-political changes occurring that may well gather force in the next few decades. The most obvious one (at least from a Western point of view) is the economic rise of the 'BRICS' (Brazil, Russia, India, China and South Africa) on the world stage. The rise of these nations may wax and wane but the rise of China and India seems inevitable. The result would be a significant shift in global power balances – unless of course neo-colonialism and/or military intervention by Western powers prevent it happening. If, as we expect, the era of Western dominance recedes, the shift in the geo-political power balance must result in a change of dominant values and ideologies that have wide implications. In such a situation, we are likely to see a very different playing field on which psychological and psychiatric systems operate – a field that, up to now, has been largely set up by post-Enlightenment Western culture.

The three previous paragraphs suggest some aspects of the possible future world we will have to live in, the helping professions, such as psychiatry, will have to contend with, and where mental health services will have to be forged. Also, at a more mundane academic level, we must address the fact that advances in the neurosciences (see, e.g., Ramachandran, 2011) are likely to impact on our understanding of the human condition – at least of the nature of 'thinking' and 'feeling' from a somatic point of view. A result of this may be that scientifically minded psychologists move closer to neurology, overlapping in practice with medical psychiatrists as specialists in understanding the complexities of the brain vis-à-vis the 'mind'; while social psychologists study social forces and structures in societies, feeding into the work of socially oriented psychiatrists who use this understanding to help people in trouble or facing misfortune, whether counted as illness or not. Counselling and psychotherapy may then be largely informed by psycho-social ways of thinking located in social studies away from their current (mainly) psycho-medical orientation. All this may be mere conjecture but something to bear in mind when considering the directions in which psychiatry may travel in the future. In my view, the search for universally valid theories around suffering and misfortune and effective ways of helping people who suffer one way or another will continue, whether the suffering is seen as being located in the 'mind' or as social suffering – although I guess that sooner or later the Cartesian mind–body dichotomy will give way to holistic thinking in keeping with modern science (Capra, 1982).

Recently, there has been much debate around the perception of psychiatry practised in the West as being in a state of crisis. Although seemingly opposing viewpoints have been proposed for its future direction – viewpoints represented by two articles in the *British Journal of Psychiatry* by Craddock *et al.* (2008) and Bracken *et al.* (2012) – in my view, the changes that the discipline undergoes are likely to be complex and to a large extent difficult to forecast, mainly because they depend very much on forces external to the subject. If it remains within the box of the narrow bio-medical illness model, psychiatry, as we know it, may well be absorbed into neurology as the neurosciences develop. However, a different progression is possible – especially if the shift in the global power balance (see above) becomes a reality. The next paragraph outlines my personal speculation, a vision of what a medical psychiatry could be like in the future.

I suggest that a psychiatry of the future will maintain 'illness' as the basis for understanding many human problems of a personal nature but illness will be seen (theoretically) as the result of a variety of influences in dynamic balance/imbalance – an illness model very different from that in psychiatry today. Once worked out, it could be one that is flexible and adaptable, underpinned by a fluidity of thought about illness that would open up into being truly culture-sensitive (that is, adaptable to whatever cultural setting it is practised in), and free of specific ideologies such as that around racism. Different societies will have variations on what may be, eventually, several universal themes within psychiatric theory; and culture will be an integral part of the way that illness will be defined and recognized in any particular setting. Explanatory models of illness will vary according to the culture in which psychiatry is practised, each and every model incorporating culture into its fabric. Any one type of explanation will not be seen as superior to another because they will all be embedded within their respective cultures but understandable on the basis of universal themes – and hence, not 'culture-bound'. There will be diversity within unity; culturally relativistic views integrated into a universalist approach.

Mental health systems incorporating the sort of flexible, theme-based psychiatry envisaged in the previous paragraph could easily come to terms with broader issues noted in the earlier paragraphs, namely the wish for people to identify both as *local* and *global*, and the multicultural nature of many soceities in the world today. Ideas and strategies from around the world would inform planners who develop services but they would be developed in association with a variery of *local* stakeholders, drawing predominantly on *local* knowledge (of social conditions, cultures and so on) and largely owned by local people and so *home-grown*.

Acknowledgement

I do feel most honoured that this book has been produced. I feel a deep sense of gratitude to the editors for the trouble they have taken in achieving such a high standard; to the contributors for their varied and thoughtful submissions; to the publishers for undertaking its production and supporting it; and to the many people who helped in the project. *Thank you from the bottom of my heart.*

References

Bracken, P., Thomas, P., Timimi, S. Asen, E., Behr, G., Beuster, C. et al. (2012). Psychiatry beyond the current paradigm. *British Journal of Psychiatry, 201*, 430–434.
Capra, F. (1982). *The turning point: Science, society, and the rising culture.* London: Wildwood House.
Craddock, N., Antebi, D., Attenburrow, M.-J., Bailey, A., Carson, A., Cowen, P. et al. (2008). Wake-up call for British psychiatry. *British Journal of Psychiatry, 193*, 6–9.
Kapuscinski, R. (2008). *The Other* (A. Lloyd-Jones, Trans.). London and New York: Verso.
Pieterse, J. N. (2009). *Globalisation and culture: Global mélange* (2nd ed.). Lanham, MD: Rowman and Littlefield.
Ramachandran, V. S. (2011). *The tell-tale brain: Unlocking the mystery of human nature.* London: Heinemann.

Index

9/11 94

Across Boundaries 3–4, 7, 150, 152
African Americans: American Medical Association's apology to 187; changes in thinking about 183–4; depression rates 93; exclusion from psychological research 58; Kardiner and Ovesey's study 28; Leff's conclusions 25–6; systematic exclusion from psychological research 58
The African Mind in Health and Disease (Carothers) 25
Ager, A. 71
Alarcon, R. D. 185
alcohol, religiosity and use of 93
Alcoholics Anonymous 93
Aldous, J. 74
Amnesty International 215
amygdala abnormalities 188
Anderson, L. M. 198
anomie 90
anti-oppression: concept analysis 145; *see also* AR/AO frameworks
anti-oppressive science 45–6
anti-psychiatry: Cooper on 43; United Kingdom's influence 44
anti-racism, and anti-oppression 145; *see also* AR/AO frameworks
anti-Semitism 47
Aotearoa, New Zealand 227–8, 230, 233; advent of Maori nationalism 234n1; mental health services inquiry 230; Native Land Act 234n2; Treaty of Waitangi 227–9; *see also* Maori culture and mental health; Maori people
Appadurai, A. 222
AR/AO frameworks: aims 145; application process analysis 148; concept analysis 145; example 150; Fernando's illustration of the micro-level application 148; focus of practice 149; holistic model of care 151–3; relevance to policy and programme development 149–50; triggers for the emergence of 148
Argyris, C. 128
assessment tools, Eurocentricity 147
astrology 208
asylum seekers: mental health outcomes of rapid integration 71; perceptions of illegitimacy 72; Silove's examinations of the impact of post-migration factors on 70
asylums 15–16, 159, 165, 205, 242
Ayurveda 15, 163, 208

Basaglia 44
Bean, R. B. 24
Bebbington, P. E. 26
Bell, C. C. 183, 186, 188
The Bell Curve (Herrnstein/Murray) 25
Benedict, R. 37, 230
Bennett, David "Rocky" 81
Bentall, R. 80
Bhabha, H. 28
Bhugra, D. 49, 248
Bhui, K. 49, 136
'Big Society' 126
bio-medical psychiatry: basis of the model 125; critical analysis 14–16; doubts about the effectiveness of 165; and the interests of the pharmaceutical industry 162
black patients, complexity of pathways to specialist care 137
Black Power (Carmichael/Hamilton) 113
Blackwood, Orville 117

Bloemraad, I. 174
Boardman, J. 80
Bojuwoye, O. 200
Bracken, P. 266
BRICS (Brazil, Russia, India, China and South Africa) 266
Brinkmann, S. 216
British Psychological Society, plan for equality and diversity 136
Buddhism 14
Building Bridges (DoH, 1995) 80
Burge, Jon 184
Burke, A. 248, 254
Burns, T. 64

Canada: barriers and access issues to mental health care in 146–7 (*see also* AR/AO frameworks); colonialist background 145; Fernando's inspiration 170; hyphenated identities 170, 173; slave industry 172
Canadian critical psychiatry: comparison with the United Kingdom 171; and the constitutional definition of Canadian identity 171; development of cultural psychiatry 171–3; and immigration policy 172; indigenous perspectives and implications 175–7; multiculturalism and the politics of diversity 173–5
cannabis 27
Capra, F. 15–16
cardiozol 194
care in the community *see* community-based model
Carmichael, S. 113
Carothers, J. C. 25
Carson, A. 92
Carter, R. T. 186
Cartesian dualism 15–16
Cartwright, S. A. 26, 183
Charles, H. 199
chemical imbalance theories 165
China 14–15, 22, 240, 266
Chinese traditional medicine 14
Christian Scientists 93, 95
Christianity 35
civil rights, and improvements in mental health care 86
Civil Rights Movement 8, 57–9, 113, 115, 183
Clinebell's pain theory 221
Clinical Psychology: "Race" and Culture – A Training Manual (Patel) 137

Clunis, Christopher 80
co-production, as example of the power of people with similar experiences 50
Cohen, D. 43
colonialism: Canadian perspective 145, 172; and the concept of race 193; and the evolution of psychiatry 194; Fernando's critical examination of psychiatry historical involvement 60–1; and the image of the anthropologist/ethnographer 36; impact on low- and middle-income countries 159 (*see also* LMICs mental health services development); and institutional racism 118; and preoccupation with race and ethnicity 35; racism as legacy of 60; South African perspective 195
Coming of Age in Samoa (Mead) 37
common sense 5, 27, 69, 71, 125
community-based model: Dutch perspective 73; and the holistic approach 152; shift towards 79–80; South African perspective 197
community development, Fernando's argument 50
community rights, vs individual rights in developing countries 163
concordance, Cooper and Powe's definition 49
confinement 15, 115, 119
Conrad, J. 37
continuity of care, fragmenting of in UK mental health services 91
Cooper, D. 43–5, 48
Counter-Psychiatry Group 44
'countries of immigration' 60–1
Craddock, N. 266
'Critical psychiatry' (Ingleby, 1980; Double, 2006) 64
critical psychiatry, focus on clinical practice 44
cultural competence: Anderson *et al.*'s description 198; Canadian perspective 177
cultural competence training, Fernando's promotion 114
cultural diversity training *see* diversity training
cultural identity: importance of in case discussion 114; importance of to indigenous people 231
Culture, Race, and Ethnicity (US Public Health Service, 2001) 185–6

culture, race and ethnicity in US psychiatry: civil rights perspective 183–4; in the cultural sensitivity era 184–5; culture-bound syndromes 185–6; current status 186–8; destructiveness of Western culture and 184; Fernando's influence 184–5; historical perspective 182–6; slavery and 182–3
cuts, impact on BME groups 61, 127

Daniel, V. E. 73
Darwin's theory of evolution by natural selection 13, 35, 145
Defoe, D. 37
Delivering Race Equality in Mental Health Care (DRE) (DoH, 2005): and the David Bennett enquiry 81; Fernando on those appointed to lead 83; fixed time frame 84–5; formal end 82; framework 81; implementation critique 82–5; implementation model 85; inception 79; intended outcomes 80; key concerns 82; limits to reforming function 82; missed opportunities 127; official launch 81; overcoming the challenges of 85; questions of tokenism 82; reasons for failure to achieve stated objectives 83; recruitment choices 83
Delphi panel 164
Denmark: Brinkmann's influence on the mental health scenario in 216; chaplaincy services for ethnic minority mental health patients 220; civil society voluntary support groups 218; critical psychiatry and psychology overview 215–17; establishment of the *Transcultural Therapeutic Team* 219; ethnic minority healthcare provision 217–18; Fernando's pragmatism and mental health services 221; recent immigration history 215; social entrepreneurship 221–2
depression, Carothers on the apparent lack of among Africans 25
Descartes, R. 15
Determinants of Outcome of Severe Mental Disorder (DOSMeD) (Jablensky *et al.*) 160
Devereux, G. 230
diagnosis: Fernando on 124–5; language and 147; political impacts 125; racial biases in 26–8, 33, 64, 73, 260, 262; social context 124–6
disability movement 50

disaster response, good practice guidelines and initiatives 139
discrimination: and mental health 95; need for a coherent ethical stance in tackling 130–1; shift in thinking about the experience of 130
disease, basis of mental ill health in 46
diversity and mental health care: Continental Europe 61–2; critical vs technical approaches 63–4; cultural sensitivity 58–60; developments in the US 57–8; global mental health campaign 65; non-Western countries 62–3; in other Western countries 60–2; psychosis and compulsory treatment 64–5; UK initiatives 61
diversity training: as core skill and requirement 134–7; critique of Western psychological theory 138–40; current training issues 137–8; holistic approach 137; literature review 134; professional bodies' equality and diversity policies 135–6; professional bodies' policies 137; users/providers collaboration 140
documentation is intervention 222
Dominelli, L. 48–9
Down, J. L. 23
Drapetomania and *Dysaethesia Aethopica* 26, 57, 183
drug abuse, association of race with 27
DSM-III, cultural perspectives 184–5
DSM-IV, cultural perspectives 185–7
DSM-V, research agenda 186–7
Dunbar, E. 188
Durie, M. 227, 229, 231–2

ECT (Electro Convulsion Therapy) 207, 242
Egypt 44, 93
emancipatory psychiatry: anti-oppressive practice 48–9; and critiques of psychiatry 43–4; Dutch context 43; holistic interventions and concordance 49–50; human rights perspective 47–8; mental illness as a social construction 46–7; policy and practice perspective 44; recovery as freedom 48
emancipatory psychiatry movement 43
Enderman, Karl Poluto 232
environment, and mental illness 114
epigenetic theory 114
equality, holistic approach 130–2
Equality Act (UK, 2010) 61, 126, 130

ethnic and cultural diversity, challenge presented to health services by 57 (*see also* diversity and mental health)
ethnic minority groups, othering process 34
ethnicity, European opposition to the notion of 62
ethnocentricity 37, 82, 116, 125, 136, 160, 170, 183, 262, 264
ethnography, classic texts 37
eugenics 22, 183
Eurocentricity 4, 36–7, 46, 137, 147–8, 153, 232, 260, 262, 264
Europe, revival of nationalism in 61
Evarts, A. B. 22
Even the Rat Was White (Guthrie) 58
exorcism 208
Expert Patient programme 50
Eysenck, H. J. 25

Fanon, F. 35, 111, 114
FANON project 254
Fearon, P. 64
Fernando, S.: advocation of "needs thinking" orientation 114; central argument 87; challenge to institutional racism 39, 230–1; Charmaine Williams interview 102–8; commitment to human rights 249; community development argument 50; conception of race and culture 128, 193–4; contribution to British psychiatry 248–52; contribution to clinical psychology 262, 264; contribution to race and mental health literature 137; critical perspective of the role of drug companies 247; on cultural sensitivity training 198; documentation of historical legacies of racism 114; on the DRE 83, 127; on the dynamism of culture 135; education 244; emphasis on service user participation and representation 264; enquiry into the diagnosis of schizophrenia 255; on the ethnocentricity of psychiatry 125; experiences in England 240–2, 245, 249; family background 244; father's influence 246; feelings on being offered an OBE 242; first research project 242; foraging a place for the disenfranchised populations of the seriously mentally ill 260–1; on future directions of psychiatry and mental health 265–7; on the holistic approach 232; and the 'iceberg' model of culture 128; illustration of the micro-level application of AR/AO frameworks 148; on the importance of cultural sensitivity in training 198; influence 170, 229–30, 248, 258–9, 264; informal approaches to the WHO 245; inspirational nature of writings 124; on the integration of Western and traditional healing systems 199–200; interviewed 102–8, 239–43; key tenets 258–9; marriage 241; mentoring practices 222; on multiple identities 131; on the notion that racism may contribute to depression 184; on personal resilience 216; perspective on *emic* and *etic* approaches 218; promotion of cultural competence training 114; on psychiatric diagnosis 124–5; on race and culture 35; on refugee mental health 70–3, 219; refusal of an OBE 256; reputation 256; return to Sri Lanka 241; social action practice 254–6; socio-cultural psychiatry recommendations 74; Sri Lankan roots 244–7; on stigma 131; Ted Lo interview 239–43; and university mental health systems 257–9; upbringing 239–40; use of the term 'liberation' 130; view of apartheid 195; Weerackody's relationship with 245–6; work in mental health 253–6
Field, M. J. 163
First Nations 14, 176, 240
First World War 46
folklore 14
Fonofale 232
forcible confinement, institutional racism and 118
Foucault, M. 15, 111, 114
France 62
Frazer, J. G. 37
Freud, S. 24, 38, 112, 230

Galappatti, A. 206
Galton, F. 22, 24
Gask, Linda 251
Gay Liberation Front 44
Germany 62
Ghodse, Hamid 251
Gilroy, P. 28
global mental health: critical views 65; misconception 165 (*see also* LMICs mental health services development)
globalization 1, 14, 137, 151, 160, 170, 265

Goldberg, D. 71–2, 75
Golden Bough (Frazer) 37
Grandparents for Asylum and Refugee Contact 218
group therapy, cultural appropriateness 163
Growing up in New Guinea (Mead) 37

Hall, S. 24, 28
Halliburton, M. 161
Hamilton, C. 113
Hampden-Turner, C. 128–9
health: non-Western views 18; WHO definition 161
Health and Social Services for Mentally Disordered Offenders and Others Requiring Similar Services (DoH/HO, 1992) 80
Health and Welfare: The Development of Community Care (MoH, 1963) 80
health literacy, acquiring 63
health pluralism 139–40
healthy migrant effect 60
Hearing Voices Network 216
Heart of Darkness (Conrad) 37
Henare, James Clendon Tau 234n3
Hertz, S. 216
Hettiarachy, P. 248
Hindu psychology 14
Hindu temple healing study 160
the holistic approach: AR/AO frameworks 151–3; the community-based model and 152; to cultural diversity training 137; Durie on 232; to emancipatory psychiatry 49–50; to equality 130–2; Fernando on 232; in Maori culture 231–4; to multidisciplinary training 123 (*see also* RECC training model); to refugee mental health 75–6
homosexuality 26–7, 35, 46, 113
hooks, b. 28
Horowitz, A. V. 114
A Hospital Plan for England and Wales (MoH, 1962) 80
Hospital Services for the Mentally Ill (DHSS, 1971) 80
Howitt, D 25
Hulgård, L. 221
human rights perspectives 34, 47–8, 50, 65, 162, 165, 197, 249
humanitarian agencies, good practice guidelines and initiatives 139
Hunter, Thomas 228
Hurricane Katrina 94

Huxley, P. 71–2, 75
hysteria 46

illness, Kleinman's explanatory model 18
immigration, countries of 60–1
India 1, 14, 24, 204, 241, 266
Indian ocean tsunami 94, 139, 206–7, 210, 245
Ingleby, D. 43–5
Inside Outside (National Institute for Mental Health in England, 2003) 79, 81, 127
institutional care, drivers of movement away from 45
institutional discrimination: English policy breakthrough 79; impacts of 123; social transmission 131
institutional racism: application to clinical care 116–18; as basis of problems of BME community 17; case examples 116–18; colonialism and 118; as consequence of post-Enlightenment ideology 35; cross-cultural relevance 116; cultural competence as a counterpoint to 118–19; and cuts in services 127; cycle of denial about 126; David "Rocky" Bennett's experience 81; and deficiencies in services 73; evidence of in the UK 115; evidence of in the US 115; Fanon's articulations 111–12; Fernando's challenge to 231; Fernando's conceptualization 111–13; and forcible confinement (sectioning) 114, 118, 242; government acknowledgement 81; historical perspective 114–15, 230–1; impact on mental health service delivery 257; impact on psychology 263; impact on refugee mental health 71; implications of police inaction as 117; interconnected issues 39; MacPherson Report's definition 111; McGill "Working with Culture" seminars 115–16; Michael and Hamilton's proposal 113; Orville Blackwood Inquiry 117; and over-diagnosis 33; and public discourse 113; roots of 171; and schizophrenia 115, 118; slavery and 118; Stephen Lawrence example 117; teaching paradigms 115–16; training implications 113–14; UK concerns and diversity initiatives 61
insulin coma 194
insurance, as barrier to mental health care 147

intelligence, racist tradition in studies of 24–5
International Pilot Study of Schizophrenia (IPSS) (WHO) 160, 253
intersectionality 33, 48
Invisible Men: Mass Incarceration and the Myth of Black Progress (Pettit) 115
Italy 62

Jacks, I. 230
Japan 14
Java 23
Jehovah's Witnesses 94
Jenkins, Rachel 251
Jensen, A. 24
Jeyaseelan, V. 199
Jim Crow policies 183
Johansen, K. 218
Johnson, S. 199
Jung, C. G. 24

Kakar, S. 204
Kaliski, S. 195
Kardiner, A. 28, 183
Kareem, J. 114
Karran, J. 50
Keating, F. 79, 81, 86
Kenya 25
King, D. 92
King Solomon's Mines (Rider Haggard) 37
Kingsley Hall 45
Kirmayer, L. J. 119
Kleinman, A. 18
Knudsen, J. C. 73
Koenig, H. 92
Komagata Maru 179n2
Kraepelin, E. 13, 23
Krause, I. B. 138
Kumar, C. 248
Kuwait 93

Laing, R. D. 43–5
language, as barrier to mental health care 147
Lawrence, E. 28
Lawrence, Stephen 111, 117
Leff, J. 25–6
Lewis, A. 23
Lindow, V. 72
Littlewood, R. 114, 254
Livingstone, D. 40n5
LMICs (low- and middle-income group of countries): concept analysis 159; development of mental health services *see* LMICs mental health services development; impact of colonialism 159

LMICs mental health services development: asylums and 159, 165; background literature 159–61; and dependence on NGOs 163; exclusion of stakeholders 164–5; future expectations 164–6; historical perspective and current scene 163–4; and informal family networks 164; and the MGMH 162, 164–5; and the pharmaceutical industry 165; realities on the ground 162–3; and regard for local conditions 163; and religious healing services 164; WHO's role 161–2
Loewenthal, K. 49
London Jewish Hospital 242
low- and middle-income countries, mental health services development in *see* LMICs mental health services development

Maclachlan, M. 138
mainstreaming, as euphemism for abolishing 85
Malinowski, B. 37
Mannoni, O. 38
Maori culture and mental health: approaches 229; colonialism and Maori freedom 228–9; emergence of Maori-led initiatives 229–30; and Fernando's challenge to institutional racism 230–1; Fernando's influence 170, 229–30, 248, 258–9, 264; first national strategic plan 232; historical perspective 228–9; holistic approach 231–4; overview 227–8
Maori people: colonial impact 227; discrimination experience 231; first recognisable assertion of sovereignty 228; over-representation in the criminal justice system 233; and therapeutic engagement 119
The Mark of Oppression (Kardiner/Ovesey) 28, 183
Mattock, J. L. 206
Maudsley, H. 23, 242
Maudsley Hospital 242
McDougall, W. 24
McGill University 16
Mead, M. 37
Mental Health, Race and Culture (Fernando) 35, 184–5, 258
Mental Health and People of Color (Chunn) 183

274 Index

mental health care, principles for good systems 161
mental health discourses, inclusion of psychosocial dimensions and wellness 113
mental health services development, in low- and middle-income countries *see* LMICs mental health services development
mental illness, as social construction 46–7
"Mental Illness in Primitive Societies" (Benedict/Jacks) 230
MGMH (Movement for Global Mental Health) 162, 164–5
migrant, term analysis 135
MIND 216, 254
mind, Western vs non-Western approaches 13–14
Minde, M. 194
Minh-ha, T. T. 37
Morel's theory of degeneration 13
Morris, J. 48
Moynihan Report 28
multiculturalism, Canadian policy 173
multiculturalism discourse, impact of in Canada 145, 173–5
multidisciplinary mental health training, central dichotomy 123
multidisciplinary training, and a holistic model of mental health practice 123; *see also* RECC training model
multiple discrimination 126, 130
multiple identities 131–2
Muslims 48, 93, 95, 206, 221–2, 239–40

National Service Framework for Mental Health (DoH, 1999) 81
Native Land Act 234n2
Nazism 24, 62
Nelson, G. 18, 137
Nest (NGO) 245
Netherlands 43, 61–2, 64, 73, 75
neurotransmitters, chemical imbalance theories 165
New Zealand *see* Aotearoa New Zealand
Nisbet, P. A. 93
noble savage concept 23, 35
non-Western psychology, examples 14

OBE, refusals 2
the Other: in canonical works of literature 37; concept analysis 34–5; ethno-racial construction 34–6; the journey from anthropology to psychiatry 37; non-Europeans as 36; post-Enlightenment representations 36
otherness, the burden of 38
Our Story: A Handbook of African History and Contemporary Issues (Addai-Sebo/Wong) 40n2
Ovesey, L. 28, 183
oxytocin 188

Pate, A. 208
pathologization, Brinkmann's model 216
Patient Protection and Affordable Care Act 57
Patterns of Culture (Benedict) 37
Pearson, K. 22
Pere, Rose 232
pharmaceutical industry 165; WHO funding issues 162
pharmacological treatments, success rates 63
Pierce, C. 183, 185
Pinderhughes, C. 183
Pinkham, A. E. 187
Pond, Desmond 248
Porot, A. 112
Portugal 62
Potatou (Te Wherowhero) 234n1
poverty 60, 70, 150, 172, 195, 209
Powe, N. 49
Pratt, M. L. 41n5
prefrontal leucotomy 194
Prichard, J. C. 23
Prilleltensky, I. 18, 137
Prince, Mary 113
professional bodies, equality and diversity policies 135–6
pseudo-science 22, 35, 37, 45
psychiatric imperialism 151
psychiatry: concept analysis 14; as expensive failure 65; Fernando on the ethnocentricity of 125; Western roots 15
psychological research, exclusion of African-American subjects 58
psychological theory, claims of racism in 137
psychotropic drugs 16, 160, 166, 194, 207
PTSD, challenging the over-diagnosis of 254
Pugh, J. F. 208

race and culture: conceptual analysis 193, 263; Fernando on 193, 263
Race and Culture in Psychiatry (Fernando) 249

Race Equality and Cultural Capability (RECC) 124
race equality in mental health policy development: breakthrough 79; critique of DRE implementation 82–5; historical context 80–1; political context 81–2; successes 85–6
racial superiority, emergence and complex set of post-Enlightenment ideologies 35
racialized communities, studies into the barriers faced by 146–7
racism: American Psychiatric Association's recognition of the effects of 186; examples of in traditional psychiatry 57 (*see also* racism in psychiatry); link to anxiety disorders 188; literature review 137; pseudo-scientific discourses 35; roots of in the United Kingdom 60
Racism and Psychiatry (Thomas/Sillen) 183
racism in psychiatry: historical perspective 22–9; mind and mental illness 23; post-war psychiatry and psychology 25–6; post-war social and cultural studies 28–9; psychological and intellectual differences 23–5; racism in diagnosis 26–8
Raguram, R. 160
'rainbow' model, of cultural differences 129–30
RECC training model: defining 'race' and cultural capability 128; and the DRE strategy 127–8; holistic approach 130–2; inspiration 123–4; models of culture 128–30; service development context 123–4; and the social context of diagnosis 124–6; training context 126
Red Cross 215
reflective discourse 113
reflective practice 50, 90, 123
reflexive practice 76
refugee mental health: and cultural identity maintenance 71; Danish perspective 217–18, 218–19; Fernando on 70–3, 219; holistic approach 75–6; institutional and societal factors 70; postgraduate training programme development 75; race and culture perspective 73–6; reflexive practice 76; scholarship 70–1; training concerns 74; UK's establishment of imaginative refugee training programs 75; user involvement 72

refugee rights, psychiatrists' efforts to protect 173
relationship skills, importance of in mental health care 91
religion, race and mental health: critique of Western psychiatry and psychology 91; race/ethnicity, culture and mental health 95–6; religious beliefs and wellness 91–4; stress and religious coping 94–5
religious and spiritual belief: commitment assessment 92; defining and operationalizing terms 91–2; and discrimination 95; health impact research 92; literature on health and 90; literature review 92–3; and political movements 96; and psychosis 93; reasons for avoiding the topic in a mental health setting 90; religious coping 92–5 (*see also* religious coping); and risk of suicide 93; and social integration 93; studies into impact on depression 93; and voluntary work 96
religious coping: definition 92; psychosis and 93; and race 94; regional perspectives 94; stress and 94–5
religious healing, Sri Lankan practices 208
religious perspectives: church attendance and resilience 90; mental health services development in LMICs 163; temple healing literature 163–4
"Resolution against Racism and Racial Discrimination and Their Adverse Impacts on Mental Health" (American Psychiatric Association) 186
Richards, G. 25
Rider Haggard, H. 37
Robinson Crusoe (Defoe) 37–8
Roma communities 61–2
Rose, N. 216
Rosenthal, B. S. 95
Royal College of Psychiatrists: and international psychiatry 249–50; Race Equality action plan 135
Rush, B. 23

Said, E. W. 28, 35, 112, 114
Samarasinghe, D. 206
Saraceno, B. 161
Sashidharan, S. 248
Sassoon, M. 72
Sathyaseelan, M. 199
Saul, J. R. 176

schizophrenia: Fernando's enquiry into the diagnosis of 255; image of 160; institutional racism and 115, 118; insulin coma treatment 194; linking of alienness to 27; mainstream psychiatry's acceptance of the universality of 230; Pinkham's research 187; racial biases in diagnosis 27, 33, 39, 64, 73, 115, 227, 233, 260, 262; social exclusion as cause of diagnoses 64; traditional healing studies 161; WHO pilot study (IPSS) 160, 253

school exclusions, disproportionate numbers of black children 39

science, use of as tool of discrimination and prejudice 45

Scientology 93

sectioning, institutional racism and 114, 118, 242

the self 14, 18, 34, 36, 38, 138, 256

self-image, and resilience to mental health problems 72, 75

Sen, A. 47–8

service users, need for mental health professional to consider experiences of 137

'seven dimensions,' of culture 129

The Sexual Life of Savages (Malinowski) 37

Shakespeare, W. 37

She (Rider Haggard) 37

shell-shock 46

Sillen, S. 183

Silove, D. 70

Singh, S. P. 64

slavery: abolition 96; Canadian perspective 172–3; and descriptions of mental illness 26–7, 57, 182–3; first black British woman to escape from 113; historical legacy 118; justifications for 23, 35, 37; and racist science 183; and the roots of institutional racism 171; Zephaniah on Empire and 2

social construction, mental illness as 46–7

Social Determinants of Health (SDH) 62

social determinants of health movement: increasing influence 62; roots 61

social exclusion, as cause of schizophrenia diagnoses 64

social inclusion, psychiatrists efforts to promote for minorities 173

social isolation, and refugee mental health 70

social psychiatry 45

social work, established approaches 48

socio-cultural psychiatry, Fernando's recommendation 74

Sodi, T. 200

Somasundaram, D. 207

South Africa, role of racism and culture in shaping mental health services 193; *see also* South African mental health/psychiatry

South African mental health/psychiatry: and the apartheid laws 195; cultural competence training 198–9; de-institutionalization strategy introduction and aims 195; and Fernando's conception of race and culture 128, 193–4; historical perspective 194–6; integration of Western and indigenous healing traditions 199–200; Minde's analysis 194; post-apartheid perspective 196–8; WHO report 195–6

Soviet Union, political abuses of psychiatry 26–7

Spain 62

spirit/mind, African ways of interpreting 14

spirit possession, as cause of mental illness 131

spirituality: concept analysis 91; defining 91

Sri Lanka 131; colonial history 205; cultural identities in 240; geographical location 205; trauma and global health programme implementation *see* TGH programme in Sri Lanka; understanding mental health in 204

Sri Lankan mental health services: availability of Western methods 207; cultural considerations in service development 209; historical perspective 205; impact of conflict and natural disaster 206–8; importance of spirituality 208; indigenous mental health practices 208–9; introduction of Western psychiatry 205; lessons of the TGH programme 210–11; WHO involvement 207

SS *St. Louis* 172

Staying Power: The History of Black People in Britain (Fryer) 40n2

stigma: a* 34, 39, 72, 76, 111–13, 115, 125, 131, 136, 146–7, 160, 163, 165, 216–17, 222; connection with the biomedical model 163; Fernando on 131;

progress in LMICs 165; racialized individuals' experience 146–7; usual response of the state in disrupting 146
stop and search 39
Street, R. 49
suicide rates, in indigenous populations 175
suicide risk, and religious beliefs 93
Summerfield, D. 65, 72
Survivors movement 44, 50
Swartz, L. 199
Sweden 61–2, 75, 90
symptoms, Hertz's explanation 216
syphilis 46
Szasz, T. 43–4, 46, 64

'Task Force on Black and Minority Health' (US DHHS, 1984) 58
Te Puawaitanga: Maori National Strategic Framework 232
Te Rau Matatini 232
Te Whare Tapa Wha 231–2
Te Wheke 232
The Tempest (Shakespeare) 37
terrorism, and the rejection of multiculturalism 175
TGH programme in Sri Lanka: Fernando's contribution 246; implementation 204; lessons learned 210–11, 246
Thatcher, Margaret 61
therapeutic community movement: beginning 242; as example of the power of people who have similar experiences 50; roots 44
Theunissen, M. 34
Thomas, A. 183
Timimi, S. 65
tokenism 75, 82, 127
Tomes, N. 46
Totem and Taboo (Freud) 24, 112, 230
'Towards a Black Psychology' (White) 57–8
traditional healing: a* 8, 38, 147, 151, 153, 199–200, 229; Hindu temple healing study 160; published studies 160–1
transcultural psychiatry: centrality of religious and spiritual understanding 90; critical analysis of Western*F psychology and bio-medical *F psychiatry 14–16; Danish perception 218; development history 249; historical perspective 16–17; ideologies 17; and intra-cultural relations 47; practical lessons 17–19; reasons for loss of momentum 251–2; Sri Lankan perspective 210–11; UK perspective 17, 90, 253; Western and non-Western cultural traditions 13; and the World Psychiatric Association 251–2
Transcultural Psychiatry Society (TCPS) 17, 44, 248
Transkulturelt Psykiatri (Alberdi/Nørregaard/Kastrup/Kristensen) 218
trauma and global health (TGH) programme: implementation in Sri Lanka *see* TGH programme in Sri Lanka; locations and components 209
Treatise on Insanity (Prichard) 23
Trompenaars, F. 128–9
tsunami, South Asian 94, 139, 206–7, 210, 245
Tuck, A. 173
Tuke, D. H. 22–3
Turkey 22, 215

UK riots: media coverage 137; racial perspective of media coverage 137
Unani 15
unconscious, as dark negative region 38
United Kingdom: challenges for mental health services in the 123; narrow model of mental health services 123; rapid post-war development of concern with minority health 60; riots *see* UK riots; roots of racism 60; roots of social determinants of health movement 61; transcultural psychiatry's arrival and influence 17; user involvement practices 72
United States: demographic perspective of minority groups 58; evidence of institutional racism 115; main source of racial injustice in health care 57; religious identity and well-being research 92–3; *see also* African Americans
user involvement, challenges to 72
user-led advocacy, as example of the power of people with similar experiences 50

Van Der Post, L. 37
Venture to the Interior (Van Der Post) 37
Villa 21 43, 45
Vogt, B. 208

Watson, J. 25

Weerackody, C., relationship with Fernando 245–6
wellness, psychosocial dimensions 113
West, C. 28
Western approaches to mental health, vs non-Western approaches 18
Western psychology: critical analysis 14–16; scope 14

Whanau Ora 233
white supremacy 38
Williams, C. 148
Wilson, W. C. 95
Wittkower, Eric 16
women, as the Other 34–5

Zen psychology 14